*f*P

AGENT

of

DESTINY

The Life and Times of

GENERAL
WINFIELD SCOTT

John S.D. Eisenhower

THE FREE PRESS
New York   London   Toronto
Singapore   Sydney

THE FREE PRESS
A Division of Simon & Schuster Inc.
1230 Avenue of the Americas
New York, NY 10020

Designed by Carla Bolte

Manufactured in the United States of America

10   9   8   7   6   5   4   3   2   1

Library of Congress Cataloging-in-Publication Data

Eisenhower, John S. D., 1922–
    Agent of destiny : the life and times of General Winfield Scott / John S. D. Eisenhower.
        p.   cm.
    Includes bibliographical references and index.
    ISBN 0-684-84451-6
    1. Scott, Winfield, 1786–1866.   2. Generals—United States—Biography.   3. United States.
Army—Biography.   4. United States—History, Military.   5. United States—History—War of
1812—Biography.   6. Mexican War, 1846–1848—Biography.   7. United States—History—
Civil War, 1861–1865—Biography.   I. Title.
E401.1.S4E5   1997
355'.0092—dc21   97-34049
    [B]   CIP

To

LOUIS D. RUBIN, JR.

During [General Scott's] long life, the nation has not been unmindful of his merit. Yet, on calling to mind how faithfully, ably, and brilliantly he has served the country from a time far back in our history, when few of the now living had been born, I cannot but think that we are still his debtor.

—Abraham Lincoln, First Annual Address

To this distinguished man belongs the rare honor of uniting with military energy and daring the spirit of a philanthropist. His exploits in the field, which placed him in the first ranks of our soldiers, have been obscured by the purer and more lasting glory of a pacifier, and a friend of mankind.

—Dr. W. E. Channing

[Scott is] the second United States general officer who has ever dared to aid and assist the open enemy of the republic in their operations against United States forces. . . . The first . . . was Major General Benedict Arnold; the second, as your finding must show, is Major General Winfield Scott.

—Edmund P. Gaines to Court of Inquiry, 1837

Another star has faded, we miss its brilliant glow
For the veteran Scott has ceased to be a soldier here below.
And the country which he honored, now feels a heart-felt woe,
As we toast his name in reverence, at Benny Haven's, Oh!

—From "Benny Haven's Oh!" (traditional West Point Song)

Contents

Prologue

H E WAS an astonishing man, one of the most astonishing in American history. For over half a century, between 1809 and 1861, he served as an active officer of the United States Army, wearing the stars of a general officer from 1814 to his death at age eighty in 1866. He was America's main source of pride in the unfortunate War of 1812 with Britain, overshadowed only by Andrew Jackson's spectacular victory at New Orleans in January 1815, after the peace was signed. For the forty years following Jackson's retirement from the Army in 1821, Winfield Scott served as the country's most prominent general. He stepped down as general-in-chief only in late 1861, six months after the beginning of the Civil War.

His accomplishments were many. Besides being the first truly professional soldier in the American military establishment, Scott conquered Mexico City in a spectacular and hazardous campaign in 1847. Later, at the outset of the Civil War, he provided the strength of purpose, military expertise, and judgment to launch the administration of Abraham Lincoln before succumbing to old age and sickness (and the machinations of Major General George B. McClellan).

The less remembered role of Winfield Scott, however, was that of the agent of Manifest Destiny, the expansion of the United States from the borders of the original thirteen colonies to the far-off Pacific Ocean. When Scott first came into service, the United States was a loosely knit federation of states, its borders and its future uncertain. It was filled with ambitious men, some of whom were not completely sold on the United States as a unified country. By the time he left, the republic filled the North American continent as a single nation, though unfortunately going through the paroxysms of civil war.

Scott was the agent, throughout at least forty years, both for the consolidation of the nation as a single unity and for its expansion. As a general, he was not the architect: it was James Madison who attempted unsuccessfully to annex Canada in 1812; it was Andrew Jackson who decided that the Indians east of the Mississippi must be moved to western lands; it was John Tyler who eventually settled the dispute with Britain over the border between Maine and New Brunswick, Canada. James K. Polk was the architect who settled most of the boundary question between the United States and Canada in 1845—and who manipulated the war with Mexico (1846–48) that expanded the nation into the southwest. James Buchanan decided to compromise with Britain over possession of San Juan Island in Puget Sound. For each of these presidents, however, the agent, the builder in contrast to the architect, was Winfield Scott.

In this role, Scott served under fourteen presidents, thirteen of them as a general officer.

Yet he became a soldier almost by chance. That is where our story begins.

1

The Bugle and the Drum

A young lawyer joins the Army.

The young soldier had heard the bugle and the drum. It was the
music that awoke ambition.

—Scott, *Memoirs*

LIEUTENANT GENERAL Winfield Scott, hero of the War of 1812, conqueror of Mexico City, and Abraham Lincoln's top soldier in the early
months of the Civil War, was born at the family farm, Laurel Hill, near Dinwiddie Courthouse, Virginia, on June 13, 1786. It was a time described by a
contemporary French observer of America, Alexis de Tocqueville, as peopled
by an "innumerable crowd of those striving to escape from their original social condition." Success rested on possession of land, driving ambitious
Americans and their government westward.

Scott was one of those so driven. He became a leading agent of America's
Manifest Destiny through his personal thirst for prominence and prosperity.
He started his quest with some advantages. His father, William Scott, was a
prominent member of the Dinwiddie-Petersburg community. A respected
former captain of the American Revolution, he was a landowner but not in-
cluded in the lists of the old Virginia plantation aristocracy. James Scott,
Winfield's grandfather, had arrived in Virginia as a political refugee from
Scotland, a lawyer who had quixotically enlisted in the service of Prince
Charles Stuart ("Bonnie Prince Charlie"), who was attempting to seize the
British throne. When the English slaughtered Stuart's Highlanders at the

Battle of Culloden in April 1746, James Scott was lucky to escape with his life. He emigrated to Virginia, settled down, married into the influential Pegram family,[1] and resumed the practice of law.

James died at a relatively early age, as did William Scott, Winfield's father. Winfield was less than six years old when his mother, Mary Mason Scott, was widowed. She was adequately provided for, however, and she did not follow the usual custom of remarrying. She raised her two sons and two daughters alone. It seemed to Scott that she raised them well, for in his memoirs he gives credit for any achievements of his own to "the lessons of that admirable parent."

Scott inherited from his forebears a remarkable physical presence. He was a handsome youth. Attention was directed to him because he was quite tall for the times, eventually reaching a height of six feet, five inches. He was well proportioned and was blessed with a strong constitution. The emotional support of his mother and his inherited physical and mental assets were his only patrimony, however, for in an arrangement young Scott thought was unjust, an estate from a namesake uncle did not devolve on Winfield but on another relative.

When his mother died in 1803, Scott was seventeen years old and on his own. Dinwiddie Courthouse and even Petersburg could not further his growing ambition. Winfield secured enough financing to pursue the classical education being offered to young gentlemen of the time in Richmond.

Scott's restlessness made his formal schooling sporadic, but he was an avid student, and from his studies he developed a fondness for philosophical ideas. The headmaster of the school in Richmond, an odd Scottish quasi-nobleman named James Ogilvie, put much emotional energy into his lectures on "the ancient classics, rhetoric, Scotch metaphysics, logic, mathematics, and political economy," and his reputation was so widespread that Thomas Jefferson himself had gone out of his way to hear him speak, afterward sending him a copy of the works of Cicero as evidence of his regard. Scott, however, was not overwhelmed by the headmaster's pedagogy. Ogilvie, he later wrote, was attempting to do too much in a limited time, and he noticed that Ogilvie's "preternatural brightness" was beginning to fade with his growing opium addiction and called Ogilvie's imitations of Cicero's compositions "magnificent specimens of art; only the art was too conspicuous."[2] Impatient, Scott left Ogilvie after a year to enter the College of

William and Mary, resolved to enter into the practice of law, which he later termed "the usual road to political advancement."

The president of William and Mary, Bishop James Madison, was a cousin of the soon-to-be fourth president of the United States, of the same name. The Madison of William and Mary was an intellectual who had studied law in both Britain and America. He was an ardent believer in Jeffersonian republicanism, so much so that he refused to acknowledge such a thing as the "Kingdom" of Heaven, referring to it as "that great republic where there was no discretion of rank and where all men are free and equal." Scott subscribed to this egalitarian philosophy enthusiastically at this time of his life. While at William and Mary he also strove to master Shakespeare, Addison, Milton, Johnson, Goldsmith, Hume, and Gibbon. He studied the works of economist Adam Smith and philosopher John Locke, and he became fascinated by the lives of great warriors such as Caesar and Scipio Africanus.

The liberal philosophical views Scott had learned from Madison never conflicted with his traditional religious beliefs. He had no patience with certain students at William and Mary who liked to call religion "base superstition" or "gross hypocrisy." On the other hand, Scott felt that Bishop Madison handled such student disaffection poorly. The bishop's impassioned denunciation of such heretics as Hume, Voltaire, Godwin, and Helvetius, Scott believed, merely whetted the appetites of the green and curious students.

By early 1807 Scott had had enough of formal schooling; he left William and Mary to join the Petersburg law offices of David Robinson, Esq., a Scotsman whom Scott's own grandfather had brought to America as a tutor for his family. Robinson, now long since in his own law practice, took three young men to study with him that year, one of whom was Scott.[3]

Robinson proved to be an ideal master for the fledgling lawyer. A man of solid reputation in Richmond, noted for his services as stenographer for the Virginia Constitutional Convention in 1788, Robinson was able to provide Scott the best possible preparation for the Virginia bar examinations. He regarded his young apprentice with affection, and Scott admired Robinson, though he disagreed with Robinson's conservative Federalist persuasion. The teachings of James Madison at William and Mary had tilted him toward Jeffersonian republicanism.

The legal duties that fell to Scott and his two associates consisted chiefly of acting as Robinson's assistants—drawing up his summonses, copying his briefs, and researching pertinent cases. These apprentice tasks were performed in Richmond and while "riding the circuit" with their mentor. Lawyers of the period traveled with the judge assigned to a designated area of the countryside, where they solicited work as counsel for disputant parties. Circuit riding required lengthy absences from home and office.

Scott and Robinson had just completed Scott's first circuit when their activities were interrupted by the electrifying news that Aaron Burr, former vice president of the United States, was to go before a court, accused of high treason. The trial proceedings were to be held in the courthouse at Richmond, and Robinson, as Virginia's most accomplished court reporter, was selected to make the official record. Robinson realized that witnessing this historic event would prove invaluable to his charges, so he set his law business aside, packed up his entire office, and took his three apprentices to Richmond.

The trial of a prominent public figure for a capital offense drew the leading forensic talents of the day. Chief Justice John Marshall presided, and Burr was defended by Edmund Randolph, one-time attorney general of the United States under President George Washington. Charles Lee, also a Burr adviser, had been attorney general under President John Adams. The prosecution was conducted by the thirty-seven-year-old George Hay, United States district attorney and James Monroe's son-in-law. Notable among the colorful list of witnesses was the forty-year-old Andrew Jackson, Burr's friend. The government's star witness was the corpulent and arrogant Major General James Wilkinson. President Thomas Jefferson, while not present, was behind the prosecution, pushing hard for the conviction of his political enemy, Aaron Burr.

Paradoxically, though the charges were grave, the atmosphere was festive, and the exuberant Scott joined enthusiastically in the carnival. During recesses he made his way around the crowds, striking up acquaintances with any prominent figures who would spare him a few moments. One such was the twenty-four-year-old Washington Irving, a reporter covering the trial for the *New York Gazette*.*

While the trial proceedings were going on, Scott stationed himself in a

---

*Irving had previously thrilled the country with his reports on the Lewis and Clark expedition of 1803–6. One of the principals of that expedition, Meriwether Lewis, was also present at the Burr trial as an observer for his patron, Thomas Jefferson.

conspicuous place, his great size attracting the notice of no less a person than the defendant himself. And as Scott watched, he developed very definite opinions of what he saw.

The charge of treason against Burr was difficult to prove. It was known that during the summer of 1805 he had visited Blennerhassett Island, in the Ohio River, and that the next year an expedition of lightly armed men, presumably sent by him, had left the same island and gone down the Ohio River. This expedition had the elements of a romantic novel: some nine boats and sixty men setting off from an island in the Ohio River privately owned by a wealthy Irish aristocrat and his young, beautiful wife. The expedition, however, collapsed almost immediately after it had commenced. In New Orleans, General Wilkinson, who was generally assumed to be Burr's co-conspirator, betrayed him, sending alarming messages about Burr's doings to Jefferson. When Burr learned that the President had called for his arrest, he turned himself in to the nearest authorities, careful to avoid falling into the hands of Wilkinson, who as commanding general might have had the power to execute him on the spot. On President Jefferson's orders, Burr was sent to Richmond for trial.

Intriguing as these circumstances were, they lacked the elements needed to convict Burr of treason as explicated by Chief Justice John Marshall, a Federalist and opponent of Jefferson. Marshall ruled that a charge of treason could be established only by proving that the defendant had committed an overt act, not merely planned to do so. Though Burr and Wilkinson were suspected of plotting to promote war with Spain, hoping to split the western states (those that lay between the Allegheny mountains and the Mississippi River) from the eastern seaboard, creating a new inland empire, Burr was able to prove that he was not personally present when his fleet of boats left Blennerhassett Island.

After Chief Justice Marshall's ruling, therefore, it came as little surprise when the jury declared the accused not guilty on September 1, 1807. Most observers conceded that, based on the evidence that had been presented, the finding was inevitable. The views of nearly all reflected their political leanings, with or against President Jefferson.

Among those disappointed in the outcome, so he wrote later, was Winfield Scott. He carried no animosity toward Burr personally; in fact he admired the way that Burr handled himself. But Scott agreed with President Jefferson's contention that Burr was guilty, the case lost because of inept handling.* And Scott had another wish, to make an example of Burr. In the absence of any execution for treason in American history, he later wrote, the people remained "untaught a most needful lesson—*that playing at treason is a dangerous game!*"

As fascinating as the Burr trial was to Scott, an incident that occurred during that time was far more important to his future. Just as the trial was getting under way, an appeal came from the governor of Virginia requesting volunteers to serve temporarily in the state militia. An emergency had arisen, caused by a naval incident at Hampton Roads, off Norfolk, Virginia, that threatened to result in armed conflict with Britain.

During the afternoon of June 22, 1807, a British frigate, the *Leopard*, intercepted an American frigate, the *Chesapeake*, as the latter was leaving Norfolk. The British captain demanded the right to search among the *Chesapeake's* crew for four deserters from His Majesty's Navy. The American commodore, James Barron,[4] refused; the *Leopard* thereupon backed off two hundred yards and poured several twenty-six-gun broadsides into the hapless American vessel. The *Chesapeake*, utterly unprepared to fight, could not resist. Commodore Barron struck the American flag and allowed the ship to be searched. The British commander removed the four men and departed. The crippled *Chesapeake*, pumping water, hobbled back into Norfolk.

The people of the United States reacted to the *Leopard-Chesapeake* affair with astonishing violence. Mobs nearly lynched a young British naval officer in the streets of Norfolk, and they destroyed the water casks of the British squadron, stored at nearby Lynnhaven Bay. "For the first time in their history," according to Henry Adams, "the people of the United States learned, in June, 1807, the feeling of a true national emotion." Public opinion forced President Jefferson, the man who "did not love the deck of a man-of-war or enjoy the sound of a boatswain's whistle,"[5] to issue a proclamation in early July requiring all British armed vessels to depart from American waters. Four days later, on July 6, he called on the governors of the states to furnish forces of one hundred militia each. The governor of Virginia called up his quota, and that appeal for volunteers reached Scott.

Scott felt an overpowering urge to play a part in the oncoming events. He excused himself from Robinson, mounted a horse, and galloped through the

---

*Burr was, Scott later wrote, "the great central figure below the bench [who] stood, in the hands of power, on the brink of danger, as composed, as immovable, as one of Canova's living marbles."

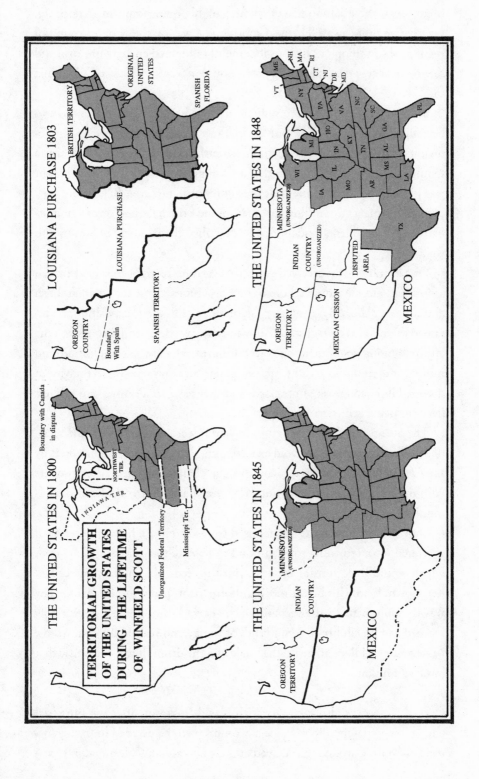

LOUISIANA PURCHASE 1803

BRITISH TERRITORY

ORIGINAL UNITED STATES

SPANISH FLORIDA

OREGON COUNTRY

LOUISIANA PURCHASE

Boundary With Spain

SPANISH TERRITORY

THE UNITED STATES IN 1848

NH
ME
MA
RI
CT
NJ
DE
MD
VT
NY
PA
VA
NC
SC
OHO
MI
KY
GA
IN
TN
AL
FL
WI
IL
MS
IA
MO
AR
LA
TX

MINNESOTA (UNORGANIZED)

INDIAN COUNTRY (UNORGANIZED)

DISPUTED AREA

OREGON TERRITORY

MEXICAN CESSION

MEXICO

THE UNITED STATES IN 1800

Boundary with Canada in dispute

NORTHWEST TER.

INDIANA TER.

Unorganized Federal Territory

Mississippi Ter.

TERRITORIAL GROWTH OF THE UNITED STATES DURING THE LIFETIME OF WINFIELD SCOTT

THE UNITED STATES IN 1845

MINNESOTA (UNORGANIZED)

OREGON TERRITORY

INDIAN COUNTRY

MEXICO

night from the Richmond courthouse to his own home in Petersburg, twenty-five miles away. The next morning he was on the parade ground of the Petersburg troop of cavalry. He somehow obtained an extra uniform and for the next few days acted the part, though never sworn in, of a Virginia militiaman.

Scott's first brief foray into military life was hardly important enough to be remembered by anyone but himself. By his account, however, an acquaintance, recognizing his natural leadership, immediately made him a temporary corporal in command of a small group of men. His detachment was placed on a small dune near the shores of Lynnhaven Bay, where they prepared to meet any landing parties from the British fleet—"several line-of-battle-ships in sullen grandeur," as he described them. There he was told to wait.

One evening Scott received word that a group of eight unarmed British sailors had illegally come ashore to buy provisions. Scott set up an ambush and captured them. Lacking any instructions as to their disposition, he retained them in his own custody, showing them lavish hospitality. As was the custom among gentlemen, he placed his captives in seats of honor around himself at their outdoor camp tables and saw that they received extra wine at dinner. His charges were impressed, and they asked if all American soldiers lived in such a gentlemanly fashion.

The authorities in Washington, however, were not so impressed. President Jefferson, anxious to avoid exacerbating the tensions brought about by the *Chesapeake* affair, ordered Scott through channels to return the prisoners with the warning, "Take care not to do it again." Scott considered the admonition "imbecile."[6]

Shortly thereafter Scott was released from the service he had never been mustered into, returning to Richmond to observe the unfolding Burr trial, which would linger on for months. But the seeds of a military career had been sown. Before his brief time in uniform, Scott had assumed that the law was the only path to the recognition he craved, but military service now loomed as a possibility to a youth full of energy and zeal. In his own words, "The young soldier had heard the bugle and the drum. It was the music that awoke ambition."

Scott did not remain with David Robinson after the Burr trial ended. Now qualified to practice law on his own, he decided to try his fortune in South Carolina. He arrived at the state capital, Columbia, in October 1807. Disappointed to learn that South Carolina law required a year's residence in the state before anyone could practice, he worked in Columbia as a lobbyist for a while but in December headed for Charleston, intending to practice law "in-doors" until permitted to appear in court. When he arrived in Charleston, however, Scott heard that on November 11, 1807, the British government had issued the latest of its "orders in council,"[7] aimed at severing all trade between the continent of Europe and those nations currently neutral in the conflict with Emperor Napoleon of France, with whom Britain was at war.

This set of orders in council was only the latest and most stringent in a series of ever-tightening restrictions that had begun once Britain, in 1805, had achieved uncontested naval supremacy over France. Napoleon, controlling all of the European continent, had responded by issuing successive decrees in Berlin and Milan, the effects of which were to close all European ports to British and neutral vessels.

The orders in council were issued only six months after the *Chesapeake* affair, and public opinion now forced President Jefferson to take firm action in retaliation. He requested Congress to pass the Embargo Act, which forbade American ships to trade with either Britain or Napoleon's Europe. On December 22, 1807, Congress complied. The willingness to enact a measure so potentially ruinous to America's shipping industry and export trade was a measure of the intensity of domestic feeling against Britain's high-handedness.

Although President Jefferson had no intention of expanding these commercial measures into military action against the British, public opinion compelled him to improve the deplorable condition of the Army and Navy. On February 26, 1808, therefore, he asked Congress to raise the Army's authorized strength by an additional five regiments of infantry, one regiment of riflemen, one regiment of light artillery, and one regiment of dragoons— an additional 6,000 men.

When word of Jefferson's requests to Congress reached Charleston, people believed that war with Britain was imminent. Perceiving a chance to obtain a commission in the Army, Scott left his law office and boarded a vessel for New York, from there making his way to Washington. He sought the help of a friend, Senator William Branch Giles, who easily arranged for the two of them to make a personal call on President Jefferson. The brash young Scott was prepared to ask for a direct commission in the grade of captain.

Scott's interview with the President was relatively short. Two other gentlemen, both members of Congress, were also present. The two congressmen, Scott observed, were "incessant talkers," and as a result Jefferson quickly became bored. He turned to Scott and asked, "Well, young man, what have you seen in Washington? Have you visited the Capitol? Whom have you heard speak?"

"I was, sir, in the House yesterday, and heard a part of Barent Gardenier's speech on the embargo."

Scott had made a diplomatic error; Gardenier, a congressman from New York, had made a bitter denunciation of the embargo, including some barbs aimed at Jefferson personally. So the President dropped the subject and turned back to the congressmen, who all the while had not ceased talking. But no matter; before Scott left, Jefferson promised that if the pending request for an augmentation of the Army was granted, he, Scott, would be commissioned a captain.

Scott had no way of knowing whether or not the projected increase in the Army would come to pass, so he returned to Petersburg to resume the practice of law. On April 8, 1808, however, Congress passed a law tripling the size of the regular Army.[8] With that increase in the Army came Scott's promised commission.

On May 8, 1808, Captain Winfield Scott of the Light ("Flying") Artillery received orders to raise a company and take it to Norfolk, Virginia, prepared to embark for New Orleans.

2

⋙⋘

A Shaky Beginning

*In his first tour of duty, Scott is court-martialed
for insubordination.*

The distribution of our little army to distant garrisons where
hardly any other inhabitant is to be found is the most eligible
arrangement of that necessary evil that can be contrived. But I
never want to see the face of one in our cities and intermixed
with the people.

—Albert Gallatin

WHEN SCOTT received word of his appointment as captain, light artillery, there was nothing ambivalent about his reaction. By return
post he sent a letter to Secretary of War Henry Dearborn accepting the
"honorable proof of confidence" and pledging "my life, my liberty and my
sacred honor" to the faithful discharge of his duties. Later that same day he
went down the street to the tailor shop and ordered a complete uniform—
sword, sash, cap, everything. When his treasure was ready, he carted it back
to his house, cleared all the furniture out of the largest room, placed two
looking glasses in diagonal corners, raised the window shades to let in the
maximum amount of light, and donned his new uniform. For two whole
hours he strutted back and forth between the two mirrors. "If any man had
seen me," he admitted later, "I should have proceeded at once to put him to
death."

His reaction was not surprising. Scott was a born soldier, and patriotism
was ingrained in his makeup, but he was also vain, and part of the attraction

of the military life was the glamour of the uniform. Though he was only twenty-two, he had already also begun to develop his lifelong weakness of taking himself too seriously. His exceptional height and build automatically attracted the admiration of strangers; people tended to defer to him, an attitude he had come to expect. However, he also possessed a generous spirit, as the British sailors he had captured on Lynnhaven Bay in 1807 could readily confirm. Though he knew that he cut an impressive figure in his dashing blue uniform, he intended to be no mere parade ground soldier. He felt that he was destined to do impressive deeds and he was ready to begin them.

Once called to duty and given his orders, Scott was expected to recruit and train his new company with very little interference or supervision. Recruiting was the primary, more tedious requirement. It was not, however, impossible given the circumstances of the times. The soldiers were paid only $7 a month, a wage scale far below that of able-bodied seamen in the coasting trade, who received between $15 and $20 a month. But the soldier's pay, plus subsistence and shelter, was steady and reliable. Since the threat of unemployment always lurked in the background at the time, the financial security provided by the military was a real attraction. And a soldier's pay could sometimes be augmented by extra-duty supplements and even commercial enterprises on the side. Some men, who were down on their luck or wished to escape their pasts, found havens in the ranks. Many of the new recruits, therefore, were foreign born, mostly Irish and Germans, who had never been completely accepted in American society.

There were many tricks that company commanders employed in their efforts to induce young men to join the ranks, and the authorities were well aware of them. Each company commander, therefore, was instructed:

> No indirect methods are allowable to inveigle men into the service of the United States; it is forbidden therefore to inlist any individual whilst in a state of intoxication, or to have him sworn until twenty-four hours after he will have signed the inlistment. . . . No negro, mulatto, or Indian is to be inlisted, nor any description of men, except natives of fair conduct, or foreigners of unequivocal characters for sobriety and fidelity.[1]

Scott threw himself into the recruiting business with gusto. Even before obtaining his uniform, he began circulating handbills in Petersburg and the countryside to drum up interest. Recruiting parties, generally headed by an officer, with two enlisted men and a couple of musicians, traveled around the country seeking areas that had not already been visited. At his company headquarters in Petersburg, Scott went through the "burdensome chores of paperwork, drilling the men he had already enlisted, chasing deserters, and still trying to enlist more men."

If recruiting tended to be a chore, training was rewarding. Scott's company[2] was to be part of the newly organized light artillery, a branch of the Army that was just becoming recognized. Artillery had, before Napoleon, been confined largely to heavy guns of high calibers, used for knocking down walls and emplacements. But Napoleon had developed the new light, or "flying," artillery, whereby the pieces took position at the front, softening up the enemy's lines from distances just out of musket range. Just that year, General Tadeusz Kościuszko had published a manual entitled *Maneuvers of Horse Artillery*, the introduction of which contained a new principle:

> The use of artillery in battle is not against the artillery of the enemy, for that would be a waste of powder, but against the line of the enemy in a diagonal direction when it is destructive in the extreme.[3]

Such ideas brought new excitement for the branch to which Scott had been assigned. The armament of his company consisted of two six-pounder guns and two five-and-a-half-inch howitzers, lethal weapons for the day, and Scott had to train his men in the intricate movements necessary to unlimber them, place them into battery, aim, and fire.

These activities occupied all of Scott's time for a full nine months, until February 1809. Then, when Scott received War Department orders to proceed to New Orleans, he marched his unit to the port of embarkation at Norfolk. There his troubles began. The vessel in which Scott and his men were to sail the seas was a "clump of a ship, half rotten, and with a master so ignorant that he did not know of the passage among the Bahama Islands called the 'Hole in the Wall.'" Much to Scott's disgust, the captain followed a course all the way around the eastern point of Cuba in order to reach New Orleans. They did not reach their destination until April 1, 1809.

At the time of Scott's arrival, the bulk of the United States Army was concentrated at New Orleans as protection against the possibility of war with Spain. Even with the augmentation of April 1808, which had increased the Army by eight regiments,[4] the total active strength of the Army came to only about 2,700 men. Over two-thirds, 2,000 men, were destined for duty under the command of Brigadier General James Wilkinson. Wilkinson was the senior of the two brigadiers in the Army, the other being Wade Hampton, whose commission was recent, dating from only the previous February.

It was only at that time, around 1809, that the Army was finally accepted as a permanent institution of the United States government. The force that Anthony Wayne had used to destroy Indian resistance in 1794 had not even been called the Army; its name had been the United States Legion, and it had been disbanded the following year after the northwest frontier, which then meant the Ohio territory, was no longer considered to be in danger. That had been followed by a "Hamiltonian Army," organized to meet a threat of war with France and to maintain internal security. But Hamilton's army met the same fate as the Legion when the threat of war subsided in the spring of 1800. President Jefferson, antimilitary though he was, had at least kept some framework of the previous military organizations. He was behind Congress's establishing a military academy at West Point in 1802, and he had made use of the military, most spectacularly in the expedition of Lewis and Clark, in westward explorations. Nevertheless, it was only the *Leopard-Chesapeake* affair, as late as 1807, that established the United States Army as a permanent institution.

Scott's first impression of the active army was far from favorable. "The army of that day," he later wrote, "including its general staff, the three old and nine new regiments, presented no pleasing aspect. The old officers had, very generally, sunk into either sloth, ignorance, or habits of intemperate drinking." This sorry condition he later attributed to the evils of political patronage, and specifically because Jefferson's Republicans, in power since the election of 1800, had almost entirely excluded Federalists from appointment to the commissioned ranks.* Further, in Scott's opinion, many of the officers who were given commissions, at least those from the New England states, lacked education, so those selected from that area consisted "mostly of coarse and ignorant men." Even so, Scott recognized a few men of talent in the Army, and he duly listed them in his *Memoirs*. To his credit, some of them were professional rivals and others were outright enemies.[5]

Part of the problem in maintaining any kind of professionalism in the officer corps was its low pay scale. Officers, therefore, like enlisted men, found it advisable to make money on the side. Fortunately, regimental duty did not demand the full time of the commander, a fact that permitted regular officers to supplement their pay with outside activities. Thus Zachary Taylor doubled as a planter; Edmund Gaines served as the local postmaster while

---

*This measure of Jefferson's was in response to John Adams's policy of appointing only Federalists. Both policies, of course, militated against the establishment of a meritocracy.

commanding Fort Stoddard; William Henry Harrison, at Fort Washington, apparently spent most of his time running his distillery. But these were all legal activities; the one man who habitually exceeded the ethical and often even the legal bounds was Brigadier General James Wilkinson himself, the commanding general at New Orleans.

Wilkinson, age fifty-two, had a spotty record as an officer during the Revolutionary War. To his credit, he had served with Benedict Arnold in the grueling campaign at Quebec during 1775 and with Washington at Trenton and Princeton at Christmas the next year. As an aide to General Horatio Gates, however, he had become involved in the Conway Cabal, a plot headed by General Thomas Conway to replace Washington as commander-in-chief. Nevertheless, Congress granted Wilkinson a brevet (honorary rank) as a brigadier general at the end of the war.

Since the Revolution, Wilkinson had been in and out of the Army, all the while indulging in often questionable business enterprises and land speculation. Among those that were open to censure was his relationship with the government of Spain, which began as early as 1787. In that year Wilkinson obtained a license from the governor of New Spain, Don Esteban Miró, which allowed him to sell produce brought down the Mississippi River. In exchange for that and other favors, Wilkinson swore allegiance to the king of Spain and provided the Spanish with a plan for closing the Mississippi to American shipping. The Spanish government adopted his plan as policy and rewarded him well. In 1788 Wilkinson secured a loan (never repaid) of $7,000 from Governor Miró, and made a profit of $5,000 by selling produce at New Orleans. In 1792 he obtained a pension from the Spanish government of $2,000 a year, which lasted until 1800. (The Spanish government, in the meantime, paid another American $1,000 a year to watch him.)

In 1803, the United States purchased the Louisiana territory from Emperor Napoleon of France, who had just wrested it from Spain. Wilkinson was one of the two dignitaries designated by President Jefferson to formally take possession of the lands. In 1805 he was placed in charge of American army forces in the West, with headquarters at St. Louis, at the same time that he was extorting another bribe of $12,000 from the Spanish throne. In 1808, after the Burr trial, he faced a congressional inquiry for accepting a bribe from Spain but escaped conviction of treason on the basis that he had been out of the Army at the time of his offense. Nevertheless Jefferson, desperate to find officers of experience, brought Wilkinson back to command the new levies of troops arriving at New Orleans as the result of the 1808 augmentation of the Army.

Wilkinson arrived at New Orleans in February 1809. Captain Winfield Scott, with his artillery company of ninety men, was among the 2,000 men converging on the city. Scott was not happy at the prospect of serving under the pudgy general, for whom he had developed a violent antipathy during the Burr trial two years earlier. Unfortunately, the young captain was unable to keep his opinions to himself. Even before leaving Petersburg, he had made a statement to the effect that he would do Wilkinson in if he ever served under the general in combat. That statement, made before Scott reported to Wilkinson, would later come back to haunt him.

On March 4, 1809, while Scott and his men were on their journey to New Orleans, James Madison was inaugurated president of the United States. For his secretary of war he chose Dr. William Eustis of Massachusetts, a man who had spent much of his professional life as a military surgeon. Eustis was poorly equipped to fill the high post he occupied, but as a medical doctor he was at least familiar with the principles of military sanitation. What he began reading about the condition of Wilkinson's troops at New Orleans alarmed him.

Wilkinson's men, he learned, were encamped in and around the city, suffering from various tropical diseases as well as a high incidence of venereal disease. Obviously the danger from venereal disease could be reduced by moving the troops away from the city, so Eustis sent Wilkinson instructions to remove his command from New Orleans to Fort Adams, a site near present-day Natchez, Mississippi, some 250 miles up the Mississippi River. Two identical confirming messages were dispatched, a week apart.

Wilkinson received these orders in early May. He agreed that his force should leave New Orleans, but he was unwilling to leave the immediate vicinity of the city; he had extensive business and social interests there, and he was busy courting a Creole belle. He therefore moved his army only a short distance, in the opposite direction, down the Mississippi to a sump hole called Terre aux Boeufs.[6]

Even before the move downriver, Scott was already disgusted with the whole scene. It had been all he could do to stomach the prospect of serving under Wilkinson, and once he reached New Orleans he began regretting his decision to join the Army in the first place. And not only was Wilkinson planning to move down into the fetid Terre aux Boeufs area; Scott and his company were being sent as part of the party designated to prepare the campsite. The young artillery captain was appalled.

Scott had seen enough of the Army's blundering. If this was what a military career meant, then he would find another vocation. So, leaving his company, he turned in his resignation and headed back to Virginia.

At Terre aux Boeufs, things continued to degenerate. The campsite was far from ready when, on June 10, 1809, Wilkinson's full force moved in. The supply of tents was minimal at best, and those available were pitched in the mud without floors. Probably due to Wilkinson's collusion with a civilian contractor, the supply of beef was rotten, described as "mouldy, black, and full of worms." The drinking water was polluted. It was therefore no surprise that within weeks Wilkinson's decision began to exact a grim price. The rains turned the camp into a morass, and dysentery and scurvy struck his men with increased virulence. By September, when Eustis forced Wilkinson to move again, the effective force had been reduced to six hundred men fit for duty—and those were busy caring for nine hundred invalids.

This time Wilkinson followed his instructions, though under protest. The trip up the Mississippi was extremely arduous, however, and with so many men seriously ill, an astounding three hundred died en route.[7] Wilkinson may have been correct in warning of the difficulties of the trip, as he later claimed, but that fact was lost, in the eyes of his superiors, in the light of his continued insubordination. Accordingly, Wilkinson was removed from command soon after his arrival at Natchez, his successor being Wade Hampton, who had become his bitter rival. Wilkinson was to report to the War Department to explain his conduct. Still he did not leave Natchez until early December, after he had recovered from a fever he had contracted himself.

Winfield Scott, back in Petersburg by late July, began preparing once again to resume his law practice. Yet for all his disgust and disappointment with what he had found in Louisiana—and his relief to leave Wilkinson's command—he was far from feeling at peace. The more he thought about his fledgling military career, the more dissatisfied he became.

Scott had been in Petersburg only a week before fresh rumors arrived that war with Great Britain was pending. That settled it. His resignation from the Army, he realized, had not yet been formally accepted by the secretary of war, so without delay he wrote to Secretary Eustis, explaining that he had changed his mind:

> I cannot for a moment think of resigning under existing prospects. The reason that put me on that determination shall be buried and forgotten whilst war, or rumors of war shall exist in our country.

A bit pompous, perhaps, but completely in keeping with the soldier's code; one does not leave service when war is impending. And Scott was never worried about consistency when his ambitions were involved; he was acting completely within character. In any event, Secretary Eustis readily put Scott's resignation aside; he was glad to retain Scott's services. He did not, however, excuse the young man from service on the Mississippi; he sent him back to his old command.

If Scott was happy to be back in uniform again, his satisfaction was soon beclouded. As he prepared to leave Petersburg, he learned from friends that Wilkinson had gotten wind of some of the indiscreet remarks Scott had made about him just before returning home to Virginia.[8] If he returned to his old station, these friends warned, he would surely be court-martialed. For Scott, this was only the more reason to return: he would go back and face his enemies. He took his time about it, arriving in Natchez only in November, probably hoping that Wilkinson would be gone. If such were his design, however, he should have tarried even longer: the general had turned over the command but was still present. Furthermore, he planned to remain at Natchez for another month.

The atmosphere at Natchez was surprisingly quiet when Scott arrived and unpacked his baggage at Washington Village. Perhaps the matter of his intemperate remarks had been forgotten! Again, however, Scott could not or would not bridle his tongue, and he resumed his tirades against Wilkinson. One of those tirades was directed toward a medical officer, William Upshaw, who was known to be one of Wilkinson's friends. One evening in the Charles Francis Hotel of Washington Village Scott declared aloud that "he never saw but two traitors, General Wilkinson and Burr." He then called Wilkinson a "liar and a scoundrel" and promised to "blow up General Wilkinson when he got back to Washington [Village]." That did it. Dr. Upshaw reported him and preferred court-martial charges against him.

The court-martial assembled on January 10, 1810. The primary charge, as preferred by Dr. Upshaw, was "conduct unbecoming an officer and gentleman."[9] But to Scott's astonishment, Upshaw had added another charge, that of embezzlement. Scott was accused of "withholding at sundry times, men's money, placed in his possession for their payment but also of issuing additional clothing to his men and charging it against them in his company book." To both charges Scott, who represented himself, pleaded "not guilty."

In his defense, Scott attempted to picture his admitted indiscretions as minor matters. Wilkinson, he argued, had been his "superior" but not his "commanding" officer when Scott's worst remarks were uttered, Wilkinson having already been replaced by Hampton. The court was unimpressed by that sophistry, but it was inclined to be lenient with Scott, as he had said no more than most of the officers and men themselves believed, including the members of the court. And the charge of embezzlement was weak in that everyone knew the regular supply system had broken down, causing all officers to do irregular things in order to clothe their men at all. Scott was certainly no thief; that aspect of him was known to all. So the court recognized the trumped-up nature of the embezzlement charge as an effort to hang one more crime on him.

It was generally agreed, however, that Scott must be found guilty of something, so when the court issued its verdict in late January 1810, it convicted Scott of "unofficer-like conduct" and sentenced him to be "suspended from all rank, pay, and emoluments for the space of twelve months." It avoided using the damning words "conduct unbecoming an officer" because that legal terminology brought with it automatic dismissal from the service. It had "no hesitation in acquitting the accused of all fraudulent intentions in detaining the pay of his men." Two days later the court recommended the remission of nine months of Scott's twelve-month suspension.

Wade Hampton, the new department commander, overrode the recommendation for reducing the sentence. Hampton bore no love for Wilkinson, but some semblance of discipline had to be maintained in his command. Scott therefore packed his bags for a second return home to Petersburg. Before leaving he challenged Dr. Upshaw to a duel, feeling that Upshaw had maliciously plotted against him. Fortunately, emotions damaged the marksmanship of both duelists; when the two paced off, turned, and fired, Scott missed completely, while Upshaw's ball only grazed the top of Scott's head.

Captain Scott then headed home, a year of suspension in his future.

3

"On to Canada!"

*War fever and mobilization bring Scott promotion
and a chance to fight.*

As in the year 1754 a petty fight between two French and English
scouting parties on the banks of the Youghiogheny River, far in
the American wilderness, began a war that changed the balance
of the world, so in 1811 an encounter in Indian country, on the
banks of the Wabash, began a fresh convulsion which ended only
with the fall of Napoleon. The Battle of Tippecanoe was a premature outbreak of the great wars of 1812.
—Henry Adams

SCARCELY MORE than a year into his military career, Captain Winfield
Scott had traveled twice to New Orleans, and during his second sojourn
there had been tried by court-martial, found guilty of unofficer-like conduct, and sentenced to twelve months' suspension from service. Such a reprimand might easily break the spirit of an officer less self-assured than he,
but on Winfield Scott it had no such effect. He saw no cause for shame in
the court's verdict; after all, most of his Army colleagues secretly applauded
his barroom denunciations of General Wilkinson, and when he left Washington Village for Petersburg, he was elated by the elaborate and enthusiastic send-off his peers had given him. Furthermore, Scott had strong inklings
that Wilkinson's successor at New Orleans, Brigadier General Wade Hampton, felt the same way.

Even so, Scott recognized that his conviction could well ruin his chances for future advancement in the Army, so on his return to Petersburg in late February 1810, he decided to forget the military and resume his interrupted law practice. He went to live with a Petersburg friend, Benjamin Watkins Leigh, who at the age of thirty was a promising jurist and a future United States senator from Virginia. Leigh was also an intellectual and a theologian, so the two young men spent many evenings together reading choice passages of English literature aloud and discussing what they had read. As one who loved a turn of phrase as well as philosophic theory, Scott was grateful for Leigh's attention. He remembered those evenings with warmth throughout his life.

Leigh's greatest contribution to his friend's future, however, was to discourage Scott's return to the law. He quickly perceived that the energetic young giant possessed great military potential but doubtful legal talents. Out of that conviction, he induced Scott to devote his time to studying the military profession, especially the tactics practiced by America's potential enemies, the British. Scott saw the wisdom in Leigh's evaluation of himself and from that time on he became a military scholar.[1]

Not all of Scott's time in Virginia was devoted to philosophy and study. He enjoyed his year of freedom and did his share of carousing in Petersburg. As time wore on, however, he began to feel a yen to return to the Army. In 1811 he wrote to a friend that, while his firm plans were to remain with the law, he had not yet given the military up completely: "Shall war come at last, my enthusiasm will be rekindled; *and then who knows but that I may yet write my history with my sword.*"

Events transpiring around him also gave Scott reason to expect that his services might soon be needed in a military capacity. The main development was a change in the attitude of the American electorate toward President James Madison's policy, inherited from Jefferson, of peaceful negotiation with Britain.[2] It was becoming all too apparent that Britain had not been appeased by a reasonable policy, certainly not enough to start treating her former colonies with anything like respect. As a result, the 12th Congress, which came to Washington in early 1811, included a new set of young radicals who came to be popularly known as the War Hawks. These newcomers, among whose ranks were such future leaders as Henry Clay, John C. Calhoun, and Richard M. Johnson, completely rejected the inhibitions observed by both Jefferson and Madison. Holding no loyalty to the past, naive and jingoistic, they were impatient with peaceful measures to maintain the nation's interests and dignity.[3] They might, it appeared, push the nation into a war that most people, including the President, would prefer to avoid.

Scott's interest in rejoining the Army was also whetted by a possibility for promotion created by the death, in early 1811, of Major John Saunders, the commanding officer of the Light Artillery Regiment. Scott's period of suspension was about to end, and he seized on the idea of filling the vacancy himself. Discounting the ridiculous idea that his court-martial conviction might present any obstacle, he wrote to Secretary of War Eustis on January 15, 1811, contending that the position should be his. After all, he argued, he had been the highest ranking captain of the regiment at the time of his suspension, and he claimed the "right" to fill that vacancy "agreeably to ordinary rules of rank & promotion." His rank of captain, he argued, had only been suspended, not voided.

Eustis ignored this cheeky argument from a suspended artillery captain. He restored Scott to his rank of captain but ignored his request for promotion to the grade of major. The secretary was in no hurry to do even that much; it was not until October 1811 that Scott received orders to rejoin his company at New Orleans.

When Scott's orders finally arrived, he made his way south to Charleston, which was then the eastern terminus of the six-hundred-mile road being constructed across Georgia, Alabama, and Mississippi to New Orleans. While there, he fortuitously met up with Brigadier General Wade Hampton, his former commanding general, who was about to make the journey from his native Charleston to his post in Louisiana. Though Hampton had disapproved the court's recommendations for leniency in Scott's suspension of rank a year earlier, he bore the young officer no rancor, and he welcomed Scott as a temporary member of his personal staff.

The overland trip from Charleston to Baton Rouge, where the army had moved, was a novel experience. From Fort Hawkins, on the Ocmulgee in Georgia, the new wagon train ran through the territory of the Creeks, Choctaws, and other Indians. On the route, the party passed only two small white settlements, one at Fort Stevens and the other at Fort Stoddard, both on the Mobile River. Once at Baton Rouge, on the lower Mississippi, Scott was appointed special judge advocate for the trial of Colonel Thomas Cushing, an officer whom Hampton had accused of demonstrating "excessive independence" of Hampton's orders. Cushing, known to be a partisan of General Wilkinson, was duly convicted. The result of Cushing's conviction was a feather in Scott's cap—and valuable legal experience. His only previous exposure to practical military law had been as a defendant.

The next six months at Baton Rouge were uneventful for Scott, but he kept a careful watch on events in Washington. During that period war was coming ever closer, spurred on by a relatively minor event in the Northwest Territory, then called Indiana.

William Henry Harrison, the aggressive, ambitious thirty-seven-year-old governor of the Indiana Territory, was becoming impatient with what he regarded as increasing Indian hostility. For the ten years he had been in office, he had conscientiously followed President Jefferson's paradoxical policies of professing friendship toward the local Indian tribes while at the same time underhandedly bilking them of their lands. He had continued to follow the same policies under President Madison, and through most of that time he had met with little resistance.

In recent years, however, the Indians, encouraged by the British, had begun to assert themselves. This new attitude was most evident among the Shawnees and their affiliated tribes, led by two brothers, Tecumseh and Tenskwatawa ("the Prophet"). These chiefs constituted a team unlike any before them, and they were unlike each other. Tecumseh was the warrior, whose current objective was to unite the fragmented Indian tribes in order to present a united stand against the whites. The Prophet was a shaman, or spiritual leader. Both were implacable enemies of the United States, greatly preferring the British (or anyone else) over the land-hungry Americans. The British exploitation of those feelings had been stepped up after the *Chesapeake-Leopard* affair in 1807, and much of the attention had been showered on Tecumseh, who was pleased and flattered.

In 1811, about when Scott was leaving Petersburg for Baton Rouge, Governor Harrison determined to destroy the main Indian stronghold, called "the Prophet's Town," where too many warriors were reported gathering for his taste. In September Harrison led an army of about a thousand regulars and volunteers[4] northward down the Wabash Valley for the 170-mile trek from Vincennes to the juncture of the Wabash and Tippecanoe Creek, on which stood the main Indian camp. There, on November 6, 1811, he was ambushed by four hundred Winnebagos, Potawatomis, and Kickapoos. His regulars and frontiersmen rallied, repulsed their attackers, and then continued on to burn the Prophet's Town. This action was later touted as the Battle of Tippecanoe.

The battle catapulted Harrison into the status of a national hero. Little note was taken of the cost. The Americans had lost 61 officers and men killed and nearly 150 seriously wounded, out of an original force of only about 800 men. The Americans recovered only 38 Indian bodies on the field, though that fact carried little meaning in light of the Indian insistence on removing their dead from the scene of any battle, regardless of risks.

The greatest significance of the Battle of Tippecanoe, however, lay in the damage it did to peace in the Indiana Territory. Tecumseh, who was not present at the battle, realized its potential impact and tried to minimize the "unfortunate transaction that took place between white people and a few of our young men at our village."[5] But the damage was done. Fear and distrust between whites and Indians along the frontier increased immensely. The Indians sought revenge; the Americans believed that the British were exploiting that thirst to agitate them against the settlers. The resulting tensions probably did more to bring on the War of 1812 than all the seamen impressed by the British navy.

The hostility between whites and Indians in the West, which found its symbol in Tippecanoe, not only made war with Britain more imminent; it also dictated the nature of the war. The conflicts of the eighteenth century had generally been limited wars, not total wars. Though the Revolution was an exception from the American viewpoint, it did not threaten the British homeland; the French and Indian War (1754–1763) did not threaten the existence of France or Britain, only the extent of their empires. Thus the War of 1812 need not have constituted a land conflict, especially if its real cause had been the impressment of American seamen. But after Tippecanoe, it was certain that the United States would attempt to invade Canada. Though an invasion was generally thought to be an easy task, it meant raising land forces, of which the United States had virtually none. The people of the West were willing to undertake that; the war would be far more popular in the West than in the East.

Though President Madison had asked Congress for an augmentation in the Army and Navy in his annual message of November 5, 1811, the first major action to increase the Army came a month later. With news of Tippecanoe on everybody's lips, Senator William Branch Giles, chairman of the Senate Foreign Relations Committee, introduced a bill to raise 25,000 regular troops, to be signed up for terms of five years, in addition to the 10,000 regulars previously requested. The 10,000 men, Giles argued, would be insufficient to conquer Canada, even with the assistance of volunteers.

Despite resistance and acrimonious debates, Congress passed the Giles bill, and Madison signed it into law on January 11, 1812.

Actually raising that army of 25,000 regulars proved to be impossible, however, because national support for war was far from solid. New England was still dominated by Federalists, who were friendly to Britain; that region would remain opposed. When a trade embargo against both Britain and France was passed (with many abstentions) in late March 1812, every shipowner on the east coast immediately sent all his ships to sea to avoid having them stuck in American ports. Evidence foretold that war loans were not going to be fully subscribed. And finally, elections held in New York and Massachusetts in May 1812 were won handily by the Federalists.

The people of the United States, moreover, were divided as to which nation, England or France, had treated this country with the least respect. A case, no doubt, could be made against either of them.[6] But out west in Indiana and along the Canadian frontier no such ambivalence existed. The British were behind the Indian troubles, the people reasoned, and the only way to eliminate British influence was to eliminate the British in North America. So when Madison and Secretary of State James Monroe learned from the British minister that his government had rejected American demands for the lifting of the orders in council, war with Britain appeared inevitable.

The decision for war against Britain was triggered on May 22, 1812, when HMS *Hornet* arrived at Washington with a supercilious "last formal notice" from the British government, leaving the choice of war or degradation in the hands of the Americans. So on June 1, 1812, Madison sent a message to Congress recommending a declaration of war. Congress debated the question in secret, apparently unconcerned as to the true state of public opinion. On June 18, 1812, the declaration of war was passed by votes of 79–49 in the House of Representatives and 19–13 in the Senate. The act was not universally popular. Opponents of the war insisted that the views of the people had not been consulted. No declaration in a hundred years, wrote an enraged Henry Adams, "showed less regard for personal and party consistency than the refusal by the Republicans of 1812 to allow society either the rights or privileges in regard to the declaration of war upon England."[7]

That same day, ironically, the British government rescinded the notorious orders in council. It was too late, and both countries were going to be forced into a war that neither the British government nor most Americans had any desire for.

Winfield Scott, in New Orleans, knew that war with Britain was approaching. Indeed, his decision to reenter the Army had been predicated on his expectation of such a war. In early February, four months before the declaration of war was passed, news arrived at Baton Rouge of the recent augmentation of the Army and the imminence of war. General Hampton, wishing to be present on the Canadian frontier, where the action would be, secured permission to return to Washington. With him, as his aide, he took Captain Scott. Hampton and his party left New Orleans on May 20, 1812, prepared for a long and tedious voyage to Washington by way of Baltimore. The ship was buffeted by storms, with the result that the journey to Maryland took a full month. Hampton, Scott, and the rest of the party were fortunate that it did not last even two hours longer. On June 20, as their ship passed through Hampton Roads, she passed close to a British frigate lying off Cape Charles, Virginia. An hour later she passed a pilot boat coming out of Hampton. Scott learned later that the pilot boat was bearing a dramatic message: Congress had declared war on Britain eight days earlier. Had the captain of the British war vessel received this word before Scott's vessel passed him, all of Hampton's party might have spent the War of 1812 in a British prison camp.

Scott was still unaware of his close call as his vessel neared Baltimore, but his impatience became nearly unbearable. At that point, the ship ran aground! Scott and a few others commandeered some small boats, made their way to North Point, and headed on foot for the city.

After some four miles in the summer heat, a sweating Scott encountered a company of militia, who were futilely trying to organize themselves for war. The chaos was heightened by the fact that they were trying to do so while drinking a keg of beer. When Scott appeared on the scene wearing the uniform of a regular, one of the militiamen spotted him. The rest gathered around, making Scott the hero of the occasion. The imbibing militiamen demanded that he mount a table and read the declaration of war, of which the text had just arrived. That he did, "in the midst of the most enthusiastic shouts and cheers."[8] This type of role put Scott in his glory, and he performed it to the hilt. He then took a gig to Baltimore, the transportation being provided by his admiring new friends.

Scott arrived in the streets of Baltimore on the evening of June 21, 1812, to find the place torn apart by riots. Worked up into a frenzy of patriotism by the word of the war declaration three days earlier, mobs of anti-British fanatics had just burned the house of a suspected British sympathizer and had burst into the offices of a newspaper that carried an antiwar slant, Alexander C. Hanson's *Federal Republican.* Since Federalists were considered almost as villainous as the British in Maryland, not only the mobs but the mayor and even the courts considered Hanson's property fair game.

That evening Scott located a couple of friends, who told him, to his surprise and delight, that he had just received a double promotion: from the grade of captain straight to that of lieutenant colonel! Scott later learned that his promotion was due, at least partly, to the effort of Senator William Giles, the Virginian who had introduced the ambitious war bill some months earlier.

The new lieutenant colonel's next assignment presented an exciting prospect: he was to be second in command of the 2d Artillery, located in Philadelphia. Its commander was to be a South Carolina colonel named George Izard. The regiment's main task, for a while, at least, would be to recruit enough men to bring it up to strength. That assignment would not be easy; despite the enthusiasm of the mobs, few men were demonstrating any desire to participate in active combat. Those in the Quaker territory of Philadelphia were among the most averse. Not even the increased bounties and promises of land grants were proving sufficient to induce men to undergo the hardships of war.

As Scott began his duties at old Fort Mifflin, on the Delaware River, word came that fighting was about to begin along the Niagara frontier. There Major General Stephen Van Rensselaer, a militiaman of northern New York, was confidently preparing to invade Upper Canada. Scott wanted very much to be part of that campaign, so he wrote, probably with Izard's permission, to his frequent correspondent Secretary of War William Eustis. He begged permission to take a small battalion of two companies ahead of the main body of the 2d Artillery, leaving Colonel Izard behind to complete the job of recruiting. Eustis, either impressed by the young man's zeal to fight or tired of hearing from him, granted permission. By September 3, 1812, seven weeks after his arrival back at Baltimore, Lieutenant Colonel Scott was on the road with two companies, those of Captains Nathan Towson and James N. Barker, en route to Buffalo by way of Albany and the Mohawk Valley.

It was not an easy trip, but Scott pushed hard. His provisional battalion reached Trenton from Philadelphia in one day, and the next day they covered twenty-five miles in a drenching rain. At Brunswick, New Jersey, they boarded a boat that took them to New York and up the Hudson River to

Greenbush, near Albany. From there they marched northwest up the Mohawk via Schenectady, Utica, and Batavia. The weather was good, and they made good time. On October 4, 1812, Scott reported to Brigadier General Alexander Smyth, commanding the regulars in Buffalo.

The war had been waiting until Lieutenant Colonel Winfield Scott should arrive. Now it could begin.

4

Captured at Queenston, 1812

An early shame befalls American arms.

BRIGADIER GENERAL Alexander Smyth, in command at Buffalo, was Scott's fellow Virginian, though an emigrant from Ireland as a child. Forty-seven years of age, he had spent his life in Virginia politics, serving as a member of the Virginia House of Delegates and later the state Senate. Despite the fact that his military career had been negligible—a peacetime colonel of the Virginia Militia—he requested and attained command of a brigade of regulars being sent to Buffalo, an action more creditable for zeal than for wisdom. And even though he lacked any previous active service, his command of a regular unit engendered in him an attitude of superiority over the militia, so pronounced as to divert his attention from the important mission of invading Canada.

Smyth did, however, receive Scott cordially, since Scott's was at least theoretically a regular unit. He sent Scott's battalion to Black Rock, a small harbor just below Squaw's Island in the Niagara River. There the young officer was to provide protection for a naval detachment that was building ships for future operations on Lake Erie.

The troops of Smyth's command, Scott soon found, were still in a state of excitement over a disaster that had occurred in Detroit some six weeks earlier. On August 15, 1812, General William Hull, governor of Ohio, had surrendered his small army of a thousand regulars and militia to a combined force of British and Indians at Detroit. The surrender constituted a grim setback to American hopes of an easy conquest of Canada.[1] It was bad enough to lose the troops but even worse to lose the store of supplies—muskets, rifles, and ammunition—items the British and Canadians were in dire need of.

Hull was castigated unmercifully by his compatriots. He was, however, as much victim as villain, an officer who had served creditably at Trenton, Saratoga, and Stony Point during the Revolutionary War but who was now advanced in age. He was only one of a group of elderly veterans that Eustis and Madison had summoned in desperation to command the American armies. It would take time and many defeats before they could all be replaced by younger, more energetic officers such as Scott.

The American troops on the Niagara frontier were not, however, discouraged by the news from Detroit. Instead they were hell-bent for revenge, determined to erase this disgrace to American arms. They would not have long to wait, for orders had already been issued for another invasion of Canada, this one at Niagara, to be executed as soon as the troops and supplies could be readied.

The invasion of Canada across the Niagara River, at Queenston, was to be the main American effort for the remainder of the year 1812. The decision to mount it came as the result of many exchanges between the President, the secretary of war, and Major General Henry Dearborn, in command along the Canadian frontier. The basic American strategy of invading Canada somewhere had never been questioned, since the chance of a British invasion of the United States, with Britain so deeply involved with Napoleon in Europe, was negligible. And Canada was vulnerable along the border. Her vast territory was largely uninhabited except for a thin strip along the great Lakes and the St. Lawrence River, and any attack in that region would be hitting into the heart of the settled part of the country. The question the American authorities faced, therefore, had been reduced to determining the place of invasion.

The frontier between the United States and Canada was, as it is today, defined by the thousand-mile waterway that stretches from Lake Michigan on the west, through Lake Huron, then Lake Erie, Lake Ontario, and finally much of the St. Lawrence River. That waterway served a double role. It constituted an obstacle to invasion from either side, of course, but its main significance lay in its value as the lifeline that joined the small settlements along its shores, which were really isolated outposts in the wilderness.

The lengthy communications line between the various Canadian settlements could be cut anywhere, but its most vulnerable area was the stretch along the St. Lawrence between Lake Ontario and Montreal, in Lower Canada (Quebec). American seizure of Montreal would neatly cut off the entire province of Upper Canada (Ontario), as its location controlled the St. Lawrence River. Montreal, therefore, was the logical American land objective for 1812, and the War Department had originally visualized seizing it by crossing three columns into Canada, one at Detroit, one at Niagara, and one via Sacketts Harbor on Lake Ontario.

Military control of both the river and the lakes was deemed a necessary prerequisite for any sustained invasion, however, and there the British and Canadians enjoyed a distinct edge. At the beginning of 1812, the British controlled the Great Lakes–St. Lawrence waterway with a collection of small fleets, which the Americans lacked. The Americans, realizing this disadvantage, had quickly begun constructing warships at Sacketts Harbor, a small fort at the eastern end of Lake Ontario that protected the naval shipyard at Navy Point. At that shipyard they began a naval construction race with the British-Canadian yard at Kingston. For the moment, the Americans had not caught up in building their fleet, so the more decisive move across the St. Lawrence to Montreal (or Kingston) was ruled out. The options of attacking from Detroit in the west or across the Niagara remained.

William Hull's planned invasion of Canada from the Detroit region had been designed to lead off the 1812 campaign. It was in that area that American militia and regulars had already been mobilized to protect against the depredations of Indian groups such as those of Tecumseh and the Prophet. After Hull's surrender, however, the attention of Secretary Eustis and general Dearborn had to focus on the projected crossing of the Niagara River at Queenston. The seizure of Queenston, admittedly, was a limited objective. Even if successfully taken, its capture would be hitting the middle, not the head of the snake. The head was at Montreal.

Yet Queenston was a worthwhile goal for the Americans. The pretty hamlet held strategic importance as the northern terminus of the so-called Portage Road, the point at which both men and supplies on the Canadian side of the Niagara River had to be offloaded from boats and carried overland around Niagara Falls on their way to Lake Erie and beyond. Occupying and consolidating Queenston would thus cut off the main British supply route between Lake Erie and Montreal. Moreover, the warm homes

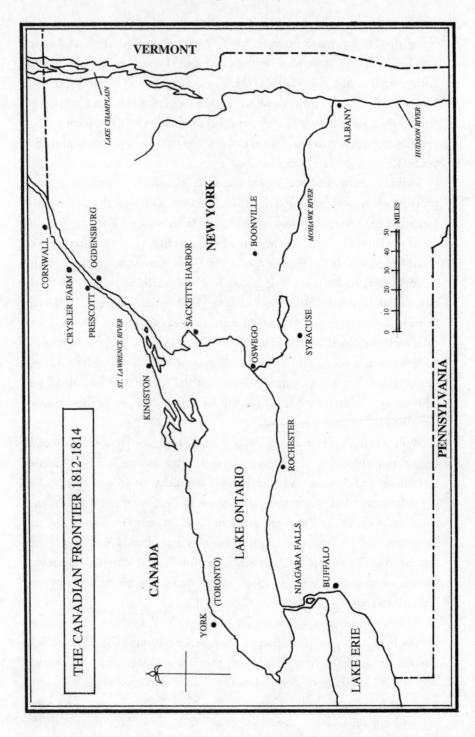

THE CANADIAN FRONTIER 1812-1814

of Queenston would provide shelter for the American militia during the cold northern winter, which in early October was already beginning to threaten.

These matters of broad policy were of little interest to Winfield Scott at that juncture. His mission to provide security for the small naval shipyard at Black Rock promised to be anything but static; something was afoot. Lieutenant Jesse Duncan Elliott, of the Navy, had conceived a plan to capture two British ships that had just sailed in from the western end of Lake Erie. The two vessels had dropped anchor in waters protected by the guns of Fort Erie, a position the British had prepared on the Canadian side of the Niagara River opposite Buffalo. One of these ships was the 200-ton armed brig *Detroit*, an American vessel that had fallen into British hands at Detroit. The other was the 90-ton brig *Caledonia*, an armed trading vessel. Both were carrying American prisoners of war in their holds. Elliott had purchased some small vessels for this project, but he lacked a sufficient boarding party and asked Scott to help him seize these British prizes.

Scott was quick to cooperate. Easily securing General Smyth's permission, he detached two companies, one under Captain Nathan Towson and the other under Lieutenant Isaac Roach. He watched the operation as, in the early morning hours of October 9, the two boarding parties, each in a separate boat, crossed the Niagara at Black Rock. In the dark, the Americans subdued the small crews of the *Detroit* and the *Caledonia* within ten minutes and freed the prisoners. Under a hail of gunfire from Fort Erie and the cheers of the Americans at Buffalo, the two ships headed back toward the American shore, only to be frustrated by a lack of winds and the very strong current of the river. The *Caledonia* eventually made her way back to Black Rock, where she would henceforth perform good service for the Americans, but the *Detroit* ran ashore on the Canadian side of Squaw Island. She changed hands a couple of times and was finally burned by the Americans. The American prisoners were brought safely back to Black Rock.

Scott did not participate actively in this action, but since some artillery shells burst around his observation post, he always remembered this highly successful venture as his first taste of unfriendly fire. The raid also heightened American morale immeasurably,[2] encouraging the Americans as they anticipated the next move, a projected crossing of the Niagara River at Queenston.

The American commander for the Queenston crossing was Major General Stephen Van Rensselaer, a citizen of high standing in New York.[3] Though inexperienced in military matters, he was assisted by a cousin, Lieutenant Colonel Solomon Van Rensselaer, who could boast some significant military experience and whose badge of honor was a scar left over from a wound he had received with Anthony Wayne at Fallen Timbers in 1794. Solomon Van Rensselaer was not only the general's chief of staff; he was also his chief executive officer and would command the Queenston expedition in every respect except in name.

The Van Rensselaers' task was a daunting one. Although the ferry site between the New York town of Lewiston and the Canadian town of Queenston was the "logical" place to cross the Niagara River, that stream presented a formidable obstacle. The river, which flowed due north from Lake Erie to Lake Ontario, was only 250 yards wide at that point, but its currents swirled dangerously from the turbulence at the bottom of Niagara Falls, five miles upstream. On the Canadian side, the village of Queenston nestled below a steep cliff that rose to its south and west. The Queenston Heights, as the escarpment was called, rose only 350 feet above the town, but it towered over the area, giving the scene a closed-in, sinister look.[4]

Solomon Van Rensselaer had no idea how many enemy were waiting for him on the opposite bank, and he was justifiably concerned that he might be attacking a force vastly superior to his own. He knew that the enemy, in whatever strength, was being supported by two heavy artillery batteries. One was a big 24-pounder at Vrooman's Point, a mile downstream to the north, and the other was an 18-pounder in a Redan about halfway up the heights behind the town. The American battery at Fort Gray, on the escarpment above Lewiston, had been unable to silence either of them.

General Van Rensselaer's entire force consisted of about 900 regulars and about 2,300 militia, with a few light cannon under Lieutenant Colonel John Fenwick. But not all of his troops were fit for combat by any standard. The militia were so ill equipped that many lacked shoes; the regulars were comparatively raw troops. Yet despite his concerns, Van Rensselaer could obtain little assistance from the other generals in the area. On October 5, 1812, he had sent a message to Alexander Smyth, at Buffalo, requesting him to attend a conference at Lewiston to discuss the matter. Smyth, though legally a subordinate, never answered his request. As a token of support, however, he promised to send a small reinforcement which, as it turned out, was Win-

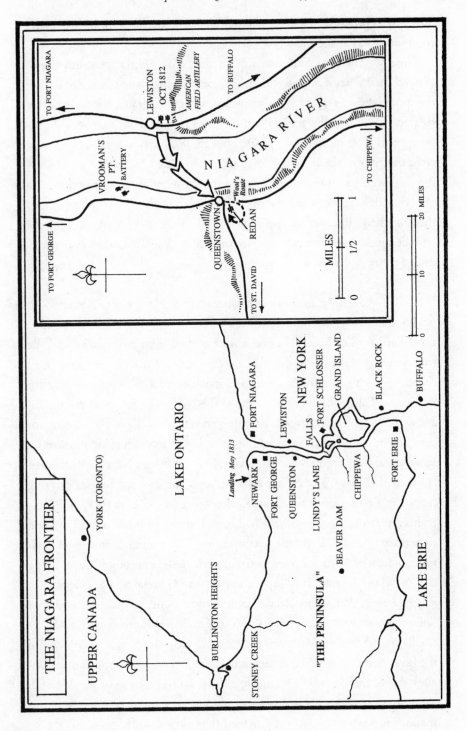

field Scott's provisional artillery battalion. Scott had just arrived in Smyth's command, and as the "new boy," he was the one most easily spared.

Time was not on Van Rensselaer's side. His militia were impatient, buoyed by the news of Jesse Elliott's successful gambit at Black Rock. Furthermore, they were living in conditions of considerable hardship. They therefore informed the general that if he did not act soon, they would simply go home. So on the night of October 10, 1812, Van Rensselaer set out to cross the river at the ferry site, over what he termed "a sheet of violent eddies." The effort came to naught when the lieutenant in charge of directing the boats deserted, crossed the river alone in the darkness, tied his boat on the Canadian shore, and disappeared from the pages of history, taking all the oars designated for the other boats with him. Van Rensselaer was determined to try again soon.

On the morning of October 11, 1812, Lieutenant Colonel Winfield Scott led his provisional artillery battalion out of Black Rock, headed northward for Lewiston. The roads were soaked from heavy rains, and the men were soon unable to drag their six-pounders through the mud. Scott therefore sent the cannon by boat to Fort Schlosser, a point just a mile south of Niagara Falls, where on the night of the twelfth he retrieved them. Unaware that Van Rensselaer was planning another crossing of the Niagara for early the next morning, Scott and his men began to pitch camp in the rain. Hardly had they begun before an infantry officer from a New York regiment chanced their way. The officer showed Scott the message he was carrying from Van Rensselaer to his commanding officer at Niagara Falls, and Scott realized that the man's regiment had been ordered to move up to Lewiston to participate in an assault the next morning. On reading the message, Scott immediately ordered his men to strike their tents. He took his grumbling command up the road at full speed to report to General Van Rensselaer.

Arriving at Van Rensselaer's headquarters, Scott quickly learned that Solomon Van Rensselaer, with some 300 militia volunteers and a slightly smaller number of regulars, was preparing to cross the Niagara River within the hour. Scott asked to be included in the first wave, but both Van Rensselaers shook their heads. The arrangements had already been settled and, more important, Scott's inclusion would automatically place him in command, since army regulations provided that a regular officer (Scott) was to be considered senior to any militia officer (Van Rensselaer) of the same rank.

That would be unacceptable. If Scott desired to waive his rank and go as second in command, they said, he might go.

Scott refused, unmoved by the fact that one of the other regular lieutenant colonels, John Fenwick of the light artillery, had waived his rank in order to participate. He also spurned an arrangement reached by Lieutenant Colonel John Chrystie, of the 4th Infantry, who would go along in command of his own troops—but would give no orders to any militiamen.

Scott's refusal to accept a subordinate status was legally sound, but the Van Rensselaers had a point. The militia were expected to constitute the backbone of this operation once they were across the river, and Solomon Van Rensselaer had far more combat experience than any of the regulars on hand. In any case, the general stood his ground, so Scott departed the conference and began placing his artillery pieces in a position above the ferry, there to support the crossing to best advantage.

From the outset, nothing went right. The participating troops, after waiting around for hours in the darkness and cold wind, finally got off in the early morning hours, the 225 regulars going first because the militia ranks were inexplicably in a state of confusion. Ten of their thirteen boats made it across to their designated landing spots, but three went out of control and drifted too close to Queenston, where boats and men were captured immediately. One of the wayward boats was carrying Colonel Fenwick.

The British garrison in Queenston was small, consisting of two "fencible"* companies of the 49th Foot and the 2d York Militia flank company, 300 men in all, with two little three-pounders. They were highly competent fighting men, however. Their commander, Captain James Dennis of the 49th Foot, quickly discerned what was happening and turned all his weapons, both artillery and infantry, on the oncoming Americans, exacting a heavy toll. Fifty-four American officers and men were killed or wounded before they even reached shore. Among the casualties was Colonel Van Rensselaer, wounded four times and barely able to give orders to seize the Queenston Heights before being carried off. Colonel Chrystie was also gone; his boat, missing an oarlock, was swept downstream in the turbulent waters.

---

*Picked men, usually two companies per regiment; might be called "commando" or "ranger" companies.

At that point, the command devolved on a scrappy little regular, Captain John E. Wool of the 13th Infantry. Wool, a former law student who had been in service only since March of that year, had already received a painful wound in the buttocks in this action, but he was still on his feet. On receiving Van Rensselaer's order he set off to capture the heights.

At first Wool was uncertain how to reach the heights. Charging directly up the slope into the face of the 18-pounder Redan, he reasoned, would be costly. His problem was solved by the lucky arrival of an officer who knew of a small fisherman's path leading up the nearly sheer cliff on the river side of the hill, out of sight of the British guns. Wool seized the opportunity and, like Wolfe at Quebec sixty years earlier, led the bulk of his men safely up the trail. Reaching the crest at a point only thirty yards from the Redan, Wool formed them up to take it from the rear.

The Redan was being manned by none other than the vaunted British commander himself, General Sir Isaac Brock, who had heard the first sounds of gunfire from his headquarters in Fort George and had lost no time in pounding down the seven-mile road to Queenston. Along the way he had paused periodically to alert his troops and get them moving along behind him. Riding through Queenston without slowing down, he had continued straight up the road to the Redan. He was busily directing fire on the Americans when he heard the sounds of Wool's troops in the woods behind him.

Brock was a front-line combat soldier, capable of performing the duties of a sergeant. He personally took a ramrod and with it spiked the fuse hole of the 18-pounder.[5] Then, with the gun's eight-man crew, he stumbled down the hill to the shelter of Queenston, where he began gathering what men he could find of the 49th Foot and the York Militia. Once he had enough men, he deployed them and headed back up the hill to recapture the Redan.

Brock's counterattack, however, was doomed. By the time he made it back up to the Redan, Wool had gathered a considerable force and at the Americans' first volley, the men of the British 49th wavered. Brock tried to rally them. Urging them forward, he rode out in front to lead the way. An American rifleman stood up, took careful aim, and shot him in the chest. Brock fell dead instantly. Brock's aide, Colonel John Macdonell, then took over command, rallied his men, and retook the position for a moment. But the odds were too great. The 49th was repulsed and the aide, like his chief, was killed in action. Captain John Wool was now in full control of Queenston Heights.

On the American side of the Niagara River, Winfield Scott was eager to join in the battle. Towson and Barker, his two battery commanders, no longer needed his supervision, having put their six-pounders into action, doing what they could to divert British fire from the Americans on and across the river. Scott therefore felt free to go back to General Van Rensselaer for permission once more to cross over and take command at Queenston. He finally secured the general's assent, and, wearing his finest full dress uniform, crossed over. He took with him only Lieutenant Roach, acting as his adjutant.

Scott had now achieved his burning ambition, to command troops in combat, and he played his part with zest. During the pause that followed the death of Brock, he was able to reconnoiter his lines and prepare them for defense, confidently expecting reinforcement at any time. As he went from position to position, he introduced himself to the members of his command. He also attempted to unspike the gun in the Redan. That 18-pounder was valuable enough to warrant the personal efforts of the highest commanders.

At one point, it appeared that Scott would be superseded in command. A gentleman in civilian clothes came up and introduced himself as Brigadier General William Wadsworth, of the New York Militia Division, who had brought a detachment across the river. Wadsworth showed no interest in taking charge of the battle, however, and when Scott courteously offered to surrender the command, the general politely turned it down, promising to support Scott to the best of his ability. That Wadsworth did, in Scott's words, "with zeal and valor."

A new crisis was now brewing. Scott's lines were established, but his men were hungry, thirsty, and low on ammunition; they had been moving or fighting since midnight. Even more alarming than the condition of his men was the sight of a column of red-coated troops marching deliberately south along the Fort George road. The commander of that column, Major General Roger H. Sheaffe, was gathering a strong force that included the remaining men of the 49th Foot, the 41st Foot, and the York Militia. It was supplemented by one hundred Mohawk Indians and a company of escaped American slaves.[6]

Scott alerted General Van Rensselaer, who crossed the river to see for himself. Realizing that reinforcements were urgent, the general hastened back to Lewiston in order to move some units forward. Meanwhile General Sheaffe and his British force took their time. Far more cautious than the impulsive Brock, Sheaffe was in no hurry, and he maneuvered carefully around to the west in order to hit the American lines with a coordinated attack. Scott, who had waited impatiently for reinforcements, finally received a hopeless message from General Van Rensselaer: "I have passed through my camp," it said. "Not a regiment, not a company, is willing to join you. Save yourselves by a retreat, if you can. Boats shall be sent to receive you."

Ultimately the blow fell. General Sheaffe, not sure of the strength of the Americans, sent an advance guard of Mohawks, led by chiefs John Brant, Captain Jacobs, and Captain Norton, to probe. When this advance guard was thrown back, Sheaffe's main body closed in. Muskets blazed; the lines seesawed back and forth; bayonets clashed. But Sheaffe's numbers were overpowering, with more reinforcements coming up from the south. Scott's men were driven down the heights to the landing at Queenston. Only about 290 of them still remained.

There the invading Americans received the final shock of the day. No boats were there to take them back across the river! The New York militia, citing the United States Constitution as their authority, had refused to cross into Canada, as that would mean fighting on foreign soil. The boatsmen, having heard the war whoops of the Mohawks on the heights above, had deserted to a man. Wadsworth's and Scott's men were now stranded.

General Wadsworth now assumed command as the senior officer present. He called a hasty council of war and advised that capitulation was inevitable; all agreed. The very act of surrendering, however, was dangerous. The Mohawks, who never accepted the inevitability of battle losses, were infuriated over the death of some of their braves. Thirsting for revenge, they were not likely to observe the niceties of the rules of war.

Concern over that danger was soon confirmed. Scott sent two sets of emissaries carrying proper white flags; nobody returned. Captain Joseph G. Totten and Captain James Gibson then volunteered to try, but Scott refused to let them take the risk without him. He would assume personal responsibility but would take them with him. His line of reasoning was typical: "Being uncommonly tall," he later wrote, referring to himself in the third person, "and in splendid uniform, it was thought his chances of being respected by the savages, who were under but little control, the best."

If Scott really believed that his gold braid would impress enraged Indians, he was sorely wrong. He and his two colleagues made their way around the town to a point where they could ascend into open view, but they did so under sporadic fire. The first enemy they encountered were two Mohawk chiefs, Captain Jacob and John Brant, who had every intention of killing the Americans. The three officers' lives were saved only by the intercession of some British officers. Once the two Indians had been brought under control, Scott and his companions were conducted to General Sheaffe, to whom Scott presented his offer of surrender. Sheaffe readily accepted its terms, but experienced a great deal of difficulty in stopping the fighting. At one point Scott asked to be sent back to his comrades to share their fate. But eventually firing ceased and the American surrender was accomplished.

It had been a fierce battle, disastrous from the American point of view. The Americans had lost 120 men and officers killed and 150 wounded; the British lost 14 killed and 77 wounded. The Indians had lost 14, most of them wounded. So went Winfield Scott's first real experience in military combat.

5

Captive

Scott spends two months as an unwilling guest of
His Majesty's Government in late 1812.

LIEUTENANT COLONEL Scott was now a prisoner of war. Unhappy as that prospect was, it could have been worse. The eighteenth-century custom of treating captive officers as guests was still being observed punctiliously, and he could expect to be treated as a gentleman—albeit under guard, of course. He had survived those dangerous first moments of capture, and he seemed to be out of danger.

Scott and his fellow prisoners were marched the seven miles down the Niagara River to the small but pleasant town of Newark (Niagara-on-the-Lake).[1] On the way, the American prisoners were marched past Vrooman's Point, where the British 24-pounder was emplaced, and passed under the walls of Fort George, which dominated the Niagara River and the American Fort Niagara on the opposite bank. General Wadsworth, Scott, and four other high-ranking officers were billeted in the back of a tavern. Their swords, which they had surrendered at Queenston, had somehow been stacked in the building's entrance hall.

As Scott and his compatriots were beginning to relax after their long period of fighting and their seven miles of marching, they heard someone at the door. The small daughter of the tavern's proprietor came in the room. Two visitors were at the front door of the tavern, she announced, who wished to speak to "the tall American." No question in Scott's mind who "the tall American" might be. Scott never forgot his gigantic size.

When Scott reached the front door, however, he met with an unpleasant surprise. The visitors turned out to be the two Indian chiefs, Captain Jacobs and John Brant,[2] who had tried to kill him only hours before at Queenston. They were still wearing their war paint, carrying knives and tomahawks, and they were obviously up to no good. Captain Jacobs was a burly fellow, almost as big as Scott. So Scott approached them cautiously.

At first the two Indians professed only curiosity. "This many times I fired at you!" Jacobs shouted, holding up several fingers. Then as if to make sure that Scott was not wounded, Jacobs grabbed Scott's arm and tried to turn him around. Scott hurled him against the wall. "Off, villain," he shouted. "You fired like a squaw!"

Both assailants grasped their knives and hatchets. "We kill you now!" Jacobs hissed.

Scott knew he was on his own. The passageway from the room where his comrades were lounging was long—several doors—and therefore out of earshot. The British sentry at the door was not in view and, Scott later mused wryly, "perhaps indifferent to consequences." So he shook himself free, dropped back to the end of the hall, grabbed one of the swords, pulled it out of the scabbard, and faced his foes. Only one man could attack him at a time in that narrow hallway, so he would be able to skewer one, even if the other eventually got him. He crouched on the ready.

The two Indians paused a moment, just long enough for the door behind them to open. In came Colonel Nathaniel Coffin, aide to the British commander, on his way to invite the American officers to dinner with the general. When Coffin saw what was happening, he seized Jacobs by the collar and at the same time drew his pistol. But the would-be assailants were not cowed by Coffin's authority, so Scott closed in, sword in hand, while Coffin shouted for the guard. Immediately the door burst open again, and the sergeant of the guard, with several men, poured in. They subdued Jacobs and Brant and shoved them out the door to the guard house. General Sheaffe thereupon doubled the guard on the Americans to protect them from other disgruntled Indians.

That evening at dinner Scott learned more about his hospitable captor. General Sheaffe had been raised in Boston. His father had been a civil employee of the Crown, who remained a Loyalist. According to custom, Sheaffe had been "adopted" by Lord Percy, later Duke of Northumberland, who was at that time colonel of the 42d Foot. He had been sent to England for his education, and the duke had remained his patron. Sheaffe himself, though not an American citizen, claimed to be anxious to avoid fighting against those he considered his "countrymen by birth," and had early requested that he be sent to some other theater of war.[3] Yet, ironically, it was this battle against the Yankees that earned Sheaffe promotion to major general and the title of baron.

General Sheaffe's consideration for Americans was demonstrated by his actions even more than his words. As soon as the last shot was fired at Queenston he sent a message to General Van Rensselaer proposing a three-day truce to allow both sides to collect and bury their dead. In the course of that truce he allowed General Wadsworth to communicate with Van Rensselaer. Wadsworth's prime need was specie—silver money—with which to pay his troops. The merchants of Newark, true Canadians, were refusing to accept American paper money, even as payment for sundries. His men badly needed such items as razors, soap, and tobacco. Sheaffe forwarded the note, appending one of his own expressing regret over Colonel Solomon Van Rensselaer's severe wound and adding, "If there is anything lacking which might be agreeable or useful to him, I beg that you will inform me." He also allowed American surgeons to cross the river to help care for wounded American prisoners.

Scott himself was caught up in this spirit of courtesy among brothers-in-arms. When he learned that General Brock and Colonel Macdonell were to be formally buried at Fort George, he sent a message across the river urging that Fort Niagara fire salutes during the funeral ceremony. The commander at Fort Niagara complied, and "there was a long-continued roar of American and British cannon in honor of a fallen hero." Sheaffe was so touched that he sent Van Rensselaer a note expressing his gratitude:

> I feel too strongly the generous tribute . . . to my departed friend and chief to be able to express the sense I entertain of it. Noble minded as he was, so would he have done himself.

But there were practical matters to attend to. One was the matter of paroling and exchanging prisoners. Sheaffe early decided to release all militia officers and men on parole—that is, their word of honor not to bear arms against Britain during the present war. The regulars, however, were to be retained until exchanged. That process involved some amusing evaluations of how valuable a man might be to either of the belligerents. In one instance, Sheaffe offered to return a militia lieutenant and a private in exchange for an Indian chief the Americans had captured on Queenston Heights. Van Rensselaer refused. Even though he himself was a dedicated militiaman, he still insisted that no militia lieutenant was worth a fierce Indian chief. But he accepted Sheaffe's offer of two regular American captains, two lieutenants, and a civilian in exchange for Captain Roletts, late of the *Detroit,* a lieutenant of Canadian militia, and a British storekeeper. Neither side demanded exact evaluations; both wanted their own men back.

Three days after the Queenston battle, Scott learned that General Van Rensselaer, disgusted with the conduct of his New York militia at Queenston, had tendered his resignation to General Henry Dearborn, in overall command of American forces on the Canadian frontier. Dearborn readily accepted; he had little sympathy for Van Rensselaer, who he thought was jealous of the regulars. Dearborn did not need to worry about repercussions from President Madison, for Van Rensselaer was a confirmed Federalist and therefore a fair target for criticism. Scott's sympathies were all with Van Rensselaer, however. Writing long after, he exclaimed,

> Nothing could have been more painful than the position of Major-General Stephen Van Rensselaer during the day at Queenstown. A citizen of undoubted patriotism and valor, with a weight of moral character very rare—but without military experience—he found himself helpless in his camp, by the machinations in the ranks of demagogues opposed to the administration and the war.

Not everyone agreed with Scott. Former President Thomas Jefferson, writing immediately after the battle, thought that Van Rensselaer should "be broke for cowardice and incapacity."[4] As it turned out, Van Rensselaer was never tried. He went on to distinguish himself in other fields of activity, but his military career was over.

General Wadsworth, one of the militiamen Sheaffe had paroled, had departed, and Scott was now senior American prisoner in Sheaffe's custody. The young officer was content enough, considering that he was a prisoner, but the situation could not last. After about a week in this congenial captivity, Scott and his 139 regulars were shipped across Lake Ontario to York aboard the *Duke of Gloucester* and the *Prince Regent.* On October 21 they began the long trip to Kingston aboard the 24-gun *Royal George,* under heavy guard of Canadian militia. At Kingston the party transferred to open boats to descend the St. Lawrence River. The river, however, was not navigable all the way; its course was periodically interrupted by rapids. When the boats reached these points, the guards directed their prisoners to disembark. Then the party would march together across the portages.

At Fort Prescott, across the river from the American town of Ogdensburg,

Scott's spirits were raised by rumors that a group of Americans at Ogdensburg were planning a raid. If that transpired, Scott and his men just might be freed. It was not an unreasonable hope. The St. Lawrence is easily crossed at that point, and intercourse between the two towns had once been common. But the rumor had no basis, and Scott resigned himself to further captivity.

Despite his determination to escape if possible, Scott's stay at Fort Prescott was as pleasant as that at Newark. His British custodian, Lieutenant Colonel Thomas Pearson, carried a soft spot for the Americans. He and his young wife had just arrived from England, and while at sea their ship had been captured by an American privateer. When the American skipper learned that Mrs. Pearson was about to give birth, he placed a sentinel at her door, left her husband to attend to her, and offered to help in any way that he could. The privateer was then taken by a British vessel and the Pearsons were released, but the colonel still harbored a deep gratitude. Though Pearson would fight against Scott in two subsequent battles, the two remained friends for life.

The old world chivalry came to an abrupt end when Scott and his fellow prisoners arrived at Montreal. They now came under the authority of Sir George Prevost, governor general of Canada, a man who detested Americans. Like Sheaffe, Prevost had been raised in the United States, but his experiences there had not been happy. He was born in New York City, the son of a Swiss officer in the British service, but throughout his youth he never developed any feelings of warmth toward the Americans—in fact, quite the opposite. So on Scott's arrival, Sir George did everything he could to humiliate the prisoners. He exhibited them to the populace, even parading them in triumph through the streets. He invited them to no dinners in his mess. The only thing good about Scott's stay in Montreal was its short duration. Prevost and Henry Dearborn had arranged for a prisoner exchange, so Scott and his men were sent on to Quebec on November 2, 1812. At Quebec the prisoners were officially paroled and scheduled for shipment on November 20 to Boston.

Scott had one more crisis to face in Canada. On the day before the American prisoners were scheduled to sail, a commission of British officers boarded their ship to screen the enlisted men in search of any suspected of being British subjects. Any men who proved to be of British nationality were deemed to be traitors to the Crown, vulnerable to the death penalty. As records were nonexistent, the only test the British officers had in order to identify alleged traitors was to listen to their speech; the vast majority of those so accused were of Irish ancestry. This was a serious issue between the United States and Britain. The United States held that any person had a right to change his or her previous citizenship in order to become an American. The British held that allegiance to the Crown could never be renounced.

The British were, of course, in control, so Scott's enlisted men were lined up on the deck of the ship without his knowledge and the questioning began. Scott was below decks at the time, but when he heard a commotion topside, he rushed out to see what was going on. Once he took in the situation, he interceded. Confronting the British officer in charge, he demanded, "What is the meaning of this procedure?"

The answer was haughty: "These men are British subjects and will be taken ashore, sent to England, and tried for treason."

"They are citizens of the United States, prisoners of war regularly paroled!"

"You are a prisoner of war yourself, sir, and you will have the goodness to go below instantly!"

"I shall do nothing of the sort," Scott shouted. Then he turned to those men who had not yet been interrogated. "You men," he commanded, "not one of you will open his mouth—not another word from you." The soldiers obeyed Scott's order despite continued threats and bullying from their captors. No more men were arrested. But before Scott's intercession, twenty-three unlucky men had already given themselves away. They were removed from the ship and later sent to Britain. As they debarked, Scott pledged out loud that the United States government would protect them. He personally would not forget the plight of those American troops.

The trip down the St. Lawrence River in the middle of winter was harrowing, as the ship's course took it north of Nova Scotia on the way south to Boston. Scott's contingent suffered severely from cold and lack of food. Scurvy afflicted some of the men, so Scott shared his own cache of supplies with the general mess, to little avail. When starvation was becoming a real threat, the ship put to shore for resupply on Cape Breton Island. An American fisherman, who ran his own little settlement, was able to meet their immediate needs. That ordeal lasted forty-six days, and Scott was glad to deposit his sick at Boston. He then headed straightaway for Washington.

With all the trials that Scott had undergone over a period of four months, foremost in his mind was the plight of the twenty-three accused men who were still in British hands. He awaited the chance to broach that matter to the American authorities at the first possible moment.

6

※※∨✕※

The Capture of Fort George

*Scott, as virtual American commander, wins his
first laurels, May 1813.*

T HE CITY of Washington that greeted the prisoners returning from
Canada was a far cry from the magnificent metropolis of today. A disgruntled junior British diplomat, writing just before the War of 1812 began,
described it as a "sorry community of bogs and gullies, broken tree stumps,
piles of refuse, potholes, and endless gluelike mud, with wells the only supply of water." Petty thieves and burglars frequented the streets, along with
pigs and cattle. The Capitol and the White House—"the two Greek tem-
ples," in the words of the young diplomat—were not yet completed. The
columns of the Capitol were too weak to support the weight of the visitors
in the gallery.[1] Yet it is difficult to exaggerate the feeling of joy experienced
by Scott and his companions as they saw this primitive capital again.

Scott arrived in Washington on January 10, 1813, just in time for a White
House reception that evening, hosted by President James Madison. Scott
was never without a full-dress uniform, and since the reception was open to
all, he attended enthusiastically. Once he had passed through the customary
receiving line, Scott found himself surrounded by a crowd of senators, congressmen, and cabinet officers, all eager to hear his stories of the Queenston
battle and of his experiences as a prisoner of war. Scott happily obliged, his
mind still dwelling on the plight of the Irish American soldiers who had
been removed from the deck of his ship at Quebec.

Scott's audience was receptive to his account of British high-handedness, and several cabinet members insisted that he make a formal report to the secretary of war. President Madison, who had joined the group, seconded the idea. That, of course, made rendering the report an official duty, and Scott went about it with zeal, submitting it on January 13, only three days after his arrival in the city.[2] The War Department immediately sent it to Capitol Hill, and on February 27 the Congress passed an "Act vesting the President of the United States with the Power of Retaliation." The act gave the President valuable authority to negotiate with the British with whatever means were available to him. Scott had now been noticed in a minor way.

During the several months that Scott had been away from Washington, the political scene had changed considerably. In November 1812, James Madison had been reelected to a second term as President, but Dr. William Eustis had resigned as secretary of war. General John Armstrong, then minister to the court of Napoleon, had been named to succeed Eustis, and Secretary of State James Monroe would be acting secretary until Armstrong could arrive.

Armstrong was a strange appointment. A New Yorker who had declared himself determined to "rescue" the government from what he considered "Virginian incompetence and narrowness," he hated and feared Monroe, especially since he suspected that Monroe, who fancied himself a military man, coveted his position. Monroe reciprocated the antagonism. General opposition to Armstrong was such that he was barely confirmed by the Senate—18 to 15—with the two Kentucky senators abstaining. Under these conditions, it has been rightly remarked that "nothing but military success of the first order could secure a fair field for Monroe's rival."[3]

With all his faults, however, Armstrong would prove to be a far stronger secretary than Eustis had been simply because he knew what he wanted to accomplish. When he took over the War Department, however, he did not reorganize it. He realized the value of the policy pursued by Eustis of refusing to appoint a single general-in-chief of the Army, because by so refraining he kept maximum power to himself. Thus Henry Dearborn, the "senior" major general and commander on the Canadian frontier, found his prestige dimmed by the fact that the Southern Department, commanded by Major General Thomas Pinckney of South Carolina, remained independent of his authority. Armstrong would obviously be very much engaged in formulating strategy for the war.

Soon after returning to Washington, Scott received another promotion. On January 29, 1813, Congress authorized an expansion of the Army by twenty additional regiments, an increase that called for six new major generals and six new brigadiers. Colonel George Izard, commanding officer of the 2d Artillery, was one of those selected for brigadier, and his advancement vacated the position of colonel of the regiment. Scott was a logical choice. President Madison was said to balk at promoting him so quickly, however, since he was still only twenty-six years old, but Senator Giles and others among Scott's Virginia friends again exerted their influence, and the President relented. Scott received official notice of his promotion to colonel in mid-March 1813.

His good fortune was somewhat beclouded, however, by a serious disagreement that had arisen between the Americans and British regarding Scott's exchange status. This was an issue that could mean life or death to him—literally. It came from a difference in the positions of the two governments regarding prisoner exchange.

Scott, along with General William Hull and Colonel John Chrystie, had been "paroled," not officially "exchanged," when they were sent home from Quebec. The parole status, a matter of courtesy and convenience, was granted to a prisoner of war on the strict condition that he would refrain from taking up arms again until officially exchanged. The penalty for violation of the statute was automatic and without exception: any parolee who had violated his oath and was then recaptured must be summarily executed. The individual parolee, of course, was a helpless pawn in the controversy. Scott, for his part, decided simply to rely on the word of his government as to whether or not he had been officially "exchanged."[4] For the time being, capture by the British would mean automatic death.

In early April 1813, Colonel Scott left Philadelphia at the head of three hundred men from the 2d Artillery. He and his command then followed the well-established route to the frontier of Lake Ontario: up the Hudson River to Albany, from there up the Mohawk River to Oswego. At Oswego, Commodore Isaac Chauncey had provided transports to carry Scott and his men westward across the lake to Fort Niagara.

It was the second time in a year that Scott had made the trip, but this time the circumstances were quite different. In the fall of 1812, he had gone as a fledgling regular officer who had never heard an enemy shot fired—and was still under a cloud from his conviction for "unofficer-like conduct." Now he had achieved command of his regiment; more importantly, he had become a veteran and even a minor celebrity. True, his total experience under fire had covered a period of only a single day, but that day of intense fighting was more than most officers had seen, and during the battle for Queenston he had conducted himself well. His opinions had been solicited by the President himself, and he had been selected over several others for his present position. He went happily.

He also went armed with theoretical knowledge. Despite the rigors of the trip, Scott began his lifelong habit of taking along his personal military library, his five-foot portable bookshelf of military writers. He took pride in those books, especially in a new French work embodying the latest in Napoleonic staff principles, Théibault's *Manuel Général du service de états-majors généraux*. He would soon, he hoped, put the manual to practical use.

While Scott was on his journey, Secretary of War John Armstrong began pushing his plans for offensive action against Canada during 1813. Dearborn, Armstrong insisted, was to move directly from Sacketts Harbor across Lake Ontario to take Kingston and, farther east, cross the St. Lawrence at Ogdensburg to take Fort Prescott. With that accomplished, Dearborn could turn eastward to take the ever-important Montreal. Dearborn had plenty of force to do that, Armstrong claimed: 7,000 regulars and militia. He estimated the enemy force in Upper Canada to consist of only 1,800 British regulars and 500 militia.[5]

There was nothing secret or particularly original about Armstrong's strategic views. Everybody recognized that the only line of communications between Upper Canada and Halifax was the waterways of the St. Lawrence River and Lake Ontario. If the Americans could sever that line, then Upper Canada would fall without a fight. "It is well known," wrote the Quebec *Gazette* in 1814, "that [the St. Lawrence] is the only communication between Upper and Lower Canada. . . . It is needless to say that no British force can remain in safety or maintain itself in Upper Canada without a ready communication with the lower province."[6]

Armstrong explained his views to Madison and his cabinet in February 1813. He claimed that the army in the north would soon have four thousand men at Sacketts Harbor and another three thousand at Buffalo. He proposed that the force at Sacketts Harbor be transported across Lake Ontario to take Kingston, only thirty-five miles away, on about April 1. Having destroyed the British navy yard at Kingston and taken what it needed from the stockpiles of supplies there, that force would then turn westward along the northern shore of the lake and take York (present-day Toronto), the capital of Upper Canada. Then, joined up with the force from Buffalo, the Americans could turn eastward toward Montreal with a secure base to their rear.

Armstrong favored this plan for several reasons, not the least of which was that it could be launched soon, six weeks before the melting ice would permit British reinforcements to arrive in the region.

But Armstrong's views met resistance from the two men who would have to execute his plan. General Dearborn and his Navy counterpart, Commodore Isaac Chauncey, meeting in their joint headquarters at Sacketts Harbor, quickly agreed that Armstrong's plan was too audacious. Sir George Prevost's force at Kingston, Dearborn wrote to Armstrong, came to about six or seven thousand men, three thousand of them regulars. He and Chauncey therefore advocated a much more modest plan that called for an extended raid on York and later, if possible, for further attacks on the western part of the Canadian frontier rather than the eastern. The west, he pointed out, was where most of the American troops were.

Armstrong assented reluctantly. His only condition, somewhat snide, was that Dearborn must command the troops himself, rather than delegate the responsibility to some subordinate officer.

By April 1813, Commodore Chauncey's booming shipyard at Sacketts Harbor had provided him with enough new ships to assure him at least temporary control of Lake Ontario. Since continuation of that control was critical to any serious American offensive operations, he had Dearborn's full support for any joint actions to retain it. Word had come in that Commodore Sir James Yeo, the British naval commander, was building a new 30-gun brig at York. The *Isaac Brock,* as the brig was to be named, would tip the balance of power on Lake Ontario in Yeo's favor whenever she joined the British fleet. Since her construction was nearly completed, Chauncey and Dearborn concluded that she must be destroyed without delay. They fitted out an invasion force of 1,600 men, to be carried by Chauncey's ships.

The expedition arrived off York on the morning of April 27, 1813. Dearborn was present, as Armstrong had insisted, but the actual landing force was commanded by Brigadier General Zebulon Pike. Pike's brigade enjoyed the protection of the gunfire from Chauncey's vessels, and since the British had only 600 men, the attack, though costly, was successful. The small British-Canadian garrison was soon forced to evacuate the town, and the *Brock* was set afire. A bonus came in the form of a 10-gun brig named the *Gloucester,* which the Americans captured intact.

The operation, however, cost the Americans dearly. They lost 320 dead and wounded. One of them, killed in a freak explosion, was General Pike himself, an officer generally considered the most promising brigadier in the Army. And now, with the stern authority of Pike gone, some of the American troops got out of hand, burning all the public buildings, including the houses of assembly. That wanton destruction had long-reaching consequences; it would later serve as justification for British excesses of a similar nature. That act signaled the beginning of the end to the code of courtesy between gentleman adversaries that had been much observed during the first year of the war.

Dearborn occupied York for ten days. He then withdrew his force. His objective had been attained.

Scott and his troops reached Oswego in early May 1813, about a week after Dearborn had raided York. At first the newcomers were unaware of what was afoot, being informed only that Dearborn and Chauncey were absent at Fort Niagara, in the western end of Lake Ontario. Nevertheless, ships were on hand to carry Scott and his men to Dearborn's headquarters, and despite unfavorable winds, Scott was able to report to Dearborn on May 13, 1813.

Fate was kind to Winfield Scott. He was coming as chief of staff to a command that was almost completely lacking in military ability and energy. Henry Dearborn, though respected as a veteran of the Revolutionary War, was a sick man, age sixty-two. Most of his top subordinates were, like him, veterans beyond their prime. Dearborn's deputy was Major General Morgan Lewis, former governor of New York and one-time chief of staff to General Horatio Gates at Saratoga. Lewis was probably the best of Dearborn's subordinates; he was said to be overfond of personal comfort, but was at least honest and frank, attributes that placed him a cut above many of the officers of the time.

Dearborn's three brigade commanders were an unpromising trio. John Chandler, like Dearborn and Lewis, had been with Gates at Saratoga, though he had long since been out of the army. The other two brigadiers were regulars, John Parker Boyd and William H. Winder. Boyd could boast some experience in combat, but not with the United States Army. Once a soldier of fortune in India, he had since emigrated to the United States and had found a soft spot in the American Army, where he was not regarded highly. Winder seemed to be a decent man, though in dire need of practical experience.

On May 10, three days before Scott arrived at Fort Niagara, General Dearborn called a council of war to discuss ways by which to follow up his limited success at York. The next obvious target was Fort George, the British-Canadian outpost right across the Niagara River from Fort Niagara, where they were then sitting. Though a position of some importance, Fort George was being garrisoned by only about 1,700 British and Canadians, as the Americans knew, whereas Dearborn's strength came to about 4,700. When the council convened, Dearborn asked for opinons on whether or not his army should attack Fort George. This reluctant group of warriors were uncomfortable, but they finally agreed on Fort George as the target for the next operation. Dearborn formally announced the decision but then did nothing.[7] He was awaiting the arrival of his new chief of staff, Scott, to convert his orders into reality.

When Scott assumed his duties, he saw at once that Dearborn's command structure was in a state of utter disarray. He therefore concluded that he would be able to run the Fort George operation himself—in Dearborn's name, of course. He met no resistance; Dearborn, in fact, immediately entrusted him with all the planning for the forthcoming assault. So in the two short weeks he had before the target date, Scott tried to organize the staff along professional lines while simultaneously drawing up a plan of attack for Dearborn's approval.

Scott attacked his problems with confidence, and for good reason. Though he could not know the exact British and Canadian strength around Fort George, he was sure that Dearborn's heavy preponderance of numbers would carry the day, especially since he was receiving the hearty cooperation of Commodore Chauncey, who would deliver Dearborn's army to its specified landing place on the Lake Ontario shore. While making plans with the Navy, Scott was impressed by a young naval officer named Oliver Hazard Perry, the new commander of American naval forces on Lake Erie. Though Perry was out of his territory on Lake Ontario, he had come to help Commodore Chauncey because the opening of the Niagara frontier was all-important to his own plans. The fleet Perry was constructing for Lake Erie was nearing completion, but it was bottled up in Black Rock, and he needed to have the British cleared from the western banks of the Niagara River before he could safely sail his ships past Fort Erie into the lake.

Scott and Dearborn were facing a competent British commander at Fort George. Brigadier John Vincent, who had replaced Major General Sheaffe, enjoyed a fine reputation as an aggressive soldier in the mold of Isaac Brock. But the odds were against Vincent and he knew it. He assumed that Fort George would soon be attacked, but he had no way of knowing where an assault would be made, whether across the Niagara River or from the shore of Lake Ontario, to the north of Newark. Dearborn and Scott made the most of the advantage accorded them by the help of the Navy. They had always intended to attack from the shores of Lake Ontario, but to keep Vincent confused, Scott placed two artillery batteries at Youngstown, just across the Niagara River from Fort George. Although those small guns could do little damage to the fort itself, their activities were meant to camouflage Scott's real intent.

On May 25, 1813, Scott published Dearborn's order. It called for an amphibious landing from Lake Ontario, the troops delivered by the Navy at a point on the Canadian shoreline about two miles west of the lighthouse at Newark. Once ashore, the landing force was to turn eastward to cut off and destroy Vincent's force. Fort George itself was of secondary importance compared to the prospect of capturing its garrison. To further ensure the destruction of Vincent's force, Scott designated Colonel James Burn, of the 2d Dragoons, to cross the Niagara at Queenston, south of the fort, to intercept any stragglers who might escape from Vincent's fleeing army.

The force at Newark was to land in column, led by an advance guard of 400 men. Scott designated himself to command the advance guard and assigned his own artillery battalion, fighting as infantry, to serve under him. Boyd's brigade was to follow Scott at a distance of three hundred yards, and in turn Boyd was to be followed by Winder. Chandler's brigade was to constitute the reserve. Though the expedition was to be officially commanded by General Morgan Lewis, Scott's position at the forefront effectively ensured that he would be able to control the development of the battle.

Dearborn signed the order readily. The amphibious expedition would leave from Four-Mile Creek* on the American side of the Niagara River and land early in the morning of May 27.

---

*Terms such as "Four-Mile Creek" denote the distance between the feature and the mouth of the Niagara River. Thus there were two Four-Mile Creeks, both flowing northward into Lake Ontario. One was in New York and one in Canada.

The Battle of Fort George

Commodore Chauncey's ships, scows, and longboats arrived off the designated shoreline as scheduled, at 4:00 A.M. on May 27, 1813. Fortunately for the Americans, the naval planning had been thorough. Chauncey and Perry had reconnoitered the beaches beforehand and had placed floating markers to identify the positions of the supporting vessels. The fog was heavy, but still the ships found their way. When visibility permitted, Chauncey's fleet began taking the enemy's shore batteries under fire.

There were two known British artillery positions on the shore, one at the lighthouse and the other one to the east at Two-Mile Creek. The *Tompkins* and the *Conquest* silenced the battery at Two-Mile Creek with solid shot and shell. The *Growler*, the *Julia*, and the *Ontario* did the same with the gun at the beacon. Chauncey watched the action from the deck of his command ship, the *Madison*. With him was Dearborn, who insisted on witnessing the assault even though not officially a participant.

At about 6:00 A.M., the boats carrying Scott's advance force cast off from their ships and headed toward shore. Soon, however, winds caused Scott's boat and several others to drift to the west. Perry, who was with Chauncey and Dearborn on the *Madison*, noticed this difficulty, jumped into his gig, picked up Scott, and guided him in steering the wayward craft. Once they were back on the path, Perry left Scott to pull for the beach.

As soon as the fog lifted, General Vincent, at Newark, knew that the blow had fallen. As he had not dared deploy all his regiments on the coast, he threw forward the Glengarry Light Infantry[8] and immediately began to reinforce it with what he could find of the British 41st Foot and the 49th Foot. The Glengarrys were waiting when Scott and his men beached their boats and started to scale the seven-foot embankment. As Scott was clambering up across the loose sand, one of their members lunged at him with his bayonet. Scott dodged the blade but lost his footing. He fell down to the beach, ruffled but unhurt. General Dearborn, on the *Madison*, saw the event and feared that his chief of staff was lost. But Scott made it up again amid heavy fighting, in which Scott, as he later recorded, lost one man in five, wounded or dead. The assault could readily have failed save for the effects of the naval gunfire, which succeeded in driving the British back from the beach.

Eventually the Glengarrys were overwhelmed. With over half their men fallen, they dropped back. Vincent ordered in other troops as they came up—a company of Newfoundlanders, five companies of the 8th Foot, some militia, and a company of Negro pioneers. This reinforcement was strong enough to force Scott back toward the beach for a moment, but he succeeded in holding along a low ridge inland from the shore. Soon Colonel Moses Porter's artillery came ashore, giving him support, and then Boyd's brigade. Faced with this force, Vincent decided to retreat.

On Scott pushed, attempting to drive between Vincent's men and Fort George. But he was too late; Vincent succeeded in evacuating the fort and moving the bulk of his troops southward before Scott could cut him off. Scott caught a runaway horse and rode out ahead of his troops to scout the town of Newark, familiar from his short time there as a prisoner. Spotting two British soldiers attempting to escape from Fort George, Scott rode them down and forced them to surrender. The new prisoners were talkative. The garrison had evacuated, they said, and they had just finished spiking the guns. They had set fuses to explode the magazines in the various bastions. Scott shouted for two companies of his 2d Artillery to follow him into the fort, and he galloped through the main gate, hoping to save the powder.

It was almost Scott's last act of heroism. One of the magazines exploded, shattering the area with stones and knocking Scott to the ground, his collar bone broken. Major Jacob Hindman, one of his artillerymen, helped Scott to his feet, and the young colonel decided that he could carry on despite his injury. Together Scott and Hindman stamped out the slow fuses before they fizzed into the powder kegs. That accomplished, Scott paused a moment to cut down the flag that had flown over the fort—he coveted such souvenirs— and then, as his slightly injured horse was still able to carry him, turned his attention to pursuing the fleeing enemy.

Scott's goal was to catch up with the rest of his advance guard, by now a mile ahead. At Five-Mile Meadows, just behind Queenston, Scott encountered Colonel Burn, who had just crossed the Niagara River with one of his companies of dragoons. Obviously not the man for the difficult task of cutting off an enemy, Burn had failed in his mission, and Scott cursed his luck for having depended on him. But on second thought, Scott realized that he was also at fault; he had not allocated Burn anything like the amount of strength necessary to accomplish so ambitious a maneuver.

Still Scott pushed on. Twice he received orders from General Lewis to halt the pursuit: twice he brushed them aside. Now, at the Meadows, he was prepared to ignore similar orders again, surmising that the general had no way of appreciating the golden opportunity that awaited them. But his intentions were frustrated when General Boyd appeared. Like Scott, Boyd was annoyed at Lewis's timid order, but unlike Scott he considered it to be mandatory. And Boyd, as senior officer, was in command. The pursuit stopped.

Vincent thus escaped with most of his force, having lost only 52 officers and men killed, 44 wounded, and 262 missing. He sent word to his garrisons at Queenston and Fort Erie to join his main body at a point five miles west of Queenston, and when all the elements concentrated at that point, he moved his unified army westward. If not completely intact, it was at least a force the Americans would still have to contend with.

In contrast to Vincent's losses, the Americans had lost relatively few, only 17 killed and 42 wounded. But more important than comparative losses was the fact that they had cleared the Niagara frontier of British and Canadian troops. It was probably the best planned and executed battle of the War of 1812.

Winfield Scott had definitely won his spurs. General Morgan Lewis granted as much, generously admitting that Scott had "fought nine tenths of the battle."[9] His success was attributable to his zeal, his energy, his audacity, and his studies. The matter of studies is not to be underestimated. With only a smattering of real experience, Scott had dominated a major battle. Senior officers had not only deferred to him; they had allowed him to run the operation almost single-handedly. He had come a long way from the anonymous artillery captain of less than a year before.

7

Muddle at Montreal

*In an abortive campaign, Scott sees the end of the
Old Guard.*

THE IMMEDIATE results of the Fort George attack were gratifying to
Major General Henry Dearborn and his chief of staff, Winfield Scott.
Newark, Queenston, Chippewa, and Fort Erie were all abandoned by the
British, and Oliver Hazard Perry was able, at Black Rock, to move his ships
out into Lake Erie, the British guns having been silenced. Perry would fight
his renowned Battle of Lake Erie the following September. But the long-
term results of Dearborn's victory were far less decisive. British General
John Vincent's army had survived the recent battle, and its continued presence in the vicinity required the Americans to choose between abandoning
Fort George and leaving a substantial number of troops to man it. Neither
prospect was inviting; the troops necessary to garrison Fort George could
be better used elsewhere in the decisive theater at the eastern end of Lake
Ontario.

Had Dearborn been able to count on Commodore Chauncey's fleet to
help him, he might still have destroyed Vincent's army by a series of landings
to the British rear, paving the way for an invasion of Upper Canada around
the west end of the lake. Short of that, the Americans could have done great
damage to British installations all around Lake Ontario, especially to
Burlington Heights. But Chauncey's help came to an end just as Fort George
was about to fall. A British fleet, Chauncey learned, had left Kingston,
bound for his all-important base at Sacketts Harbor. So Chauncey left for

the eastern end of Lake Ontario as soon as he had put Dearborn's army ashore.

Chauncey's information turned out to be all too true. Spies and illegal trade abounded in all towns on the American-Canadian frontier throughout the War of 1812, and each side was kept well informed about the activities of the other. As soon as Chauncey had left Sacketts Harbor for Niagara, therefore, word had reached Sir George Prevost and Commodore Sir James Yeo at Kingston. They immediately marshalled the entire British fleet on Lake Ontario, with 700 British regulars, and set out to attack Chauncey's base and occupy it. Failing that, they could at least destroy the new ship under construction there, the *General Pike*, a 28-gun frigate which was nearing completion.[1] They had left Kingston on May 25, 1813, just before the assault on Fort George.

At Sacketts Harbor, which the British fleet reached in the early morning hours of May 29, the invaders found themselves pitted against 900 American defenders, 500 militiamen on the beach and 400 regulars entrenched on the heights behind. Prevost and Yeo landed their assault force at the base of Horse Island, a peninsula that led to the beach, and after a sharp fight dispersed the American militiamen. The American commander, Colonel Jacob Brown, handled his men well, however, and the British paid dearly. When they reached the crest of the ridge, they met the American main line of resistance, 400 regulars occupying Fort Tompkins and Fort Pike. After a hard fight, Prevost decided to withdraw his invasion force.

The British inflicted much damage, however. In the course of the fighting, some poorly aimed but fortuitous British shells passed over the heads of the soldiers on the ridge and fell among the ships at Navy Point in the rear of the American position. American sailors, unaware of what was happening, thought the shells had been fired by a victorious British force, so they complied with previous orders and set fire to the *General Pike*. Once they discovered their mistake, the tars extinguished the fires, but not before considerable damage was done to the sails and rigging. Completion of the *Pike*, the ship on which Chauncey had placed all his hopes, was delayed for six very important weeks. Commodore Chauncey arrived at the battle scene too late to participate.

Dearborn did not give up plans to capture Montreal in 1813, even though he was now forced to confine himself to land operations in the vicinity of Fort George. He immediately moved his headquarters from Fort Niagara to

Fort George, and then, without waiting to hear of the outcome at Sacketts Harbor, sent Morgan Lewis with a task force in hot pursuit of Vincent. Lewis's effort, however, could only be described as pathetic. His men took so long getting on the road that Vincent had moved his newly concentrated force to Forty-Mile Creek before Lewis could make contact. Lewis marched only five miles south, stopped, and turned back to Fort George.

Four days later, on June 2, Dearborn and Scott organized a serious expedition, a task force of four infantry regiments, reinforced with artillery and dragoons. Brigadier General William Winder, in command, was to proceed westward along the Lake Road in the general direction of Vincent's position at Forty-Mile Creek. The day after Winder left, Dearborn sent General Chandler, with a slightly smaller force, along the same road. Chandler and Winder arrived at Forty-Mile Creek at the same time, only to discover that Vincent had fallen back in the direction of Brunswick Heights. They continued the pursuit, and on June 5 they reached a place called Stony Creek. Apparently content with their achievements so far, they bivouacked for the night and relaxed, posting only a very light guard.

Unfortunately for the Americans, their carelessness did not go unnoticed. When Vincent discovered Winder's vulnerability, he led 700 men to the edge of the American camp during the night and in the early morning overpowered the three sentries. In the process, however, a few exuberant British soldiers began shouting, alerting the Americans. Once aroused, the Americans gave a good account of themselves, and in the melee the British reported losing about 212 men, including 55 missing. The Americans reported only 55 killed and wounded, but 113 missing in action, most of them captured. Among those who fell into British hands were both brigadier generals.

With Winder and Chandler gone, Colonel James Burn, who had disappointed Scott at Queenston a week earlier, assumed command, called a council of war, and decided to retreat, a movement the Americans carried out in such haste that they left their dead unburied on the field. Once out of the range of British guns, Colonel Burn stopped at Forty-Mile Creek, where he awaited orders. A distraught Dearborn, back at Fort George, turned to Lewis and sent him, assisted by Scott, to assume command of the leaderless task force. But by now British Commodore Yeo's fleet was in the vicinity, threatening Lewis's rear, so Lewis, on arrival, decided to retreat all the way. Scott was placed in command of the rear guard, the point of greatest danger.

He later claimed that his presence did much to relieve the fears of the frightened troops. He conducted the operation without interruption.

Henry Dearborn now collapsed. Suffering from a combination of age, indecision, anxiety, and that mild kind of typhoid called "lake fever," he instructed Scott to issue orders designating General Lewis as temporary commander of the Niagara army. He then restricted his activities to writing plaintive letters to Secretary Armstrong and to looking over Lewis's shoulder. Lewis himself was soon recalled to Sacketts Harbor, and he was succeeded in command by Brigadier General John P. Boyd.

Dearborn's humiliations were not quite finished. With his approval, Boyd sent out another expedition of 500 men to Beaver Dam, a point seventeen miles southwest of Fort George, to destroy the Decou house, suspected of being a base for marauding parties. The task force, actually more of a raid, was to be commanded by Lieutenant Colonel Charles G. Boerstler, 14th Infantry, a cantankerous individual who viewed Scott with envy and loathing. Unwilling to accept a verbal order from Scott, Boerstler demanded orders in writing, under the pretext that he harbored misgivings about the mission. Scott, as Boyd's chief of staff, readily wrote the orders in Boyd's name.

Boerstler's bad humor could have been forgiven had he been successful in his mission, but unfortunately he was not. He marched his task force out of Fort George on June 23, 1813, and arrived at Beaver Dam on the morning of the 24th. Meeting a party of about 200 Indians, he quickly decided to retreat—only to find his escape route blocked by a mere handful of Canadian militiamen. As Boerstler vacillated, a British officer from the 49th Foot, Lieutenant James FitzGibbon, appeared and demanded his surrender, threatening massacre by the Indians. Boerstler abjectly complied, surrendering 540 men to a force of 260 Indians, British regulars, and Canadian militiamen.[2]

The Boerstler affair signaled the end of Henry Dearborn's tenure at Niagara. Much to the relief of his command, he left Fort George under orders on July 15, 1813, still bewildered at what had gone wrong. But the officers of the Army of the Niagara, recognizing the old general's "high moral worth, patriotism, valor, and military distinction" during the Revolution, sent him off as a hero. Scott, the designated speaker, enthusiastically comforted Dearborn with kind words. Scott's effort, he later remarked with satisfaction, "did much to soothe a wounded heart."

Scott left his position as chief of staff very shortly after Dearborn's departure, returning full time to the command of his 2d Artillery, which he had never relinquished. While on duty as chief of staff, however, he came in contact with two men who would play roles in his future life. One was a British officer, a sturdy lieutenant colonel who had been in the forefront of Glengarry resistance to Scott on the beaches of Newark. Scott's first awareness of John Harvey, General Vincent's adjutant, did not portend well for a later friendship, as it came in the form of an exchange regarding the troublesome matter of Scott's status as a former prisoner.

Among the spoils taken by the British at Stony Creek was a document, signed by Scott, which was brought to Vincent's attention. Scott was still a parole breaker in British eyes, and Vincent directed Harvey to write a letter to General Lewis asking whether the "W. Scott" who had signed the paper was indeed the Scott who had been taken at Queenston on the previous October 13. If so, the message went on,

> it is impossible that he can be recognized in any other capacity than a British prisoner of war, he having given his parole of honor, (of what value is now proved,) not to serve again until regularly exchanged. Lieut. Colonel Scott cannot but be aware, however, of what the custom and usage of nations have prescribed should the chance of war again place him in our hands.[3]

Lewis did not answer the letter directly, referring the matter to Dearborn, who wrote to Prevost. Prevost, in a letter to Dearborn, remained adamant on the subject, and the United States government, equally adamant, still refused to take Scott off duty.

Scott bore no resentment toward Harvey because of his message; despite the slur, he saw it as written in his best interests, as giving fair warning. He decided to answer Harvey's unanswered missive over the signature of his own assistant chief of staff. In a message addressed directly to Harvey, he confirmed that he was indeed the officer referred to in Harvey's letter. He added, however, that he placed "implicit faith in the assurances of his government and as a good soldier obeys its mandates regardless of consequences." That ended the matter for the moment.

The other man who came to Scott's attention at this time was Brigadier General Peter Buel Porter, a militia general who had succeeded Alexander Smyth in command at Buffalo.[4] Porter was an ex-congressman, one of the War Hawks, and the chairman of a congressional committee recommending preparations for war in early 1812. Though now out of Congress, he retained strong political connections with President Madison, Secretary Armstrong, and New York Governor Daniel Tompkins. Porter's weakness as a soldier was not a faint heart; it was an overactive spleen. Fearing no retribution for insubordination, Porter vented his frustrations about the state of chaos in the Niagara district by writing vituperative letters to both Armstrong and Tompkins. He spared Scott in his tirades, probably because Scott had performed well, but it was well known that he disliked Scott intensely, principally because of Scott's obvious disdain for militiamen. Boyd learned of Porter's attacks but decided that he could do nothing. Scott recognized Porter, however, as a man to watch out for.

In late July 1813, Chauncey's valued frigate, the *General Pike,* joined his fleet, and this preponderance in strength encouraged the commodore to undertake other joint operations. He had his eye focused on Burlington Heights, the main British stronghold on western Lake Ontario. He asked Scott to provide the troops, so Scott, having secured General Boyd's permission, loaded up, with 200 men of the 2d Artillery, on Chauncey's schooner, *Lady of the Lake.* The joint task force sailed on July 29. When they arrived at Burlington Bay, however, they found the position heavily defended, so they abandoned the attack and reembarked, bound for York.[5]

At York the joint operation was more successful. The British had not rebuilt the defenses destroyed by Zebulon Pike earlier in the year, and the town did not resist. Chauncey emptied out the storehouses while Scott freed all political prisoners in the jail, some of whom were Americans. Scott, however, "left all felons—persons charged with offences against morals—to abide their fate."

The incident at York carried a personal touch, significant for the future. After the American expedition had left York, Scott discovered that the sailors had loaded some trunks belonging to British officers and men. On going through one of them he found some official British papers, which he set aside to return to General Sheaffe. In another he found a "miniature of a beautiful lady, set in gold, taken out of another trunk that had upon it the name of Colonel Harvey." So the sentimental Scott, concluding that this likeness must have been the colonel's young bride, bought it from the sailor who had taken it and returned it to Harvey, along with the papers going to General Sheaffe.

While all this was going on—indeed, even before the capture of Fort George in May 1813—Secretary of War John Armstrong had an irksome problem to deal with, the status of Major General James Wilkinson, still commanding at New Orleans.

The people of the Crescent City had long since had enough of Wilkinson and now, through their senators, they were demanding his removal. President Madison did not feel able to resist them, so in early March he directed Armstrong to issue an order for Wilkinson to leave New Orleans. His new assignment would be to Sacketts Harbor, where he was to serve as Dearborn's chief of staff. Armstrong knew that Wilkinson was indolent and even disloyal, but he carried a strong bond from the days when he had fought alongside Wilkinson in 1777. He was therefore careful to spare his old comrade's feelings. On March 12 Armstrong wrote, "The men of the North and East want you. Those of the South and West are less sensible of your merits. . . . Come to the North, and quickly. If our cards be well played, we may renew the scene at Saratoga."[6]

Wilkinson was a scoundrel but not a stupid one; he knew when to retreat. He left New Orleans on May 19, within three weeks of receiving Armstrong's letter. In no apparent hurry, he arrived in Washington on July 31, already late in the summer. In the meantime, however, Dearborn had been relieved as commander on the Canadian frontier. Wilkinson, by default, was now the commanding general, rather than a mere chief of staff, as Armstrong had intended.

On August 20, Wilkinson arrived at Sacketts Harbor to take command. He immediately called a council of war, inviting the senior commanders in the region—Morgan Lewis, Brigadier General Robert Swartwout, Colonel Jacob Brown, and Commodore Isaac Chauncey. Under a directive issued by Armstrong, the group decided to launch a campaign that autumn down the St. Lawrence River to take Montreal. The plan would require that all the regular forces, including those on the Niagara, be concentrated at the eastern end of Lake Ontario. For some reason Wilkinson decided that he should visit Fort George and conduct Boyd's brigade in person back to Sacketts Harbor. He arrived by water at Fort George on September 4, 1813, and stayed for nearly four weeks.

Wilkinson's arival at Fort George placed Scott, who had once been punished by court-martial for calling Wilkinson a traitor, in an awkward position, to say the least. Nevertheless, Scott rose above his chagrin and, as the commander of the 2d Artillery, paid a courtesy call on his new commander.

The enigmatic Wilkinson accepted Scott's promise to "continue to execute, with zeal and alacrity, all duties that might be assigned to him"—or at least he pretended to—and when he took the bulk of the regular forces back to Sacketts Harbor, he left Scott in command of the fort.

Scott now had an independent command, consisting of seven hundred regulars and a detachment of militia. His mission was to rebuild the dilapidated Fort George, and he did it well. After Wilkinson's departure at the end of September, Scott worked his men day and night to that end. Yet, despite the honor of exercising independent command, Scott yearned for action. He therefore secured Wilkinson's approval of his proposal to join the Montreal campaign once he had rebuilt the fort.

On October 11, 1813, Scott wrote a long and ingratiating letter to Wilkinson, summarizing what had happened since Wilkinson had left. The enemy, Scott wrote with a touch of bravado, had "neglected" him by failing to attack. The British, in fact, had evacuated their previous position five miles from Fort George and had retreated to Burlington, leaving the whole peninsula open.

Scott attributed the British retrenchment to the disaster that had befallen British General Henry Procter at the Battle of the Thames, near Detroit, where the Americans under General William Henry Harrison had destroyed Procter's army. The influential Indian chief Tecumseh had been killed at that battle, and only about a quarter of the nine hundred British in Procter's army had been able to join Vincent at Burlington. Scott added, tactfully, that Wilkinson's expected expedition to Montreal was already drawing British regulars from the Niagara frontier.

These developments, Scott presumed, permitted him to turn the command at Fort George over to the militia and march his regulars to Sacketts Harbor. His position at Fort George was no longer justified, and he wished to join Wilkinson "in time to share in the glory of impending operations below." He intended to leave on October 13 for the mouth of the Genesee River (present-day Rochester), there to await the vessels "you were good enough to promise me." He boasted that he had been working day and night to improve the defenses of Fort George, and "flattered" himself that he had also improved the discipline of the garrison.

Two days later Scott left Fort George in the hands of Brigadier General George McClure, a militia general who had been appointed by General Peter Porter, at Buffalo. As Scott expected troop transports to meet him at the Genesee River, he encumbered himself by taking along the sick and wounded from the fort. His disciplined troops covered the sixty-mile trip in good time, but on arrival at the rendezvous point he was shocked to find no troop carriers waiting for him, only a single dispatch vessel, *Lady of the Lake*. Wilkinson had dissuaded Chauncey from sending even part of his fleet away from the eastern end of Lake Ontario for four days.

Denied water transport, Scott's weary men had a long, hard march ahead of them to Sacketts Harbor, made longer by the lack of direct roads in northern New York. From Rochester their route took them south all the way to Utica, on the Mohawk River, where their route turned north. When Scott finally reached that settlement, he was delighted to encounter Secretary of War John Armstrong, who was on his way back to Washington from Sacketts Harbor, where he had been since September 5, nearly two months earlier. In talking with Armstrong, Scott learned what had transpired during that time.

Armstrong's stay at Sacketts Harbor, which overlapped Wilkinson's, had been difficult because the two men disagreed violently as to which British position in Canada should be attacked next, Kingston on Lake Ontario or Montreal on the St. Lawrence. Armstrong favored Kingston, a major base, critical to the British resupply of Upper Canada. Wilkinson, on the other hand, argued for Montreal, partly for the bizarre reason that he suspected the motives of Armstrong. The matter had become academic in mid-October, however, when Sir James Yeo returned to Kingston with a strong enough naval force to render an American attack infeasible for the moment. The only reasonable objective then was Montreal, which might be approached down the St. Lawrence if Commodore Chauncey's small American fleet of warships could protect the army's rear. With that argument settled, Wilkinson's army set sail in small boats from Sacketts Harbor on October 17, bound for Grenadier Island, at the entrance to the St. Lawrence from Lake Ontario. Though their destination was only eighteen miles away, storms and high winds prevented the fleet from reaching that point until November 5.

Wilkinson had organized his army of 7,000 men into two divisions, plus a reserve. One of his divisions was commanded by Morgan Lewis, and the other was without a commander for the moment, slated for General Wade Hampton at such time as he joined Wilkinson from Plattsburgh, New York. Until Hampton should arrive, the two brigades of the division (Robert Swartwout and Jacob Brown) would operate independently. Wilkinson's reserve was commanded by Colonel Alexander Macomb, and his artillery by a veteran of Fort George, Colonel Moses Porter.

Secretary Armstrong, Scott soon learned, had no real hope for the success of the campaign. The British and Canadians were known to be in considerable strength around Montreal, and the two American commanders, Wilkinson and Hampton, openly hated each other. Hampton, the Army's "other" major general, had expected to serve under Dearborn when he had arrived at Plattsburgh the previous July, and when he had learned of Wilkinson's succession to Dearborn's position, he had attempted to resign. Armstrong had promised Hampton that, as one of Wilkinson's division commanders, he would receive orders only from Armstrong himself—a weird promise that Wilkinson had never accepted—but Hampton would remain in his position only under that arrangement.

Armstrong himself was part of the problem. Not only had he kept Hampton as a division commander under unworkable arrangements; he had demonstrated his pessimism on October 16, when he sent a message to the quartermaster general to prepare winter quarters for 10,000 men at a place near French Mills, in American territory south of Montreal.[7]

In that pessimistic frame of mind, Armstrong had left Sacketts Harbor as soon as Wilkinson's force had departed for Grenadier Island on October 17, convinced that the expedition was doomed to failure.

How much of all this Armstrong shared with Scott is unknown, but the secretary was impressed by Scott's eagerness to fight, an attribute seldom seen on the St. Lawrence until then. He therefore gave Scott permission to turn his command over to a subordinate and proceed ahead by himself to join Wilkinson, accompanied only by an adjutant. Scott seized this opportunity eagerly.

Scott rode for thirty hours without a break through the forests of northern New York in a sleet storm, arriving at Waddington, on the St. Lawrence. He then turned back westward for another twenty miles to Ogdensburg, where he reported to Wilkinson on November 6. He had been on the road nearly a month.

On November 7, the day after Scott joined Wilkinson's army, the American flotilla ran past the British guns that threatened from Fort Prescott. It then prepared to continue downstream to shoot the eight-mile rapids called Long Sault. After that, according to the original plan, Wilkinson was supposed to be reinforced by Wade Hampton's 4,000 men at St. Regis. Together, the combined force of 11,000 men might stand a chance of seizing Montreal despite the anticipated hazards. Its chances of success depended on three assumptions: (1) that the command would be aggressive, (2) that Chauncey's blockade of Kingston would be effective, and (3) that Wade Hampton would push aggressively to St. Regis and join Wilkinson as planned.

To protect the army from the fire of hostile troops on the north bank of the St. Lawrence, Wilkinson sent Lewis's division, without its division commander, across the river from Ogdensburg to Prescott, thence down the Canadian side to Montreal. When a bedraggled Scott met the army at Ogdensburg, he was sent across the river to join Macomb's brigade, which was in the lead of the army's march. Macomb assigned Scott to command the advance guard, a position which, though it did not call for an officer of Scott's rank, still elated him. He was exhilarated by the cheers the troops gave out when they learned that they were to be led by the hero of Fort George. Scott started the vanguard eastward immediately.

On November 10 Scott's advance guard reached a place known as Hoople Creek,[8] behind which was a British force of 800 men—about the size of his own—which he later learned was commanded by the redoubtable Major James B. Dennis, 49th Foot, who had successfully defended Queenston against the Americans the previous October. Scott, seeing that Dennis had a strong position, decided to flank it to the north, hoping to trap and annihilate it. Dennis, however, detected the American movement and pulled out of his exposed position in time. Scott was able to cut off and capture only the rear of Dennis's column; most of the rest escaped.

The main action of the Montreal campaign, however, took place at the rear of the column. Chauncey's blockade of Kingston turned out to be ineffectual, and a British amphibious force, carrying a battalion of infantry under Lieutenant Colonel Joseph Morrison, 89th Foot, landed at the head of the St. Lawrence, where it soon caught up with Boyd's brigade, Wilkinson's rear guard. From his sickbed, Wilkinson ordered Boyd to turn around and destroy this annoyance.

Colonel Morrison, Boyd's experienced opponent, had only 800 men, about half the number available to Boyd, so he stopped, took up a strong position, and allowed Boyd to break his forces trying to dislodge him. Boyd handled his troops badly, committing each unit piecemeal as it arrived on the scene. Each one disintegrated in turn, the men falling back on the boat landing on the river. Boyd's own brigade, the last one, followed the others, and eventually all the Americans were evacuated across to the south bank.

The Battle of Crysler's Farm, as the fight came to be known, has been called "the least credible of the disasters suffered by American arms during the war." And yet some American forces fought well; Edmund P. Gaines elicited even Morrison's admiration. And Crysler's Farm did not, in itself, end the effort. Though Boyd had failed to dislodge a greatly inferior force, the heavy British casualties he inflicted put an end to their pursuit. Wilkinson's army continued down the St. Lawrence River and ran the rapids at Long Sault on November 11, emerging at St. Regis at the other end.

There the campaign ended, not from enemy action but from the failure of the Americans to coordinate their efforts. When Wilkinson's main body reached St. Regis, where they were supposed to meet Hampton, the commander learned that Hampton was not there and had no intention of ever arriving. Rankling under unreasonable orders that Wilkinson had sent him, discouraged by a small but humiliating defeat he had suffered at the hands of a British force at Chateauguay, south of Montreal, on October 22,[9] and lacking transport to carry necessary supplies, he sent Wilkinson a letter on November 8 advising that he was falling back on Plattsburgh for the winter. That ended even the remotest prospects of success. Wilkinson's army retired to Frenchman's Creek, just across the New York border, there to spend a miserable, even dangerous winter.

Campaigning for the year 1813 was over. The Americans had achieved some minor successes. They had raided and destroyed York, the capital of Upper Canada; they had won a significant victory over the British at the Battle of the Thames; they had seized Fort George; and Oliver Hazard Perry had ensured the safety of the western flank by his significant naval victory on Lake Erie. But the objective of the United States was not defensive; it was to invade and take at least a part of Canada. In that the Americans had failed, partly because of their inability to secure control over Lake Ontario but mostly because corrupt and incompetent officers had failed to make the best use of available resources.

There was, however, one favorable result of the 1813 failures. President Madison and Secretary of War John Armstrong now realized full well the price the United States was paying for incompetent leadership. Fortunately, a few officers had come out with enhanced reputations in the various operations. So during the winter and spring of 1813–14 the Old Guard—Wilkinson, Dearborn, Boyd, Lewis, and other Revolutionary relics—were relegated to the trash heap of military command. Young, energetic officers such as Jacob Brown, Alexander Macomb, George Izard, Edmund Gaines, and Winfield Scott would now rise to the positions of high command.

8

❧❧❧

Victory at Chippewa

"Those are regulars, by God!"

WHEN JAMES Wilkinson's army staggered into French Mills, on the American side of the St. Lawrence, Colonel Winfield Scott found himself in a situation similar to that at Terre aux Boeufs, Louisiana, nearly five years before. Once more Wilkinson had placed his men in a position where they faced hardships, this time freezing cold and starvation. During the ten weeks the army camped at French Mills, sickness took over 200 lives; 2,800 men—over a third of the army—were unfit for duty. Even Wilkinson later acknowledged that "the mortality spread so deep a gloom that funeral dirges were countermanded." Wilkinson must have come by that knowledge through reports; he had departed the scene almost immediately after his army arrived.

And once again, as in Louisiana, Scott was spared much of the ordeal, for he was almost immediately ordered to return to Washington after only a month at French Mills. He made his way back, arriving in Washington by Christmastime, 1813. Scott had more reason to be elated on being called to Washington than mere personal comfort, important as that might be. President Madison himself had sent for him, as he was now considered one of the few trustworthy officers of the Army. The President gave evidence of Scott's elevated status by consulting with him, in the company of Secretary Armstrong, three times during his stay in Washington.

In Scott's absence, in fact even before he returned to Washington, tragic news came in regarding the situation on the Niagara frontier. Brigadier General George McClure, the militia general who had assumed responsibility for Fort George from Scott in October 1813, had managed to lose everything the Americans had fought for the previous summer. Admittedly understrength—he had only 324 men with whom to defend Fort George, Fort Niagara, Black Rock, and Buffalo—he certainly had some justification for abandoning Fort George, but in so doing he committed a blunder, the seriousness of which bordered on the criminal: he needlessly and without warning burned the Canadian town of Newark, next to Fort George, a deed that neither the British nor the Canadians ever forgave.

The act was cruel and unnecessary. Though the American government had long recognized that Newark might have to be destroyed because of its proximity to Fort George, McClure's act could not be justified by military necessity, for while he was burning both Newark and Queenston, he left the fort itself intact, with valuable supplies in it. The people were given no chance to save belongings that might have protected them from the cold of a Canadian winter.

The new British commander, Lieutenant General Gordon Drummond, was enraged when, in early December 1814, he came upon the scenes of devastation at Newark and Queenston. He exacted a grim revenge. His troops crossed the river and destroyed and pillaged Fort Niagara, Buffalo, Black Rock, Fort Schlosser, and even Lewiston. McClure later described the taking of Fort Niagara:

> On December 18 a British force of 550 men surprised the American sentries at Fort Niagara, extracted the password, and then secured access to the fort. . . . "Our men," said General McClure, "were nearly all asleep in their tents, the Enemy rushed in and commenced a most horrid slaughter." The British inflicted eighty casualties (mostly by bayonet) and took 350 prisoners, while suffering fewer than a dozen casualties themselves.[1]

Fort Niagara remained in British hands for the duration of the war.

These developments in western New York caused a near panic among the Americans in that region. So concerned were they that they sent a deputation to President Madison urging him to take energetic action to stabilize the American position at Buffalo. Among their requests, one was bound to give Scott pleasure. John Nichols, a former congressman from Virginia, asked Madison on behalf of the group that Scott be sent to the Niagara frontier in command.

Madison agreed with the high opinion the New Yorkers held of Scott, but he was unwilling to go so far as they asked. He was conscious of Scott's youth, and he had already selected Jacob Brown to be overall commander in the region. Brown, a few years older than Scott, was a New Yorker who had distinguished himself at Sacketts Harbor and in every action since. Madison agreed to send Scott to Niagara, but not as overall commander. He was to be promoted to the grade of brigadier general and given a brigade in Brown's army. It was a compromise satisfactory to everyone.

Scott left Washington for Buffalo in late January 1814. At Albany, along the way, he was instructed to stop off to urge Governor Daniel D. Tompkins, on behalf of the President, to raise additional militiamen from New York. Scott was also under instruction to wait at Albany until his promotion to brigadier general was published as part of the overall reorganization of the Army. It was necessary, in order to command a brigade, that his rank be equal to that of any of the militia officers serving under him.

Delays in publishing the promotion list in Washington caused Scott to remain in Albany longer than had originally been intended. He bided his time cheerfully, working at the nearby arsenal during the day and attending social events in the evenings. His time in Albany was, in fact, principally notable for his activities outside of duty hours. After hours he met with Governor Tompkins and his leading Republican politicians in the evenings, including a rising star by the name of Martin Van Buren, who was encouraging the people of New York to keep supporting the war. President Madison had apparently recognized a zeal for politics in Scott and he had confidence in Scott's loyalty. Acting as an unofficial representative of the President was a heady jump for a young man of twenty-eight, who only two years earlier had been a captain suspended from duty for "unofficer-like conduct." Scott had always made full use of political friends in pushing his military career, but this was his first experience in handling political matters himself.

The promotion list that confirmed Scott as a new general officer arrived in late March 1814, and it represented an admirable improvement in the high ranks of the Army. George Izard, Jacob Brown, and Andrew Jackson were designated as the three new major generals; Alexander Macomb, Edmund Pendleton Gaines, Winfield Scott, and Eleazar W. Ripley were to be the new brigadiers. The vacancies had been created by a clean sweep of the old tier of generals. Wilkinson, after leading one more fiasco against a position at La Colle, Quebec, was finished; Henry Dearborn, Morgan Lewis, and of course William Hull were already on the shelf. The average age of the eight generals on the Army's rolls in June 1812 had been sixty years; two years later the new crop averaged only thirty-six. The quality of the units would reflect this new energy.

The day on which Scott received notice of his promotion to brigadier turned out to be memorable for another reason, his first real acquaintance with Aaron Burr. Martin Van Buren had asked Scott to his home for dinner that evening, and Burr, one of Van Buren's houseguests, was to be there. Scott and Burr got along amiably, and when they were partners at whist after dinner, Burr said, "General Scott, I have seen you before." Scott, though he remembered the occasion quite well, stammered with embarrassment, "Have you, Colonel? And where was it?" The courteous Burr, whose piercing brown eyes were fixed on Scott, played a card, and in his courtly yet careless tone, and with his characteristic short, sharp phrases, answered, "At Richmond, in the court room, at my trial. You stood on the lock of the door above the crowd. I noticed you at the time: it was on the first day."[2]

Soon after receiving word of his promotion, Brigadier General Winfield Scott, the youngest general officer in the United States Army— and doubtless the cockiest—left Albany for Buffalo. On March 24, 1814, somewhere east of Buffalo, he chanced to meet up with the newly appointed Major General Jacob Brown and Brigadier General Eleazar Ripley, who were together leading some 2,000 troops from French Mills to the Niagara frontier. The three joined up to ride into Buffalo.

Brown had by now assumed command along the Canadian frontier, with his headquarters at Sacketts Harbor. He had organized his army, as had Wilkinson before him, into two divisions. One, the so-called Right Division, was under General Izard, at Plattsburgh, New York. The Left Division, also known as the Army of the Niagara, was on the Niagara frontier, with headquarters at Buffalo. Rather than appoint an officer to command it, Brown had decided to take personal command of this force himself. The Army of the Niagara was a small force; it consisted of only six newly organized infantry regiments[3] and a command of artillery.

While the Army of the Niagara was getting settled at Buffalo, the American strategy for the 1814 campaign on the northern frontier was still being debated, with the arguments sounding like dreary repetitions of those advanced the previous year. Though Kingston remained the critical objective for offensive action, attacking it from Sacketts Harbor still required naval supremacy on Lake Ontario, and unfortunately for the American cause, Commodore Chauncey was no Oliver Perry. So deeply concerned was he about the threat posed by Sir James Yeo that he relegated joint army-navy action to bottom priority. Yeo himself was not much better from the British viewpoint. Neither commander ever dared to put the question of naval superiority to the test in one great battle, both appearing to be content with a stalemate, in which the possessor of the latest ship enjoyed only a temporary edge.[4]

Secretary of War John Armstrong, who always favored direct joint action against Kingston, wanted the President to order Chauncey to take more risks, but Armstrong's status in the President's cabinet had sunk so low as a result of the 1813 frustrations that he was unable to exert much influence on either Madison or Secretary of the Navy William Jones. The best Armstrong could extract from Jones was a promise to make an effort "some time after July 10," four months off. Before that time arrived, however, new developments made aggressive action even more unlikely. Napoleon had been defeated at Leipzig in late 1813, and his abdication of the French throne freed British reinforcements for action in America. The Americans would now have to face the flower of the British army.

The delay in taking the field did carry one important benefit, however: it provided Brown with time to whip his green troops into shape. He could not personally spend all his time preparing that army, and he was honest enough to recognize that Scott's technical knowledge of drill and discipline exceeded his own. So soon after their arrival at Buffalo, Brown placed the entire Army of the Niagara in Scott's hands for training while he returned temporarily to his main headquarters at Sacketts Harbor.*

Scott was now in his element. Though he was comfortable and eager in the presence of the prominent men of the East, it was on the training field that he reigned supreme. He set up a training camp near Buffalo and went to work.

Scott spared nobody as he began the formidable task of training these newly recruited troops to be "regulars," able to stand up to the British. Least of all did he spare himself. He first organized the camp by emphasizing in

---

*This included Scott's brigade.

daily routine matters such as outposting, night patrolling, guards, sentinels, camp sanitation, police, rules of civility, etiquette, and courtesy—"the indispensable outworks of subordination." Not all the soldiers were ready to accept this level of discipline. To prove to his men that he meant business, Scott made an example of five convicted deserters. He lined them up before a firing squad, all five standing before their newly dug graves. Four of the men met their doom. The fifth, a mere boy, was spared; Scott had directed that the muskets fired at him should be loaded with blanks. It is unlikely that the boy ever deserted again.

Scott conducted the tactical instruction of each arm using a copy of the French *Reglement*,[5] a product of his library, starting with the officers. He personally assumed that phase of training himself, always appearing for drill in full dress uniform, ready to work for up to ten hours a day. When he decided that his officers were sufficiently expert at the intricate drill moves of the day, he supervised their instruction of their men. This routine went on for three months. By the end of that time, Scott could boast that "confidence, the dawn of victory, inspired the whole line."

In May he wrote,

> I have a handsome little army of about 1,700 "total" to wit: the 9th, 11th, 21st, and 25th regiments and two companies 2d artillery. . . . I am most partial to these regiments. The men are healthy, sober, cheerful, and docile. The field officers highly respectable, and many of the platoon officers are decent and emulous of improvement. If, of such materials, I do not make the best army now in service, by the 1st of June, I will agree to be dismissed the service.[6]

On May 14, 1814, an event occurred that relieved Scott's mind on at least one account. The governments of the United States and Britain had begun a series of talks to find peace terms that would be acceptable to both sides, thus putting an end to the war. Though those talks had failed for the moment, the fact that the Americans now had some British prisoners to offer enabled the conferees to effect a general exchange and cancel all existing paroles (except for the twenty-three Irishmen of Scott's old regiment). From this time on, Scott's status was no longer a matter of controversy. He would be treated as a normal prisoner of war if captured.

General Brown returned to Buffalo on June 5, 1814, ready for action, and two days later, on the seventh, the President and his cabinet in

Washington decided that the invasion of Canada that year should once more be launched from the west, on the Niagara frontier. Commodore Chauncey had pleaded illness as an excuse for deferring an attack on Yeo until the middle of July, so Armstrong wrote to Brown suggesting that, to "give immediate occupation to your troops," he cross the Niagara River at Buffalo, take Fort Erie (garrisoned, he said, by only three or four hundred men), push northward to seize the bridge at Chippewa, and then determine the next move. Brown, thus inspired, prepared for action.

Brown's Left Division was the most professional formation the United States had fielded since the Revolution nearly thirty-five years earlier. The two regular brigades were commanded by Scott and Ripley, officers of proven performance in battle. The third brigade commander, Peter Porter, for all his pretentiousness and lack of military knowledge, would probably become a capable commander. The troops, at least the regulars, were highly trained in the intricate movements so necessary to bring maximum fire to bear on an enemy.

Brown decided to allocate the six regular regiments that Scott had trained a bit unevenly, giving Scott four regiments, the 9th Massachusetts (642 officers and men), the 11th Vermont (577), the 22d Pennsylvania (287), and the 25th Connecticut (619).[7] To Ripley he assigned the 21st Massachusetts (917 officers and men) and the 23d New York (496). Scott's numbers were 50 percent greater than those of Ripley (2,100 as compared to 1,400), and his four commanders, in contrast to Ripley's two, clearly gave Scott the bulk of the regular force in the army.

Peter Porter's situation was different. Assigned to raise his own force of militia, he found recruiting difficult in New York, so his brigade consisted of only six hundred Pennsylvanians, augmented by the attachment of about six hundred Six Nations Indians. Further, his men had not undergone the rigorous training at Buffalo that summer, due partly, one suspects, to his dislike for and jealousy of Scott. In March, before he was certain that Brown instead of Scott would command the Army of the Niagara, Porter had written Governor Tompkins, complaining,

> If, as has been distinctly insinuated, a young officer [Scott] of the regular army is to be promoted to take command . . . I trust in your friendship to apprize me of it and relieve me of the unpleasant consequences of such a measure.

Porter had conceded, however, that it was now impractical to complain because of Scott's obvious "military acquirements." Porter conceded Scott's military prowess but could not abide his youth and ill-disguised condescension, if not contempt, for militia.

Brown took his army across the Niagara River in the early morning hours of July 3, 1814. Scott's brigade landed near Fort Erie in the dark and rain. Despite those conditions, Scott found the exact cove he had been seeking and, always in the vanguard, he jumped over the edge of the boat to lead his men ashore. But instead he disappeared into a hole in the uneven bottom, encumbered by a heavy cloak, high boots, and sword and pistols. His men managed to save him, and he resumed his place of leadership, soaked but with no damage to anything but his dignity. Locating a better spot, he led his men ashore. The few British pickets, who had been firing a few shots, had left. Everything else went smoothly. Ripley's brigade landed a mile or two on Scott's right, and later in the morning Porter came ashore, his Indians maneuvering around to the west to seize the rear of the position. The three brigades converged on Fort Erie at about noon, and its garrison surrendered by 5:00 P.M. that day. It consisted of only 170 men.

At Fort George, British Major General Phineas Riall[8] learned of the landings early in the morning of July 3. Like Isaac Brock before him, he headed southward on horseback, gathering forces as he went along.[9] With about 2,500 officers and men, including Indians, he formed a battle line behind the Chippewa River, a major obstacle, there to await the American advance.* Two flank companies of the 100th Foot were sent ahead as advance guard. They were under the command of Lieutenant Colonel Thomas Pearson, Scott's hospitable prison guard of late 1812.

Once Fort Erie was taken, Brown sent Scott northward in an attempt to seize a crossing over the Chippewa River before the British could arrive in force. Scott did not begin his northward advance until the morning of Independence Day, however, so Pearson's British covering force made contact with him only a couple of miles from Fort Erie. Pearson fought a skillful delaying action, from creek to creek for the sixteen miles up to Street's Creek, uprooting the floorings of the bridges over each waterway. Scott, on his part,

---

*Chippewa was a major position for the British on the Niagara Peninsula. The town of Chippewa, a little over two miles above Niagara Falls, was the southern terminal of the Portage Road around them. Since the Chippewa River, to its south, represented a formidable obstacle, it was not only a natural defensive position for the defending British but also a logical objective for Jacob Brown's Americans.

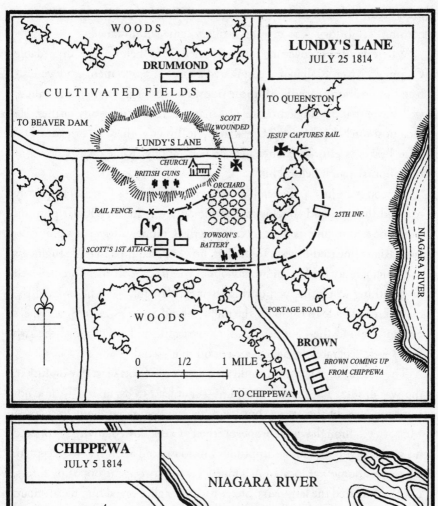

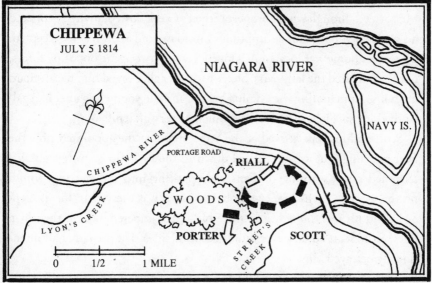

prevented Pearson from demolishing the abutments and stringers by bombarding each bridge as soon as his artillery came within range.

When Pearson's covering force rejoined Riall behind the unfordable Chippewa River, Riall had accumulated a force of 2,000 men, who were already in position. Faced with those odds, even the aggressive Scott halted, well aware that his single brigade was inadequate to pursue any farther. He took position behind Street's Creek to await Brown's other two brigades. Despite Pearson's efforts, Scott had marched rapidly; Ripley was still about three hours' march behind him.

At 7:00 P.M., July 4, General Brown arrived at Street's Creek. He quickly scanned the field and concluded that the only way to carry Riall's position would be to outflank its right by crossing the Chippewa River at a point beyond Riall's line to the west. To do that, however, required that his engineers construct a hasty bridge, and that would take time. Scott therefore believed that nothing would happen during the next day, July 5, so he ordered the men of his brigade to camp for the night behind Street's Creek. Since Riall's position behind the Chippewa River was a mile and a half away, the two forces were separated by a large area of no-man's-land.

The next morning, July 5, could well have been Scott's last day of duty in the War of 1812. The danger to his life—or at least to his liberty—came not from the guns of the enemy but from his own vanity and guilelessness. A Mrs. Street, through whose property Street's Creek flowed, invited Scott and his staff to her house for a sumptuous breakfast, and Scott readily accepted. The Street home was located in a lonely place between the opposing forces, but Scott trusted the lady. Mrs. Street had, after all, begged him to safeguard her house from looting the evening before, and the young brigadier had gallantly done so. She must, Scott reasoned, be very grateful!

Scott and his staff arrived at the Street house at the appointed time the next morning, but as they settled down to the first cup of coffee, an aide screamed out a warning; Indians were pouring into the clearing from a nearby woods. Their intent was obvious, so it was every man for himself; Scott and his men bolted from the table and scampered back to their own lines. Still, Scott could never quite accept the idea that the lady had intentionally betrayed him.

The rest of the day promised to be quiet. Scott's men were still weary from a long day of marching and fighting, so their commander planned a belated feast to celebrate Independence Day. He prevailed on the quartermaster depot at Fort Schlosser across the Niagara to send special rations for the occasion. Then, after all had eaten their fill, Scott decided to hold a dress review to "keep his men in breath." He was unconcerned about reports that parties of hostile Indians were in the woods to his left; the task of cleaning them out had been assigned to Porter's militia, not his brigade. Scott therefore marched his brigade over the single bridge crossing Street's Creek. After all, the flat ground in the wide field ahead would be ideal for a review.

As the head of Scott's column crossed the bridge, Scott was feeling content. It was only 4:00 P.M., and many hours of daylight remained. All of a sudden, a figure came galloping out of the brushwood to Scott's front, headed toward the bridge for the rear. On second glance Scott realized that the fugitive was General Brown himself. Brown did not pause. "You will have a battle!" he shouted. Scott was puzzled, unaware that Brown was rushing back to bring up Ripley's brigade. His confusion was soon dispelled by the sight of Riall's army south of the Chippewa. Riall had left his defenses and had come out to meet him.

Scott had to make a quick decision, whether to wait for Brown's entire force or to fight with only one brigade, which he could see was slightly smaller than Riall's. The decision was a foregone conclusion; he had no intention of staying in a defensive position behind Street's Creek. He had trained this brigade, and he would fight it out with the British on an equal basis! Forgetting his parade, he sent Towson's three artillery pieces to the head of his line and crossed the bridge, one unit at a time.

During that uncomfortable period when Scott's column was crossing the bridge, Riall's field guns opened up.[10] Shells began falling among Scott's men. But the men of Scott's brigade never faltered, even though they took a few losses. Scott felt justified and encouraged. He placed Towson's artillery pieces on his right, next to the Niagara River, and built up his line by placing each infantry battalion, as it crossed the bridge, on the left of the battalion ahead. Eventually Scott's line was drawn up opposite Riall's, the two sides just out of musket range.

Riall had taken a risk in coming out from his prepared positions, for he had no way of knowing that he would meet Scott alone. He might well have encountered Brown's whole army. He moved forward, expecting to encounter only untrained militia, who experience indicated would flee at the first volley. He did not realize that the forces in front of him were regulars; their undyed gray·uniforms, of a kind usually issued to militia, misled him.

Riall soon realized his error. As Scott's troops stood up under his artillery fire, Riall is said to have uttered, "Those are regulars, by God!" Still he pressed on.

Scott and Riall both advanced at the same time, the two lines alternately stopping to fire and to move forward. At first Riall anchored the right of his line against the woods to the west, where his Indians had temporarily routed Porter's brigade. Scott soon discovered, however, that Riall had cut loose from that anchor, thus exposing his right flank. Against that body Scott sent Thomas Jesup's 25th Infantry, and that unit drove back the right portion of Riall's force.* The left half of Riall's force remained.

At that point, Scott took the risk of splitting his forces. He formed his remaining three infantry regiments into two "battalions," the left consisting of McNeill's 11th Infantry and the right comprising the 9th and 22d, under Leavenworth. Leaving space between those two forces, he ordered them to face inward. He presumed that Riall would mass his troops against his own weak center, and he could catch Riall on both flanks.

The maneuver worked. As Riall ordered the Royal Scots and the 100th Foot to charge, Towson's artillery managed to put Riall's guns out of action. Towson could now place his fire on the enemy's left flank from Scott's right. Caught in both artillery and musket fire from their flanks, the British lines gave way, retreating from the field after suffering losses of 515 dead, wounded, and missing. When Ripley's brigade finally arrived, no more British were in sight. The battle had lasted less than an hour.

The triumph at Chippewa was not an overwhelming victory, because Riall had escaped. Nevertheless, it could not have come at a better psychological time for the American cause. Representatives of the various New England states were about to meet at Hartford in order to discuss seceding from the Union or even taking up arms against it! News of Scott's victory, the first time that American troops had defeated British regulars, put all such ideas to bed.

As Scott described the impact of Chippewa in later years,

History has recorded many victories on a much larger scale than that of Chippewa; but only a few have wrought a greater change in the feelings of a nation. Everywhere bonfires blazed; bells rung out peals of joys; the big guns responded, and the pulse of Americans recovered a healthy beat.

*In doing so, Jesup was forced to make a bayonet charge to disperse Canadian sharpshooters in the woods, which Porter had failed to clear. Fredriksen, "Niagara, 1814," p. 88.

9

❧❦❧

Wounded at Lundy's Lane

Scott nearly pays with his life for his early rashness.

The world has seen mightier armies moved over more memorable fields, and followed by louder notes of the far-resounding trumpet of fame; but a bloodier scene for those engaged, a severer trial of courage and of discipline, or one whose action was more closely associated with the sublime and beautiful in nature, the world has not seen.
—Edward D. Mansfield, *Life and Services of General Winfield Scott*

We boast of a "Great Victory," but in my opinion it was nearly equal on both sides.
—Colonel Hercules Scott, 103d Foot, British army

THE BATTLE OF Chippewa, fought on July 5, 1814, was only a preliminary skirmish in the ambitious campaign being planned by Major General Jacob Brown. Beyond Chippewa lay Burlington, York, and eventually Kingston. True, Brown's—really Scott's—victory at Chippewa had been hailed across the United States as the first real success attained by American troops against British regulars, but the results, while satisfying, had not been decisive. General Phineas Riall's brigade had not been destroyed; it would still be a force to reckon with in any future plans.

Brown's first requirement, before continuing on with the campaign, was of course to dislodge Riall from his strong position behind the Chippewa

Creek. He did not find that challenge very difficult. His engineers soon located an acceptable bridge only a mile west of Riall's position, so when Riall learned that the Americans were crossing with superior numbers, he hastily evacuated his position. Uncertain of Brown's strength, he temporarily abandoned the whole Niagara front except for Fort George and Fort Niagara. For the moment, until he could be reinforced, he contented himself with holding those two bastions while moving his brigade westward from Queenston, through St. Davids. He assumed a defensive position behind Twenty-Mile Creek, a strong obstacle behind which he could defend Burlington—if it came to that.

At this point, with Riall in retreat before him and flushed with his recent success at Chippewa, Jacob Jennings Brown was at the apex of his military career as a field commander. At age thirty-nine, this Quaker from Bucks County, Pennsylvania, had reached his important position by sheer merit. In command of the militia at Sacketts Harbor a year before, Brown had conducted the defense with such zeal and energy that he had been promoted to the grade of brigadier general in the regular army just after the battle. His reputation had been unmarred when he participated in Wilkinson's half-hearted campaign toward Montreal in late 1813. In recognition of his abilities, Brown had subsequently been placed in command of the entire Canadian front, succeeding the disgraced Wilkinson. Always a fighter, though not highly qualified technically, Brown had taken personal command of the Army of the Niagara even though he could have delegated it to someone else. He and Scott made a good team; Brown had no need to deny Scott the lion's share of the credit for the Battle of Chippewa, and in return he enjoyed Scott's full loyalty.

When Riall withdrew from Chippewa Creek, Brown decided to follow him with two brigades—Scott's and Ripley's—as far as Queenston. There, on the heights defended by Scott nearly two years earlier, he established camp at the abandoned British position and sent scouting parties to bring back information on the conditions at Fort George and on the strength of Riall's army. But he dared not try to move on Burlington, much less York, without help from Commodore Chauncey's Lake Ontario fleet, because leaving the waters of the lake open to the British would allow them to reinforce Lieutenant General Sir Gordon Drummond whenever they chose.* So on July 13, 1814, Brown wrote Commodore Chauncey:

> I have looked for your fleet with the greatest anxiety since the 10th. I do not doubt my ability to meet the enemy in the field, and to march in any direction over his country, your fleet carrying for me the necessary supplies. There is not a doubt resting in my mind but that we have between us the command of sufficient means to conquer Upper Canada within two months, if there is a prompt and zealous co-operation and a vigorous application of these means.[1]

Chauncey delayed answering Brown's urgent message, pleading illness but still unwilling to turn over his command to anyone else. Brown, therefore, could only move up to Fort George and from that vicinity send out more reconnaissance parties. Those patrols seem to have neglected scouting in favor of looting, and one party unnecessarily burned the town of St. Davids, thus fueling the fires of resentment that were already raging between the Americans and the Canadian populace.

Brown held off from attacking Fort George, however. Thanks to the efforts that Scott had exerted in strengthening its walls the previous year, he would need siege guns to reduce it—guns he did not have. Moreover, Canadian irregulars were harassing his supply lines, and he had received word that Riall had been reinforced.

As each day passed, Brown's position near Fort George became more and more tenuous. His information regarding British reinforcements was borne out; in fact 700 British regulars had joined Riall as early as July 9. And in addition to the troops Riall had on the spot, General Drummond was coming to the Niagara front to take personal command, bringing with him such crack troops as Colonel Joseph Morrison's 89th Foot, the victors of Crysler's Farm. More British regulars, farther distant, were reportedly on the way. Even without Drummond's reinforcements, Riall, who had now inched back to Ten-Mile Creek, could reply in strength if Brown ever decided to attack the garrison of Fort George.

On July 23 Brown received a final blow to his ambitious plans. A message from Sacketts Harbor advised him that he could expect no help from Chauncey. Scott, undeterred by the lack of naval support, asked permission

---

*Drummond had been appointed lieutenant governor of Upper Canada in late 1813, with headquarters in York.

to take his single brigade around the western end of Lake Ontario and seize Brunswick. Brown, however, refused permission and removed his entire army to the position behind the Chippewa River, where Porter's brigade was awaiting him.

July 24, 1814

For both the British and the Americans on the Niagara Peninsula, Sunday, July 24, was a day of groping. General Brown arrived on the familiar ground of the Chippewa battlefield with Riall following him at a considerable distance. When Riall reached Lundy's Lane, a position about three miles to the north of the Chippewa, he stopped.[2]

On that same day, Sir Gordon Drummond arrived at York from Kingston. Told that the Americans had established a supply base at Lewiston, he decided to attack at once, moving down the east bank of the Niagara River, sending Colonel G. P. Tucker (1,500 men), reinforced with 400 men from Morrison's 89th Foot, from Fort Niagara to Lewiston. Once at Lewiston, Tucker was to cross the Niagara at Queenston, hoping to catch Brown in a trap between Tucker and the rest of his army, still on the west bank. (Drummond did not realize when he issued his order that Brown had already withdrawn to Chippewa Creek.) Drummond was taking a risk in dividing his army, with a major river between his two wings; his so doing reflects the contempt he still held for Brown's Army of the Niagara.

Late in the afternoon of the 24th Drummond himself sailed the few miles across Lake Ontario from York to Fort George.

July 25, 1814

On arrival at Fort George, General Drummond learned of Brown's withdrawal to the Chippewa. On the morning of July 25, therefore, he changed his orders to Tucker and Riall. Since it was no longer possible to trap Brown by crossing over the Niagara at Queenston, he ordered Tucker to cross the Niagara and join Riall. As Drummond himself was coming southward with reinforcements, he expected to concentrate his army at Lundy's Lane by the end of the day. Riall had reached Lundy's Lane that morning with the 800 men of Pearson's Light Brigade, and Tucker, with 300 men of the 41st, 200 Royal Scots, and some Indians, was crossing the Niagara. A fourth British force, still at Twelve-Mile Creek, was Colonel Hercules Scott's 103d Foot, a few hours behind.

Jacob Brown, at Chippewa, was unaware of Riall's presence at Lundy's Lane. His first word of enemy on his front came from Colonel John Smith, commander of the militia unit that had fled from Lewiston under pressure from Tucker. Brown's worst fear centered on the safety of Fort Schlosser and Buffalo. The only way to save them, he reasoned, would be to attack on his own front and force the British to return from the east bank. The aggressive American general therefore decided to take the offensive. Ever optimistic—and ignorant of what lay in his path—he hoped, if the countryside to his front was clear of enemy, to push on to Burlington. To that end, Brown's men devoted the day of July 25 to preparing for the next day's march.

Some time during the afternoon of the 25th the commander of the 9th Infantry, Major Henry Leavenworth, noticed some unusual activity at Lundy's Lane, and he reported it to General Brown. Brown, unconvinced, took no action. But Leavenworth insisted, and to corroborate his report, he asked Major Thomas S. Jesup, of the 25th Infantry, to confirmed what he had seen. Jesup did so, whereupon Brown, deciding to act, called for Brigadier General Winfield Scott and ordered him to proceed north as far as Queenston. Scott's mission was not to bring on a battle; it was "to report if the enemy appeared, and to call for assistance if that were necessary." Scott, always eager for action, left Chippewa in late afternoon among much enthusiasm and clatter.

The Battle of Lundy's Lane

The distance between the Chippewa and Lundy's Lane is less than four miles, so Scott arrived at Niagara Falls, a little over halfway, fairly soon after setting out. As the head of his column neared a tavern overlooking the falls at Table Rock, he spied three British officers leaving in haste, taking just a moment to cast a defiant salute in his direction. As the officers headed northward, Scott entered the door, seeking information. The widow Wilson, the owner of the tavern, seemed to be cooperative, or at least indifferent as to what she passed on. A British force of about 1,100 men and two guns, Mrs. Wilson said, was gathering along nearby Lundy's Lane. If that were true, Scott would have every reason to be cautious.

Scott, however, was skeptical. Still convinced that the bulk of Riall's army was on the east bank of the Niagara headed for Fort Schlosser, he decided that he could brush aside the "remnant" force in front of him. He moved his brigade ahead—into an ambush. The lady had been telling the truth. Colonel Pearson, still commanding Riall's advance guard, had assumed a position along the ridge over which Lundy's Lane ran, and by now Riall's entire brigade had joined him.

The British position was a good one. The lane ran along the top of a rise sufficiently high to provide observation in all directions. Its left flank lay on the Portage Road to Queenston, which it joined at nearly a right angle. It then ran almost due west, atop the hillock, for a half mile, after which it bent gradually northward. On the hillock, only about a hundred yards west of the Portage Road, stood a Presbyterian church, a low frame building, and on its east side stood its churchyard, already old with weatherbeaten wooden slabs and rude brown headstones. South of the church, toward Chippewa, the area was clear, providing almost nothing by way of cover and concealment for an attacking force. It was in that area, south of the church, that Scott's brigade was trapped in withering fire from nearly three directions.

Scott was now in a quandary. It was impossible, he quickly concluded, to retreat; if he did so his men might panic, the fear spreading to other parts of the army. So he deployed his brigade to attack Riall's position from the south, across a large clearing, in order to feel out the position. Then he cautiously moved forward.

Phineas Riall, on the lane, was impressed with Scott's aggressiveness. Only a portion of a larger force, he reasoned, would dare move against his line under these conditions. The rest of Brown's command, with the other brigades, must be close at hand. So at about six o'clock, he ordered Pearson's brigade to begin evacuating the position, sending word back to Colonel Hercules Scott to stop his march and return to Twelve-Mile Creek.

At that point General Drummond arrived on the scene, leading several regiments of reinforcements. Colonel Tucker's task force reached the field at about the same time as Drummond, bringing the combined strength of the three forces to 3,000 men. Drummond assumed personal command, stopped the withdrawal, and began placing the units in position, his movements screened by Pearson's covering force, the only British troops still on the hill.*

---

*Drummond placed Glengarry Fencibles (light infantry), with some militia and Indian scouts, on his extreme right, in the orchards. He placed two big 24-pounder field guns, with three Congreve rockets, in the cemetery of the Presbyterian church on the crest of the hill. The main line, running

Scott was now in serious trouble. He had launched his aggressive move on Lundy's Lane when he was facing only Pearson's covering force. Had Drummond and Tucker not appeared soon thereafter, Scott's bluff would probably have been successful. But now, faced with Drummond's buildup, his brigade was in a trap. He rejected the idea of a retreat, however. Such a move was against all his instincts, and his men were so pinned down by heavy fire that they could not show themselves without unacceptable slaughter. So Scott left most of his command in place along the base of the hill and sent a message back to Brown urging him to bring up Ripley's and Porter's brigades. He also sent his reserve, Jesup's 25th Infantry, into the woods on the right, there to report back and engage whatever enemy would be found there. When Ripley's brigade arrived from Chippewa, Scott's men had been bled for over two hours—from about 6:30 P.M. until nearly 9:00 P.M.[3] Out of his original brigade of 1,300 men, he now had only 400 effectives.

Scott's losses might have been even greater had it not been for the aggressive action of Major Thomas Jesup of the 25th. Jesup did more than merely reconnoiter; he pushed ahead on a narrow pathway through thick woods until he found the Canadian militia unit that Drummond had posted between the Portage Road and the river. Undetected, Jesup's men fired a point-blank volley and followed it up with a bayonet charge that netted over a hundred prisoners and the regimental ammunition cart. At the junction between the Portage Road and Lundy's Lane a scout reported that he had seen a "glittering entourage" of British mounted troops up ahead. Jesup's men surrounded and subdued the group, discovering that one of their prisoners was Major General Riall himself. Riall was seriously wounded in the arm.

Jesup was now in a quandary over having captured such a prominent British officer. His battalion was "so burdened with prisoners," he later wrote, "as to render it impossible to convey my intentions into execution without

east-west, was held by the 8th Foot and parts of the 1st and 41st regiments, backed up by Morrison's 89th Battalion and some detachments from the 19th Dragoons. Down to the left of the 8th Foot, beyond the Portage Road and extending to a point about 200 yards from the steep escarpment over the Niagara River, he placed a detachment of Canadian militia. As local militia came in, Drummond sent them to the woods on the right to reinforce the Glengarrys in the orchard. "No better ground for receiving an attack," writes the expert Ernest Cruikshank, "could be found for many a mile. The entire number of all ranks . . . was 1,637, of whom about one-half were Provincial troops." Cruikshank, *The Battle of Lundy's Lane*, p. 31. Fredriksen, pp. 131-32.

first putting the prisoners to death." But Jesup, though he felt that "duty demanded such action," could not bring himself to carry out such a measure, and many of his prisoners therefore escaped.[4] But Scott later approved Jesup's restraint, instructing him to treat Riall with the utmost courtesy.

It was now about 9:00 P.M., almost completely dark except for a small sliver of moon. Brown's first action on arrival was to relieve Scott's brigade and place it in reserve. When Scott evaluated the situation, he concluded that his losses, especially in officers, were so severe that the units were no longer cohesive. He therefore consolidated all his regiments except Jesup's into one "battalion," which he placed under the command of Major Henry Leavenworth. From this time on, the spotlight would shine on Brigadier General Eleazar Ripley, and Scott would play a supporting role, his men temporarily in reserve. At this point, Drummond had probably 2,600 men on the field; Brown had 1,900.

The second phase of the battle was about to begin. On surveying the scene, Brown stepped in and took personal command. Deciding that the British artillery in the Presbyterian churchyard was the main source of American casualties, he ordered Ripley's brigade to assault it. Ripley broke the brigade down into two separate task forces, sending the 23d Infantry, with himself assuming personal command, around to the right. The 21st, led by Colonel James Miller, was sent directly against the guns in the churchyard. Together these regiments totalled about 750 men.

The attacks succeeded. Ripley's 300 men attacked straight up the Portage Road, attracting the enemy's fire at about 150 yards from the hill, while Scott led Miller's 21st Infantry along the covered approach he had earlier discovered. Concealed by the light shrubbery and the darkness, Miller's men were able to approach within a few yards of the British battery. Then, with a sudden rush, they fixed bayonets and rushed the guns, killing the British gunners where they stood. Drummond's 2,600 men—or their commander—seemed paralyzed. And at the same time, Ripley's men broke the British left, causing the 89th, the Royal Scots, the 8th Foot, and the 41st Foot to retreat a half mile before stopping to reform.

Drummond believed the American numbers to be greater than they actually were. Nevertheless, he made a valiant effort to regain his former position. Though he had lost all of his artillery, his exhausted men made three distinct and bloody efforts against the heights. Losses on both sides were heavy in the hand-to-hand fighting. After an hour, Lundy's Lane remained in American hands. Brown needed only one fresh battalion to ensure his victory.

Having reorganized the survivors of his former brigade into a single battalion, Scott was anxious to put it back into the battle. He left it in reserve for the moment while he rode back and forth, ignoring a wound in the side which he had sustained earlier from a rebounding cannon ball. While desperately looking for a place to commit his men, he had two horses shot from under him. Eventually he decided that the area most in need of re-inforcement was Major Jesup's position, on the Americans' right flank, which was under severe pressure; Jesup was only tenuously hanging on. So Scott and Jesup hastily began conferring.

All of a sudden Scott fell, hit in the shoulder by a one-ounce ball that shattered the bone. Two of his men, not sure that he was alive, dragged him to a place of safety and placed his head behind a tree. Scott immediately re-vived. Unable to raise his head from the loss of blood, he was no longer in any condition to command. Someone found an ambulance and the brigade commander, in great pain, was removed to the camp behind the Chippewa. The War of 1812 was over for Winfield Scott.

By this time, the battle of Lundy's Lane had degenerated into a mass of confusion on both sides. Unfortunately for the Americans, Jacob Brown was wounded by a Congreve rocket at about the same time as Scott. Of the three senior regulars on the field, only Ripley was unhurt; the com-mand of the troops on the hill therefore devolved on him.

As Brown was being carried off the field, he encountered Major Jacob Hindman, the divisional artillery commander, hurrying forward with wagon loads of ammunition. Brown stopped Hindman and gave what would later be a controversial order: "We will all go back to camp," he an-nounced. "We have done all that we can." When Ripley received that order, faithful soldier that he was, he did not question its wisdom or Brown's right to order it when out of action. He withdrew all the troops remaining on the field, even though undisturbed by Drummond. Lundy's Lane remained bare for a while, but when Hindman returned at about midnight to recover the guns he had captured earlier, he found the hill had been reoccupied by the British. Drummond had launched one final probe, only to discover that no Americans were left. He repossessed his guns and claimed victory.

Which side "won" the slaughter at Lundy's Lane has long been a source of pointless controversy. Military tradition holds that the commander who possesses the battlefield at the end of the day is the victor, and certainly on that basis Drummond's claim of "victory" is incontestable.[5] But in 1814 Americans would not stand for such a viewpoint. The battle, so the argument went, was finished at around midnight, at which time Ripley, on Brown's orders, simply returned to camp. Drummond's act in returning to take possession of his guns was not a legitimate part of the battle. As to the infliction of casualties, the issue was certainly a draw. The British had lost 876 killed, wounded, and missing whereas the Americans had suffered 861.

All such claims of tactical "victory" are irrelevant, however. The fact is that the Battle of Lundy's Lane was a strategic success for the British and Canadians. It effectively halted the American invasion of Canada. Admittedly, it also foreclosed any British-Canadian invasion of the United States, but it was the United States, not the British, that was hoping to alter the status quo.

American occupation of Canadian territory did not come to an immediate end in the early morning hours of July 26, 1814. Both sides remained in the vicinity of Lundy's Lane for a short time, and then, aware of British reinforcements on the way, Ripley wisely withdrew. He marched the Army of the Niagara back to Fort Erie, from which point the Americans had moved northward only three weeks earlier. Drummond followed him cautiously.

At this point, Drummond's luck ran out. While the Chippewa–Lundy's Lane campaign had been going on, American engineers had been busy building up Fort Erie, clearing out fields of fire, and making it a position of strength, in contrast to the run-down structure it had been in early July. On Brown's order, Brigadier General Edmund P. Gaines, commanding Brown's fourth brigade at Sacketts Harbor, hurried to replace Ripley in command of the army for the period of Brown's convalescence. His arrival raised spirits.

Drummond then tried to reduce Fort Erie without incurring the losses of a frontal assault. First he tried to take Buffalo, across the Niagara River, in hopes of eliminating Fort Erie's sole source of supply. An expedition under Colonel John Tucker to that end failed miserably, principally due to the ingenuity of the American commander at Conjota Creek. Thereupon Drummond settled down for a serious siege. It was August 4, only ten days after Lundy's Lane.

The siege of Fort Erie was badly conducted on Drummond's part, and the worst disaster came to the British and Canadians on August 15, when an ill-advised assault failed with losses of a thousand men. Many of those deaths were caused by an accidental explosion in one tower of the fort that had been temporarily occupied by British troops. Those losses were higher than those the British and Canadians suffered at Lundy's Lane.[6]

An even worse disaster hit Drummond on September 17, just as he was preparing to leave the scene. General Gaines had been wounded, and the aggressive Brown had come from a sickbed to take personal command once more. He planned and carried out a sortie that was spectacular in its success. Drummond's besieging force, reduced by sickness and battle casualties, left Fort Erie in American hands.

But even the under-publicized American successes at Fort Erie came to naught eventually. General George Izard, who finally succeeded to the command, realized what a running sore Fort Erie was, and he eventually evacuated the fort and destroyed it. He returned his troops, uncontested, to Buffalo.

Winfield Scott had no role in any of this. Of indirect personal concern to Scott, however, was the widespread acclaim accorded to Edmund Gaines by a grateful President and public. Regardless of his actual performance, which was not studied critically, Gaines was brevetted to the rank of major general and given kudos akin to Scott's. It was the beginning of a lifelong rivalry.

10

Hero

A young general basks in his status as a
national hero.

WINFIELD SCOTT was hovering near death. The musket ball that
hit him at Lundy's Lane had passed through his left shoulder and
shattered the bone. Yet, despite his excruciating pain, he never lost some degree of control over the events immediately surrounding him. When he and
a few other wounded officers were rowed in a flat-bottomed boat to Buffalo
on the morning of July 26, he was conscious enough to insist on being conducted only by convalescing militia. No able-bodied men, especially regulars, were to be used for that task!

For a few days Scott lay half dead in the makeshift hospital at Buffalo. He
would never recover complete use of his shoulder, but for the moment neither he nor his doctors were concerned with the future use of the arm. They
worried about the danger of infection and gangrene, both of which all too
often set in with severely wounded men. Realizing that Scott needed better
care than they were able to provide in Buffalo, the doctors soon moved him
to the nearby town of Williamsville.

At Williamsville, Scott was surprised and gratified to learn that the
wounded being treated there included two prominent British prisoners.
One was Major General Phineas Riall, whose arm had been amputated to
save his life, and the other was Lieutenant Colonel John Moryllion Wilson,
a man destined to be Scott's lifelong friend. Exhibiting his usual solicitude
for his British enemies, Scott gave orders from his sickbed that the surgeon
previously scheduled to accompany him should accompany Riall and Wil-

son to Albany instead. Scott went even further; he dictated a letter to Jacob Brown complaining about the poor quality of medical treatment the two Englishmen had received. He admonished his superior that "the honor of the army is concerned in this." He also arranged for both British officers to be placed on parole and returned to Britain.

When Scott and the doctors concluded that he was out of danger, he began his arduous journey back east. He was too weak to make the journey all at once, however, so he was first moved to the home of James Brisbane, of Batavia, New York. From there he was transferred to the Geneva, New York, home of John Nicholas, the transplanted Virginian who had demanded Scott's assignment to Niagara the previous year.[1]

Even at Geneva, however, Scott lacked the advanced medical care he would need. That could be supplied only by his own personal physician, the appropriately named Dr. Philip Syng Physick, and Scott pushed on to reach him, traveling on a mattress in a spring carriage. At every point along the line he was praised lavishly, as the "only representative," he noted, "that they had seen of a successful, noble army."

Scott's most prestigious honor was bestowed on him when he reached Princeton, New Jersey. Newly promoted to the brevet (honorary) rank of major general,[2] he arrived at Princeton College just in time for commencement day. The trustees and faculty learned of Scott's arrival, so they sent a deputation to Scott's quarters and invited him to attend the ceremonies. As he could not yet walk, they carried him to the platform in Nassau Hall. The valedictorian amended his address, the theme of which was "the duty of a patriot citizen in time of war," to personalize his remarks in honor of Scott. At the end of the ceremony, Scott was given the honorary degree of master of arts.

In late September, Scott finally reached Philadelphia after a trip of nearly two months. His arrival was greeted by Governor Simon Snyder, heading an honor guard comprised of a whole division of Pennsylvania militia. There, under the care of Dr. Physick, he settled in for a long, slow recovery.

Scott's name was now on the lips of all Americans. During that autumn of 1814, his luster far outshone that of any other officer, even those senior to him. Jacob Brown, Scott's commander on the Niagara Frontier, did not seem to mind, however. He had, in fact, generously attributed the victory at Chippewa, the one clear-cut American triumph of the Niagara campaign, almost uniquely to Scott. The only other officer so lauded, Edmund

P. Gaines, fell short of Scott in public accolades. Gaines's partisans might claim that his actions at Fort Erie were as important as those of Scott, but the circumstances surrounding Scott's achivements were emotional, not intellectual. For just as the public was celebrating Scott's victory at Chippewa, it learned that the new hero had been seriously wounded, perhaps mortally, at Lundy's Lane. The handsome young personification of Mars had fallen heroically.

Scott's public acclaim was extraordinary. On November 3, 1814, the Congress requested the President to cause a gold medal to be struck for presentation to Scott, "in testimony of the high sense entertained by Congress of his distinguished services, in the successive conflicts of Chippewa and Niagara [Lundy's Lane], and of his uniform gallantry and good conduct in sustaining the reputation of the arms of the United States." The legislature of New York directed the governor, Daniel D. Tompkins, to do the same. The next year Scott's native state of Virginia voted its thanks for his services, with an appropriate sword.

Certain problems could be foreseen in Scott's meteoric rise to fame, however. The most obvious of these had to do with his youth, inexperience, and immaturity. Despite his proven qualities of leadership in battle, he had much to learn in administrative matters. Along with his youth, his brashness was bound to give him troubles in getting along with others in the upper echelons of the Army. Those who doubted Scott's ability to adjust gracefully to the sudden role of national hero had a great deal on which to base their misgivings.

It would be some time, however, before these problems would become obvious. Scott first had to recover from his wound, and his duties had to be of a limited nature. While he was recuperating, Secretary of War Armstrong called on him to draw up recommendations for a prospective invasion of Canada in 1815. His views on broad military matters were now sought by Secretary of State James Monroe, Senator Martin Van Buren, and even by President Madison himself.

In early October 1814, a prestigious military surgeon, Dr. William Gibson, declared Scott fit for limited active duty, so he left Philadelphia and proceeded to Washington. There he was placed in command of the Tenth Military District, which included all of Maryland and northern Virginia, recently held by the luckless William Winder.

This was no empty assignment. After the Niagara campaign of 1814 the focus of the war had shifted from the northern frontier to the Chesapeake

Bay area. Dramatic events had been occurring there even while Scott was being moved from Buffalo on his journey to Philadelphia.

With the banishment of Emperor Napoleon to Elba in May 1814, King George III and his government were determined to punish "Jonathan," as the Americans were called. The Americans, the British claimed with much justification, had taken advantage of Britain's preoccupations in Europe to further their own ends across the Atlantic. Provocations for revenge, if such were necessary, were readily at hand; the malicious burnings of civilian towns along the Niagara frontier—York, Queenston, and Newark on the Canadian side and Lewiston, Fort Schlosser, and Buffalo on the American—had engendered bitterness on both sides. The British decided that retaliation, to be really felt, had to be administered close to home, in the middle Atlantic states. The Chesapeake Bay region was chosen.

The British government therefore sent three infantry regiments of "Wellington's Invincibles" to the Chesapeake in addition to those sent to Canada. There they were incorporated into a powerful naval force under Admiral Sir Alexander Cochrane and his fiery subordinate, Admiral George Cockburn, who had been plundering and burning American fishing villages with impunity for some time. On August 20, 1814, Cockburn landed a British army of about 4,000 men under Major General Robert Ross at Benedict, on the Patuxent River, Maryland. Ross immediately set out in the direction of Washington.

The British had caught the Americans totally unprepared. It was only on July 2, six weeks earlier, that President Madison had established the Tenth Military District to resist such a move. To command it, Madison and Armstrong had chosen Brigadier General William Winder, who had somehow escaped serious censure for his ineptness at Stony Creek the previous year.

Winder, while he turned out to be a poor choice, had been given an impossible task. His troops were untrained, and he was given almost no support or direction. His authority was continually being undercut by two cabinet secretaries, John Armstrong and James Monroe, who insisted on accompanying him on the battlefield itself. Most disastrous, his requests for troops fell on deaf ears. He expected 15,000 troops from the District of Columbia, Pennsylvania, Maryland, and Virginia, but only 5,400 men, including about 1,000 regulars, marines, and sailors, ever appeared.

Winder assembled this motley army at Bladensburg, a town only nine miles from the outskirts of Washington. There, on August 23, 1814, they were reviewed by the President and his cabinet. The next day, August 24, 1814, they were attacked by Ross's force and completely routed. American casualties—eight killed, eleven wounded—were so light as to make the episode appear almost comical. The British continued on to Washington, burned the Capitol and the White House, and returned to their ships unmolested. The United States government had scattered all over the region; President Madison in Virginia, Winder and Monroe at Montgomery Courthouse (Gaithersburg), and Armstrong at Frederick.

The British triumph was soon to end, however. American forces under Major General Samuel Smith blocked an attempt to sack Baltimore, and British failure to take Fort McHenry inspired "The Star-Spangled Banner." But American pride had been badly wounded, and a general feeling of humiliation and gloom descended on the American populace. John Armstrong, the principal scapegoat, resigned his position as secretary of war.

Everyone knew, however, that Armstrong was not solely responsible for the defeat. All realized that United States forces in the region sorely needed strong leadership. No wonder the Madison administration welcomed the presence of a recognized professional soldier, Winfield Scott. As the new commander of the Tenth Military District, he could be counted on to ensure that Washington and Baltimore would not be subject to such a humiliation again.

By the time Scott assumed command at Washington, the immediate threat had passed. Admiral Cochrane's fleet had sailed for Halifax to refit in late September, leaving the small detachments of British troops in the Chesapeake area immobilized. And even they were removed in mid-October.

The departure of the British forces from the Chesapeake, however, did not mean that peace was at hand. Neither Scott nor anyone else in the government could foresee that the American commissioners in Ghent—Henry Clay, John Quincy Adams, and Albert Gallatin—would be able to sign an honorable treaty with Britain any time soon. So Scott, despite his weakened condition, made inspection visits to the defenses at Washington and Fredericksburg, Virginia, both considered vulnerable points. Then, as the year 1814 ended without further threats, Scott reduced the strength of the garrisons under his command by sending the militiamen home.

In the meantime he set about building personal friendships among political leaders. He continued to cultivate Senator Martin Van Buren, who was concerned with the defense of the New York frontier in the campaigns projected for 1815. When the senator sought Scott's views on ways to improve the New York militia, Scott responded enthusiastically. He drew up a plan based on a careful system of classifying potential recruits. In October he rhapsodized that "with this force we may think of carrying the war to the walls of Quebec by the first of November, 1815." Scott also suggested that Van Buren, despite his innocence of anything military, might enter service "at any rank he fancied."[3]

With the winding down of the threat to Washington, the War Department began considering his next assignment. Scott's shoulder wound appeared to be sufficiently healed; Dr. Gibson was asked whether Scott was again fit for field duty, specifically to join General Andrew Jackson at New Orleans. The doctor turned thumbs down; the trip would be too long, he declared. So Scott was assigned to administrative duties, which he performed with zeal.

One pleasant assignment involved chairing a board to overhaul the current system of drill and tactics. A congressional resolution, under the sponsorship of Congressman William Lowndes, set up such a panel, naming Scott specifically as president. He worked diligently on that assignment, replacing Duane's *Handbook for Infantry* and other manuals being used at the time. The panel's new system of field regulations resembled the Napoleonic system, which Scott had been using at Buffalo the previous year.[4]

Another board, also chaired by Scott, was less agreeable. It was convened to consider what disiplinary action, if any, should be taken against General Winder for the defeat at Bladensburg, which had opened the way for the burning of Washington. The inquest was not initiated by the Army, but many super-patriots, demanding a scapegoat, had been howling for Winder's scalp, and an inquiry had to be made. By the time the board met, however, the din had abated. Armstrong, the principal target of criticism, had already resigned, so the board happily dropped all charges against Winder; commanders had little stomach for condemning one of their own.

In early August 1814, even as Admiral Cochrane and General Ross were landing in the Chesapeake, a peace conference between the British and the Americans had convened at the Belgian town of Ghent.

The atmosphere between negotiators, however, was one of recrimination, not of reconciliation. The British public now transferred all the venom they had previously directed toward Napoleon Bonaparte onto American President James Madison, and the positions of their representatives reflected that feeling. So far apart were the British and Americans, in fact, that the conference appeared to be in danger of collapse from the moment it opened.*

Despite what appeared to be poor prospects, however, British foreign secretary Lord Castlereagh was anxious to avoid assuming the onus of a failed conference. If he maintained too adamant a position, the previously unpopular war might become popular in the United States—and correspondingly unpopular in Britain. Therefore, while not much went on for a while, the conference continued.

At first the Americans were on the defensive. Albert Gallatin, one of the delegates, had advised President Madison that the Americans should be satisfied with an acceptance of the status quo ante, and the President had adopted that as his objective. But Castlereagh, sensing military triumph in America, insisted that boundaries should be adjusted in accordance with the territory in the possession of the two sides. He therefore did not rush, expecting his military commanders to occupy the territories Britain would later demand.

The positions of the two sides always reflected the latest news from the battlefronts. When word of Bladensburg and the burning of Washington arrived on October 1, the negotiators assumed that those British victories would soon be followed by others. Word of the British defeat at Baltimore and the perceived British rebuff at Lundy's Lane soon followed, however, casting the military situation in a light less and less lopsided in the British favor.

The last news of military significance came in late October. Sir George Prevost, with 15,000 men, had begun a major operation up Lake Champlain, intending to occupy great tracts of American territory, perhaps even as far as Albany. But the British had sustained utter defeat on September 11, 1814, when their fleet, under Captain George Downie, was destroyed by American Captain Thomas MacDonough in Plattsburgh Bay (Lake Champlain), and their army under Prevost was stalemated by a vastly smaller American army under Brigadier General Alexander Macomb. Prevost withdrew to Montreal under disgrace. (The Duke of Wellington refused to take the command replacing him.)

---

*British foreign secretary Lord Castlereagh was less vitriolic than the people he represented, but he still delayed sending negotiators to the conference until he had announced the dispatch of 20,000 men to Canada, a force deemed more than adequate to overpower any force the Americans could muster.

With this military impasse, the negotiations at Ghent wound down to an end; the participants simply ignored some of the questions that could not be agreed on, such as British fomenting of unrest among the Indians. The Treaty of Ghent, effectively restoring the status quo ante, was signed on Christmas Eve, 1814, and a ship was dispatched bearing the news. On February 11, 1815, the vessel arrived in New York harbor with word that the war was over.

A week later, President Madison issued a proclamation of peace, and the people rejoiced. Never mind that the treaty included no British concessions on impressment of seamen, the ostensible cause for the declaration in 1812.

Scott received the news of peace with mixed feelings. He realized that the treasury was empty, that commerce was at a standstill, and that the war had caused sectional bitterness that even threatened a rupture of the Union. From the standpoint of the good of the United States, the end of hostilities could only bring a sense of relief. Yet Scott would have been superhuman—which he certainly was not—had he not been disappointed that peace had brought his prospects for promotion to an end. Rumors had been circulating that three names were being seriously considered for promotion to the grade of lieutenant general, those of Andrew Jackson, Jacob Brown, and Winfield Scott. Congress, however, had not yet taken action, if it ever intended to, and the end of the war would put such action out of the question. A disappointed Scott wrote disingenuously to Monroe, "I exceedingly lament that Congress should be indisposed to create the rank of Lieutenant-General. . . . [W]hat reward can a government bestow on Maj. Generals Brown and Jackson? Rank is the first wish of a soldier; but a major-general has nothing to acquire."[5] He neglected to mention—but it was all too obvious—a similar reward for Winfield Scott.

But ambitious as he was, Scott pursued his ends with the future in mind. Immediately after the end of the war, certain members of Congress recommended Scott for the position of Secretary of War (which he had been filling on a temporary basis since the previous September). Scott knew better; he was only twenty-nine years old, and the position of secretary, or even acting secretary, would put him temporarily, but only temporarily, over such future regular army superiors as Jackson and Brown. Scott discouraged that move decisively.

Scott was now in for a personal demotion of sorts. At about the time he was writing to Monroe, word arrived that Andrew Jackson, on January 8,

1815, had scored a one-sided triumph over a major British force under General Sir Edward Pakenham at New Orleans. Jackson had placed his militia—the 7th Infantry was his only major regular unit—in a strong defensive position, which the British commander, like Riall at Chippewa, had attacked almost contemptuously. As a result, the British lost 2,000 men as against Jackson's loss of a little over a dozen.

The Battle of New Orleans, though fought after the Treaty of Ghent was signed, represented by far the most decisive American victory of the War of 1812. That victory gave a sweet taste to those Americans, especially the War Hawks, who had been frustrated by defeat after defeat during the previous two and a half years. Andrew Jackson was now the undisputed darling of the public. Scott, while still highly honored, was relegated to second place.

In the spring of 1815, Scott was assigned to a board that would have a direct effect on his future career: a panel to reconstruct the officer corps of the reorganized army. Jackson was named as the senior member of the board, but both he and Brown were delayed by the exigencies of travel. The work of the board, therefore, was done largely under Scott's direction.

The panel's first task was to select the six general officers to be carried on the permanent list. That phase was a cozy affair, and the result of the deliberations was a foregone conclusion: the members of the board simply selected themselves. Jackson and Brown were named as the two major generals, while Macomb, Gaines, Scott, and Ripley were to be the brigadiers, all with brevets (honorary rank) as major generals. The only matter of possible contention was the order of precedence among the brigadiers. The sequence in which the names appeared dictated seniority among them until some later promotion list should make alterations—which was not expected. The final sequence was based on the date that each officer had received his original promotion to brigadier. Scott's and Gaines's dates of rank were the same, Gaines coming first alphabetically.

The panel's second task, that of reducing the Army from its authorized wartime strength of 65,000 men to its peacetime strength of 10,000, was far more difficult. This cutback was particularly hard on the men who had served as officers. The position vacancies for the commissioned ranks had been filled, even though wartime recruiting had never brought the enlisted ranks up to authorized levels. Many officers, having spent several years in the Army, had cut themselves off from the trades that had supported them before the war, and modern compensations such as retirement pay, pensions, and bonuses were still things of the distant future. The cutback did, of course, afford the opportunity to get rid of much dead wood, but that advantage did not outweigh the pain.

Once the board had completed its difficult work, Scott felt that he deserved a leave of absence from his duties. He hoped to travel in Europe, being particularly anxious to visit France. At the time Scott conceived the idea, Emperor Napoleon had just returned to France from his exile on Elba, and Scott expected him to remain in power for some time. Anticipating renewed warfare on a grand scale, he hoped to witness action between the massed armies of France, Russia, Prussia, and Britain. Keenly aware that his own command experience had been limited to directing a single brigade, he longed to be exposed to larger operations. Quite possibly he also desired to broaden his acquaintance with influential foreigners; there was nothing narrow in Scott's personal ambition.

He submitted a request for a three-year leave of absence to the acting secretary of war, Alexander J. Dallas. Dallas readily approved, but stipulated that Scott must travel as "an interested neutral spectator" only. He was not to be given any official status by way of introductions to foreign officials. Nevertheless, Scott had many personal contacts and his papers were soon full of such letters from prominent citizens, both in and out of government.

Scott hoped to be able to present himself to the Duke of Wellington at some point, but his primary destination was France, which he planned to reach by way of a British port. So he recruited a young militia officer as aide and secured regular rank for him. General Winfield Scott and Major John Mercer sailed from New York on July 9, 1815.*

The sailing ship on which Scott was traveling made good time, crossing the Atlantic in eighteen days. When the passengers disembarked in Liverpool, they were met with startling news: Napoleon had been decisively defeated at Waterloo, Belgium, on June 18, 1815, and was now a prisoner of the British in Plymouth harbor. Paris, they learned, was now occupied by a joint command of British, Prussian, Austrian, and Russian troops, under the overall command of the Duke of Wellington. Scott therefore wasted no time

---

*On the dock at New York Scott was overjoyed to meet twenty-one of the the twenty-three soldiers of Irish descent who had been sent to Britain in late 1812. Two had died of natural causes. Scott, *Memoirs*, 1:81.

in Britain; he and Mercer sped through England and within a few days arrived in Paris.

The Paris that met Scott's eyes presented a far different spectacle from what he had originally expected. Instead of a dazzling capital with inhabitants exultant over the return of their emperor, he found the people sullen and depressed. Foreign troops—over 100,000 of them—were occupying the streets. Foreign dignitaries of whom Scott had read were readily accessible to the gaze of all. Scott made his way through that scene and proceeded to make his presence known. As the third-ranking general of an independent country, he was welcomed by the occupying powers.

His relations with the different nationalities varied, however. At one point he learned that a group of British officers were planning a celebration of the anniversary of the burning of Washington the year before.[6] Scott bided his time but then, in January 1816, he organized a party of Americans to celebrate Andrew Jackson's decisive defeat of General Pakenham's troops at New Orleans a year earlier. Even though the dinner was to be held just across the street from the main British hotel, the occasion passed without disorder. One of the toasts presented that evening was particularly provocative toward the British:

> Major General Andrew Jackson and his heroic army, who, this day a year ago, near New Orleans, defeated thrice their number of the best British troops, commanded by Sir Edward Packenham, the brother-in-law of the Duke of Wellington.[7]

Scott had made his gesture of defiance, but he was disappointed that the editor of the French newspaper refused to print that particular toast. He therefore took matters in his own hands. He wrote a complete account of the evening and had it printed in a British newspaper in the form of an advertisement.

Scott made other contacts. He was particularly anxious to visit Tadeusz Kościuszko, the Polish patriot and friend of the United States. Kościuszko was too sick to receive him but sent a letter of lavish compliment, enough to satisfy any young general's ego. As to the French, Scott was keenly partisan in favor of those who had helped the Americans. The greatest of these was the Marquis de Lafayette, now under a cloud in Bourbon France because of his participation in the French Revolution. Scott visited Lafayette and the two men spent several days together. Perhaps out of loyalty to

Lafayette, Scott went out of his way to show distaste for the Bourbons. At one of the frequent and colorful reviews of troops, he refused to remove his cap as the Bourbon troops marched by. Nothing was said about the affront, however.

Scott made a point of visiting the Louvre nearly every day after his arrival in Paris, as that museum presented a rare opportunity to see exceptional works of art. Masterworks from all over Europe, taken from their homes and placed in the Louvre during Napoleon's reign, were now being removed for return to their previous owners. The French King, Louis XVIII, had secured permission to have copies made of them, however, and a group of artists, mostly young women, were working to that end. One day Scott spied the Russian czar, Alexander I, attempting to make pleasantries with the artists as they worked. The Gallic *patriotes* refused to respond; Alexander was simply one of these "enemies of France." Scott also saw such figures as Emperor Francis of Austria, the king of Prussia, General Gebhard von Blücher, and the venerable Baron Wilhelm von Humboldt.[8]

One of Scott's informal objectives in Europe was to measure the degree of friendliness toward the revolutionary movements in Mexico and South America, where the local populations were rising against their Spanish masters. Scott crossed the channel to Britain in late January 1816, and there he was able to meet with a group of prominent Mexicans. Their leader, General Francisco Xavier Mina, was trying to raise funds to finance another Mexican uprising in the steps of the failed Hidalgo revolution of 1810.[9] Scott relished reporting the encounter to Monroe.

While in London Scott became acquainted with the United States minister, John Quincy Adams. Adams was unusually solicitous to the younger man, obtaining for him a ticket of admission to the Strangers' Gallery of the House of Commons, from which vantage point he could witness British legislative government in action. Scott dined at the American legation and was able to give Adams's son, Charles Francis Adams, some information on the battles of Chippewa, Fort George, and New Orleans, with which he could defend himself against the taunts of the British schoolboys.

Scott left Britain in the middle of April 1816, nine months after his arrival in Europe. Even though his original plans had called for a visit of three years, he was ready to return home. He made no note of meeting with Wellington while in France, though the Iron Duke must surely have noticed his defiant celebration of Jackson's victory at New Orleans. He arrived at Baltimore on May 10, 1816, "a little improved," he later wrote, "both in knowledge and patriotism."

On his return home, Scott was assigned to command the Third Department of the Northern Division, U.S. Army,[10] whose territory stretched from New York City, where he kept his headquarters, all the way to the Niagara.[11] Little was occurring at the time. The quiet of peacetime was beginning to descend on the Army.

11

Domestic Bliss and a
Feud with Jackson

Scott meets his match in a vicious war of words.

O N TUESDAY evening, March 11, 1816, Miss Maria Mayo was married to Major General Winfield Scott at Bellville, the home of Colonel John Mayo Jr., near Richmond. The courtship was shrouded in mystery. The bridegroom was said to have been wooing the comely and vivacious Miss Mayo for years, but the bride, the toast of Richmond society, denied that rumor. She had not even met Winfield Scott, she once declared, until after he had become a general.

Such details were of no consequence. This occasion was touted to the country as the dream union, a joining of a national hero and the young woman who was called "not only beautiful both in face and figure but intelligent, witty, cultivated, charming—and modest withal."[1] The wealthy and prestigious Mayo family would unite with the most eligible bachelor in the United States. But in Richmond society, the matter was not so simple. Colonel Mayo was the great-grandson of William Mayo, who in 1737 had surveyed both Richmond and Petersburg at the behest of William Byrd II— and who in his own right was a wealthy engineer and owner of a mill and a tobacco kiln. John Mayo was not impressed with Scott's pedigree, a matter far more important to him than Scott's current fame. As a member of what had become one of the First Families of Virginia, the colonel was said to view Scott as an upstart. Nevertheless, he gave his grudging permission and granted the young couple the use of his home at Elizabethtown, New Jersey, across the Hudson from Scott's headquarters in New York City.

Scott was too busy to leave on a honeymoon immediately after the ceremony, but later in the summer he managed to get away for three months, taking his bride to the traditional honeymoon spot of Niagara Falls and showing her the scenes of his former triumphs—no doubt in excruciating detail. Their trip took them down the St. Lawrence River, along the road where Scott had been marched as a prisoner of war four years earlier. In the fall they settled down at Elizabethtown, which was to be their home, off and on, for the next thirty years.

The union was fruitful. Early in 1818 came the birth of Maria Mayo Scott, named after her mother. Other children followed in quick succession; by 1825 the Scott family included three daughters and two sons. Two more would follow in later years. Family life was relatively serene; the nation was at peace; communications with the outside world were slow; and Scott was contented in his new command of the Third Department.

By the act of 1815, the Army had been reduced from its authorized wartime strength of 65,000 men to 10,000. The commanders would be two major generals, Jacob Brown in the north and Andrew Jackson in the south. Four brigadiers were assigned under the major generals. Scott's command, the Third Department, which encompassed all of New York State and much of the northeast, came under Brown.

Once Scott had his duties in hand, they did not fill all of his time, so as one who needed to be busy,[2] he secured General Brown's permission to draw up a system of general regulations for army administration, which he called his *Military Institutes,* something woefully lacking in that relatively new institution. To assist him Scott drew heavily on manuals he had used himself, the French *Législation Militaire* and the English *General Regulations.* The *Institutes* included rules for administration, instruction, service, police, and other matters. Together with some minor dabbling in politics and a foray into the press on the subject of temperance, the *Institutes* kept Scott occupied for a while.

It was also at this time that Scott began to develop his intimate relationship with men of influence in New York. As the commanding general of the Third Department, he was automatically an accepted member of New York society, a role that he relished. As many years of his life were to be spent in Elizabethtown and New York, those relationships would profoundly affect his life from that time on.

Professionally, however, these quiet years were marred by a series of controversies that largely grew out of Scott's youth and rapid elevation to high army rank. He was naturally the envy of other officers who, though lesser known, had also performed meritoriously. Even more troubling, however, was the effect that his rapid rise had on Scott himself. It whetted his appetite for even more recognition, often to his detriment.

An army too long at peace is always a hotbed of restlessness and petty squabbles. As the War of 1812 faded into history, old jealousies lived on and new ones developed, even among former comrades. One of Scott's inveterate detractors, old James Wilkinson, devoted much of his *Autobiography* to castigating Scott. In late 1814 Wilkinson underwent his final court-martial. Although exonerated of wrongdoing for lack of evidence, he was soon honorably discharged from the Army. At least that particular blackguard was no longer a force to be reckoned with. The more important jealousies, however, arose among the relatively young generals who had salvaged America's military fortunes after two years of defeats. The fate of the Army—and of the country—would rest in their hands for decades to come. The most celebrated of these squabbles arose between Scott and Andrew Jackson who, though seventeen years Scott's senior, had not yet reached the age of fifty.

Scott had never quite adjusted to the fact that Jackson, after the Battle of New Orleans, had become the primary hero in the public eye, with himself relegated to second place. In early 1815, soon after Jackson's singular triumph, Scott wrote Secretary of State James Monroe, referring to Jackson as "that favorite of fortune," questioning some aspects of Jackson's campaign, and remarking that "M. Gen'l. Jackson and the Western militia seem likely to throw all other generals & the regular troops into the background." But Scott did not express any reservations about Jackson in public. He remained circumspect whenever Jackson's name was mentioned. He and Jackson dwelt in different worlds—the West and the East.

In mid-1817, however, an unfortunate incident provoked a controversy between Jackson and Scott that, though patched over, never really healed. In March 1817, as the administration of James Madison was drawing to a close, Acting Secretary of War George Graham committed a serious breach of military courtesy toward Jackson, whose command stretched over the entire western portion of the then United States. Through either carelessness or the pressure of time, Graham ordered an engineer officer to leave his posting on the upper Mississippi River and report immediately to Washington— this without sending a copy of the order to Jackson.

Jackson, at Nashville, had tolerated similar actions before, as he recognized that his command was spread over great distances, and because the

War Department had always sent him copies of such orders. But when Jackson learned of this action only by reading about it in a New York newspaper, he wrote an angry letter to President James Monroe denouncing the breach of custom and requesting an apology. Monroe, however, was busy organizing his new administration, and he neglected to answer.

Jackson awaited a reply for more than six weeks. Then, on April 22, 1817, he issued a general order to the Southern Command prohibiting his subordinates from obeying "any order emanating from the department of war, to officers of the division . . . unless coming through [Jackson] as the proper organ of communication." The order castigated the War Department's "provocation," claiming that acquiescence would be a "tame surrender of military rights and etiquette, and at once subvert the established principles of subordination and good order."

Jackson's defiant action could not be justified on any legal basis; indeed the very existence of Jackson's command was contingent on the authority of the secretary of war. But Jackson declined to admit his shaky ground, and when his order became public knowledge, he refused to recant. Old Hickory's *pronunciamento* became a tantalizing topic of conversation in both military and civilian circles.

One evening, when Scott was a dinner guest at the home of a prominent citizen of New York, he found himself in after-dinner discussion with De-Witt Clinton, governor-elect. In deference to the positions of these two prominent men, others in the group fell silent and allowed the two to hold forth. When the subject inevitably turned to Jackson's recent actions, all turned to Scott, as the authority on things military. Scott obliged by expounding his views, and Clinton made his own contribution. Somewhere along the line the word "mutinous" came up. Scott later blamed Clinton for the use of the word itself, though he never denied that he had agreed. The exchange was little noted at the time; it was presumed to be private.

But not everybody at the dinner was a well-wisher. An unidentified guest described the incident in a scurrilous, unsigned letter that was sent to the editors of the *Columbian* newspaper. The *Columbian* printed the letter, whereupon someone—probably the writer himself—forwarded it to Jackson under the cover of another unsigned letter. The anonymous author(s), describing Scott as the "organ" of the government, made the most of the affair:

> The War Office gentry and their adherents, pensioners, and expectants have all been busy, but no one, of sufficient mark for your notice, more than General

Scott who, I am credibly informed, goes so far as to call the order in question an act of mutiny.

Andrew Jackson could well have ignored this anonymous correspondence, as it deserved no respect. But the hero of New Orleans was sensitive on this subject, and he refused to let it pass. On September 8, 1817, he wrote Scott a correct but ominous letter that described the circumstances and then concluded,

> I have not permitted myself for a moment to believe, that the conduct ascribed to you is correct. Candor, however, induces me to lay them before you, that you may have it in your power to say how far they may be incorrectly stated.
>
> If my order has been the subject of your animadversions, it is believed you will at once admit it, and the extent to which you may have gone.

Jackson's letter arrived at Scott's headquarters as Scott was returning to New York from an inspection trip to the Northwest. Disturbed, he studied the article and quickly saw that the author of the unsigned letter had been totally confused on the details but had not been mistaken on the essence.[3] Scott had indeed referred to Jackson's "dictatorial system" and "doctrines of obedience." That realization put him on the defensive, and the defensive was no place for Winfield Scott ever to be.

On October 4, he sent Jackson a reply that could not have been better calculated to send Old Hickory raging. After denying authorship of the letter in the *Columbian,* he elaborated in defense of his viewpoint, his words degenerating into an intricate explanation of legalities. Trying to be thorough, he appeared condescending. He then added a gratuitous distinction between Jackson's position as his *superior* officer—which, as a major general, Jackson was—and the position of his *commanding* officer, which Jackson was not. Scott seemed to forget that this line of argument had gotten him nowhere in his earlier contretemps with James Wilkinson.

Scott's letter only worsened the situation. On receiving it, Jackson turned his rage from the War Department to Scott. Forgetting the relatively academic question of his original "mutiny," Old Hickory could now think of nothing but Scott's patronizing tone. He castigated his fellow general officer without restraint: "The circumstances of your wearing the badge and insignia of a soldier," he wrote, "led me to the conclusion that I was addressing a gentleman." Had he earlier realized his error, he went on, he would have "viewed you as too contemptible, to have held any converse with you on the subject." He called Scott a "bully," his rhetoric "tinsel." In closing, he called Scott one of those "intermeddling spies and pimps of the War Department," ending with an implied challenge: If Scott felt aggrieved, "any communication from you will reach me safely at this place."

Scott was as brave a soldier on the battlefield as was Jackson, and more audacious as a commander. But he lacked Jackson's personal savagery, and in situations like this, he was no match. Fortunately for all, he was for once deliberate in his response, consulting friends before answering. The main problem was to fashion a response to Jackson's indirect but unmistakable challenge to a duel. He realized that he could never gain from a duel with Jackson; either he himself would be killed, or else he would kill a great national hero. Even if the second alternative proved to be the case, Scott would be tarred with the same brush as Aaron Burr was ten years earlier for mortally wounding Alexander Hamilton in a similar affair of honor.

Scott therefore delayed answering until after the turn of the year. Then he wrote declining the challenge on the basis of "religion" and also from patriotic scruples. "My ambition is not that of Erostratus, the killer of a defender of his country," he wrote.[4] But he knew that Jackson would not be mollified by this somewhat subtle compliment, so he concluded ruefully,

> I should think it would be very easy to console yourself under this refusal, by the application of a few epithets, such as coward, &c., to the object of your resentment, and I here promise to leave you until the next war to persuade yourself of their truth.

As Scott had predicted, Jackson was not placated. He passed Scott's letter around to friends, attaching his own sneering comments. He did not, however, take further action against Scott. The new secretary of war, John C. Calhoun, alarmed by the exchange, tried to end the squabble by prohibiting "all publications relating to transactions between officers, of a private or personal nature." And President Monroe, trying to settle the question that had caused the brouhaha, notified Jackson that the government would insist on obedience of its orders under all circumstances. At the same time the President promised that orders concerning individuals would be sent through proper headquarters when possible; otherwise copies would be sent to the commanders involved. Jackson, clearly in the wrong, did or said nothing further.

Now Jackson and Scott both felt aggrieved. Jackson published a pamphlet containing the entire correspondence for circulation among his friends, and Scott answered with one of his own. The two exchanged accusations in the public press. But by the end of May 1818, with Jackson deeply involved in preparations for the First Seminole War in Florida, both prima donnas seemed to lose interest. Jackson continued his swaggering attitude toward Scott, and the rumor came around to Scott that Jackson was telling his friends that he would "cut Scott's ears off" if ever they met in person.

That threat was all right so long as Scott and Jackson had half a continent between them. Providentially, the gap was preserved for another three years.

12

❧❧❧❧

Ridiculous Resignation

Scott loses his bid to head the Army.
He nearly does even worse.

THE YEAR 1821 introduced a period of frustration in Scott's life, a low
point of his career. True, he received well-deserved accolades for the
work he had done on the *Military Institutes,* but when that work was completed, he found himself without a constructive way to occupy his mind.
More disturbing than that, however, was the fact that a recent cutback in
general officers would make it impossible for him and Maria to remain permanently in Elizabethtown.

In December 1820, Secretary of War John C. Calhoun, complying with a
directive from the House of Representatives, submitted a plan to reduce the
strength of the Army from its present 10,000 officers and men to 6,000.[1] His
approach was to keep the Army's structure essentially unchanged, reducing
it by lowering the number of privates assigned during peacetime to each organization. In time of war, the reasoning went, the privates could be quickly
recruited and assimilated into the existing units (nine infantry regiments
and five of artillery) without the need for recruiting new units or calling up
militia. The total strength of the two branches would be 6,300.

Calhoun was sanguine about this plan, boasting,

Without adding an additional officer or a single company, [the infantry and ar-
tillery] may be augmented . . . to 11,558; and pending hostilities, by adding 288
officers . . . they may be raised to the respectable force of 4,545 of the artillery and

14,490 of the infantry, making in the aggregate 19,035 officers, non-commissioned officers, and privates.[2]

From a military viewpoint, this was a sensible scheme, one followed by the European powers throughout the nineteenth century. It also served a selfish purpose for the professionals; it retained most of the officer positions, especially in the higher grades. It was defeated by pressure from the militia, however, who were well organized politically. It would, they reasoned, reduce the need, in time of war, to rely heavily on volunteer units. In the law that was passed in March 1821, therefore, Congress required that the structure itself be reduced to four regiments of artillery and seven regiments of infantry. The law also required that the number of major generals be reduced from two to one, and brigadiers from four to two.

Once the shock of this rebuff had worn off, the War Department began planning how to comply. The adjustment in major generals turned out to be surprisingly easy. President James Monroe offered to appoint Andrew Jackson governor of Florida, a prestigious post. Old Hickory seized the opportunity; he was developing political ambitions and was just as glad to leave the regular army. He would stay a while in Florida and then go on to other things. His departure left Jacob Brown as the only major general.

Cutting back the brigadiers was more of a problem, because all four of them wished to continue. A solution of sorts was finally reached. Winfield Scott and Edmund Gaines were to retain their previous ranks. Alexander Macomb, though previously the senior brigadier, was enticed to accept reduction to the grade of colonel in exchange for the coveted post of Chief of Engineers. He was also granted the privilege of exercising his brevet as a brigadier, including a brigadier's pay. Only Ripley was given no recompense; he resigned in a huff.

But if Scott survived the reduction in general officers, he could no longer count on keeping his comfortable berth in New York. Under the new organization, the Army was split into two commands: the Western, with headquarters in St. Louis, and the Eastern, with headquarters in New York. With the blessing of the War Department, Scott and Gaines came to a compromise: Scott would stay in New York till 1823, two years hence. The two would then exchange posts, with Scott replacing Gaines in St. Louis, and the latter returning to New York.

In late 1823, Scott headed westward to take command in St. Louis, in accordance with his agreement with Gaines. On the way he went by Washington, hoping there to mend his fences with Andrew Jackson. Scott was leery of approaching Jackson directly, so he planned to make their meeting appear to be a matter of chance. He would approach Jackson in the halls of the Senate, where Jackson would be taking his seat for the first time. As Scott had been accorded the "privilege of the floor" of the Senate, he had a unique opportunity to meet his old adversary face to face.

When Scott arrived at the Capitol, he quickly recognized Jackson in the Senate, and he began maneuvering around the Senate floor, giving Jackson every chance to accost him, either in a friendly or hostile manner. To his disappointment, however, Jackson gave no hint of reciprocating. For several days nothing happened.

By December 11, 1823, Scott's time in Washington was drawing to a close, so he addressed a note to Jackson pointing out that he had been in Jackson's presence for six days "without having attracted your notice." But then he came to the point:

> As this is the first time in my life that I have ever been within a hundred miles of you, and it is barely possible that you may be ignorant of my presence, I beg leave to state that I shall not leave the District before the morning of the 14th inst.

Jackson answered immediately. From Scott's "ambiguous" letter, he said, he had concluded that it "was written with friendly views." He added an equally oblique invitation: "Whenever you shall feel disposed to meet me on friendly terms, that disposition will not be met by any other than a correspondent feeling on my part."

Scott was relieved by this cordial reply, as he had half expected a rebuff. He lost no time in calling on Jackson in his Senate office where he was, as he later wrote, "graciously received." He left happily for the West the next day, confident that the rift between him and Jackson had been healed.[3]

Though his clash with Andrew Jackson was Scott's most trying controversy, he managed to run afoul of others as well. Two of these incidents would result in challenges to duels—both, ironically, issued by Scott himself.

The first of these was of little lasting consequence. It involved Scott's perception of DeWitt Clinton's role in fomenting his misunderstanding with Jackson. In one of the pamphlets that Scott issued to his friends in response to those of Jackson, he gratuitously accused Governor Clinton of instigating the anonymous letter to Jackson that had begun the troubles. Clinton promptly answered with an article in the *Columbian*. A vitriolic exchange followed, and in a fit of exasperation Scott challenged Clinton to a duel, his "religious aversion" to such affairs notwithstanding. Clinton refused the challenge on the basis of "official duties," an argument sustained by the constitution of the state of New York. Then, in a nine-page letter, Clinton continued his diatribe, calling Scott a "ruffian, outside the pale of honorable men." The New York Democratic press supported Clinton's refusal to fight, saying pointedly that the governor should refuse Scott's challenge—at least until Scott accepted Jackson's.

As with Jackson, Scott again came out second best. He had indeed found some falsehoods in Clinton's accusations, but his own blunder had been worse: Clinton had been innocent. Scott later apologized to Clinton, but by that time both men had lost interest. The two operated in different spheres, and the matter was allowed to die.

Scott's other feud was with his peer, Brigadier General (Brevet Major General) Edmund P. Gaines. Because of the length of time it would go on, it was the most significant of Scott's feuds. And as was so often the case, the issue was one of rank: after the recent reorganization, which of the two was to be regarded as the senior?

The matter was not so petty as it may sound, for precedence was important to both officers. The choice of assignments between New York and St. Louis had fortunately been worked out, but now that General-in-Chief Jacob Brown was obviously dying, both coveted Brown's position. The nod would most likely go to the brigadier general considered senior.

Both had certain rationales to support their claims. Scott and Gaines had been made colonels of the regular army on March 12, 1813, and both had subsequently been promoted to the grade of brigadier general on March 9, 1814. Gaines's claim to seniority, therefore, was based on the fact that his name preceded Scott's on both promotion orders. Scott's argument centered on brevet rank, in which his promotion to major general, a reward for his performances at Chippewa and Lundy's Lane, preceded that of Gaines, which was based on his handling of the battles around Fort Erie. Most contemporary opinion favored Gaines's position, preferring regular rank as the basis for further promotion; Scott argued vehemently in favor of brevet.

Unfortunately, the War Department was weak in its handling of this conflict. Though department officials cautiously favored Gaines's position, nobody in authority seemed willing to stop Scott from appealing to political friends—and to the press—to trumpet his cause. As a result, Scott and Gaines fought the battle out with letters berating each other, one exchange resulting in Scott's challenge to a duel, properly refused by Gaines. The War Department, in an effort to defuse the issue, gave both parties the pay of major generals. But that sop did not end the dispute, which continued throughout the rest of the two men's association. The hard feelings would cease only with the death of Gaines in 1849.

The year 1824 saw the end of the relatively stable political dominance of the "Virginia Dynasty" of American presidents—Jefferson, Madison, Monroe. The presidential field that year was open, and the flock of contenders included Secretary of State John Quincy Adams, Senator Andrew Jackson of Tennessee, Senator Henry Clay of Kentucky, Senator John C. Calhoun of South Carolina, Governor Clinton of New York, and William H. Crawford of Georgia. All called themselves "Democratic Republicans"; the Federalists had gone out of contention for failing to support the War of 1812.

When the actual election was held in late 1824, none of the candidates received a majority. Andrew Jackson led the field, receiving 90 electoral votes, but Adams, with 84, was close behind. The rest of the electors split between Crawford and Clay. In accordance with the Constitution the election was therefore thrown into the House of Representatives, and after an incredibly long period of suspense and connivings, the House elected John Quincy Adams to be President of the United States on February 13, 1825.

On that same Sunday evening, President and Mrs. James Monroe entertained Washington dignitaries in the White House for the last time. The House action had been completed only that day, and nobody was quite sure how the volatile Jackson, deprived of office despite his popular majority, would react. Much to everyone's relief, Jackson was on his good behavior. He shook hands with all the guests—President-elect Adams, Vice President–elect John C. Calhoun, Henry Clay, Daniel Webster, the portrait painter and inventor Samuel F. B. Morse, and many others.

The guest of honor that evening was the venerable Marquis de Lafayette, who was making a triumphant tour of the United States as the "nation's guest." But to President Monroe's embarrassment, the crowd paid little attention to either the guest of honor or the other dignitaries. Everyone clustered around the hero of New Orleans. Outside the doors of the White House, crowds of citizens also wanted a look at Old Hickory. So determined were they that the thin line of United States marshals were inadequate to stop them. The barricades gave way; people thronged into the White House from the streets, bringing many unwanted guests.

Among the guests caught up in the swirl of humanity that surged through the ground-floor rooms of the White House was Major General Scott. The society matron who later wrote up an account noted with wry humor that the handsome Winfield Scott had eight hundred dollars picked out of the pocket of his resplendent uniform.[4]

With the inauguration of John Quincy Adams, Scott saw an opportunity to close the issue between himself and Gaines—favorably to himself, of course. Once he returned from St. Louis to New York (December 1825), he took advantage of the friendship that had begun in London ten years earlier. He began bombarding President Adams with his arguments, always at great length. On December 12, 1825, he visited Adams in the White House to press for a decision in the matter. Adams was personally sympathetic but amused by Scott's presumption. In his diary he noted Scott's insistence that "the correct answer to the question involved was so plain and easy that no intelligent or impartial mind could hesitate concerning it." In the course of the futile discussion, Scott called attention to a letter that John C. Calhoun, then secretary of war, had written him in 1822, promising him Brown's position when and if the latter should become incapacitated. When Adams informed Scott that the duplicitous Calhoun had written an identical letter to Gaines, the big general was crestfallen.

The conflict reached a new level of intensity on March 30, 1827. Secretary of War James Barbour called on the President bearing a letter he had recently received from Scott, together with a pamphlet, presumably written by Gaines. Scott's letter was full of invective, directed not only at Gaines but at the secretary himself. Barbour was now out of patience and recommended convening the cabinet to discuss how to put the two obstreperous generals in their places.

Adams agreed. The next day he discussed the problem with all five members of his cabinet.[5] That body concluded that trying both officers by court-martial was a tempting thought but not feasible. The two offenders had not quite exceeded bounds to the point where a clear-cut case of insubordination could be made against either one of them, and an acquittal would make matters worse. Furthermore, the 1828 presidential campaign was just beginning, and both generals had popular followings among the electorate.

Adams decided that Secretary Barbour should write each a strong letter admonishing him to improve his conduct. If either should answer in an insubordinate manner—which was halfway expected from Scott—then a court-martial should be convened. Barbour wrote the letter, and the two prima donnas quieted down.

On February 24, 1828, Jacob Brown died, leaving the position of major general open. The Scott-Gaines conflict now had to be dealt with. Immediately the political wheels began turning. Gaines made the first error; within thirty-six hours of Brown's death, he called on President Adams and demanded the appointment to the new vacancy. Gaines assumed that only he and Scott were in contention, but in that he was sadly mistaken. Senator William Henry Harrison, a hero of the War of 1812, was interested in the position, and Alexander Macomb, who had once been the senior brigadier general of the Army, was also available. Nothing in law or regulation forbade the President from naming anyone he chose.

Of Adams's cabinet, four favored the appointment of Scott.[6] In addition, Scott had powerful congressional friends from Virginia in the persons of William S. Archer and Charles F. Mercer, both of whom called on Adams to plead his cause. But equally powerful support developed not for Gaines but for Macomb, the unobtrusive chief of engineers. Macomb, among his other attributes, was the popular son-in-law of Treasury Secretary Richard Rush, and Rush's persuasiveness with Adams was great, perhaps even crucial. In any event, the prized position fell to Macomb.

Scott received the news of Macomb's appointment to the major generalcy while he was on an inspection trip in the West. Securing a quick leave of absence, he hurried back to Washington to confront President Adams again with renewed arguments against the Macomb appointment. Adams was not impressed: "a repetition of the argument in his controversy with General Gaines," he wrote dryly in his diary. But Scott was not yet through. Roger Jones, the army's adjutant general, overheard Scott declaiming in public that he intended to resign his commission in the Army. Jones reported the incident to Adams, further fueling Adams's impatience with Scott.

Scott now gave up on Adams, concentrating his efforts on Acting Secretary of War Samuel Southard. On May 30, 1828, he declared his intention to resign from the Army if Macomb was not tried for his presumption in assuming command. If the President declined, he went on, he asked that he himself be relieved of command and "ordered before a court-martial for this my refusal to obey the orders of my alleged junior, and therefore inferior officer."

Astonishingly, President Adams's patience still held out. He instructed Southard to notify Scott that Macomb's assuming command of the Army had been done on the President's order, so obviously Macomb could not be arrested. Scott was ordered to return to his post in St. Louis.

Scott's bluff had now been called, and he backed down. Even if his cause had not already been lost—which it was—the appointment of a new secretary of war, Peter B. Porter, only made it worse. Porter had harbored a distaste for Scott ever since the two men had commanded brigades under Jacob Brown back at Chippewa and Lundy's Lane. He would not be sympathetic.

In late 1828, President John Quincy Adams again faced the electorate, opposed by Andrew Jackson. Adams never stood a chance; he was swamped by a popular vote of about 650,000 to 500,000, for an electoral edge of 219 to 83. That development put a final end to Scott's tiresome efforts. In all probability he would never have gotten his way with the stony but patient Adams, but at least he dared to argue with Adams. With Jackson he did not.

The new secretary of war, John H. Eaton, was sympathetic to Scott—or at least to keeping him in service. So in March 1829, he offered Scott a face-saving device; Scott could have a furlough in Europe with his family and take some time to think things over. Scott agreed, and in May 1829 he sailed. In Europe he visited old friends and acquaintances, not the least of whom was Lafayette, a fact that possibly applied some balm to his emotional wounds. He arrived back in the United States with a more tractable attitude, and on November 10, 1829, he wrote a letter of capitulation to Secretary Eaton claiming that his friends deemed it "incumbent" on him to sacrifice his convictions and feelings. He had, therefore, "brought myself to make that sacrifice, and withdraw the tender of my resignation now on file in your department." Eaton was quick to respond. No other development, he wrote,

> "was cherished, or was hoped for, but that, on your return to the United States, you would adopt the course your letter indicates, and with good feelings resume the duties of which she has so long had the benefit."

Winfield Scott's military career had been saved from his own overweening pride.

13

※※∨∈≪

Black Hawk War, 1831

*Scott proves that his heroism is not confined
to the battlefield.*

ON JULY 4, 1831, James Monroe died in New York City at the home of his daughter and her husband. Winfield Scott was by Monroe's side during the former president's last days. Scott, now back in command of the Eastern Division, had always held a high respect for Monroe, whom he considered the mainstay of James Madison's cabinet during the War of 1812, and Scott had leaned heavily on Monroe for assistance and advice in the difficult years following the war. He wanted to be with his friend and fellow Virginian whenever he might be needed.

During that same year, Scott was appointed to head the Board of Visitors at the United States Military Academy at West Point. He was not a graduate, but some of his closest friends were among its sons, particularly Joseph Gardner Swift, the first graduate of that institution (Class of 1802). Scott early developed a proprietary feeling toward the Academy. For one thing, he loved the scenery. West Point's flat plain, carved out of rugged, forested hills, looked down on the powerful Hudson River churning below, and the view upriver toward Newburgh was and is breathtaking to behold. But even more than the physical beauty of West Point was the fact that the Academy stood as the symbol of military professionalism—the core of Scott's very being.

While visiting West Point in 1831, Scott made a point of attending classes; his was not to be a cursory board of visitors. Among the cadets he encountered was Erasmus D. Keyes, a young man destined to be Scott's personal aide and protégé. An unconventional kind of soldier, Keyes would never quite fit the military mold. In common with the better-known Ethan Allen Hitchcock, Keyes would contribute to history mainly through his firsthand observations of more prominent military figures, especially of Scott. Keyes's observations began that day in the classroom:

> General Scott was a little past the middle life, but still in the perfection of his bodily and mental powers. He was six feet four and a quarter inches tall, erect as an Indian chief, with an eye of wonderful force and expression. His features were regular, his nose nearly straight, although a slight curve added essentially to the air of command which is peculiar to the masters of slaves, whether they be black or white. His martial bearing was enhanced by the remembrance of past exploits, by constant adulation, by self-content, and many feasts.

He added that Scott's face was "marked with more lines than I observed at a later date."[1]

Keyes's observations had much to be said for them. At age forty-five, Scott took himself very seriously, cultivated a presence of command, and thought of himself as older than he actually was. His lined face bore the marks of hard service, frustration with his superiors in Washington, and the tragic deaths from illness of both of his sons, John Mayo Scott in 1820 and Edward Winfield Scott in 1827.

In the summer of 1832, Winfield and Maria's relatively quiet life at Elizabethtown, New Jersey, was shattered by orders from President Andrew Jackson to proceed west to Illinois, where a local affair between the settlers and the Indian tribes was now being referred to as the "Black Hawk War."

Black Hawk, the Sauk leader of the rebellion Scott was ordered to quell, was 65 years of age, older than the usual revolutionary. The tribes he led, the Sauks and the neighboring Foxes, had for years been peaceful fur traders and farmers. In recent years, however, even though they traded with the whites, they had grown increasingly bitter because of white encroachments on their land. Black Hawk's disillusionment with the whites had begun as early as 1804 (if not before), when he saw Governor William Henry Harrison, pretending to entertain the Indian chiefs, induce his half-drunk guests to sign a treaty ceding fifty million acres of land to the United States. The Sauks and Foxes originally believed that the whites wanted only to use the land for hunting; instead, the Indians found that they were giving away their homes.

Black Hawk, thoroughly hostile to the whites, had joined Tecumseh soon after the signing of the 1804 treaty, later becoming a member of Tecumseh's inner circle. He fought against the whites alongside the Shawnee chief during the War of 1812 and reportedly had been with Tecumseh when the latter died at the Battle of the Thames in 1813.

After the War of 1812, Black Hawk returned to his village, raising crops during the summer and hunting over a wide area during the winter. Each year, as he and his braves returned in the spring, they found some new violation of their homes: their lodges burned, their cornfields fenced in, and—worst of all—their cemeteries molested. Black Hawk's pleas to the U.S. government fell on deaf ears, in part because not all the Sauks and Foxes were solidly behind him. Keokuk, a younger man, advocated submission to the white man.

In the summer of 1830 the U.S. Government General Land Office announced confiscation of the land on which Black Hawk's village stood. That was more than the proud chief could stand for long, so in April 1832 he brought a band of a thousand men, women, and children to Rock Island, Illinois, threatening to retake the town. His band of 600 braves included, in addition to the Sauks and Foxes, some Kickapoos, Winnebagos, and Potawatomis. The local settlers, frightened, appealed to John Reynolds, governor of Illinois, who in turn called for volunteers to repel the invasion. The Black Hawk War had begun.

General Edmund P. Gaines, in whose territory Illinois lay, sent Brigadier General Henry Atkinson, a noted explorer of the West, to deal with Black Hawk. Atkinson, a capable soldier, was a good choice, but he had only 220 regulars with him. By the time he arrived by steamboat at Rock Island, he found that Black Hawk had already occupied the ground with 2,000 braves. Atkinson thereupon called on Governor Reynolds for help and was soon reinforced with 1,700 militia.[2]

Black Hawk never hoped to hold out permanently against the aroused settlers; there were now 170,000 of them in the Illinois Territory. So after a time he and his braves retreated up the Rock River, hoping unrealistically that the British might come to their aid. They were pursued by a force of 1,500 mounted riflemen under the command of General Samuel Whiteside, with Governor Reynolds along.[3]

Over Whiteside's protests, Governor Reynolds sent a small force of 275 mounted militia, under Major Isaiah Stillman, ahead of the main body to "coerce" the rebellious Indian. Stillman's force caught up with Black Hawk at a point on the Rock River near the northern boundary of present-day Illinois.

Black Hawk, with only about 40 braves, had decided to surrender, but the excited and nervous militiamen, reportedly half drunk, opened fire on Black Hawk's emissaries, killing two, the others fleeing back to the momentary safety of Black Hawk's force. Black Hawk, now determined to sell his life dearly, set up an ambush, caught Stillman's men as they came forward into the trap, and rose up to charge. Stillman's terrified militiamen turned and ran, never stopping along the twenty-five miles back to their main body.[4]

The well-named "Battle of Stillman's Run" caused the local government to become thoroughly alarmed. Black Hawk exploited his astonishing success by marching up and down the Illinois countryside, looting and pillaging. Then he faded away for the moment into the swamps of southern Wisconsin.

On receiving word of this humiliation, an angry President Andrew Jackson decided to send his foremost general, Winfield Scott, to quell the uprising, ignoring the fact that Illinois lay in the territory assigned to Gaines's Western Command. The affront to Gaines probably caused Scott little pain, but he was much concerned over the slight to his old friend Atkinson, a man he respected from the days of Terre aux Boeufs in 1809. Jackson's orders were not discretionary, however, and by the end of June, Scott had ordered a force of nine companies of regulars to proceed to Buffalo, where he would later join them.

Before leaving New York, however, Scott took time to provide for his family. A cholera epidemic was sweeping the eastern seaboard, reportedly making its way up the St. Lawrence River, and New York City itself was being threatened by the deadly disease. Scott therefore sent his wife and children to West Point, there to await his return, under the watchful eye of his friend Captain Ethan Allen Hitchcock, commandant of cadets. Scott then went to New York to consult with a prominent physician, Dr. Thomas G. Mower, to learn what he could about the nature of the disease. Nobody, including Mower, knew much about cholera, but the doctor was able to provide Scott with some remedies, apparently palliatives.

His business with Dr. Mower accomplished, Scott took a boat up the Hudson River. At West Point he picked up a small group of recently graduated cadets, taking them with him as observers. Scott was delighted with the arrangement; here was another chance to instruct the young. Furthermore, the contingent included the sons of such friends as Senator John Crittenden, Jacob Brown, and Alexander Macomb.

Immediately on reaching Buffalo, Scott chartered four lake steamers to take his force to Chicago. Two of the vessels would carry officers, troops, and equipment, including him and his staff. The other two would carry provisions. All four crossed Lake Erie and soon headed for Detroit.

By the time Scott arrived at Detroit in early July 1832, the much-dreaded cholera had already struck. Two men had died aboard his own ship, and the disease seemed likely to spread. The alarmed city authorities persuaded the ship's captain to anchor out in the lake, so Scott simply moved his headquarters, plus a company of uninfected troops and the West Point cadets, to another vessel and continued on. His small flotilla continued northward into the St. Clair River, toward Lake Huron. By the time they reached Fort Gratiot, forty miles north of Detroit, scores of men had come down with cholera. Scott landed and removed the victims, some of whom burst out and fled into the woods, never to return.

Scott, however, concealed his fears. He immediately sent his contingent of cadets back to West Point and continued on with 220 men, determined to reach Chicago. For a while, no other cases of cholera broke out, but when his boat passed the Manitou Islands, in Lake Michigan, more cases appeared. Scott left three sick soldiers and two crewmen on Mackinac Island and then continued on, hoping that the crisis was past. It was not, however; the disease broke out again. By the time Scott and his men landed at Chicago on July 10, 1832, 1 officer and 53 men out of his original 220 were dead and another 80 were prostrated. Three members of Scott's staff were down, though none fatally.

If Scott had never accomplished another thing, he could be remembered for his conduct at this time. Combatting a hidden force that could strike a man down without warning and subject him to an excruciating death, Scott never wavered in seeing to the welfare of his men. He visited them, applied the remedies that Dr. Mower had taught him, and inspired the troops by his presence and seeming lack of fear. That bravery was not shown by everyone. Scott was disgusted to see the ship's surgeon panicking, gulping down a bottle of wine, and going to bed. The man was sick, Scott later admitted, though he added that the doctor "ought to have died."[5]

Scott would never allow casualties, whether from disease or bullets, to dissuade him from his mission. He had come to Illinois to assume command, and he intended to do so as soon as he had enough troops fit for duty. On July 29, 1832, he set out with a small escort toward Galena, Illinois, which he reached on August 3. He pushed on to Prairie du Chien, arriving four days later. There Scott learned that Black Hawk's band had been destroyed only a few days earlier at Bad Axe. The victorious commander was Henry Atkinson.

After the fiasco at Stillman's Run in mid-May, Atkinson, after one false start, had assembled a force of 350 regulars and 950 militia and followed Black Hawk up the Rock River to a place near present-day Madison, Wisconsin. On August 3, Atkinson closed in on Black Hawk at the juncture of the Bad Axe River and the Mississippi as the Indian was attempting to escape across the Mississippi.

Like so many Indian slaughters, the battle resulted from a misunderstanding. As Black Hawk's suffering people sought to cross the river in makeshift rafts and canoes, they tried to confer with the captain of an American ship, the *Warrior*. But in the absence of a common language, the jittery crewmen opened fire and the Indians shot back. When Atkinson's men arrived, they presumed that a battle was raging, and they inflicted a merciless slaughter on men, women, and children. Some Indians who attempted to swim the river were drowned. Most of those who made it to the other side were killed and scalped by the Sioux, their bitter enemies. The scene was described by the Indian agent:

> The Indians were pushed literally into the Mississippi, the current of which was. at one time perceptibly tinged with the blood of the Indians who were shot on its margin and in the stream. It is impossible to say how many Indians have been killed, as most of them were shot in the water and drowned in attempting to cross the Mississippi.

Black Hawk himself, spurned by his people as a failed commander, escaped with a small band of warriors, only to be captured by the Winnebagos, taken south to Prairie du Chien, and turned over to the commander, Zachary Taylor.[6] He never returned to power. Henry Atkinson's reputation was fully restored among the Americans, and he happily left for St. Louis and the resumption of "normal" duties.

Scott's mission was not yet complete, however. As the new commander in the region, he was responsible for arranging a treaty with the Indians. To that end, he mustered out the Illinois militia and on August 10 left aboard the *Warrior* for Fort Armstrong, on Rock Island, where he would meet with delegations from the Sauks, Foxes, Winnebagos, and Sioux. Then disaster struck again; the cholera returned in full force.

Scott took action at once. He notified all the Indians gathering for the conference to stay away and "not approach him till a new summons." Then, at Fort Armstrong, an incident occurred that Scott long remembered with admiration for what he considered the Indians' high sense of honor.

At that time Scott was holding three Sauk prisoners, convicted of murdering three enemies, Menominees. The men were undoubtedly guilty, but their act of vengeance completely conformed to Indian custom. Sympathizing with the Indians' plight of being held responsible to the white man's law for deeds done according to their own mores, he took advantage of the cholera epidemic to set the men free, supposedly to return after the cholera epidemic had passed. "If I permit you to seek safety in the prairies," he said, "will you, when the cholera shall have left the island, return here to be dealt with—probably hung—as a civil court may adjudge?" The Indians said they would. Scott arranged a signal for their return, and they left.

When the cholera abated, Scott hung out the agreed-upon signal and to his evident astonishment the three murderers returned. Scott placed them on parole pending an appeal he made to Washington on their behalf. He was happy that they were, on duly constituted authority, released.[7]

In early September the cholera had subsided for good, and it was now safe to begin the process of drawing up a treaty to end the Black Hawk War. Parties of Sauks, Foxes, Winnebagos, Sioux, and Menominees came to the vicinity of Fort Armstrong, ready to parley. Leading the Sauk tribe was Keokuk, described by one admirer as "a master spirit, then in the prime of life, tall, robust, manly, and who excelled all the surrounding red-men in wisdom and eloquency of council."[8] Keokuk was potentially useful to Scott. Besides being a natural leader, he was the one most favorably disposed to conciliation. So Scott used his influence with the visiting Sauks to elevate Keokuk once again to the preeminent position he had enjoyed before being temporarily displaced by Black Hawk. Without a great deal of difficulty this was accomplished.

The issue could not be hurried, however. Even though the Indians were coming as the losers in the previous fighting, they insisted on doing things their own way. As Scott held individual conferences with the heads of the various tribes, those chieftains did not approach him diffidently. Instead, they came to every conference "with the loud tramp and shout, which seemed rather the clangor of war than the forms of ceremony. When a council was to meet, they came at a furious charge; suddenly dismounted, arranged themselves in order, and then, between lines of soldiers, entered the pavilion with the firmness of victors, but with all the deep solemnity of a funeral." That was all well with Scott. He was always willing to treat the vanquished with respect, especially if doing so ensured a conciliatory attitude on their part.

The ceremonies lasted for several weeks. When the participants were not in formal session, the soldiers and the Indians associated in a convivial atmosphere. Chief Keokuk starred in Sauk pantomimes—rehearsed, precise renditions of former battlefield triumphs, against both prey and foe. For the edification of the mixed audience of Indians and whites, Keokuk presented his recollection of a raid on an enemy camp. The pantomime included the long, arduous march, the killing of the enemy sentries, the stealthy approach to the enemy village, and the final triumphant assault. It was a demonstration that Scott always remembered with unusual vividness.

When the time for the formal parleys began, Governor Reynolds, by protocol, should have been the principal United States spokesman. He deferred, however, to Scott, who accepted center stage with enthusiasm. Scott planned to concentrate primarily on the Sauks and Foxes, the main culprits in the recent fighting, and secondarily on the Winnebagos, accused only of being in complicity with them.

Scott took pains to conduct each session in what he considered a spirit of "forbearance and liberality." To the modern reader it was hardly that. He opened each council with a severe reproach, accusing the tribes of failing to restrain Chief Black Hawk. This failure, he asserted, had resulted in an "unjust war upon the unoffending white settlers," thus making the Indians liable to forfeiting as much of their territory as the conqueror might choose to claim as an indemnity. The Indians, possibly at the urgings of Keokuk, did not refute Scott's one-sided version of events, even when he came forth with his most remarkable pronouncement:

> Such is justice, between nation and nation, against which none can rightfully complain; but as God in his dealings with human creatures tempers justice with mercy—or else the whole human race would soon have perished—so shall we, commissioners, in humble imitation of divine example, now treat you, my red brethren! who have offended both against God and your great human father, at Washington.

The results of the treaties were far from generous. The Sauks and Foxes were forced to give up six million acres of land, the main part of present-day Iowa. In return, the United States granted Keokuk about 400 square miles on the Iowa River. Scott further agreed to pay the Indians a sizeable amount of money each year for thirty years, to satisfy the debts of the tribe, and to employ a blacksmith and gunsmith for them. The Winnebagos, the accomplices, were required to cede five million acres, a large part of present-day Wisconsin. As a sop, they were granted annuities similar to those granted to the Sauks and Foxes.

Despite the severe terms of the treaties, their signing was celebrated raucously by all. Artillerymen put on an impressive display of fireworks, including some displays fired from mortars, much to the delight of the Indians. A lively dance followed, the soldiers and Indian braves dancing together. The modest Indian women, it was recorded, enjoyed the proceedings from the sidelines.

Scott had come through a difficult ordeal well. He had shown a striking degree of courage and a determination to care for his men in his handling of the cholera epidemic. Secretary of War Lewis Cass, delighted, commended him warmly in writing.[9] So it was with a sense of satisfaction that he headed home in mid-October 1832. At Cincinnati, on the way back, however, Scott had one more scare: he came down with symptoms of cholera himself. It was only a light case, however, and by the time he arrived in New York he had recovered sufficiently to attend a sumptuous feast. Wine flowed freely and many compliments were paid to Scott personally. But when he boarded the boat for the trip up the Hudson River to West Point, the symptoms—or something resembling them—came back in full force.

Melodramatically, Scott gave orders from his bed that the boat should continue up the river past West Point so he could die alone, without infecting his family. Two hours later, however, the symptoms of cholera disappeared, giving rise to a suspicion that Scott had simply eaten or drunk too much. Unabashed, Scott changed his orders, the boat docked at the West Point landing, and Scott hurried up the hill for a joyful family reunion.

14

Watching the Nullifiers

Andrew Jackson storms at South Carolina;
Scott defuses the crisis.

AFTER HIS return from the Black Hawk War, Scott was hoping to
spend some time at West Point with his family. He was not to be accorded that respite; in early November, only a few days after his arrival, he
received a message from the War Department ordering him to proceed at
once to Washington.

The order came as no great surprise, for Scott was well aware that the
long-simmering trouble with the "nullifiers" in South Carolina was approaching the boiling point. If the issue were to result in a clash of arms between that state and the federal government, he felt sure that his services
would be required. The area, after all, was included in Scott's Eastern Command. He left for Washington as rapidly as he could.

The nullification episode of 1832 had been triggered by the tariff
act of that year. Tensions between the agricultural South and the rapidly in-
dustrializing Northeast had been growing since the end of the War of 1812,[1]
caused largely by a series of tariff bills, backed by the North. High tariffs
benefited northern industry by making it competitive with Britain, whose
industrial plant still put out better products at lower prices. That worked to
the disadvantage of the Southerners, whose economy was always struggling.
Southern resistance to early tariff bills had always been strong, but the measures they resorted to had been relatively restrained. By 1830, however, following the "tariff of abomination," certain Southerners were so angry that

they had begun challenging the authority of the central government. A nullification movement, which held that a state possessed the constitutional right to nullify acts of the federal government, had found its leader in Vice President John C. Calhoun, once an avid nationalist. Calhoun, ambitious for the presidency, had fallen from Andrew Jackson's favor over personal matters* and had adopted the doctrine of nullification as his political base.[2]

Calhoun had seized upon the tariff act of November 1832 as his rallying cry. South Carolina was willing to follow his leadership by refusing to collect the tariff. If necessary, Calhoun was ready to declare South Carolina a sovereign state, seceded from the Union. As Scott headed down the Hudson for Washington, Calhoun was in the process of resigning his office as vice president of the United States.

On arriving in Washington, Scott proceeded at once to the War Department. Disappointed to find Secretary of War Lewis Cass absent from his office, he went from there to the White House. He may still have been uncomfortable around Andrew Jackson, but he never considered reporting to General-in-Chief Alexander Macomb for instructions in the secretary's absence.

At the White House, the President received Scott graciously. He brought Scott up to date on the latest word from South Carolina, which he expected to might try to leave the Union. He was far from rigid, he explained, regarding the tariff issue itself, but he intended to maintain the supremacy of the Constitution as the law of the land, completely rejecting any theories that might permit a state to withdraw from that Union.

Scott's mission, Jackson went on, was to stabilize the political-military situation at Charleston, thus buying time for cooler heads in Washington and Charleston to work out a political compromise. Having outlined the situation, Jackson solicited Scott's military opinion of what should be done.

Scott, who had given the matter considerable thought, was prepared with a ready answer. The two federal garrisons at Charleston, Fort Moultrie and Castle Pinckney, must be reinforced immediately to prevent them from

---

*The basic cause of the rift was Jackson's learning of Calhoun's condemnation of his questionable invasions of Florida in 1819. The immediate trigger was the touchy matter of Peggy Eaton, the attractive, flirtatious wife of Jackson's secretary of war, John H. Eaton. Jackson was highly displeased when Mrs. Calhoun, along with other officials' wives, snubbed Mrs. Eaton, for whom Jackson adopted the role of protector. Eaton resigned and was succeeded by Lewis Cass in 1831.

falling into nullifier hands. The arsenal at Augusta, Georgia, was important to keep, filled as it was with supplies and equipment. That arsenal was vulnerable, located right across the Savannah River from Hamburg (Aiken), South Carolina. He further recommended that a sloop-of-war and some revenue cutters be sent to Charleston.

Jackson approved Scott's recommendations and placed him in temporary command in that area:

> Proceed at once and execute those views. You have my *carte blanche* in respect to troops; the vessels shall be there, and written instructions shall follow you.

Scott left the White House elated, almost stunned by Jackson's friendliness. Jackson had even invited him to stay for dinner! Scott had begged off that invitation to allow an hour with his old friend John Quincy Adams. Jackson had not appeared offended. He nodded approvingly. "Never forget a friend," he said.

Scott's desire to visit former President Adams was completely sincere. Though Adams had nearly cashiered him from the Army four years earlier, Scott held no grudge, his admiration for the elder statesman undiminished. Still Scott did not feel free to disclose the real purpose of his trip to Charleston, even to his friend Adams, trying to portray the assignment as routine, nothing to alarm the nullifiers. The canny Adams was not taken in, but he approved Scott's going to Charleston to "watch the nullifiers." John Calhoun, he volunteered, would give way in any confrontation with Andrew Jackson. Calhoun, he predicted, would "show the white feather."

Scott arrived at Charleston on November 22, 1832. His ship was able to land at Fort Moultrie, on Sullivan's Island, without being immediately detected. Though he intended to control matters in Charleston from three miles across the harbor, his presence was soon discovered, and it was regarded with some suspicion and a good deal of defiance. One irate writer, in a letter to the Charleston *Mercury*, noted that Scott's arrival and that of two revenue cutters on the same day bore "a most portentious relation to each other" and foreboded land and naval operations at once. The letter insisted, however, that the prospect had not "produced the panic that it was doubtless intended to beget." The result was indignation rather than alarm; there was "no power in the United States" that would dare try to subdue the South Carolinians. But the letter offered some solace, the possibility that Scott himself was at heart a nullifier: "He comes of a race easily infected with such [nullification] opinions: and certainly did once, in his own person, nullify the Department of War."[3]

Two days after arriving at Charleston, Scott learned that a South Carolina convention had met at Columbia and declared that the recent tariff acts were null and void, not binding on "this State or its citizens." That long-threatened step raised the level of the crisis. The convention, however, was not yet ready to take the state out of the Union; it prudently left room for a peaceable settlement, setting February 1, 1833, as the day on which the declaration should go into effect. That caveat gave at least two months in which the issue might be put to rest.

Scott's first priority at Charleston was to secure the federal forts and garrisons from the threat of sudden seizure. The garrison of each installation had to be brought up to strength and adequately supplied, especially with food. The men would have to be trained and alerted. Accordingly, he withdrew all the small detachments of soldiers around the area into the garrisons of Fort Moultrie and Castle Pinckney. He ordered construction to strengthen the forts themselves. He even required all regular officers to renew their oaths of allegiance to the United States, replacing some whom he regarded as untrustworthy. That done, he set out to make contact with leading unionists such as influential South Carolinians Joel Poinsett and James Louis Petigru.[4] These men, he hoped, might provide him some warning of impending attack.

All this took time, more time than a "routine inspection" would normally require. Scott therefore pretended to be immobilized by a sprained ankle—how convincingly is questionable—and used that infirmity to justify lingering at the garrisons. Once satisfied at Charleston, he moved on to check the garrisons at Augusta and Savannah. Reports from friends in Charleston helped him to evaluate the temper of the citizenry from a distance, in relative peace.

Scott was a social being, with a zest for the company of prominent men, especially of political leaders. In the past he had made friends with many leading South Carolinians, some of whom were now among the ranks of the nullifiers. These friendships helped him in his efforts to defuse personal antagonisms and to convince his old friends of the basic good will of the federal government. One of these contacts was William Campbell Preston, of whom Scott was genuinely fond. To this man, one of the nullifiers, Scott wrote from Savannah, assuring him that there was nothing ominous about the recent arrival of two or three companies of troops at Charleston. They had come only to ensure that the forts in the harbor shall not be wrested from the United States. The President, he presumed, would

> stand on the defensive—thinking it better to discourage than to invite an attack—better to prevent than to repel one, in order to gain time for wisdom and moderation to exert themselves in the capitol at Washington, and in the state house at Columbia.

Scott's letter may have influenced Preston, as that gentleman later took steps to modify some of the extreme nullifiers' positions.

The crisis continued to heighten. On December 10, 1832, President Andrew Jackson issued a proclamation terming the actions of the South Carolina convention an "impractical absurdity." The alleged power for a state to annul, the proclamation went on, was "incompatible with the existence of the Union." It warned those who thought South Carolina could peaceably leave the Union in strong terms:

> Disunion by force is treason. Are you really ready to incur its guilt? If you are, on the heads of the instigators of the act be dreadful consequences. . . . Your first magistrate cannot, if he would, avoid the performance of his duty.

Even this strong proclamation, however, failed to deter the nullifiers in South Carolina, at least on the surface. The new governor, former senator Robert Hayne, penned a counter-proclamation, and South Carolinians openly broke into two camps, the nullifiers and the unionists.[5] Both sides began procuring arms and studying manuals on tactics. The Columbia *Times* predicted that twelve thousand Carolinians would be ready by February 1 "to serve their commander-in-chief" against the unionists and the federal government. Thousands of volunteers from other Southern states, the editor predicted, would come to the aid of their friends in South Carolina. The unionists also prepared for conflict. Joel Poinsett, the unionist leader, wrote gloomily that he considered it difficult to avoid a civil war.

Jackson then raised the stakes in the face-off. He sent Congress a proposal that became known as the Force Bill, which authorized him to use military force to collect government revenue in Charleston Harbor. Its opponents rose in wrath against the "Bloody Bill." Senator John Tyler of Virginia was among the most passionate denouncers. On the floor of the Senate the future president painted a picture of Charleston as a "beleaguered city," the whole state of South Carolina becoming a "conquered province," with her cities leveled, her daughters in mourning, and her men "driven into the swamps where Marion found refuge."

Meanwhile Scott continued his public relations campaign. He mingled with nullifiers and unionists, always careful to exhibit what "humility and forebearance" he could muster in his dealings. He urged his troops to do likewise, especially the boat crews, whose trips to the city from Fort Moultrie brought them daily into personal contact with the merchants:

> In walking the streets let us give place to *all* citizens. Bad words and even casting mud upon us, can do no harm. We shall show our courage by quietly passing along. I rather think that I should disregard even a few brickbats, and *remember, my gallant fellows, that you are no better than your old commander.*

Scott took other measures. He invited hundreds of Charleston citizens to dock at Fort Moultrie for a visit every week. Scott mingled with his guests, always assuring them that the strong defensive works had been reinforced only because "in the unhappy excitement prevailing, some unauthorized multitude, by a sudden impulse, may rush us, in ignorance, and to their certain destruction." Scott also issued dinner invitations to those prominent citizens whose good will he deemed most valuable.

During January 1833, a rare opportunity to demonstrate good will toward the Charlestonians presented itself. A fire broke out in a local sugar mill, and Scott, from Fort Moultrie across the river, saw the smoke and instantly acted. He sent three hundred volunteers, unarmed, in rowboats over to Charleston to help put out the flames. At the same time he sent Major Julius Heileman, a great favorite in the city, to inform the mayor of what he was doing.

At first Scott's gesture was rebuffed. Heileman reached the mayor's office before the troops arrived, and found that magistrate resentful rather than grateful. He loudly refused any help from federal soldiers. The desperate owner of the mill, however, cared more for saving his property than he did for politics, so when the first troops arrived, he welcomed them. "Here, major," he shouted, "for God's sake save my sugar refinery!"

Fortunately, the officer in charge, Major Sam Ringgold, was astute as well as energetic. Drawing on a joke that was current in the town, he shouted to his men, "Do you hear that, lads? We'll go to the death for the sugar!" Ringgold was aware that a former South Carolina governor, James Hamilton, had made a fool of himself over his resistance to federal customs officials intent on confiscating an illegal consignment of sugar he had ordered from Cuba. Losing all sense of perspective, Hamilton had shouted passionately to a mob of nullifiers, "If Uncle Sam put[s] his robber hands on the boxes, I know, my fellow citizens, you'll go to the death with me for that sugar!" Anyone but the most rabid nullifier could see inanity in "going to the death for that sugar."

So the citizens laughed as they helped the men put out the fire. Their wives came forth with bread, cheese, and cider—Ringgold refused the offer of liquor. The episode, over fairly quickly, had a salutary effect. In one move it saved Charleston from a serious fire and raised the respect of the Charlestonians for the federal soldiers.[6]

As Scott and his men kept tempers in check at Charleston, the nullification crisis gradually petered out. Virginia, assuming a leadership role that the other states did not invite, sent a mediator to South Carolina in an effort to ease the situation. The mediator happened to be Scott's old friend and mentor from his outcast days of 1810, Benjamin Watkins Leigh. When Leigh arrived at Charleston in early February, he began consulting with Scott, with the nullifiers, and with the unionists. Both sides of the tariff issue eventually regained their senses.

In early February 1833, the United States Congress solved the impasse by passing a bill that had been drafted jointly by Calhoun and Henry Clay. That act mollified the nullifiers to a large extent because it provided for reducing the hated tariffs drastically. But there were face-saving aspects for the federal government also. The act was passed contingent on the governor of South Carolina's agreeing first to withhold nullification until after that session of the United States Congress. And at the same time Congress passed President Jackson's Force Bill. With passage of the new tariff act, the South Carolina legislature rescinded the nullification ordinance.

Scott had made a major contribution to the resolution of the nullification crisis. His strength of purpose, coupled with his moderation, created a great deal of respect for the federal government among the Charlestonians. The lack of open fighting between his men and the local citizenry helped the course of sanity eventually to prevail. Years later, Leigh gave him credit. Calling Scott's mission extremely delicate, he attested,

From the beginning to the end [Scott's] conduct was as conciliatory as it was firm and sincere, evincing that he knew his duty and was resolved to perform it, and yet that his principal object and purpose was peace.

He added that Scott had been "perfectly successful, when the least imprudence might have resulted in serious collision."

And yet Scott was in for disappointment. Proud of the work he had done, he reported to the White House on his return north only to find President Jackson relatively cool to his accomplishment. He offered only what an anguished Scott later described as "a few terms of measured praise." Jackson's aloofness reawakened Scott's old suspicion, that "the reconciliation between the parties in 1823, was, with General Jackson, but external."[7]

15

Enter Erasmus D. Keyes

Observations of an irreverent aide.

FOLLOWING THE nullification crisis of 1832–33, Scott was allowed to live with his family in Elizabethtown, New Jersey, where he remained for four years. It was a period of relative tranquility. Scott found the duties associated with administering the Eastern Command less than taxing, and his leisurely schedule allowed him time to study and to dabble in matters on the side. Having witnessed the devastating effects of drunkenness on his soldiers, he took a keen interest in the temperance movement. He also did some investing in the New York stock market, with only limited success. Most significant for the future, he began developing an interest in politics. He joined the new Whig Party, along with Daniel Webster and Henry Clay. Though the Whigs had been established primarily as a confederation of all elements opposed to the administration of Andrew Jackson, the party had quickly developed a complexion of its own. In New York, at least, it became recognized as standing for government by the Better Sort.

Such political activities were not uncommon for army officers in those days; indeed political connections were assumed to have a significant effect on an officer's prospects for promotion. At this point, politics had not become Scott's major preoccupation, so his activities were not considered any great obstacle to his being given strictly military duties.

This kind of life was not new to Scott; it was similar to his activities during the previous decade. The difference lay in the fact that Scott's earlier years had not been chronicled. This period might also have been lost to memory had Scott not acquired, in October 1833, a Boswell in a new junior aide, Lieutenant Erasmus D. Keyes. Keyes was an aggressive, ambitious, and irreverent young officer, the same man who, as a cadet, had observed Scott during the general's visit to a West Point classroom over two years before.

Scott did not welcome Keyes as a member of his personal staff when the lieutenant first reported for duty. He considered Keyes's sixteen months of commissioned service a totally insufficient period for any graduated cadet to serve before being cast into the atmosphere of high command. He accepted the young man only reluctantly, on the urging of Lieutenant John Mercer, the aide who had been with Scott ever since the two had made an extended trip to Europe in 1815. Though acceding to Keyes's appointment, Scott still treated the new addition to his official family with a cold formality for some time, giving him no more attention than he would a piece of furniture.

A friendship later developed between Scott and Keyes, however. It began with a trivial incident. Ordered to dine one evening with the general, the young aide sat quietly as Scott conversed with another guest, Lieutenant William De Hart. Wishing for the salt, Keyes tactfully asked De Hart, not the general, to pass it, even though the cellar was closer to the general. That kind of deference to age and rank fitted Winfield Scott's notions of the proper demeanor of a junior officer. He turned to Keyes and said, "Young gentleman, you showed tact in asking Mr. De Hart for the salt instead of me, as he is more nearly your own age."* From that time on, Scott began to look up from his papers and acknowledge Keyes's presence when the young officer approached him on an official matter.

In person, Keyes saw Scott as a fussy man who demanded much, especially from his personal servant, David. David, whom Keyes regarded as an interesting character himself, was "black as Spanish ink, five feet six inches tall, strongly built, visage purely Ethiopian, so straight that a plumb line falling from the back of his head would drop clear of his body to the ground." He was also a devoted servant who organized his master's effects according to a system of his own. He stayed with Scott through thick and thin, despite Scott's querulous ways. At least twice a week, Keyes recalls, he would hear Scott exclaim angrily, "Damn you, David! You hide everything I've got, and then you hide yourself."

Scott felt completely justified in expecting a great deal of personal atten-

---

*All quotations in this chapter come from Erasmus Darwin Keyes, *Fifty Years' Observation of Men and Events.*

tion. He was partially disabled, he claimed, by the lingering effects of the wound he had incurred at Lundy's Lane. But most of his demands bore no relationship to that questionable infirmity. The tobacco he chewed had to be kept at a certain moisture, brought out only when called for. He called often for a glass of water, tinged with a little gin—or even a weak mint julep, though he had no inclination to drink very much.

One of Keyes's duties, as a personal aide, was to accompany the general to church, where Scott comported himself as the model of dignity and propriety. There was nothing dour or self-effacing in Scott's approach to God. Keyes describes him as "cheerful, grateful, and exuding benevolence, as befitted the offspring of a generous nature." Scott always thanked his Creator for his physical health, strength, and sturdy moral sense. "When he entered the temple of the Lord," Keyes concluded, and "stood erect before the Altar, his motive was to show that he had not neglected the talents confided to him."

Keyes found much to admire in the general. Despite Scott's foibles and eccentricities, Keyes early noticed a generosity of spirit that drew both men and women to him. He possessed a formidable mind, which was never idle. He was "a constant and general reader, who studied common, civil, statute, and military law, being familiar with all the standard writers on the subject. He could read French well, allowing him to translate French military works into his own language."

Scott's most serious problem remained his vanity. Long before Keyes appeared on the scene, this weakness had earned Scott the enmity of such men as Wilkinson, Gaines, and Andrew Jackson. Keyes had his own idea of what was involved:

> The chief ruling passion of the general was ambition and its uniform attendant, jealousy. In matters of rivalry he was easily vexed, and when the thing pursued was of great distinction, he seemed to go out of his own skin into that angry porcupine with every quill standing fiercely on end. . . . He would pour out his venom against his rivals in terms which showed him skilled in the jargon of obloquy.

If Keyes viewed Scott with reservations, he felt only unqualified admiration for the general's wife, Maria Mayo Scott. Claiming to have enjoyed "the acquaintance of many of the grandest and most gifted dames of all the Christian nations of the world," he remarked, "I remember none who, in breeding and accomplishments, were the superior of Mrs. Scott." He was also struck by the beauty of Scott's sixth child and fourth daughter, Adeline

Camilla Scott, who was "endowed with the expression of angels." As a professed student of Raphael, Guido, and Murillo, Keyes rhapsodized, "Never did I behold the likeness of a child more lovely in shape and countenance than Miss Adelaide [sic] Camilla Scott, as she appeared in the early morning of her life."

The relationship between the general and his wife had certain boundaries. Keyes noted that Scott always referred to his wife with pride and affection, but "as he and she were each the centre of attraction to great numbers of people, they were often separated."

The Scotts were indeed often separated. But Scott was nonetheless a faithful husband to Maria, apparently never even tempted to stray. At the time Keyes reported for duty, the general was so popular that in every city he visited he was greeted by immense crowds, "frequently beset by women, who clustered around him like summer flies." Keyes was amused by the fact that Scott treated all of them alike. "Thin-lipped, sharp-nosed vixens, loud-talking viragos, stately matrons, sentimental damsels, joyous maidens, faded and dejected spinsters, prancing widows, fussy housewives, willing dames and scandal mongers would all leave his presence content with having been gently spoken to by the great general." An aggressive hostess, especially one who might be harboring some hidden desires, could frighten him. And when the rather inane question once came up about the relative virtues of married women and old maids, Scott sided with the old maids. Keyes could only conjecture that single women accorded him even more lavish admiration than did the married.

Scott's relations with women, however, were of secondary importance in his life, which was lived in a society dominated by men. A remarkably small number of men ran the country in those days. Keeping control of the new nation to themselves, they alternated their roles among such positions as United States senator, state governor, and landed property owner. Scott's position as the second highest ranking officer of the Army gave him ready entrée into such groups, and since his headquarters were located in New York City, already the country's largest and wealthiest city, he had ample opportunity to continue and enlarge on his friendship with most of the important men on the national scene.

These men were often the dinner guests of a notable host, Mr. Gouverneur Kemble, who entertained them at his home about thirty miles north of New York City. Kemble was a lifelong bachelor, and his dinners were nearly always stag parties, notable not only for the list of attendees but also for the quality of his table. To an epicure such as Scott, who could discuss food even more voraciously than he could eat it, dinner at Kemble's table was a delight. It included "many small dishes, besides fat turkeys and domestic fowls, of which the only danger was of eating too much." Scott particularly appreciated Kemble's wines, especially the port and the sherry. Disliking champagne, Scott always drank just one glass, sufficient for ceremonial purposes. He passed up the cigars in favor of Kemble's gold snuff-box, which stood at the end of the table.

The conversations at Kemble's dinners were wide-ranging, covering "the policy of governments; the habitudes engendered by climate, race, and occupation; the laws and rites of various nations and ages; sculpture, painting and achitecture, and all the vast domain of science, history, politics, parties, civil and military biographies, poetry, and manners." Only religion and matrimony were delicately omitted as subjects. The close associations thus fostered served a national purpose, as when Scott's friendship with William Campbell Preston, developed under such circumstances, had proved invaluable to him at Charleston in 1832. Above all, Scott found the atmosphere highly congenial.

Yet these gatherings were only part of Scott's ways of conducting business. When duty called, Keyes observed, "Scott's mental, physical, and moral nature conspired to form in him a habit of promptness and constancy. He foresaw the requirements of his professional and pecuniary engagements and attended to them fully. Until the duty to be done and the task in hand were executed and completely finished, he would allow himself neither rest nor pleasure, night or day, in sickness or in health." Scott seldom complained about the hardships of travel, which in those days tested the endurance of most men. During one trip, Keyes and Scott were together on the road in stagecoaches or sleighs for fifty-four nights. During that time Scott showed no uneasiness except at the frequent delays, which always annoyed him. "No necessity or incident of duty seemed to trouble him, and in its performance Job himself could not have been more patient."

The need to make a transition to duty came in 1836, when military developments in Florida brought an abrupt end to the pleasures of gentlemen in society. He returned to a life of strenuous activity, with good will. For Scott was first and always a soldier and a patriot.

16

❧

Frustration in Florida, 1836

Old World tactics fail in the swamps of Florida.

> Moving from swamp to swamp in search of an enemy that never
> appeared, dying by battalions with fever and exposure, never able
> to bring on a decisive engagement with the elusive natives, never
> daring to separate into small groups without being exterminated
> by savages who sprang from the soil . . . the little army of less than
> 1,000 regulars tried to clean out a vast country occupied by over
> 3,000 Indians . . . at the price of misery, disease, and death.
> —William A. Ganoe, *History of the United States Army*

IN THE AFTERNOON of Monday, December 28, 1835, two companies of
American soldiers under the command of Major Francis L. Dade were
nearing the end of a seventy-five-mile march from Tampa, Florida, to Ocala.
It was presumed to be a routine march; Dade and his troops anticipated no
difficulties. The mission, to be sure, had an ominous aspect; they were being
sent to provide additional security to Fort King, as Ocala was then called,
because of a recent outbreak of troubles between white settlers and Seminole
Indians. But that fact was no real cause for alarm; Seminole bands had previously limited their maraudings to isolated families and small detachments
of troops; they had never hit troops of company size. The two companies
were happily anticipating the party that Dade had promised to give them on
reaching their destination. Because of the cold, they marched wearing their
overcoats, which were draped over their cartridge boxes. The troops, mostly

artillerymen employed as foot soldiers,[1] marched in double file, preceded by an advance guard and a rear guard, but no flank security. The thick forests along that stretch, Dade decided, made that precaution unnecessary.

Dade and his men were marching into an ambush. Unbeknownst to him, his column had been watched from the bushes ever since it had left Fort Brooke, at Tampa. The Indians had held off from attacking because Chief Micanopy, the leader of the group, had been reluctant. When Dade reached a bottleneck in the road just southeast of Wahoo Swamp, however, Micanopy yielded to the urgings of his chief lieutenants* and gave the word.

The first volley of Seminole bullets killed Major Dade and about half his commmand instantly, and the remaining Americans were doomed. Captain George Washington Gardiner, second in command, did his best and succeeded in delaying the final moment by driving the attackers off, throwing up a small triangular log breastwork, and bringing his single six-pounder artillery piece into action. But by 4:00 P.M., soon after Micanopy resumed the attack, not one white American remained on his feet. Three soldiers later escaped after playing dead, but the only one in any condition to tell the story was Private Ransome Clarke, who after a harrowing trip made it back to Tampa.

Thus began the Second Seminole War, a conflict that stretched beyond the Dade massacre in the closing days of 1835 for nearly seven years. The Seminoles were only one of the tribes affected by the Indian Removal Act of May 1830, which called for moving all the Indians east of the Mississippi to lands in the West. Others included, among the main ones, the Creeks, the Choctaws, the Cherokees, and the Chickasaws. As these tribes were moved at various times—sometimes resulting in wars—it was almost inevitable that Scott would be drawn in, and indeed he was for parts of three years. But of all these movements, the most costly by far was the government's effort to move the Seminoles.

Though little noted in our country's history, the Second Seminole War involved at one time or another a total of 41,000 American troops, who strove to move some 5,000 Seminoles to western reservations, at a cost, to the small regular army alone, of over 1,300 dead. It cost the nation nearly

---

*"Alligator" and "Jumper," whose Seminole names were Halpatter Tustenuggee and Ote Emathla respectively.

$120 million.[2] The war was the most difficult and costly of any the United States has ever waged against any of its Native American tribes.

The high cost in men and matériel necessary for waging the Second Seminole War was due to the terrain of Florida—swamps, thickets, hummocks—which worked to neutralize superior U.S. firepower, discipline, and sometimes even numbers. For most Americans the climate was inhospitable. Florida's terrain was described by one army surgeon as

> the poorest country that ever two people quarrelled for . . . a poor, sandy country in the north; and in the southern portions nearly all wet prairies and swamp . . . a most hideous region to live in; a perfect paradise for Indians, alligators, serpents, frogs, and every other kind of loathsome reptile.[3]

Even more formidable than the terrain was the ferocity of the Seminoles themselves. These so-called wild people were not the aborigines of Florida; the people who first inhabited Florida had long since perished from disease. The Seminoles were offshoots of the Upper Creeks of Georgia and Alabama, who had migrated to Florida in about 1770, bringing with them a number of runaway Negro slaves. At first they had prospered as farmers and plantation owners, but they had met with nothing but grief once the United States attained possession of Florida from Spain in 1819. The Treaty of Moultrie Creek (1823) had concentrated them on an interior reservation, devoid of access to the ocean, on which much of their commerce had previously depended. Then, in 1832, the fraudulent Treaty of Payne's Landing had provided for their removal to lands in the West in accordance with federal law.

Such abuse at the hands of the white man was a common story to the Indian tribes in the eastern United States. But the Seminoles, whose whole identity as a people stemmed from the land they occupied, were adamant in their determination not to give it up. As characterized by one of their chiefs as early as 1826, it was land where "our navel strings were first cut and the blood from them sank into the earth, and made the country dear to us."* In their resistance to being moved away, the Seminoles were led by the fiery, charismatic young Osceola, a man of unusual ability. Osceola was mild-mannered on the surface but extremely proud. When the Indian agent General Wiley Thompson, his one-time friend, put him in chains to calm him down during a fierce argument over the Treaty of Payne's Landing, Thomp-

---

*Tuckose Emantha, also known as John Hicks.

son not only sealed his own doom but ensured that Seminole resistance would be conducted to the death.[4]

On January 20, 1836, three weeks after the Dade massacre, Brevet Major General Winfield Scott, in Washington on routine business, first learned of the crisis then gripping Florida. Secretary of War Lewis Cass had just received the grim word of the Dade massacre, and as Scott sat riveted, Cass described not only that story but many other events as well.

The Dade massacre was not the only grim news from Florida. The reason that Osceola had been absent from that action was a previous commitment, a determination to perform another act of violence personally. On that same afternoon of December 28, Osceola and a small band had murdered General Thompson just outside the gate of Fort King. Thompson was an important man, ironically a man who had defended the Seminoles against government encroachment and who had once been a warm friend of Osceola's. He had thought that he and Osceola had reconciled after he had humiliated the chief by putting him in chains during the treaty dispute, but Osceola had only feigned contrition and remorse. He would not rest thereafter until he exacted his revenge.

A third report involved an old friend of Scott's, Brevet Brigadier General Duncan L. Clinch. Three days after the Dade massacre, though totally unaware of it, Clinch and militia Brigadier General Richard K. Call had led some 250 regulars and 500 militia on a raid intended to destroy a rumored Seminole hideaway in the Cove, a swampland behind the Withlacoochee River, near present-day Crystal River. There they had been confronted by a sizable body of Seminoles led by Osceola. Clinch had taken his regulars across the Withlacoochee in the face of Osceola's fire. As the militia were unable to give effective support, it looked for a while as if Clinch's men would meet the same fate as those of Dade. Ultimately, however, he had thrown the Seminoles off balance by launching a bayonet charge, allowing time for the militia to come to his assistance. Once all his men were safely back behind the river, Clinch had taken his regulars and militia back to Fort Drane. His losses had been 4 killed and 59 wounded; those of the Seminoles were probably lighter.[5]

The episode, while minor, had significant consequences. It caused bad blood between the regulars and the militia, particularly between Clinch and Call, as they blamed each other for the near disaster. Of much greater importance was the fact that a milestone had been passed. Unrest among the Seminoles had now blossomed into full-scale war.

While this was going on during the late months of 1835, the authorities in Washington tried to minimize the growing troubles in Florida. As of January 2, 1836, Congress had voted only $80,000 to meet the emergency. By January 29, however, with the news of the Dade disaster, the figure had risen by another $500,000. President Andrew Jackson now considered the situation serious, and he responded by once again calling for Winfield Scott to take command.

After bringing Scott up to date, Secretary Cass asked abruptly, "How soon can you be ready?"

Scott's answer was quick and typical. "This evening."

Despite Scott's dramatic response, Cass knew it would take some time to prepare the instructions. While his orders were being drawn up, therefore, Cass, Scott, and Adjutant General Roger Jones studied the letters and reports that were coming in from Florida. By midnight Scott's orders were ready. He was pleased to note that they reflected the President's confidence in him. Though the instructions admonished him to call for only the smallest possible number of troops, they also said,

> I would not have you hesitate for a moment in calling out such a number of militia as will enable you, with promptitude and certainty, to put an immediate termination to these difficulties. . . . This subject is therefore committed entirely to your discretion.

Scott left Washington by ship the next evening, bound for Columbia, South Carolina, by way of Charleston. By now he had formulated a general plan for action against the Seminoles, based on what he had learned in Washington. The plan assumed—as did all plans at that time—that the main Seminole population of 4,000 to 6,000 men, women, and children was located in the swamps behind the Withlacoochee, the Cove, where Clinch and Call had encountered such difficulties. Consequently, Scott planned to descend in overwhelming force on that spot. To do so he planned to send three strong columns converging from three directions. Each column was to search the countryside for Indian warriors as they marched toward this heartland.

Much of this scheme was dictated by what was already in place. American troops were already concentrated at Fort Drane[6] in the north, about twenty-five miles from the Cove, and at Fort Brooke (Tampa), about a hundred miles distant. To supplement those two forces, a third column could be

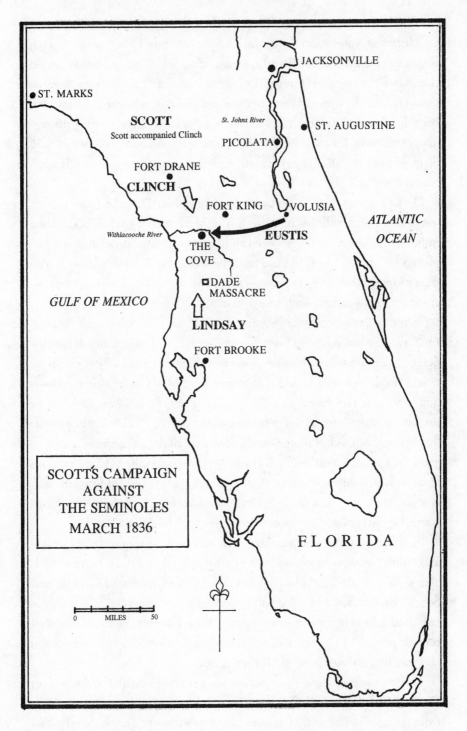

JACKSONVILLE

ST. MARKS

SCOTT
Scott accompanied Clinch

St. Johns River

ST. AUGUSTINE

PICOLATA

FORT DRANE
CLINCH

FORT KING

VOLUSIA

*ATLANTIC
OCEAN*

Withlacooche River

EUSTIS

THE
COVE

DADE
MASSACRE

GULF OF MEXICO

LINDSAY

FORT BROOKE

SCOTT'S CAMPAIGN
AGAINST
THE SEMINOLES
MARCH 1836

F L O R I D A

0   MILES   50

launched from the east coast of Florida, where a major supply base was being established at Volusia, on the St. Johns River south of Lake George. Clinch would command the northern force, and Colonel William Lindsay would command the force at Tampa. The third column, leaving from Volusia, would have to be brought from out of state. For that mission Scott selected Brigadier General Abraham Eustis, who was presently commanding the regular garrison at Charleston. All three forces would need volunteers, and Scott would have to arrange for them with the respective governors. It was a reasonable plan.

On January 29, 1836, Scott arrived at Columbia. There he asked Governor George McDuffie to increase Eustis's detachment of South Carolina militia to regimental strength—ten companies totaling 600 men, to be employed as infantry. At that time Scott believed that mounted troops, who were more difficult to raise than infantry, would not be required. The governor set out to comply with his request.

Two days later Scott was in Augusta, Georgia, conferring with Colonel Lindsay, who had come up from Tampa. When Lindsay described how difficult the terrain was in Florida, Scott raised his estimates of the troops he would need. Not only would 5,000 men be required to subdue the Seminoles; he now concluded that "the greater part of the force ought to be mounted." Advised that the desolate countryside of Florida could provide little by way of food or forage, he decided that all the troops would have to carry their rations with them. Accordingly he requisitioned 320,000 rations to be delivered during the next three months to his two main forward bases at Picolata (supply base for Fort Drane) and Volusia, both on the St. Johns River. He also ordered 250,000 rations to be sent to Tampa Bay.

In making his final troop estimates, Scott asked the governors of Georgia and South Carolina to provide two regiments each and the governor of Alabama to provide one. He suggested that the governors of Georgia and South Carolina, the states providing two regiments, might wish to incorporate their militia regiments into brigades. If so, however, he asked that they provide only the brigade staffs, not the brigade commanders. Scott desired no more brigadier generals in his command.

The strongest of these three columns was to be Clinch's brigade at Fort Drane, which Scott called his "right wing." Its mission was to hit the Cove from the north. The second column, Lindsay's force at Tampa, Scott called his "center wing." It was to march on the Cove from the south. The third column, Scott's "left wing," was commanded by Eustis, who was to disembark at St. Augustine, march southward to Mosquito Bay (Daytona Beach), then turn westward to Volusia. In planning this rather intricate maneuver, Scott hoped that all his troops would arrive at the Cove simultaneously. To do so, all three columns would have to be under way by March 8. Speed was essential, as his militia were signed up for only three months. Most would have to be discharged soon after the end of April.

Scott drew on his formidable experience in the field to come up with this plan, which under conventional military conditions would have been a sensible, if somewhat intricate, arrangement. The mighty St. Johns River, which flows northward for many miles, only a few miles inland from the peninsula's east coast, provided an ideal supply route for most of the way. The plan's chief weakness was its timetable, far too optimistic for this large, dense wilderness. Scott believed that he had adequately taken local conditions into account, and in that belief he was supported by Duncan Clinch, the man who knew the Florida situation best. Scott had every hope of success.

Nothing, however, went according to plan. Scott was delayed at Savannah because the steamer chartered to carry him to Picolata* was slow in arriving. He encountered bureaucratic obstacles, such as a ban against issuing United States government equipment to militia—a ban he declared he would ignore. When his steamer finally did land at Picolata on February 22, he found that only one regiment of South Carolina volunteers had arrived in Florida. Further, the seven companies of the Georgia mounted men destined for Fort Drane would not be getting there until the end of the month.

The supply situation was slow in improving. On February 22, Scott complained that none of the patent rifles he had ordered had arrived, and that he was also short of knapsacks, camp kettles, and tents. As was his habit, he did nothing to hide his frustrations from Washington. "In this state of disappointment and vexation," he wrote, "I shall endeavor to borrow of South Carolina, say, 1,500 muskets and accoutrements and twice as many knapsacks, but it is doubtful whether South Carolina has them to lend." Still, he hoped to get his columns moving out by the eighth of March.

---

*Picolata, a small village on the St. Johns River, eighteen miles west of St. Augustine, had been a landing place for supplies for many years. It was the usual crossing place for people going from St. Augustine to western Florida.

Scott's greatest vexation, however, was still ahead of him, in the person of his old bugaboo, Brevet Major General Edmund P. Gaines. The grizzled, lean, outspoken banty-rooster had heard of the Dade massacre as early as January 15, 1836, while on a visit to New Orleans. As the western coast of Florida was normally included in his own Western Command, Gaines immediately called on the governor of Louisiana to provide him with a regiment of volunteers, for he was determined to go at once to Clinch's aid. Five days before Scott's meeting with Secretary Cass at Washington, Gaines was already busily preparing to leave New Orleans for Tampa.

It took time, however, for the Louisiana governor to raise the troops Gaines had requested. Gaines also needed to assemble shipping for his force. It was February 3, therefore, before he and his command of 1,140 regulars and volunteers were loaded up, bound for Tampa by way of Pensacola. On reaching Pensacola two days later, Gaines received a message informing him that Scott had been ordered to take command of all troops in Florida, including the western part. Gaines, the order continued, was to proceed to the Texas border, where Sam Houston's rebels were preparing for war against the Mexican president, Antonio López de Santa Anna.*

Gaines, however, had no intention of abandoning his expedition. He had, as he put it,

> made a pledge to the Governor and volunteers of Louisiana—a voluntary pledge—that I would not require this fine corps to go further than myself would go and that I would stand by them as long as they would stand by me in our contemplated efforts to take or destroy our red and black enemy in East Florida.

When Gaines arrived at Tampa Bay three days later, a message confirming his previous orders awaited him. By now, however, he had gone much too far to back down. Besides, Scott's present whereabouts were unknown to him, and the countryside was still in peril from Indian maraudings. He decided to push into the interior of Florida. Leaving a small detachment at Fort Brooke, Gaines departed on February 13 with about a thousand regulars and volunteers, following Dade's route toward Fort King.

A week later, Gaines's column arrived at the grisly scene of the Dade massacre. Up to that time only the testimony of Private Ransome Clarke had told the story. Now the whole tale lay before them.[7] Gaines, however, did not delay long at the scene. He buried the dead with due ceremony

---

*The Alamo, in San Antonio, fell to Santa Anna on March 7, 1836.

and continued his march that same day. By February 22, as Winfield Scott was landing at Picolata, Gaines and his troops arrived at Fort King. Even in that wilderness, a suitable guard of honor was turned out to meet the general.

Now Gaines himself was in for a shock. At Fort King he learned that the 120,000 rations Scott had ordered for delivery there had not arrived. In dire need of food for his hungry men, Gaines therefore sent a packhorse train to Fort Drane requesting that Clinch send him 14,000 rations. Clinch could spare only 12,000, but Gaines was glad to get even that many.

Scott, at Picolata, heard of Gaines's presence at Fort King during the evening of February 25. Shocked, he fired off a testy message to Clinch:

I have heard with equal astonishment and regret that Major-General Gaines, without reference to my arrangements, perhaps in ignorance, possibly in defiance of them, should have made a premature movement from Tampa Bay, and having arrived within 20 miles of Fort Drane, should have called for nearly three-fourths of the subsistence in deposit at that place, on which I have relied for the movement of the right wing, in concert with other parts of the army.

He added, "If [Gaines] should prefer to remain, he must obey my orders."

Even while he was writing it, Scott's message was already overtaken by events. For Gaines, having received his rations, was at that moment leaving Fort King, headed back to Fort Brooke. To reach his destination as fast as possible, and perhaps hoping to encounter some enemy along the way, he decided to follow the route that Clinch and Call had taken at New Year's, straight from Fort King to the Withlacoochee, through the Cove. He arrived at the river two days later.

If promoting a battle with the Indians was his hope, Gaines succeeded. At a point near the river crossing site where Clinch and Call had previously run into trouble, Gaines ran into even more. Even before he could get any troops across the Withlacoochee, he was attacked by a large force of Seminoles. Hastily the general threw up a breastwork for defense, naming it Fort Izard in honor of Lieutenant James F. Izard, the first American killed in this fight. Sporadic fighting continued at Fort Izard for eight full days. In the course of it, a Seminole bullet hit Gaines in the lower lip, knocking out two front teeth.[8]

In the meantime Scott was beside himself. On March 1, receiving no reply from Clinch, he wrote a second letter, his famous "starvation letter."

Even if you had sufficient stores on hand, and means of transportation, I should, under the circumstances, command you to send no subsistence to [Gaines] unless to prevent starvation; but you have neither. Let him therefore, in time, extricate himself from the embarrassment he has placed himself in by marching upon Volusia, where I have no reason to doubt that 20,000 rations, sent hence on the 27th ultimo, have safely arrived. As he appears to have retreat open to him, or is in no peril to prevent his taking that step, you, of course, will make no detachment or movement to join him.

In the meantime Clinch was to give Gaines nothing more "for further false expeditions."

Duncan Clinch was now in a quandary. Scott's orders were unmistakable, but Scott was still at Picolata, sixty-five miles away and out of touch, while every day the news of Gaines's plight on the Withlacoochee grew worse. So Clinch used his judgment: Gaines's desperate condition, he reasoned, took precedence over future tactical plans. On March 5, therefore, he left Fort Drane for the Withlacoochee.

Gaines's men claimed afterward that their only problem on the Withlacoochee was hunger, and that they had not considered retreat. That may be so. In the meantime, they had used up their corn and had begun eating their horses. Despite their later bravado, the garrison was relieved when, on the evening of the fifth, a cry came from someone in the Indian camp wishing to hold a parley. Gaines refused to appear concerned, so on his instruction, the officer of the guard replied that if the Indians wanted to confer, they should come in the morning, carrying a white flag.

At about ten o'clock on March 6, a group of fully armed Indians drew themselves up behind Gaines's camp about five hundred yards off. Two Seminoles came forward under a white flag, and Gaines sent a staff officer out to meet them. Speaking to junior officers—Gaines would never talk with the Indians personally—the Indians promised to fight no more if Gaines would leave the Withlacoochee. The American officers answered mostly with warnings of the size of force that would be turned loose against the Indians unless they put down their arms. The Indians retired.

That afternoon another Indian contingent, which included Osceola himself, came across. They were tired of the war, they claimed, and wanted only to live peacefully. But they refused to be moved from Florida to the West; they would have to be allowed to stay in their homes. Gaines replied that if Osceola and his warriors withdrew and agreed to attend a council on government call, they would not be molested—a hollow promise considering that it was Gaines, not Osceola, who was under siege.

At that point, the Indians commenced to disperse. Clinch had arrived! The Seminoles were soon "beyond the reach of gunshot, and were out of sight and over the river."

Edmund Gaines and his men were saved. Sobered, he turned over command of his force to Clinch and returned to Fort Drane, determined to leave the Florida theater alone, accompanied only by a small escort. He also issued a pompous order of the day, extolling the virtues of his officers and men. In it he made the ridiculous claim that he and his men had brought the Seminole War to an end.

Gaines waited at Fort Drane one night too long. He was in a hurry to leave, as he was aware of Winfield Scott's imminent arrival, and he had no desire to meet his rival face to face. On March 13, however, Scott appeared, frustrated and exhausted after the difficult sixty-five-mile trip from Picolata. Gaines would have to spend an evening with him.

The scene at Fort Drane was later described by a keen observer, a diminutive Englishman named John Bemrose. Bemrose, unaware of the animosity the two men had for each other, wrote in some wonderment that, although Scott and Gaines acted in a relatively civilized manner toward each other, "I noticed a cold salutation passed between them. There was no companionship and evidently there existed a distaste, a repelling power proving that when interests clash, two of a trade seldom agree."

Scott, Bemrose noted, was "one of nature's finest specimens of the *genus homo* . . . decidedly the finest man I ever saw. He stood six foot four inches high. There was a slight stoop of one shoulder owing to a shot received at the Battle of Plattsburg [Bemrose meant Lundy's Lane], where he was the hero of the day, taking command of the American army after General Brown was carried off the field." Calling Scott "most certainly a clever general, patriotic and brave," Bemrose admired Scott's obvious concern for the wounded. "He was more than a daily visitor to the hospital," Bemrose wrote, "and his custom was to bring with him limes and oranges and other little dainties for those who bore their sufferings manfully."

But Bemrose also noted certain other, less admirable things about the general. "General Scott," he wrote, "had brought with him a band of choice musicians." They came "with appurtances to match, marquees of furniture, . . . giving our surroundings the appearance of sudden refinement. Thus he had decked out everything with the panoply of war . . . quite unsuitable for Indian bush fighting. He had three large wagons, laden with superb furniture and all things comfortable for himself and staff. There were wines and other luxuries in [such] profusion that one would imagine it was the train of some Indian nabob."[9]

Edmund Gaines left Fort Drane overland for Tallahassee and Mobile the next morning, still believing that he had ended the Florida war—one of the more optimistic statements of all time. His expedition to Fort King and the Withlacoochee had set Scott's plans back, because his troops had consumed many of the rations Scott had been counting on, and the thousand men that Gaines had left behind were not fit to go back into the fight. Yet the setback may not have been so serious as Scott later claimed, because his own troops from South Carolina, Alabama, and Georgia were still streaming into the Florida ports when Gaines departed. That meant delays, and Scott's force did not move out until later in the month.[10] Eustis left St. Augustine on March 15, but Lindsay did not receive orders to move until March 21.

The resulting campaign turned out to be a complete anticlimax to all the preparations that had preceded it. Scott's commanders soon found that survival had to take precedence over seeking out the enemy. The distances over uncharted ground, the heat, and the need to cut paths through the vast, tangled forests were too much for their men to overcome.

Scott and Clinch reached the recently christened Fort Izard on schedule, and they crossed the Withlacoochee River without great difficulty. Inside the Cove, they encountered one band of Seminoles on March 31, but after that they failed to find any concentration of Indians to fight—a swamp here, a hummock there, a small group of Seminoles somewhere else, but no enemy drawn up for battle. The right wing reached the far end of the Cove by April 1, 1836, exhausted and without a serious military encounter.

Eustis did good work in clearing out the Seminoles east of the St. Johns, but by the time he crossed the St. Johns at Volusia it was March 26, only a day before he was expected at Piklakaha. He finally reached his destination, moving through heavy rains and uncharted wilderness, on March 31. The next day he encountered Scott, from whom he learned that Lindsay had arrived at Chocochatti on March 21, waited for three days, and then returned to Fort Brooke.

Clinch and Scott, together with Eustis, arrived at Fort Brooke on April 5, relieved to be back at a base but aware that they had achieved nothing. They had killed a few of the enemy, but they had fought mostly terrain and hunger.

Scott's three wings had encountered no concentrated force of Seminoles to defeat. Their rations were low, they were exhausted, and their volunteers were due for return home within weeks. Scott's only choice was to abandon the chase, march his three wings back to their ports of embarkation, release the volunteers, and then consider the next step.

Scott was highly disappointed. He realized that his efforts to subdue the Seminoles had failed, at least for the moment. His volunteers would soon be due back to their homes, and in order to reach the ports by which they had arrived in Florida, they would have to retrace their steps. His three columns could beat the bushes on the way back, but they could not spend much time in doing so.

Scott's report to the Adjutant General, which he had ready by April 12, 1836, was a remarkable document. It laid forth every particular in excruciating detail, accounting for the activities of every small unit, down to company level. Although it complained of supply shortages, it was utterly factual except for its superfluous (and inevitable) attack on Edmund Gaines's Order No. 7, which declared that his force had won the Seminole War on the Withlacoochee.

The more significant part of Scott's report described his plans for the three wings of his army as they headed back to their respective starting points. Clinch's right wing was to return to the Cove, resupply at the mouth of the Withlacoochee River, and then return to Fort Drane. The center, under Lindsay, was to march up the Fort King Road, search the headwaters of the Withlacoochee, and then return to Fort Brooke.

Abraham Eustis was once again given the most difficult task. His left wing, reinforced by Colonel Persifor F. Smith's Louisiana Regiment, was to march southward to Pease Creek, search for concentrations of Seminoles, and recross the peninsula by a new route from Pease Creek to Volusia and St. Augustine.* Scott would accompany Lindsay, at least to the Withlacoochee River.

After losing the services of the volunteers, Scott would be left with only 789 effectives in all of Florida. These regulars he planned to distribute

---

*Persifor Smith and his Louisianans were to return from Pease Creek to Fort Brooke for shipment back to New Orleans.

among Fort Drane, Picolata, and St. Augustine. On April 13 and 14, all three wings of the army moved out according to Scott's plans.

Scott arrived back at Picolata on April 30, 1836. Aside from the successful arrival of his troops, he could report only that "nothing of importance has been achieved." But he still felt, in his report, a need to attack Gaines even further. This time he blamed Gaines for dispersing the Indians who had been concentrated in the Cove. The Indian villages he had been seeking, he asserted, had originally been there but had left "even while the parley was going on with General Gaines on the 7th of March, moving off to the southeast. . . . The wily chiefs profited by the information; sent off their families and dispersed their warriors into small parties."

Along more constructive lines, he turned to the future. To find the Indian villages and scour the country, he estimated, 3,000 troops would be needed, 2,400 of them mounted. He had no particular desire to conduct the operation himself: it would be a duty he would "neither solicit nor decline." But then he overstepped the bounds of good sense: "Of the above force, *3,000 good troops, (not volunteers)* five hundred will be necessary to garrison five posts for the deposit of supplies."

Scott may have expected such a remark to remain a secret between himself and the Adjutant General, Brigadier General Roger Jones. If he did, he was woefully unrealistic. The contents of the report inevitably became public knowledge, and the remark about "good troops, not volunteers" was painful to patriotic Americans who, whatever their shortcomings, had come from civilian life to struggle through swamp and forest under his command. Even so, the reaction among Floridians was not yet severe, except for some sniffing remarks describing Scott as a regular who had, in one writer's words, "drawn [his plan] upon the carpet before his comfortable fire."

Two weeks later, however, Scott exacerbated the bad feeling by issuing General Order No. 68, expressing disgust for the continuing fear that still gripped many Floridians, huddled close to the forts for safety. Their panics, he wrote,

> are infinitely humiliating. Within a few days, just five Indians penetrated a neighborhood in the heart of Middle Florida,[11] and committed a murder. Instead of giving pursuit, the inhabitants abandoned their plantations and fled to Tallahassee and Monticello. . . . a panic is rife throughout the country.

He went on to declare that

no General, even with extensive means, can cure a disease in the public mind, so general and degrading, without some little effort on the part of the people themselves.

That did it. The Floridians now focused their wrath on Scott himself. He was burned in effigy in Tallahassee, the target of his recent remarks, and Major Leigh Reed, a powerful local politician whom Scott had criticized, attacked him with vitriolic articles in the local newspapers. Scott's unpopularity with the Floridians had come not from his lack of military success but from the destructive effects of his pen.

Fortunately for Scott's peace of mind, he was spared any more service in Florida. On May 23, just as he was getting himself deeper in hot water with his trusty pen, he received a letter from Secretary Cass ordering him to leave Florida and proceed to the Chattahoochee River, between Georgia and Alabama, where a serious Creek uprising was under way. The governors of both states had been writing letters to the War Department urgently requesting Scott's services.

Scott left Florida with little regret.

17

Scott Faces a Court of Inquiry

Scott loses a friend but triumphs over Jackson's
last effort to humiliate him.

S COTT ARRIVED at Savannah on May 22, 1836, in good spirits. He had
spent the last three weeks at St. Augustine sick in bed with a fever, but he
had now experienced a miraculous improvement in his physical condition.
He was also buoyed by a message from Governor William Schley welcoming
him to Georgia. Schley described recent Creek depredations and concluded
in flattering terms: "We [Georgians] know so little of military matters, and
the economy of an army, that your presence will be quite acceptable."

Scott now felt himself again. "Thank God!" he wrote a friend.

> Here an enemy may be reached, perhaps 10,000 strong! Nothing is wanted but a
> sufficient force, and the Georgians and Alabamians are assembling. I may have
> everything to create in regard to subsistence and everything to organize. So much
> the better—I like difficulties, and I hope to know how to conquer them. . . . I am
> nearly well. By the time I arrive at Augusta I shall be able to ride 40, or march 30
> miles a day on foot. Thank God for a good constitution and a cheerful mind!

The general realized, however, that he now depended once again on volunteers from Georgia and Alabama, so he set out to mend his fences with
those he had offended. On May 26, at Augusta, he wrote to Governor
Schley that he would be late in arriving for a conference at Milledgeville,
the state capital. He had been advised to delay his journey twenty-four
hours, he said,

to give time to counter a strong prejudice against me, growing out of a letter of mine to the Government, recently published. To effect this object, the noble commander of the Augusta battalion, lately under my command, has addressed me a letter, to which my reply, I think, cannot fail to be satisfactory.

The situation in Georgia and Alabama bore some resemblance to that Scott had faced in Florida. In both cases, the local Indians were resisting efforts of the federal government to move them westward, in their frustrations raiding and destroying white settlements. The military problem in dealing with the Creeks, however, was much easier. Though the Creeks were numerically stronger than the Seminoles, they enjoyed none of the terrain advantages that made the Seminoles so formidable. The country surrounding the Creek nation was relatively open, with roads capable of carrying the supplies that Scott ordered. The temporary commander in west Georgia, moreover, was Brevet Major General Thomas Jesup, Scott's warm friend and professional ally ever since Jesup commanded a regiment with such distinction under Scott at Lundy's Lane. There was no danger, it was thought, of any personal rivalry developing between the two generals; everything boded well.

Scott met with Governor Schley and General Jesup at Milledgeville on May 28, 1836. Their concerns were not exactly the same. The governor was primarily concerned about protecting civilians from the Creeks, who were raiding Georgia from Alabama along the forty-mile stretch of the Chattahoochee between Columbus and Roanoke (present-day Omaha). Scott shared that concern, of course, but he focused on destroying the Creek forces before they could send organized bodies southward into Florida, which was still very much on his mind.

As in Florida, Scott was planning an organized, coordinated campaign. Aware that supplying the troops with food was the paramount problem, he ordered 250,000 rations from the quartermaster base at New Orleans, to be sent up the Apalachicola and Chattahoochee rivers to bases near Columbus, and an additional 100,000 rations to come by wagon from St. Augustine.

Scott's scheme of maneuver was elaborate. With Florida still on his mind, he planned to send strong forces southward along the Chattahoochee from Columbus on the Georgia side and from nearby Fort Mitchell (Phenix City) on the Alabama side. At Irwinton (Eufala), Alabama, some of the Georgians and regulars would cross the Chattahoochee and attack the Creek nation from the south and east, cutting them off from their escape route to Florida.*

Both Jesup and Schley professed to agree with Scott's plan, so Jesup left on June 1 for a dash through Creek territory to Montgomery. There he was to assume command of Alabama forces, organize the incoming recruits of the Alabama militia, and then, once Scott had ordered the attack, march down the western bank of the Chattahoochee. His force would be augmented by a body of friendly Creek warriors.

Difficulties, however, soon set in. When Jesup reached Tuskeegee, he found that some of the Alabamians had already taken the field.[1] The attitude of Alabama Governor Clement C. Clay, moreover, was uncertain; Jesup was far from convinced that Clay really intended to put the Alabama militia under his command. Jesup's report of June 8 ended cryptically: "If a movement be determined on, I will send you information of it by a runner."

From the outset, therefore, Scott feared that the governor of Alabama planned to attack the Creeks independently of Scott's instructions, without turning his volunteers over to Scott's command. That was disturbing enough, but even worse was the impression that Jesup himself seemed reconciled to such a development.

The problem was again one of timing. Scott's plan, while thorough and prudent, failed to take into account that Creek warriors were killing citizens of lower Alabama every day and that Governor Clay was being inundated by letters of strong protest from those endangered.

In the meantime, Jesup acted on his own. Probably with the concurrence of Governor Clay,[2] he left Tuskeegee on June 10, two days after his letter to Scott, and instead of enveloping the Creeks from the south, went straight eastward through the heart of Creek territory, arriving at a point fourteen miles from Fort Mitchell, across from Columbus. Six days later he attacked the main camp of the principal Creek chief, Eneah Mathla, with spectacular success, capturing the chief himself along with three hundred Creeks. He sent word of his victory to Scott, along with an urgent request for rations.

The military campaign against the Creeks had been completed easily, but the war of words was just beginning. Scott sent no congratulations on Jesup's

---

*Scott could count on 3,000 men from Georgia, and he expected Governor Clement C. Clay of Alabama to provide another 2,000. He also had 1,000 regulars, including some marines, coming by rail from Charleston. Scott to Clay, 31 May 1836. U.S. Congress, Senate, Exec. Doc. No. 224, p. 415.

success. Instead, he wrote a plaintive letter on June 17 saying that he was "infinitely astonished and distressed to hear of your near approach, and in a starving condition, at Fort Mitchell." He accused Jesup of "seeking private adventures" in violation of his own plan of operations. Comparing Jesup's move to that of Gaines upon Fort King, he concluded, "My grief and distress are at their utmost height!"

By the next day, Scott realized that he had been too harsh in his previous day's message. He now conceded the importance of protecting the Alabama settlements and promised to send rations to Fort Mitchell. He was, however, still unhappy that Jesup had acted outside of his own orders.

Jesup claimed at first that he regretted earning Scott's "disapprobation," though he insisted he had acted within the "spirit" of Scott's instructions. He had attacked, he wrote, only to "stay the tomahawk and scalping knife, and prevent the devastation of entire settlements." He then went to Fort Mitchell personally, expecting to meet Scott there, only to find that Scott had come and gone. A series of letters then passed between the two former friends, the situation intensified by the lack of prompt communications, each writing two or three messages before receiving a reply to the first one. Finally, on June 20, an infuriated Jesup wrote a letter to Francis Blair, editor of the *Washington Globe*. Describing the scene as "the Florida scenes enacted all over again," he repeated the claims he had previously made to Scott and concluded by saying that, if Scott did not arrest him first, he would apply to be relieved, for "[Scott's] delay has been destructive to the best interests of the country." He then added an extraordinary paragraph asking Blair to "let the President see this letter."

Ironically, Scott had now, too late, come to appreciate what Jesup had accomplished. In a letter, he wrote to Jesup, "As to my confidence in your high honor, intelligence, and capacity for war, nothing has ever shaken that." And to Adjutant General Roger Jones, he wrote asking that all the letters he had written criticizing Jesup be withdrawn from the record. He also sent a force southward to intercept those three hundred Creek warriors who had escaped Jesup's attack a few days earlier.

Jesup was not placated. Very shortly after receiving Scott's conciliatory letter, he again broke channels—officially this time—by writing directly to the secretary of war, repeating much of what he had written before.

The epistolary clash, however, soon came to an end. On July 6, Scott received a mysterious letter from General-in-Chief Macomb ordering him back to Washington.

At first, Scott gave his orders to Washington little thought. He had no idea that either the president or the secretary of war had any reservations about his performance in either the Seminole campaign or the Creek War. He therefore turned over command of the Army of the South to Jesup with a good will. It was only when his ship docked at Norfolk that he began hearing rumors that he had been relieved of his command for cause. Never admitting throughout his life that he had made even the slightest mistake in either campaign, he headed for the nation's capital determined to get to the root of the matter.

Scott was not a man to hold back. On his arrival on July 20, he headed straight for the office of the secretary of war, expecting to confront Lewis Cass. But attaining satisfaction was to prove elusive. With the Jackson administration winding down to a close, the secretary had left his office for good, leaving behind the department's chief clerk, Cary A. Harris, as acting secretary. Harris was a public servant, in no mood to make enemies, so when Scott confronted him with the rumors he had heard, Harris produced from a back drawer the evidence he was looking for, Jesup's letter to Francis Blair, with, on the bottom, an endorsement in Jackson's handwriting,

> Referred to the Secretary of War, that he forthwith order General Scott to this place, in order that an inquiry be had into the unaccountable delay in prosecuting the Creek War and the failure of the Campaign in Florida. Let General Jesup assume the command.

This was Scott's first official knowledge of Jesup's unethical dealings—or of Jackson's reaction, for that matter. So Scott, in his anguish, attempted to see the President in place of Cass. But Jackson had left for Nashville, where he planned to stay nearly three months at the Hermitage, away from his desk. So Scott took off to New York in pursuit of Cass. While there, he was able to check in with his own headquarters—he was still in command of the Eastern Department—but Cass could not be found; he had left for Detroit.

Scott's futile efforts to find anyone in authority were not kept secret. The Whig press took delight in it. One writer, Charles King, for example, wrote an article dubbed "A Major-General in Pursuit of the Government," implying strongly that nobody was in charge in Washington. And when Jesup's letter to Blair was published in the *Globe* on July 29, the impropriety of Jesup's action was given due notice. None of this public sentiment, however, did anything to dissuade Jackson from putting Scott before a court. For a while, Scott could not find out whether he would be facing a court-martial or a court of inquiry. He would have favored the former even though a court-martial, which implied wrongdoing, perhaps criminal, placed his career in more jeopardy than a mere inquiry. Scott, being completely sure of the rightness of his case, would risk the court-martial, as its very seriousness would give the accused greater rights to subpoena witnesses. It turned out, however, that the hearing was to be only a court of inquiry. The War Department's General Order No. 65, issued on October 3, 1836, specified at first that the court was

> to inquire and examine into the causes of the failure of the campaigns in Florida against the Seminole Indians, under the command of Major General Scott, in 1836; and the causes of the delay in opening and prosecuting the campaign in Georgia and Alabama against the hostile Creek Indians.[3]

Ten days later, however, the court's responsibilities were enlarged. Word reached Jackson that Edmund Gaines, after sending in his official report on the Seminole campaign on July 4, had simultaneously given a copy of it to the press. Jackson, who had been sour on Gaines for some time, took immediate action: he simply added Gaines's name to that of Scott as subjects of the court's investigations.

Since it would require weeks to assemble the witnesses, many of whom had to travel great distances to participate, the opening of the proceedings was delayed until November 28.

When at last the court opened, its first order of business was to deal with a protest issued by Gaines from Mobile, dated October 30. Gaines objected to the composition of the court, specifically to the presence of General-in-Chief Alexander Macomb, its president. Gaines also demanded that the venue of the court be moved from Frederick, Maryland, to Mobile. Those demands gave Scott a great opportunity to get off on the right foot. In his opening statement, he indicated that he was pleased with the composition of the court. All three of its members, Major General Macomb, Brigadier General Henry Atkinson, and Colonel Hugh Brady, were friends.[4] The court therefore elected to overrule both of Gaines's objections. Macomb declared himself willing to withdraw from that portion of the court pertaining to Gaines, but the court would have none of it. Moving the proceedings to Mobile was out of the question. So Gaines refused to attend the first meetings of the court, sending Captain E. A. Hitchcock, who had been his adjutant in Florida, to represent him during his absence.

On December 6, Scott's defense, which he conducted personally, began. He commenced by submitting depositions taken from officers who had been supply officers during the Florida campaign. These depositions, in the form of questions and answers, described the shortages of horses, wagons, and provisions, especially of foodstuffs. The testimony of Colonel James Gadsden, one-time quartermaster of the Army of Florida, later Scott's adjutant, was particularly telling.

The deposition submitted, Scott began interrogating Colonel William Lindsay, who had been in command of Scott's center wing, marching from Tampa toward the Cove. Lindsay was strong in supporting Scott's contention that supply had been totally inadequate in Florida. He also backed up Scott's declaration that the war had not been ended by Gaines on the previous March 10—a point that hardly needed proving.

The next day, General Abraham Eustis took the stand. His testimony was particularly useful to Scott's cause by illustrating the difficulties of crossing the Florida peninsula, where he had met resistance from the Seminoles and also suffered from a shortage of transportation:

Scott: Was there a full supply of hard bread for witness's column on the St. Johns, at the commencement of his advance on Pelaklikaha, or was he obliged to substitute a portion of flour, and had any bacon arrived before the commencement of that march?

Eustis: The column under my command never had a full supply of hard bread. It was not to be obtained. I had no bacon. I was of course obliged to take a portion of flour.

Scott: Did the enemy met with by the troops under the witness's command show a disposition to treat or surrender, or the reverse?

Eustis: The appearance of the enemy was always announced to me by their firing upon my advanced guard. There was no disposition shown to treat with us, or to have any communication with us.[5]

Eustis finished, there followed a series of witnesses, largely supply officers, many of them no longer in service.

On December 22, Scott put his star witness on the stand. Brigadier General Duncan Clinch, since resigned from the service, answered questions pertaining to the quality of the volunteers who had been available and also to the conditions under which they marched, including the quality of the drinking water along the way. He answered Scott's first pointed question favorably:

Scott: Whilst he was within your observation, did you observe any deficiency in the zeal, activity, or judgment of General Scott, in the prosecution of the campaign against the enemy?

Clinch: I did not. He was always active, and sometimes, I thought, rather over-zealous or restless in pushing on the operations of the campaign.

He attributed the failure of the campaign principally to the "want of energy and military forecast in the late head of the War Department." Clinch had never forgiven Cass for replacing him with Scott.

The next day, however, Clinch gave Scott a small defeat, unimportant as it was:

Scott: What influence had the movement of General Gaines against the Seminole Indians in 1836, on the results of the campaign conducted by Major General Scott against the enemy in Florida in the same year?

Clinch: I am of the opinion that the movement of Major General Gaines's command through Florida did not materially affect the operations of Major General Scott. General Gaines's command did consume several thousand rations; but the material of that command was of the best kind, and would have been of advantage to the commander of any army.

Also to Scott's disappointment, Clinch testified that the troops Gaines had brought with him, both regulars and Louisiana volunteers, "were an acquisition, as they were experienced regulars, and gallant and efficient volunteers from Louisiana."

Finally the time came for Scott to make his final statement. He was upset by being called to account far more than he was worried about his career. Always the historian, he opened with a reference to classical history:

When a Doge of Genoa, for some imaginary reason, imputed by Louis XIV, was torn from his government and compelled to visit France, in order to debase himself before that inflated monarch, he was asked, in the palace, what struck him with the greatest wonder amid the blaze and magnificence in his view? 'To find *myself* here!' was the reply of the indignant Lescaro. And so, Mr. President, unable, as I am, to remember one blunder in my recent operations, or a single duty neglected, I may say, that to find myself in the presence of this honorable court, while the army I but recently commanded is still in pursuit of the enemy, fills me with equal grief and astonishment.

But Scott was still, even in this strange circumstance, not inclined to offend President Jackson who, he judged, could still do a great deal of damage to everyone present in that courtroom. So he spent the next paragraph of his statement almost eulogizing Jackson:

> And whence this great and humiliating transition? It is, sir, by the fiat of one, who, from his exalted station, and yet more from his unequalled popularity, has never, with his high displeasure, struck a functionary of this Government . . . who was not from the moment withered in the general confidence of the American people. Yes, sir, it is my misfortune to lie under the displeasure of that most distinguished personage. The President of the United States has said, 'Let General Scott be recalled from the command of the army in the field, and submit his conduct in the Seminole and Creeks campaigns to a court for investigation.' And lo! I stand here to vindicate that conduct, which again must be judged in the last resort, by him who first condemned it without trial or inquiry.[6]

Scott's summary was a powerful argument, over 14,000 words in length. And it was convincing. He began by going down the list of ten factors which he believed had made his mission to Florida impossible; the brief terms of enlistment for the volunteers, the Gaines intrusion, the lack of transportation, the shortage of supplies, rations, and forage were among them. He mentioned the heat, the filthy drinking water, and the need to transport wounded in precious cargo space. Not to be omitted were the lack of information about the nature of the country, the lack of sufficient scouts, especially Indians, and the lack of roads.

Scott could not finish without a castigation of Gaines, who had called his plans for the March campaign "too elaborate and too European." Describing Gaines as "an old officer who delights to see himself in print," Scott asked, in answer to the "European" accusation, whether it was criminal to import professional knowledge. Gaines, he surmised, possibly thought that wars should be waged without plans.

Sandwiched in between testimonies regarding the Florida campaign, Scott was also conducting his own defense against charges of delay in the Creek campaign during June and the early part of July 1836. On December 19 he submitted a deposition from Major Edmund Kirby, once paymaster of the army, who had been an aide to Scott during that campaign. To Scott's standard question regarding his own performance, Kirby testified, "The General manifested great and incessant solicitude for the arrival of the necessary arms and other supplies, to enable the troops to take the field." Others were included, all either Georgians or regular army officers. But Scott's main defenses were from the big guns: Governor William Schley of Georgia and Major General J. W. A. Sanford, commander of Georgia troops during the Creek campaign. Schley's deposition established that apparent agreement had existed beween him, Scott, and Jesup when the three had gone from Milledgeville to Columbus the previous May, before Jesup had left for Montgomery, Alabama. He also attested that Scott had kept him completely informed of all his plans at that time.

Schley's testimony, helpful as it was, was overshadowed by that of General Sanford in contending that the Georgia troops were in no condition to fight before Scott actually put them into motion:

Scott: Up to about the time that the witness marched with part of his division towards the place called Roanoke. . . . what portion of the division was without arms and accoutrements?

Sanford: Of the troops remaining under my immediate command, less than one-third were armed, and these variously and indifferently with shot-guns, rifles, and muskets. Our miserable deficiency was most strikingly displayed to my view when, upon the occasion of an alarm, and it was expected that the enemy would be upon us in full force, I had the mortification of beholding within my lines fifteen or sixteen hundred men with no weapons of defense beyond their side-arms, clubs, and club-axes.

....

Scott: If the whole disposable force of Georgians, Alabamians, and regulars, with the friendly Indians acting as auxiliaries, had been placed in line below the enemy, and had operated up the country, whilst the frontier settlements of Georgia and Alabama were guarded by competent detachments, is it not probable that fewer of the enemy would have escaped across the Chattahoochee in the direction of Florida, than actually did so escape, and also that the war would have been finished earlier than it actually was?

Sanford: Had the first plan of operations been fully adopted, the troops now mentioned would have been able to have carried it out. The enemy being encompassed in every direction by superior numbers, defeated in his hopes of escape, and defeated in the field, must have immediately sued for peace, and the war would have very probably terminated without those straggling parties which invaded Georgia the latter part of July last.

Finally, to prove the impropriety of the calling of the court of inquiry, Scott obtained a deposition from Francis Blair, the editor of the *Washington Globe.* Blair was candid in his answers. They established beyond a doubt the impropriety of Jesup's letter to him—implying somewhat the impropriety of President Jackson's calling the court to meet.

All in all, Scott's defense regarding the Creek campaign was a strong argument. Still it had weaknesses. None of the deponents was from Alabama; all were Georgians, who had seen matters Scott's way from the beginning. Jesup, Scott's antagonist, had no opportunity to cross-examine witnesses, as he was busy with his own campaign against the Seminoles in Florida, where he had gone from Georgia. But this was a court of inquiry, not a court-martial. So Scott's defense was not questioned.

In the meantime, Gaines was injuring his own cause—and aiding Scott's—by his intemperate conduct before the court. In his statement of defense, he compared Scott to Benedict Arnold. He called Scott's conduct at Camp Izard

> the atrocious machinations of the second United States general officer who has ever dared to aid and assist the open enemy of the republic in their operations against the United States forces employed in the protection of the frontier people. The first great offender was Major General Benedict Arnold; the second, as your finding will show, is Major General Winfield Scott.

The court took due note of this intemperance.

By the end of January 1837, the catfight at Frederick was over, and the court reached its findings for submission to the President. The conclusions were foregone, as all the testimony had been brought in by the defendants and no cross-examination had taken place. So, not surprisingly, both Scott and Gaines were exonerated of any serious errors or wrongdoings. The court placed all the blame for the failures on circumstances out of the army's control. The court further judged that Scott, though "amply clothed with authority to create the means of prosecuting the Seminole War," had been brought in too late in the year to achieve success. "The season," it declared, "was too far advanced for him to collect, appoint, and put in motion his forces until a day too late to compass the object." Citing Scott's "great diligence and energy," it ascribed the failure to "want of time to operate, the insalubrity of the climate, the impervious swamps and hammocks that abound the country . . . and absence of all knowledge by the General of the topography of the country, together with the difficulty of obtaining the means of transporting supplies for the army." It concluded that "Major General Scott was zealous and indefatigable in the discharge of his duties, and his plan of campaign was well devised, and prosecuted with energy, steadfastness and ability." Amid these encomiums, however, the court administered Scott a wrist slap:

> As connected with the Seminole campaign under Major General Scott, in 1836, the attention of the court has been called to the tone and language of his "Order No. 48," dated the 17th of May, and of his letter of the 11th of May to the Adjutant General, the first reflecting on the people of Florida and the latter on the conduct of Major Read, of the Florida volunteers. The tenor of these are not considered a military offense, but an indiscretion that it were better to have avoided.

The court was equally generous when it came to evaluating Scott's role in the Creek campaign. Of course that was easier; the Creek campaign had been a success.

Scott's rivals did not fare so well. Although neither Gaines nor Jesup was criticized for their military actions, the personal acts of both were condemned. In the case of Gaines, the court's wording was noncommittal:

> The court, therefore . . . is of the opinion that the failure of the campaign should rather be attributed to the want of means of subsistence to prosecute the war, than to the contingent result of a sortie [against the Withlacoochee].

It was not kind, however, regarding the words Gaines had used against Scott, comparing him to Benedict Arnold. It called that language "unbecoming his, Major General Gaines's, high rank and station—remarks and assertions which the court condemns in the most decided terms of reprehension."

The court also took a swipe at Thomas Jesup, even though he was not on trial. In connection with Scott's recall from Georgia, it referred to Jesup's

> letter bearing the date of the 20th of June, 1836, addressed to F. P. Blair, Esq., at Washington, marked *"private,"* containing a request that it be shown to the President—which letter was exposed and brought to light by the dignified and magnanimous act of the President in causing it to be placed on file in the Department of War, as an official document. . . . Conduct so extraordinary and inexplicable

on the part of Major General Jesup, in reference to the character of said letter, should, in the opinion of the court, be investigated.

Those findings, while reasonable, were courageous. Both Gaines and Scott were known to be in disfavor with President Jackson, and Jesup, whose conduct had received a serious reprimand, had been castigated.

On receipt of the report, Andrew Jackson did not avail himself of this opportunity to be magnanimous. On February 18 he penned a letter to the secretary of war for transmittal to General Macomb, asserting that "the facts found by the Court are stated in a very general form, and without sufficient minuteness and precision." Therefore, Jackson wrote, he was remitting "the said proceedings to the Court, to the end that the Court may resume the consideration of the evidence" and take further hearings with "distinctness and precision" for the information of the President. As to the wording on Jesup, Jackson wrote, the court's opinion was "totally unauthorized by the Order constituting the Court." The circumstances of Scott's removal from Georgia and the "propriety or impropriety of the conduct of Major General Jesup in writing the letter" were not submitted to the court as matters of inquiry. The President therefore disapproved the opinion and remitted it for further consideration.

Upon receiving this rebuff, however, Macomb and his colleagues acted with even more courage—or insubordination, according to the viewpoint. The court added exhaustive sequences of facts and events to its former report, deleted that portion pertaining to Jesup's letter to Blair, and resubmitted the report on March 8, 1837, without a single change in its findings regarding either Scott or Gaines. The members of the court knew, of course, that they were safe from Jackson's wrath. Martin Van Buren had been inaugurated President on March 4, four days earlier, and he had no stomach for continuing this pointless exercise. He approved the court's findings and sent its members back to their normal stations.

Scott was content. He had been more than exonerated for his role in Florida; he had even been praised. In one sense the court's action had been a personal triumph over Andrew Jackson, who Scott always assumed had been persecuting him despite his earlier manifestations of friendship. Writing nearly thirty years later, Scott still seemed defensive:

The emphatic verdict of acquittal in this case, openly approved by hosts of [Scott's] supporters, administered to President Jackson the first wholesome rebuke he had received in that office. He was made to feel that it shook the public faith in his supremacy.

His role in Florida over, Scott returned to his headquarters in New York and his home in Elizabethtown. He was elated over the prospect of a public dinner "in honor of his triumph before the court."

18

⋙⋙⋆⋘⋘

The Great Pacificator, 1838

Scott's military prestige helps avert another
unnecessary war.

Scott's exploits in the field, which placed him in the first rank of
our soldiers, have been obscured by the purer and more lasting
glory of a Pacificator and of a Friend to Mankind.
—William E. Channing, 1841

ANDREW JACKSON had left the presidency and was back in retirement at the Hermitage, near Nashville. With Old Hickory's departure
from the national scene, Scott's position in the Army was now more comfortable. The new President, Martin Van Buren, was a personal friend,* and
the new secretary of war, Joel R. Poinsett, was a South Carolina unionist,
Scott's collaborator during the nullification crisis of 1832.

Scott could never be a member of Van Buren's inner circle, however. His
increasing ties with the opposition Whigs were indissoluble, and since Van
Buren was the protégé of Jackson, the bugaboo of the Whigs, a political association was impossible. Van Buren and Poinsett were broad-minded men,
however, and Scott could expect a cordial relationship with both.

It had been barely a year since Jackson and Cass had sent Scott to Florida,
but the citizens of New York City welcomed him back as if he had been gone
a very long time. When he first set foot at his headquarters, Mayor Cornelius

---

*Scott always claimed credit for first suggesting that Van Buren run some day for the presidency, a
delusion the Little Magician probably desired Scott to think.

Van Wyck Lawrence and a group of prominent citizens invited him to attend a dinner they were planning to hold in his honor. He accepted happily. Only days after his acceptance, however, disaster struck the financial markets of the country. The uncontrolled financial speculation that had almost doubled real estate and stock prices in a very few years collapsed. A lot at Broadway and 100th Street, New York, previously priced at $480, now sold for $50. In view of this cataclysm, Scott sensed that this was no time for personal aggrandizement. He wrote the committee that

> feeling deeply for the losses and anxieties of all, no public honor could be enjoyed by me. I must therefore, under the circumstances, positively, but most respectfully, withdraw my acceptance of your invitation.

The members of the committee were not offended; they were grateful to be spared an evening of false gaiety. They drew up a resolution declaring that Scott's withdrawal from the dinner demonstrated his "sympathy with all that regards the public welfare, and of his habitual oblivion of self, where the feelings and interests of others are concerned."

Other forces once again curtailed Scott's respite in New York. Serious trouble between the United States and Britain had erupted on the Canadian border, which meant another call for his services.

The new troubles between the United States and Canada were concentered at first around the area of Buffalo, New York. In Upper Canada, across the Niagara River, reformers who called themselves the Patriots were agitating against what they viewed as the tyranny of the British government. As no response came from Britain to grant the Canadians more representative government, the Patriots set their sights on total independence. The independence movement did not involve great numbers; it was not strong enough to make much headway without support from American citizens along the border. Unfortunately for relations between the United States and Britain, certain groups of Americans did rally to the Patriots' assistance. Most of that assistance took the form of financial support, but some Americans were willing to go even further, to take up arms in the Patriot cause. Some did so out of genuine sympathy for the Canadian rebels, but others were simply acting out earlier dreams of conquest in that region.

The activities of these meddling American citizens caused acute embarrassment to the United States government. President Van Buren, always an Anglophile, was personally repelled by the prospect of a third war between the two countries and fervently wished to eliminate any occasion for a quarrel. He was, however, limited in what he could do. Almost the entire regular army of the United States was still fighting the Seminoles in Florida, so he lacked the physical means to prevent his own citizens from getting involved across the Niagara River.

The crisis continued to grow. The Patriots in Upper Canada, beaten by British and Canadian authorities in the field, retreated across the Niagara River and took refuge in New York, where they began recruiting volunteers in Buffalo. Many who joined their ranks were American citizens,[1] headed by "General" Rensselaer Van Rensselaer, a son of the Solomon Van Rensselaer who had commanded the American invasion force at Queenston. Bands of Patriots then crossed the border from New York to Navy Island, between Buffalo and Niagara Falls, and there built a fortification on British soil. At the same time they optimistically declared the "independence of Canada from Britain." They procured the steamboat *Caroline,* which they used to deliver supplies to Navy Island from Fort Schlosser, on the New York side.

The crisis erupted into flame during the night of December 29, 1837, when a detachment of Canadians, loyal to the British, crossed the Niagara River from Chippewa Creek and stormed the *Caroline,* which was tied up at Fort Schlosser. They captured the steamer, set fire to it, and turned it loose to tumble over Niagara Falls.

One American was killed in the action, and the people of the New York frontier jumped to the erroneous conclusion that wounded Americans had been aboard the *Caroline* when she drifted over the falls. Patriot sympathizers made the most of the inaccurate information. They displayed the one body they had recovered, implying that it was that of one of those wounded who had supposedly gone over the falls.

Public sentiment in western New York immediately rose to the point where war was possible. An aroused American public refused to accept the Canadian argument that the *Caroline* was a pirate ship. Scott later claimed that as many as 200,000 Americans in the region had succumbed to the war fever.

On the evening of January 4, 1838, President Martin Van Buren hosted a political dinner at the White House, the purpose of which was to extend the olive branch to the Whigs for cooperation in this hour of national financial crisis. Most of the guests were prominent Whigs, and among them was Winfield Scott, who happened to be in Washington on a visit from his New York headquarters.

The President was late that evening, so late that the guests were becoming restive. Some of the Whigs began joking with their Democratic friends, asking whether the President had gone to resign his office. All the guests were, Scott later sniffed, "equally ignorant, merry, and hungry."

Eventually the President joined the group. Drawing Senator Henry Clay and General Scott off to one side, he whispered, "Blood has been shed." Then, turning to Scott, "You must go with all speed to the Niagara Frontier. The Secretary of War is now engaged in writing your instructions."

Scott left Washington early the next morning, bound for Albany and thence to Buffalo. His concern was not to negotiate any long-term peace; his urgent task was to prevent hot-headed Canadians from invading and sacking Buffalo, using a search for Canadian and American Patriots as an excuse. Lacking any regular troops on the northern frontier, the President had authorized Scott to call on the various governors for volunteers. Scott quickly decided that only the state of New York could help him on this short notice, as all the current difficulties were occurring at Buffalo. At Albany, Scott paused to visit Governor William Marcy, his friend from the days at Gouverneur Kemble's dinners. He prevailed on a somewhat reluctant Marcy to travel with him up the Mohawk to the frontier. By their personal presences, Scott argued, the governor and the general could most easily expedite the mobilization of the New York volunteers.

Scott and Marcy were able to take the new railroad train only as far as Utica, where the line terminated. There they bundled up and rode in open sleighs for the rest of the trip. They arrived at Buffalo, almost 220 miles to the west, late on January 7, only three days after Scott had first received his instructions in Washington. In his hurry, Scott had gone on without waiting for his staff. Following on his heels were Colonel John E. Wool, Colonel William J. Worth, and his aide, Lieutenant E. D. Keyes. The three arrived together the next evening after Scott.

The situation at Buffalo was every bit as serious as Scott had been told before leaving Washington. War with Britain was generally considered inevitable by those on the scene, and the Patriots and their supporters were eager for action. A serious Canadian incursion into Buffalo was not the immediate problem, however. The urgent need was to quell the activities of the American Patriot sympathizers.

Scott wasted no time. On January 13, just after his arrival at Buffalo, he visited Niagara Falls, there to view the scene of the *Caroline*'s destruction and to be seen doing so. He then sent Colonel Worth out to Navy Island to make contact with "General" Van Rensselaer, who was still holding out in that fort.* In the course of the conversations with Worth, Van Rensselaer agreed to return to Black Rock in order to talk with Scott.

Scott, who had at first held some sympathy for the Patriots, did not talk politics when the two men first got together. Instead he started out trying to convince the young rebel that his cause was hopeless from a military viewpoint. Van Rensselaer's men lacked organization and discipline; his water transportation was inadequate to support any sort of sustained operations. If he were able to land his troops at all on the Canadian shore, his little band would soon be cut to pieces.

As the discussions went on, Scott began to grow weary of Van Rensselaer, and he began to vent his anger at the young man's temerity in violating the laws of his own country. He admitted that he could take no direct action as yet, but as soon as a new law authorized him to do so, Scott would, as he put it, "lay my hands upon him and the others" in the capacity of *posse comitatus.*[2]

The warning had an effect. Van Rensselaer evacuated Navy Island the next day and arranged for his heavy guns to be removed from it. He set up a new camp just outside Buffalo. Van Rensselaer was later arrested by American authorities, only to be released immediately on bail.

A potentially dangerous—and totally unexpected—crisis then loomed, only a couple of days after Scott's interview with Van Rensselaer. It was caused largely by a misunderstanding. After the *Caroline* was sunk and burned, the Patriots on Navy Island had chartered a small craft, the *Barcelona,* to resupply them. Even after leaving the fort on the island, they still tried to keep the boat for other purposes. Scott saw this as an undesirable development, and since he was amply supplied with cash, he managed to outbid the Patriots and put the *Barcelona* in the service of the United States. He sent an agent to bring the ship to Buffalo for future use on Lake Erie. On January 15, however, he learned that the British authorities on the Canadian side were bent on de-

---

*Mr. Clinton Salt Brown, who was raised in Buffalo, advises that the Niagara River seldom freezes south of the rapids approaching Niagara Falls.

stroying her. Three British schooners had invaded American waters, apparently intending to take the *Barcelona* under fire when she came into view from the strait behind Grand Island (American).

Scott's dander was up at this violation of American waters. He sent a letter to "The Commanding Officer of the Armed British Vessels in the Niagara" advising that he and the governor of New York were on hand at Buffalo to "protect our own soil or waters from violation." He protested the presence of British vessels in United States waters and warned that he would be "obliged to consider a discharge of shot or shell from or into our waters, from the armed schooners of her Majesty, an act seriously compromising the neutrality of our two nations."

Scott then placed artillery batteries on the New York shore, trained point-blank on the British vessels, ready to fire. In case the British violated American "neutrality," that land-based artillery would damage, if not destroy, their vessels.

The responsibility for war or peace had thus been placed directly in the hands of the local British commander. But in so doing Scott had committed a serious blunder: he had failed to inform that commander that the *Barcelona* was now the property of the United States government. The British commander would feel humiliated if he allowed an American to force him to refrain from firing on a pirate ship.

As the *Barcelona* sailed up the Niagara toward Buffalo on January 16, Scott was waiting at Black Rock, ready to open fire with his artillery. The impending crisis was averted by the actions of a British officer who was with him. When that officer learned of the *Barcelona*'s status, he promptly left the scene to inform the British commander. The *Barcelona* came and went undisturbed beneath the muzzles of the British guns.

Scott still had to dissuade the Americans on the frontier from pursuing their aggressive designs. He was admirably fitted for that task. As the local hero from the War of 1812, he had not been forgotten. In his public appeals, impressive in his array of gold braid and utterly convinced of the rightness of his cause, he was in his element. He pulled out all the stops of emotion in addressing the public:

> Fellow citizens,—and I thank God that we have a common government as well as a common origin,—I stand before you without troops and without arms, save the blade by my side. I am, therefore, within your power. Some of you have

known me in other scenes, and all of you know that I am ready to do what my country and what duty demands. I tell you then, except it be over my body, you shall *not* pass this line—you shall *not* embark.[3]

His efforts were successful. He gave the citizens pause when they realized that he was there to prevent, not promote, conflict. The more sober citizens remembered his deeds of bravery on the frontier almost a quarter century earlier. Thus, while Scott had no means of suppressing the hotheads other than rhetoric and diplomacy, he made the most of those limited tools. He received a warm reception, "drawing forth," as he later descibed the scene, "the applause of listening multitudes."

When Scott believed he had successfully completed his mission, he departed, leaving the Buffalo frontier under the direct command of Colonel William Worth. He retraced his steps to Albany, where he was lavishly feted in the state capital, and then he returned to New York.

He stayed in New York only one night. Had the weather been better, he would not have remained even that long. When he arrived at his living quarters at the Astor House, he found a message from Worth advising that a new outbreak of troubles had erupted on the northwest frontier, this time in Ohio. There another group of Patriots was preparing to invade Canada, and Scott's presence was needed once more to prevent such a move.

Scott was ready to be back on the road for Buffalo that same evening, and he sent word at once for his aide, E. D. Keyes, to join him. Luckily for the less than zealous Keyes, whose quarters were in Brooklyn, the message did not reach him before ice had closed off the Hudson River. So Scott, Keyes, and Scott's servant, David, did not get off until the following evening at 7:00 P.M.

This trip to Buffalo and beyond was notable for its grueling travel conditions. Scott and his party were able to travel the first thirty miles without difficulty, but snow soon began to fall. It was 2:00 A.M. before they reached a tavern near West Point, where they stayed the night. The next evening they pushed on.

Scott made it a point to begin each day's journey in the evening after dark and to continue on until the night's objective had been reached. It was easier, somehow, for Scott and David to manage this schedule than it was for the young aide, who lacked their ability to sleep amid the jolts of the road. Keyes would usually wake up for good at dawn and watch Scott and David as they slept on. Scott, Keyes reported, "had the look of a tawny old lion slumbering quietly, but David's black visage would twitch as if he was uneasy. David was like a branch that had been wrenched from a tropical tree and carried up to the frozen zone—he was out of place."

One morning, however, Keyes managed to sleep longer than Scott. They had been three successive nights in a stage coach and were making their way slowly through deep snow. When Keyes opened his eyes, he saw his chief regarding him with "compassion"; his own face, Keyes later admitted, was probably "sorrowful to behold at the moment." Quietly "the general took out from his pocket a handful of parched corn and dropped five or six grains into my hand, one after another, his eye fixed on mine with an expression of affection like that of a mother watching her suffering child."

Scott and his party reached Monroe, Michigan, on February 25, 1838. It had taken only a week after leaving New York, which was an astonishing pace. There he found that Colonel Hugh Brady, in charge in that area, had the situation under full control and was in hot pursuit of the local Patriot force. So the general returned to Cleveland and not long after was back in Albany. There Scott collapsed, the fatigue and irregular eating finally proving too much for him. After a week of recuperation, he took his party back to New York, arriving around March 21.

The Patriots' efforts now petered out. The Canadian government promised to take severe action against any Patriots they captured, whether Canadian or American. President Martin Van Buren cooperated by issuing a warning: any Americans apprehended by the British while engaged in criminal violations of law need not look to their own country for protection. The crisis was over.

Involvement in peacemaking was a new path for Winfield Scott. He took to it readily. From that time on, his admirers could see him as more than a brilliant general, impressive as that might be. He was now also the "Great Pacificator."

19

≫━✠━≪

Along the Trail of Tears

*A sympathetic Scott fails to alleviate the pain of the
Cherokees as they head west.*

> They never showed their grief in noisy demonstration, not by
> tears, but it could be seen with chilling effect in the lines of sad-
> ness which despair had engraven on the faces of nearly all of
> them. For a moment I regarded myself as a trespasser, as one of a
> gang of robbers, and in my effort to justify my position the spec-
> tre of Avarice arose upon my imagination.
> —E. D. Keyes, *Fifty Years' Observation of Men and Events*

THOUGH WINFIELD Scott never admitted that his conduct of the
Seminole campaign had been anything less than exemplary, he nevertheless retained a certain dissatisfaction, a sense of incompleteness, with regard to that failed mission. Desiring another chance to bring the war to a
close, he wrote Secretary of War Poinsett in September 1837, asking to be re-
assigned to Florida. After all, he argued, Florida lay within the area of his
Eastern Command, and most of the troops normally assigned to him were
deployed there. Moreover, Thomas Jesup, who was currently up to his ears
directing that struggle, was junior to him.

Poinsett and President Martin Van Buren refused even to consider Scott's
request. Sending "Old Fuss and Feathers," as Scott was sometimes called, to
replace Jesup or to reassume command over him would be a sure guarantee
of more trouble. They left him in his headquarters in New York.

On April 6, 1838, however, a mere month after Scott returned from his three-month mission on the Canadian frontier, he received another mission. He was to supervise the removal of the Cherokees from their present homes in the southeastern United States to new locations in Arkansas and Oklahoma, beyond the Mississippi. His deadline would be tight: the move must be completed by May 23, only six weeks away.

When Scott told his friends in New York about his new task, some of them were concerned; he had burned his fingers in the Florida campaign, and they rightly feared that Indian removal, wherever it occurred, offered no opportunity for a soldier to enhance his reputation. It was, in fact, fraught with hazards. But Scott was unworried, at least in public. No call to duty ever fazed him, and he dismissed the fears of his friends with his usual cheery rejoinder: "I like difficulties." He proceeded to Washington, where he was allowed to write out his own instructions, the President signing his draft immediately.

Before leaving the capital, Scott received a visit from Chief John Ross, who at the age of forty-eight had been the Cherokee "principal chief" for the past ten years.[1] Ross was only one-eighth Cherokee by blood and spoke the Cherokee language only imperfectly, but he was performing a task the bulk of his people wanted done: attempting by legal means to persuade the authorities in Washington to cancel the impending removal. Ross saw hope in his cause, despite the harsh fate that had already befallen other tribes, especially the Seminoles. Opposition to the removals among the American public was growing. Former president John Quincy Adams, who had now become a representative from Massachusetts, was using the removal issue as a major part of his campaign to resist Jackson-type measures and to promote human rights. The removal act of 1830 had been passed by only a very narrow margin despite all the pressure that Jackson had mustered. The vote had, moreover, been cast along sectional lines. So Ross persisted.

Ross pressed Scott passionately with the Cherokee viewpoint, trying to dissuade the general from undertaking an "illegal" mission. Scott, however, had his orders. Despite Ross's troubling arguments, he could only listen but then go ahead with his plans.

Scott then headed south to the governmental Cherokee Agency, at Athens, Tennessee, where he drew up his strategy for the removal. Basically, his concept was, "By the strength of numbers and measures, to make resistance hopeless." Territories in parts of four states were involved: Georgia, Alabama, North Carolina, and Tennessee. Scott divided the area into three operational sections: the western, central, and eastern. In each he planned to set up a number of large collection camps, in which the Cherokees would be concentrated for the first phase. Later the Indians would be transferred in groups to debarkation points on the major waterways of the region, from which they would be sent to the West by riverboat. Scott was careful to specify that the collection points were to be provided with shade, water, and security.

To enforce such a plan on an unwilling people, Scott needed a strong military force. General-in-Chief Alexander Macomb appreciated that need and assured Scott that adequate numbers of regular troops would eventually be provided: the 4th Infantry, the 4th Artillery, and six companies of dragoons from Florida, 3,000 men in all. These regulars were to be commanded by Colonel William Lindsay, who had earned Scott's confidence in the Florida campaign. Lindsay had preceded Scott to Athens and had already done much preparatory work—stocking supplies and setting up separate collecting posts—but the regular troops were scattered and could not arrive immediately. The various collecting posts, twenty-three in all, would have to be manned temporarily by militia. Still Scott believed he had all the resources he needed.

On May 8, 1838, Scott issued a proclamation to the Cherokees that he believed would bring them thronging to the collection points. "Cherokees!" he proclaimed, "The President of the United States has sent me, with a powerful army, to cause you, in obedience to the Treaty of 1835, to join that band of your people who are already established in prosperity on the other side of the Mississippi." He had no power to delay the move, he continued; they must be on the move before the next moon passed away. His army had overpowering strength, but his soldiers were their friends. He ended by reminding them that he was an "old warrior" who had seen much carnage and was hoping that the Cherokees would not force him to see them suffer by disobeying the order to move. "May the God of both [Cherokees and whites]," he wrote in finishing, "preserve them long in peace and friendship with each other."[2]

Scott no doubt believed every word of this proclamation, and he was therefore astonished when he realized a few days later that his words had failed to make any significant impression. The Cherokees, he now learned, were still counting on Chief John Ross to induce the Van Buren administration to cancel the removal or at least delay it. So long as the Indians retained any hope of success on Ross's part, Scott's edict would be ineffectual. As May

23 approached, therefore, only a few families reported to the collection points. A full 12,000 still remained behind in their homes.

Scott was furious. He was not so angry with Ross as he was with the War Department, for continuing to listen to him. "I cannot suppose," Scott wrote to Poinsett, ". . . that the Department would, without reference to me, so soon take the whole subject out of my hands." He complained that his proclamation had initially received favorable response among the Indians, but that rumors of action in Washington had destroyed its effect. Scott still failed to appreciate the depth of the Cherokee determination to resist.

Of the five southeastern Indian tribes, the Cherokees presented the best case for remaining on their lands. As they had assimilated white ways—religion, language, and clothing—they were viewed as "the most highly civilized of all." Like their Seminole kin in Florida, they were farmers. Some were wealthy, with impressive plantations; many were slaveholders.* In contrast with the Creeks, they had sided with the United States in the War of 1812, and at least two of their principal chiefs, John Ross and Major Ridge, had fought alongside Andrew Jackson at Horseshoe Bend in early 1814. One of their intellectuals, Chief Sequoia, had developed a Cherokee alphabet, and with it they had, in 1828, drawn up their own constitution, based on that of the United States. They had established their own newspaper, the *Cherokee Phoenix*.[3] Their chiefs, most of whom were of mixed blood, were known almost exclusively by their anglicized, not their native Indian names.[4] Based on their close integration in the white community, the Cherokees had every reason to desire—and expect—to be allowed to live where they were, unmolested.

Unfortunately, the Cherokee homeland was located in areas heavily populated by whites.[5] When the settlers began to covet their land, therefore, the victims were overpowered by sheer numbers. Of the four states involved, Georgia, where gold had been discovered on Cherokee land, was the most insistent on removal; it had passed an act on December 19, 1829, incorporating much of the Cherokee Nation into Georgia. It preceded Andrew Jackson's removal act of 1830 by almost a year. Georgia's governor, George R. Gilmer, did not consider the law to be radical in the slightest degree, and

---

*The institution of slavery, despite its odium, was a sign of social acceptance in those days, a "white" institution.

without waiting for the final passage of Jackson's Indian act, he began agitating for Cherokee removal immediately.[6]

Jackson, sympathetic to Georgia's position, began a gradual removal that same year, 1830, sending small parties from Georgia to Arkansas by boat from Gunter's Landing (present-day Guntersville), Alabama, all the way to Oklahoma.[7] Prominent among those who migrated early were the celebrated Chief Sequoia and Chief John Jolly, the adopted stepfather of Sam Houston. From that year on, the Cherokee Nation would be split between the western and eastern branches.

But despite the small movements westward, the vast bulk of the Cherokees remained adamant against moving to the West. Unable to mount armed resistance like that of the Seminoles in Florida, and unable to dent the determination of Andrew Jackson, they resorted to action in the United States Congress and the courts. There they met with legal but not practical success. Chief Justice John Marshall declared the several Indian nations to be "distinct political communities, having territorial boundaries within which their authority is exclusive." Andrew Jackson, however, responded defiantly. "John Marshall," he said, "has rendered his decision; now let him enforce it."

The split among the Cherokees became more pronounced by the emergence of a small group of Cherokee leaders known as the Ridge-Boudinot faction. Major Ridge, whose first name derived from the military rank Jackson had given him in the Creek War, was the titular leader of this group, a sixty-year-old man deeply respected in his tribe. His son, John Ridge, had been educated in white schools, as had his nephew, Elias Boudinot. Both John and Elias had married white women from Connecticut, whom they had met when they went to school there. Elias Boudinot was the editor of the *Cherokee Phoenix* in New Echota, Georgia. This group, unlike the Ross faction, advocated migration.

The Ridge-Boudinot faction were not traitors, nor were they dupes of the whites. Through many years they, like John Ross, had fought fiercely to keep the Cherokees in their eastern homes. Finally, however, they had despaired of attaining justice from the government in Washington. They also opposed Ross's idea that the Cherokees might apply for American citizenship in order to stay on their lands. To the Ridges and Boudinot, despite their American wives, "amalgamation" into the white society of Georgia was "too horrid for serious contemplation."[8]

The rift became official on December 29, 1835, the day after Dade and his men were massacred by the Seminoles in Florida. On that day the Ridge-Boudinot faction met with the Reverend J. F. Schermerhorn, the United States representative to the Indians, and signed the controversial Schermerhorn Treaty, which called for the movement of the eastern Cherokees to western lands. As remuneration for their abandoned property, the United States agreed to pay the sum of $5 million for the whole of the Cherokee lands in the East. Unfortunately for all, the treaty did not represent the views of the bulk of the eastern Cherokees.

Once the Schermerhorn Treaty was signed, President Andrew Jackson recognized it. He also realized that he would need a military man to enforce it. As Scott was involved in Florida, Jackson appointed Brigadier General John E. Wool, hero of Queenstown, to supervise the preliminary plans. But Wool sympathized with the victims of this enterprise. On February 18, 1837, after meeting with the Cherokees, he reported that they were "almost universally opposed to the treaty and maintain that they never made such a treaty." He described the "heartrending" meeting bluntly, bitterly concluding,

> If I could, I would remove every Indian tomorrow beyond the reach of the white men who, like vultures, are watching, ready to pounce upon their prey and strip them of everything they have.

Wool's attitude, predictably, infuriated the Georgians and Alabamians alike. The governor of Alabama trumped up charges accusing him, among other things, of usurping the powers of civil tribunals. A court of inquiry vindicated Wool in September 1837, but the proceedings left Jackson without a military commander. He left the Cherokee removal problem to his successor, Van Buren, who called on Scott the following April.

Along with the resistance of the Cherokees, Scott was suffering other vexations. None of the 3,000 promised regulars, he learned, would arrive in time for the first roundup of Cherokees into the collection points. He would therefore be forced to use his 4,000 militiamen. In the absence of voluntary moves by the Indians, the militia would have to roust them from their homes. He set the date for the first phase, the removal of Cherokees from Georgia, for May 26, 1838. The roundups in Tennessee and Alabama would take place ten days later.

While facing these practical matters, Scott was feeling troubled about the justice of the removal itself. There was no question that he would do his duty, but he was shaken by the fact that an executive decision had decreed an action that many Americans considered inhumane and even illegal. And, thanks partly to the efforts of his old friend John Quincy Adams, the question was dividing along sectional lines, with the New England states blaming the landowners of the South for insisting on carrying it out. Mutual distrust and resentment between Southerners and Northerners was an unpleasant by-product.

Scott's ill humor came to the attention of his outspoken aide, E. D. Keyes, an unabashed Yankee himself. One day a young artillery captain under Scott's command requested a leave of absence to visit his wife, who was seriously ill. Scott not only refused to grant the leave; he also couched his refusal in insulting terms. Keyes knew that the captain, a New Englander, had been complaining about the unjustness of the removal and imputing it to "Southern politicians and land grabbers." Keyes delayed in transmitting Scott's orders, claiming difficulties in getting the letter copied, until the general had benefited from a good horseback ride and a chance to calm down. During the ride Keyes broached his question: "General, don't you think the letter you wrote to the Captain was a little severe?" Scott answered abruptly: "You think so, do you?" Nothing more was said for the rest of the ride. On return, however, Scott tore the letter up and wrote another. He still, however, refused the captain's request for a leave of absence.[9]

In all the impasse facing him, Scott could only reassure the Cherokees of decent treatment. His instructions to the militiamen who were going to enforce the initial move to the collecting points left no doubt of his sincerity along that line. His official order, issued on May 17, emphasized how important it was that the soldiers, in executing their duty, do so in a humane manner. He reviewed the high points of Cherokee history and admitted candidly that four-fifths of them were against moving to the West. Calling any acts of harshness and cruelty utterly "abhorrent to the generous sympathies of the whole American people," he admonished his troops not to fire on any fugitives they might apprehend unless they should "make a stand to resist."

He spared no details: Indian horses or ponies should be employed to carry those Indians who were too sick or feeble to march. "Infants, superannuated persons, lunatics, and women in a helpless condition will all, in the removal, require peculiar attention, which the brave and humane will seek to adopt to the necessities of the several cases."

The date for the enforced removal of the Georgia Cherokees was kept confidential in order to prevent large numbers of people from escaping into the hinterlands. When the plan was put into effect on May 26, 1838, the fear of flight proved groundless; the Cherokees refused to leave their homes until forced. The process of removing the victims was carried out in a manner far less generous and humane than Scott had visualized. Many of the militiamen entrusted with the task stood to benefit from the removal, as they had already laid claim to the Indian properties. As a result, the scenes of uprooting were chaotic at best and brutal at worst.

One contemporary account describes Indian families being routed at dinner by gleaming bayonets, driven along weary trails to the stockades, and turning back to witness their "homes in flames, fired by the lawless rabble that followed on the heels of the soldiers to loot and pillage," their livestock driven off even before the soldiers had started the Indians on their journeys.

The abuse continued even after the Cherokees had arrived at the embarkation points. Many captors were reported to be driving the people "with whooping and bellowing, like cattle, through rivers, allowing them no time to take off their shoes and stockings." The Cherokees gave some futile resistance. At Ross's Landing some of the people refused to board the boats, so "the soldiers rushed in and drove the victims into the boats regardless of the cries and agonies of the poor helpless sufferers." Families sometimes became separated when children were sent off and parents left behind.

Scott and his small staff tried to supervise these activities by traveling from place to place, but the distances were too great for them to observe much. Apparently they saw none of the extreme abuses, for Scott was surprisingly sanguine when he reported on the operation. Though he later admitted to "painful anxiety" as he watched the Georgia troops collect the Indians, he claimed that "food in abundance had been provided at the depots, and wagons accompanied every detachment of troops." Based on his limited observation, he congratulated the Georgians for having "distinguished themselves by their humanity and tenderness." Though he admitted that he had "never witnessed a scene of deeper pathos" as thousands of men, women, and children, some of them sick, were brought into the collection camps, he laid a good bit of the blame at the feet of the Cherokees for "obstinately refusing to prepare for the removal." Many arrived, he reported, "half-starved, but refused the food that was pressed upon them."[10]

The operation, however, was at least bloodless, and nearly all of the Cherokees were soon collected. Most were taken to intermediate holding areas at first, to be transferred to the points of departure. The three points of departure were the Cherokee agent's office at Athens, Tennessee;* Ross's Landing, Nashville; and Gunter's Landing, Guntersville, Alabama. All three points were located on navigable rivers, along which the Cherokees could be comfortably delivered by water.

By mid-June 1838, about three weeks after the movement of Cherokees from Georgia had begun, most of the regular troops promised by Poinsett and Macomb had arrived. Scott therefore felt free to discharge his militiamen. He sent them home with the thanks of the United States for "promptitude, zeal, and humanity" and then, with his regulars, set out to complete his task. With the Cherokees cleared out of Georgia, Scott now hoped that those located farther west, in Alabama, on hearing of the "just, and humane, even caring" treatment their brethren had enjoyed in Georgia, would leave their homes and report voluntarily to the camps by the twentieth of July.

Scott was doomed to sustain another disappointment. By July 13 he discovered that the Cherokees in the west had likewise done nothing to prepare for such a move. It therefore took his regulars another ten days to round them all up.

By August 1838, only 3,000 Cherokees had left Georgia and Tennessee by water; an estimated 13,000 still remained at the camps. The hot season had arrived, and the rivers were at such low levels that they were no longer navigable. Scott was therefore faced with the grim prospect of sending the refugees overland, under guard, in the dreaded heat of the summer. He was saved from that prospect by the arrival of a deputation of Cherokee chiefs who asked that he delay their departure until the end of the hot weather. Scott saw the merit in their request, so he stretched his authority and held those Cherokees who were still in the camps until the first of September. In the meantime he took steps to maintain order and sanitation, even persuading some Indians to submit to vaccination. He also rigidly regulated the sale of whiskey.

In mid-July John Ross had given up trying to influence Washington. But on his return he carried with him authority for the Cherokees to travel west under their own auspices, unarmed, and free of supervision by United

---

*This was a camp on the Hiwassee River. Scott described this spot as "a camp twelve miles by four; well-shaded, watered with perennial springs, and flanked by the Hiwassee."

States troops. The chiefs, elated over this removal of their shackles, agreed to supply their own subsistence and provide their own supervisors. Scott was much relieved to have this burden taken off him, and he awarded to the Cherokee Council the contract to remove the 11,000 people still in his camps. Having made this arrangement, he sent out a message admonishing all the people living along the route of march to show the Indians "sympathy and kind offices."

Although this agreement served the best interests of the Cherokees and the soldiers, it aroused the protests of white contractors, steamboat owners, and others who were profiting by providing food and services to the government. So Scott once more became a target of abuse, even though he was completely in the right. One of the protesters was old Andrew Jackson himself, who wrote from the Hermitage on August 23 to Felix Grundy, United States attorney general:

> The contract with Ross must be arrested, or you may rely upon it, the expense and other evils will shake the popularity of the Administration to its center. What madness and folly to have anything to do with Ross when the agent was proceeding well with the removal on the principles of economy that would have saved at least 100 per cent from what the contract with Ross will cost. . . . The contract with Ross *must be arrested* and General [Nathaniel] Smith be left to superintend the removal.

Scott did not flinch in the face of the protests, however. He observed that the morale of the Indians was improving under their own leadership, and his own soldiers were glad to be relieved of the responsibilities of the move. He was well aware of the increased costs to the government that the Ross contract entailed, but in his mind the "almost universal cheerfulness" among the Cherokees was worth it.

By this time Scott's mission was largely completed. Yet, despite the fact that his wife Maria was reportedly ill, he determined to accompany one group of Cherokees overland to Arkansas informally, only as an observer. Each contingent followed a slightly different route, depending on its starting point. Scott chose to join the first "company" of a thousand people, including both Cherokees and black slaves, which left Athens for the overland route to Arkansas on October 1, 1838. Its route was from Athens, overland by way of Murfreesboro, Nashville, and Hopkinsville (Kentucky) to a passage between the Ohio and Mississippi rivers, thence to Jackson, Springfield, and

Cape Girardeau, all in Missouri, and finally Batesville, Arkansas. Some of the Cherokees with whom Scott traveled were provided for sufficiently, wearing the clothes of prosperous planters, carrying their belongings in wagons. But most of them were bedraggled.[11] Since by agreement they traveled unguarded by United States troops, Scott released three of his five regiments of regulars, sending them to New York and Florida, where they were needed.

Scott's involvement with the move ended on October 23, 1838. An urgent message from Poinsett awaited him at Nashville, ordering him back to Washington. The Patriots were making trouble again on the northern frontier. He left immediately for his third trip as a peacemaker to that region.

The story of the Cherokee removal is known in history and legend as the Trail of Tears, partly because of the injustice of the whites in uprooting a whole people and partly because of the sufferings and the high death rate of the miserable Indians and blacks as they staggered across the country in winter weather.* Out of the 13,000 people who started moving in October, nearly 2,000 died. The total deaths during the collection period and the long weeks of waiting in the camps came to 4,000.

In the years that followed, the Cherokees were to establish a flourishing community in Oklahoma and Arkansas, but the bitterness engendered in them by their treatment at the hands of the white man, which culminated in the Trail of Tears, did not quickly subside, if it has to this day.

Shortly after the Cherokees arrived on the Arkansas River, in Oklahoma, an unofficial Cherokee council met to try Major Ridge, his son John, and Elias Boudinot in absentia. The bitter survivors of the trek condemned this faction, whose members had avoided hardship by emigrating early by water. The council decreed death for all three in accordance with an old Cherokee "blood law," which forbade dealing with the white man on pain of death. Three assassination parties were sent out, and the Ridges and Boudinot were brutally murdered.

Scott was spared the horror and sadness of the latter stages of the Trail of Tears. He had performed his duty; the Cherokee move had been bloodless and as comfortable as it was in his power to make it. He had sincerely intended to share their hardships on the trip west. The Cherokees still remember Scott as the one American who tried to minimize their grief as best he could.

---

*The first company left on October 1, the last as late as November 23. Arrivals in Arkansas and Oklahoma were between January 4 and March 23, 1839.

20

☙❧

Diplomacy and Politics

Scott and a British friend avert war between their countries
for a second time.

> As a statesman, especially in that department of statesmanship
> which exerts itself to uphold the dignity of a nation in its inter-
> nal and external relations . . . neither the exercise of official vigi-
> lance and power nor the complexity of negotiations ever fatigued
> him, nor was watchfulness ever at fault. In discussing interna-
> tional questions with the representatives of foreign powers . . .
> Scott displayed an amount of information and *finesse* as a diplo-
> matist which was surprising.
> —E. D. Keyes, *Fifty Years' Observation of Men and Events*

THE RENEWED troubles on the Canadian border were explosive, so explosive that Scott gave up any plans to visit his wife, Maria, who was ill
with a bronchial condition. A Washington physician had recommended
that she go abroad, where the spas of Europe would be favorable for her condition. Without trying to meet with Scott, she took their four surviving
daughters—Virginia, Cornelia, Adeline Camilla, and Marcella—and departed for Europe. Scott would live as a bachelor for the next five years.[1]

Scott went to the frontier by way of Frankfort, Kentucky, and Columbus
and Cleveland, Ohio, arriving at the latter on December 5, 1838. At Frankfort and Columbus he made arrangements with the respective governors for
volunteers, ones chosen from those known to be "uninfected" with the virus
of hostility toward Canada. He also picked up federal deputies and United
States marshals, men who possessed the civil authority to arrest agitators—

which they would do under Scott's instructions, it was understood. Scott approached his new assignment with serene confidence. The Patriots, as he saw the situation, had merely "taken advantage of his absence in the South" to renew their attempts to break into the Canadas.[2]

The Canadian border, as Scott discovered when he reached Cleveland, was in a state of high agitation. A group of Patriots, based in the United States, had recently raided the city of Windsor, across the St. Clair River from Detroit, and in the action the Canadians had captured four of them and shot them without a trial. The American public was in such a fury as to challenge even Scott's abilities as a pacifier.

Once more Scott was called upon to face down the agitators with words. At Cleveland, Sandusky, and Detroit he addressed impassioned crowds, calming them down enough so they would leave the question of war or peace to the authorities in Washington. They were too excited, however, for him to approach them directly. First he gave assurances that he would be with them in case of war. Together they would go "into it headforemost, and the man who stands in the front rank will find me standing shoulder to shoulder with him!" The people loved such bombast, even calculated bombast, and gradually they became content to listen to arguments for due process in the course of national affairs. Scott spent several weeks engaged in such activities on the frontier. He went eastward from Buffalo to Albany, and kept going until he reached northern Vermont.

In the meantime, a dispute in Maine was beginning to constitute a far greater threat to peace than even the actions of the hot-headed Patriots. In Maine those contemplating war were not mere rabble-rousers or fanatics; provincial and state governments were ready to fight. The issue was the boundary between Maine and the Canadian province of New Brunswick, one of the loose ends set aside in the efforts to attain peace after the Revolutionary War and subsequently ignored in the Treaty of Ghent ending the War of 1812.

The so-called "disputed territories" were not prime farmlands; they were unpopulated empty forests. In general, the territories covered the area south of the St. Lawrence River, west and south of the St. John River, and north of the Aroostook.* Though nobody cared much for the land itself, both sides

---

*The St. John cuts through the disputed territory when it flows west to east. When it then turns southward, it runs through New Brunswick, east of Maine.

coveted the timber that grew on it. On January 23, 1839, Governor John Fairfield reported at least five instances of Canadian timber poachers in the area, and a few days later he sent a posse in to stop them. Canadian provincial troops from New Brunswick intercepted the posse, however, and captured Rufus McIntire, the American agent who had been sent to represent Fairfield. In the confused melee the American posse managed to capture the Royal Warden of the territory.

A few days later, in mid-February, Fairfield notified the Maine legislature of what had happened and informed them that he had sent reinforcements to bolster his beleaguered posse. British Major General Sir John Harvey, lieutenant governor of Canada, responded by calling up a force of 1,000 Canadian militia. The populations on both sides of the border were now up in arms, ready for war to satisfy their honor.

Scott was in Vermont when he learned of the governor's message to the Maine legislature, and he realized at once that something would have to be done. Lacking instructions to cover this turn of events, he prudently left for Washington. He arrived in the nation's capital on February 23, 1839, without, as he put it, "having been in a recumbent position for eighty hours." Presumably he had slept sitting up in his carriage, as always.

Everyone in the Van Buren administration, Scott later recalled, was alarmed at the prospect of getting into a war that nobody wanted but that nobody would back away from. Matters were made much worse by the lack of any sort of plan. Nothing had been done to prepare for war with Britain; both countries had been glad to ignore the issue of the disputed territories for the twenty-four years since the end of the War of 1812. All Van Buren could issue by way of instruction was that Scott do all he could to avert an "untoward mistake." Scott was not optimistic. "Mr. President," he warned, "if you want war, I need only look on in silence. The Maine people will make it for you fast and hot enough. But if *peace* be your wish, I can give no assurance of success. The difficulties in the way will be formidable."

The President's reply was terse: "Peace with honor."

Though Scott was anxious to get back on the road to Maine, he was detained for a few days to help push two pieces of legislation through Congress. Both bills were important. One authorized the call-up of 50,000 militia for terms of six months, instead of the three months that had tied Scott's hands in Florida. The other was to grant him a sum of $10 million credit for use in negotiating a settlement on the frontier.

Acting as a legislative lobbyist may have seemed a strange role for a military man, but Scott was becoming an influential political as well as a military figure. The financial panic of 1837 had swept the Whigs into control of the Congress, and the testimony of Scott, as a recognized Whig and the country's most prominent general, was bound to carry weight. Beyond doubt his efforts at least contributed heavily to the administration's success in getting the wherewithal to support its actions on the border.

Scott left Washington accompanied only by his assistant adjutant general, Captain Robert Anderson, and his aide, Lieutenant Keyes. By March 2, 1839, the three were in Boston. There Scott was lavishly feted by the governor and invited to speak before the legislature, which he did graciously. He was not, however, much concerned with that appearance. The Massachusetts legislators were no problem to him; it was the seething emotions of the "down-easters" of Maine that Scott had to contend with.

When Scott arrived at Augusta, Maine, he was quickly made aware that the enthusiastic crowds were greeting him as a potential war leader, not as a peacemaker. A couple of Scott's former soldiers from Lundy's Lane made themselves conspicuous, and one, as Scott later put it, advertised him as "the greatest man-killer extant;—one who had killed off, in Canada, more men than Great Britain had there in that war." More significant than the enthusiasm of a hot-headed veteran, however, was the statement of a member of the Senate Chamber of Maine, who declared just before Scott's arrival: "I speak advisedly when I say, that if the contemplated visit of General Scott to Maine is only to persuade a withdrawal of our troops from the disputed territory, or a relinquishment of our present position, he might as well stay away."[3]

This universal mindset was too strong for Scott to resist at first blush, so he decided to bide his time. When asked to make a speech to a boisterous crowd, he declined. He acknowledged the cheers and then, with unaccustomed modesty, saluted and went his way.

As with all these disputes on the Canadian frontier, Scott was well aware that he was not addressing the long-term arguments over the disputed territory himself: that would be the task of the governmental leaders in London and Washington. His sole goal was to damp down the passions then flaming so that the statesmen of both Britain and the United States could address the issues calmly. Even that limited objective would be difficult to attain.

Three echelons of government were involved. One was the national level—Washington and London—at which both sides sincerely sought peace. Another was the state/province level—Maine and New Brunswick—where Scott's problems would be complicated by local political attitudes. The third level of government was the military, which included the ranks of militia signed up for the purpose by the governors of Maine and New Brunswick.

The two national governments had already made one effort to stave off the crisis. On February 27, President Van Buren sent a message to Congress that introduced a memorandum of understanding signed by the secretary of state and the British minister in Washington. Full of flowery and pious sentiments, the memorandum called for a temporary solution, agreeing that pending further negotiations,

> Her Majesty's officers will not seek to expel, by military force, the armed party which has been sent by Maine into the district bordering on the Aroostook river; but the government of Maine will, voluntarily, and without needless delay, withdraw beyond the bounds of the disputed territory any armed force now within them.
>
> The civil officers of Maine and New Brunswick, who had been taken into custody by the opposite parties, shall be released.

Though this agreement secured the release of the civil officials of both sides, the citizens of Maine found its provisions far too conciliatory; to them it practically constituted surrender. And they had a point; the memorandum committed the Americans to do exactly what the British were demanding, to withdraw from the disputed territory; all the British agreed to was to desist from attacking them while they were doing so. Washington had not been much of a help.

The body that needed to be convinced to support Scott's peaceful course was the Maine legislature. Before Scott could begin any negotiations with the British military (who would make the ultimate decisions on the other side), he had to be assured that any promises he made would be subsequently honored by those for whom he was negotiating. Arranging such assurances would be complicated by considerations of internal American politics.

At that time the Democrats, in the Andrew Jackson tradition, were generally more disposed to an aggressive foreign policy than were the Whigs.[4] The situation in Maine, however, presented a special case, for the local population was so aroused as to supplant traditional party attitudes. No Maine politician, Whig or Democrat, dared to appear "soft" on the disputed territory issue. Neither could any party be counted on to support a peaceful solution, much less take the lead in promoting it. The most that could be asked was for both to place full trust in Scott to act for them.

Obtaining the trust of both parties was a difficult matter, for neither wanted a member of the other camp to obtain credit for any satisfactory solution.* Here Scott as an individual had an advantage; his party affiliation was not widely known outside Washington; he was thought of as a general, indifferent to politics. The local Whigs were therefore somewhat skeptical of him. After all, had he not been sent on this mission by a Democratic president? Scott found himself being received coolly among them.

Scott immediately began intriguing with the recently elected governor, John Fairfield, a Democrat, who was one of the very few on the scene who knew that Scott was really an ardent Whig. With Fairfield's knowledge and concurrence, Scott arranged for a Whig friend, Congressman George Evans, to host a dinner in his honor, the guest list to include both the governor and the most influential legislators of both parties. At the table, Evans placed Scott among the Whigs and the Democrats around the governor. At first the Whigs were somewhat unfriendly, but at an opportune time, Evans came around and whispered in the ear of one that General Scott was "as good a Whig as the best of them."

The resulting surprise gave Scott his entrée. A genial man around the dinner table, generous with good fellowship and compliments, Scott was soon completely accepted by legislators of both parties. "A feast is a great peacemaker," Scott later wrote, "worth more than all the arts of diplomacy." By March 20, 1839, the Maine legislature had passed a resolution placing the border question in the hands of the "national authorities," which meant the President's representative, Scott.

Fortunately for both sides in this border dispute, the key military players were two reasonable major generals, Winfield Scott and Sir John Harvey. So long as these two men could keep their heads—and keep the militia under their commands in line—blood over this trivial matter would not be shed. Happenstance played a favorable part. Harvey, though Scott's enemy on the Niagara frontier in 1813, had since become his personal friend. (The friendship had been prompted, no doubt, by Scott's magnanimous gesture in purchasing and returning the stolen picture of Harvey's young bride after the raid on York.) The two men had corresponded from time to time.

---

*Recent elections in Maine had put the governor's seat and the majority of the legislature in Democratic hands, though the Whig minority was a strong force to contend with.

On March 21, 1839, Scott sent a message to Sir John in which he himself assumed the onus of making the first move toward conciliation. In a formal and flowery letter, Scott said he

> had the honor . . . to invite from his Excellency Major-General Sir John Harvey, Lieutenant-Governor &c, &c., a general declaration to this effect: That it is not the intention of the Lieutenant-Governor of Her Britannic Majesty's Province of New Brunswick . . . to take military possession of [the disputed] territory, or to seek, by military force, to expel therefrom the armed civil *posse* or the troops of Maine.

"Should the undersigned have the honor to be favored with such declaration or assurance," the letter went on, he undertook to deliver it to the governor of the state of Maine and did "not doubt" that the governor would authorize him to send back a corresponding pacific declaration to the effect that

> it is not the intention of the Governor of Maine . . . to interrupt the usual communications between that province and Her Majesty's Upper provinces; and that he is willing, in the mean time, to leave the questions of possession and jurisdiction as they at present stand.

With that understanding, Scott's letter went on, the governor of Maine would quickly withdraw Maine forces from the territory, leaving only a land agent with a small civil posse to protect the timber that had already been cut. Scott added a warm personal renewal of his "ancient high consideration and respect."[5]

Happily for everyone concerned, Sir John Harvey had no more desire for war than did Scott. On March 23, he wrote Scott a warm letter, far more relaxed than Scott's to him. Addressing him simply as "My dear General Scott," he expressed his "gratification" and added,

> My reliance upon *you*, my dear general, has led me to give my willing assent to the proposition which you have made yourself the very acceptable means of conveying to me; and I trust that as far as the province and the state respectively are concerned, an end will be put by it to all border disputes, and a way opened to an amicable adjustment of the national questions involved. I shall hope to receive the confirmation of this arrangement on the part of the State of Maine at as early a time as may be practicable.

Harvey appended a more formal acceptance of Scott's proposal.

That exchange of messages completely defused the situation. Within three days the Maine legislature had accepted the truce, and the governor at once disbanded the militia. It remained for Secretary of State Daniel Webster and Lord Ashburton, three years later, to arrive at a diplomatic compromise in the treaty that bears their names. A useless war had been averted, and the accomplishment was Scott's almost alone.

Sir John Harvey was certainly of that opinion. Shortly after the end of the negotiations, he wrote Scott saying, "I have long entertained a secret wish to procure for you a *tender* at least of some mark of the distinguished estimation in which your character and services ought to be held by the Sovereigns of England—if your institutions should present no difficulty." Unfortunately for Scott, American institutions did present difficulties, and he was forced—regretfully, no doubt—to refuse. The constitutional provision against accepting foreign presents and titles was being scrupulously observed.

When Scott left Augusta in early April 1839, his reputation was at an all-time high. Almost single-handedly he had prevented a needless war between the United States and Great Britain, both at Buffalo and in Maine. Though President Martin Van Buren and the Democrats would soon have cause to downplay his services for political reasons, his name was once more before the public as a hero.

On the way back to New York, Scott and his party stopped for a week at Boston. At a dinner given in Scott's honor, the general met a distinguished Unitarian preacher, William Ellery Channing. At age sixty, Channing wielded great influence in theological circles, being known among other things for having coined the term "Unitarian." Declining health had forced him to give up many of his functions as a practicing clergyman, but his influence with the pen far outshadowed any he might have had in a pulpit.

To Lieutenant Keyes, the new friends made a strange pair, the robust giant and the "dwarf" sitting in rapt conversation, with the dwarf doing most of the talking. Scott was always fascinated by ideas new to him, and after the remarkable two-hour session with Channing he declared that he had been "conversing with a Grecian sage." Channing reciprocated Scott's admiration, and when Channing delivered a celebrated "Lecture on War" the following autumn, he devoted a full two paragraphs to Scott's virtues. Channing was a pacifist, and he saw Scott as an accomplished warrior who had become a man of peace:

To this distinguished man belongs the rare honor of uniting with military energy and daring, the spirit of a philanthropist. His exploits in the field, which placed him in the first ranks of our soldiers, have been obscured by the purer and more lasting glory of a pacifier, and a friend of mankind.

There is so much of noble generosity of character about Scott, independent of his skill and bravery as a soldier, that his life has really been one of beauty and interest.[6]

Channing's words may have been ornate, but in an age given to flowery prose, they were not a source of amusement. By and large—with notable exceptions such as Andrew Jackson, Edmund Gaines, and Thomas Jesup, to be sure—the American public agreed with Channing, and Scott's career began to be concentered around Washington, with its politics and power.

The first sign of this new development came in 1839, even before Scott had completely finished his task in the Maine woods. In late March a Whig journal carried an article that launched Scott's overt career as a presidential candidate. After an introduction that rivaled the wording of Channing, the writer asked rhetorically,

Why, we repeat, should not General Scott, the soldier, the civilian, and the true-hearted American,—be the next president of the United States by the voice and acclaim of the people thereof?

Despite the fact that any praise always pleased him greatly, Scott had shrugged the proposal off. Sentiments similar to those of the Whig journal had been expressed when he was on his way to Maine, and he had declared himself "utterly indifferent" as to whether or not he would ever reach the presidency—he made no pretensions, he asserted, and there were already candidates enough.

After the triumph in Maine, however, Scott's name came to be mentioned more often in connection with the 1840 campaign for the White House. He did not question the motives of these expressions of support. Tending toward the naive, he had no real way of knowing which of his glowing admirers were truly sincere.

The noises being made on behalf of Scott the Whig had no effect on the generosity of President Martin Van Buren, who invited the general to a sumptuous dinner at the White House upon his reporting in early April

1839. And for some months Scott's duties reverted to military activities. He sought permission to hold a large encampment, including most of the regular army, at Trenton, New Jersey, in order to restore some of the discipline, drill, and military appearance the troops had lost while fighting the Seminoles in the swamps of Florida. In June he was sent on a trip to Wisconsin, this time to parley with the Winnebago Indians. This trip failed. At a meeting on July 12, the Indians refused to sign away their rights to hunt on the grounds south of the Wisconsin River. Scott did not stay around and try to enforce the ultimatum he had issued to them. Perhaps he saw the futility in such an effort, or perhaps he was in a hurry to get back to New York.

August 1839 was an active period for Saratoga Springs, New York, a favorite place for the prominent to escape the summer heat, always a mecca for the influential. That year the prominent political leaders, both Democrats and Whigs, were on hand at the same time. One of the privileged group was Philip Hone, a fifty-nine-year-old New Yorker who had attained great wealth in his auction business. A lifetime admirer of Scott's, Hone greeted Scott's arrival on the scene with enthusiasm:

> Monday, August 12 [1839]. This is the meridian of the Saratoga season. All the world is here: politicians and dandies; cabinet ministers and ministers of the gospel; officeholders and office-seekers; humbuggers and humbugged; anxious mothers and lovely daughters. . . . A little circle was formed this evening in the grand saloon which occasioned much serious speculation. It consisted of the three prominent candidates for the next Presidency: Mr. Van Buren, who returned this morning, Mr. Clay, and the gallant Gen. Scott, whose star is rising fast. Each had fair ladies receiving his attention, and many good-natured jokes were passed between them. 'I hope I do not obstruct your way,' said the President to Mr. Clay, who was endeavoring to pass. 'Not here, certainly,' replied the veteran in politics and politeness.

Van Buren did not need to fight for his party's renomination; that was assured him. The two Whig rivals were Henry Clay and Scott. Clay, the party's nominee seven years earlier, was the odds-on favorite; his backing in the South was solid, but his support in the North was wavering because of his status as a slaveholder. So thin was Clay's candidacy in New York, in fact, that the state's two leading Whigs, Governor William H. Seward and Thurlow Weed, were casting about to find someone with whom to oppose him. Scott seemed to be the logical man to play that role. Though Seward was the governor, the forty-two-year-old Weed was the more influential politician of the two; he had, in fact, been given credit for Seward's election as governor in 1836. Known as one who "derived great satisfaction in bringing capable [Whig] men into public service," he was thought to consider bribery and legislative favors as "legitimate party instruments," though even his worst detractors along those lines never accused Weed of accepting bribes himself.

Weed was interested in the manifestations of strong support for Scott out in western New York, and for a while he considered Scott his best hope for defeating Clay's nomination by the Whigs. In June, therefore, Weed asked Millard Fillmore, another prominent New York politician, to make a trip to that region to check out public sentiment. Fillmore reported back in Scott's favor but recommended that his name be introduced first in the eastern portion of the state. When such a possibility was explored, Weed soon concluded that Van Buren was too strongly entrenched in the minds of eastern New Yorkers; Scott would be unable to draw the Democratic vote in the east. Even before the great gathering at Saratoga in August, Weed had lost much of his zeal for Scott.

Scott, however, had now been bitten by the presidential bug, and his interest grew even as his actual prospects ebbed. He dropped his former pretenses of indifference to his political chances. In a trip to Detroit in November 1839, he mixed politics with his military duties. Though what he saw was not encouraging, he had by then become convinced that he would win. Attempting to make light of his aspirations, he wrote to William J. Worth, "Should I *not* be nominated, we shall both be in high humor and make crack both a bottle and a jest at our ease; in the other case I shall need you much to comfort me." He even planned to accept the nomination from the "heart of the old Dominion."[7]

Actually, Scott's prospects were already moribund. Old friends could view the situation in a realistic light. One of the most telling was Colonel J. Watson Webb, editor of the Whig *Courier and Inquirer,* who wrote that nobody wished Scott more success than did he, but warning,

> do not, as you value his fair name, suffer yourselves to be made the tools of selfish and designing men . . . who are prepared to sacrifice both General Scott and the Whig party of the Union, to secure the triumph of their own private and selfish views.

By the time the Whig convention opened in Harrisburg on December 4, 1839, four men were being considered. One, Daniel Webster, dropped out of the running, leaving Henry Clay, Winfield Scott, and William Henry Harrison. By this time, Thurlow Weed had decided to push the candidacy of Harrison, despite the fact that the 42 delegates of New York were declared in Scott's column. Together Weed and the former followers of Webster formulated a ruse that prevented a stampede to Clay, the leader; each state, in voting, must do so in private, and the results of each such private ballot would be unanimous. When the delegates met in the Lutheran church of Harrisburg, the first ballot came up Clay 102, Harrison 91, Scott 57. Since those opposed to Clay were more adamant than were his supporters, ballot after ballot was taken with no candidate ever receiving a majority. Scott never came close; his best showing came on the next to the last ballot, where he scored the 62 votes of the delegates from New York, New Jersey, Connecticut, Vermont, and Michigan.

Finally the logjam was broken when Virginia, previously solidly for Clay, swung over to Harrison. Weed saw his chance and swung New York's 42 votes to Harrison, giving the hero of Tippecanoe 148 delegates to Clay's 90 and Scott's 16. The convention then began a series of offers of the vice presidential nomination to at least five men, finally settling on John Tyler of Virginia, who was said to have been weeping over Clay's defeat. The choice would go unnoticed today except for the results: a little over a year later Tyler would ascend to the presidency on the death of Harrison after only a month in office.

In company with Clay, Senator John Crittenden of Kentucky, and Senator George Evans of Maine, Scott sat in the Astor Hotel in New York playing whist while waiting for the returns to come in. When the four received word of Harrison's victory, Scott concealed his disappointment, but Clay did not. He physically struck Scott, whom he blamed in part for his defeat, and then had to be dragged bodily from the room. The blow hit Scott on the shoulder that had been wounded at Lundy's Lane, and possibly as a secondary outlet for his disappointment, he sent a challenge to Clay through Crittenden. Crittenden, horrified at the prospect, was able to extract an apology from Clay.

Worse than the disappointment of failing to achieve "another brevet" was Scott's feeling of betrayal by Benjamin Watkins Leigh, his old friend from his Petersburg days back in 1809. Leigh had recognized Scott's military rather than legal potential when he was exiled from the Army; he seemed to feel the same way nearly thirty years later. Scott, however, held a different view, later describing Leigh as having become a "slave to his profession," thereby losing interest in any viewpoints other than those of Richmond. But it was well that Scott was not nominated in that year when the Whig prospects were so promising. His greatest military triumph would have been denied him had he won.

21

General-in-Chief at Last

Fulfilled ambition and the presidential bug.

ON JUNE 29, 1841, Major General Alexander Macomb, the general-in-chief of the United States Army, died in Washington at the age of fifty-nine. His had been an exemplary if somewhat colorless career. His joint victory at Plattsburgh, with Commodore Thomas Mac Donough, had done much to secure satisfactory terms for the United States in the peace conference at Ghent. Since then, as chief of engineers and general-in-chief, Macomb had performed his duties diligently and without fanfare—and apparently without rancor at being overshadowed in the public mind by his colorful subordinate, Winfield Scott.

Scott was the logical choice to succeed Macomb as general-in-chief, but he was aware that his lifelong rival, Edmund Gaines, still coveted the position. He therefore acted quickly. Having received the word of Macomb's death while at his headquarters in New York, he deferred a trip to Mackinac Island and dictated a message to Secretary of War John Bell that was far from subtle: "I take it for granted that my name will be sent, in a day or two, to fill the vacancy [resulting from] the death of Major-General Macomb." He went on to repeat his dreary arguments of 1828, insisting that he had always been *"one step higher"* in ordinary rank than General Macomb and forty-eight days his senior as Major General by brevet." He went on to claim that he held "the same seniority" over General Gaines as of that date.

Secretary Bell may have groaned over this reopening of old wounds, but the Tyler administration, brought into office by the death of the late president William Henry Harrison, was in much confusion. The secretary was therefore in no mood for a fight. He sent a memorandum to President John Tyler recommending Scott's appointment. Tyler approved forthwith.

Scott realized that his new duties would be trying, because he was determined to inject some meaning into what had always been the innocuous and artificial office of general-in-chief. When that position had been established in 1821, its occupant had been given little control over the staff and, even worse, his advice was seldom sought by his civilian superiors, the secretary of war and the President. Orders were sent out with the designation "By order of the Commanding General," but they were actually processed by the adjutant general under the direction of the secretary of war, and Macomb had been forced to make a special effort even to see them. Macomb's efforts to integrate himself into the real chain of command have been described as "almost pitiful."[1] Even though Scott's personality could be expected to give his new position more influence than it had previously enjoyed, the fact remained that Gaines, as commander of the Western Command, and Jesup, as the quartermaster general, would both be reporting directly to the secretary of war, not to him—at least in peacetime.

When Scott assumed command of the Army in 1841, about 12,600 men were on its rolls, an artificially inflated strength stemming from the requirements of the continuing Seminole War. Within a year, however, the war came to an end.[2] Brevet Brigadier General William J. Worth, with the approval of the President, simply declared on August 14, 1842, that "hostilities with the Indians in Florida have ceased." The Seminoles, whose entire number in Florida had declined to about 300 people, of whom only 112 were warriors, were granted a temporary reservation south of Pease Creek, where they settled down to peaceful pursuits. The Army was happy for an end to the debilitating Seminole War, but the price in terms of strength reduction would be high. On August 23, 1842, nine days after the official announcement of peace, Congress reduced the Army by 4,000 officers and men, from a strength of 12,539 to only 8,613.

Even Scott's position as general-in-chief was not above threat from Congress. In 1842, several movements developed in Congress to cut back on Scott's pay and emoluments, some even advocating abolition of his position. Scott's friends, however, banded together to stop any such movements. In the House of Representatives, former president John Quincy Adams expressed disgust on the floor of the House at the idea of cutting the general's wings. Standing by his old friend, "Old Man Eloquent" trumpeted that he thought it a

> very ill reward for the great and eminent services of Scott during a period of thirty-odd years, in which there were some as gallant exploits as any in our history could show, and in which he had not spared to shed his blood, as well as for more recent services of great importance in time of peace—services of great difficulty and great delicacy—now to turn him adrift at his advanced age.

If Scott had received from the government "thousands of dollars more than he had," Adams finished, "Scott would not have received one dollar which he did not richly deserve at the hands of his country."

Representative Charles J. Ingersoll, an old friend of Scott's and a free-thinking Jacksonian Democrat from Philadelphia, agreed with Adams, citing Scott's services at the forefront in the War of 1812, the "man who had struck the first blow in that struggle through which alone this Government had been preserved."[3] Scott's pleasure was heightened by the fact that Adams and Ingersoll never agreed on any other matter throughout their long political careers.

One man who would normally be expected to side with Scott in such a conflict was President John Tyler, his fellow Virginian. But Tyler did nothing. He had approved of Scott's appointment as general-in-chief, but that was as far as he would go in Scott's behalf. Tyler, a Southern states'-rights Whig, had quickly found himself at loggerheads with the rank and file of the Whigs, who tended to view Clay, not him, as the head of the Whig Party. Scott, because of his long association with the New York branch of the party, was no political supporter, even though he was conscious, as a general officer, of his obligation to refrain from attacking Tyler in public.

Even on matters pertaining to the Army, Tyler did not seek Scott's opinions. The relations between the general and the White House were rendered even more awkward by the fact that Scott was clearly an active candidate for the Whig nomination in 1844. As early as 1842 President Tyler became suspicious that Scott's trips to assess the conditions of his troops had more behind them than his military requirements, that they were indeed tinged with politics. Tyler thereupon shut down Scott's practice of visiting summer militia encampments. To Scott this was a sure way to ensure the nomination of Henry Clay by the Whigs. In August 1842, he wrote lugubriously to his campaign manager, Thaddeus Stevens:

I am cooped up here, a prisoner confined to the District [of Columbia]. Mr T. gave me permission to be absent a week in May, in the direction of Pennsylvania. Hearing of the kind attentions shown me, I found, on my return, that he had given directions not to let me "go reviewing" again. Can any man be more desperately bent on the nomination of Mr. Clay?

Not surprisingly, Scott had little good to say about Tyler, regarding him simply as a man elected to the vice presidency on a Whig ticket who had later turned coat when that high office had devolved on him with Harrison's early death. Scott wrote in later years,

Of Mr. Tyler's administration of the executive branch of the Government, but little will be said here. He soon committed the grossest tergiversation in politics, from the fear of Mr. Clay as a competitor for the succession, and to win that for himself, all the patronage of the Government, all the chips, shavings, and sweepings of office, down to the lowest clerkship, the posts of messengers and watchmen, were brought into market and bartered for support at the next election. To the honor of the country, Mr. Tyler was allowed to lapse into a private station.

With John Tyler so unpopular among both Whigs and Democrats—both considered him a traitor to their respective causes—it was inevitable that Whig politicians would become preoccupied with their party's candidate for the presidential election of 1844. As the nominee was certainly not going to be Tyler, they turned, almost to a man, to Henry Clay. Scott, however, commanded some support, especially in Pennsylvania, where the powerful Thaddeus Stevens, as early as 1841, had begun plugging his name. Scott was interested in promoting what chances he had, and he soon began corresponding with Stevens. He refused Stevens's request for a "campaign biography" of the general, but did write a long, uninspiring letter setting forth his general political views. He also developed a friendship with Senator John J. Crittenden, the man who was rapidly becoming the recognized kingmaker in the Whig party.

In his own fashion, Crittenden was as colorful a character as Scott. Only a year younger than Scott, age 57 in the fall of 1844, Crittenden had attended the College of William and Mary at about the same time as Scott but had stayed on to finish his degree. He served in the Kentucky militia during the War of 1812, participating in a minor role at the Battle of the Thames in 1813.

No professional soldier, Crittenden was elected to the Kentucky legislature while still in uniform.

Crittenden had become a booster of his fellow Kentuckian Henry Clay in 1824 and since then had never denied Clay his support except for those years in which he believed Clay's chances for election to be hopeless. Though he was appointed by John Quincy Adams to the Supreme Court in the last days of February 1828, his nomination was dropped on the inauguration of President Andrew Jackson, at which time Crittenden ran successfully for the United States Senate, where he served until President William Henry Harrison appointed him attorney general in 1841. Known as a whiskey-drinking, cigar-smoking, whist-playing bon vivant, Crittenden had the capacity to earn and keep the trust of many different men. One of these was Winfield Scott, whom he had accompanied on a fact-finding trip to Lockport, Pennsylvania, in 1841.*

Despite his friendship with Scott, Crittenden was never tempted to support the general at Clay's expense. Accordingly, Crittenden played the broker between Clay and Scott, always the Clay loyalist but attempting to keep Scott in good humor. That chore was not difficult, as Crittenden genuinely liked the blustery political ingenue. Scott, generous in nature, accepted Crittenden's position.

In early July 1842 Crittenden wrote to Clay advising him of developments on the political scene. The Whig delegation from Pennsylvania, he had heard, was intending to nominate Scott as the candidate for president on the first ballot, to be cast at the end of the month. However, the Pennsylvania leaders had confidentially informed him that they would support any Whig ticket eventually selected; therefore, their support for Scott was tantamount only to a vote for a "favorite son." Crittenden added that Scott would be better off if the Pennsylvanians supported Clay on the first ballot, as such a token nomination, "in the midst of so universal and ardent a sentiment in your [Clay's] favor, would place him [Scott] in a very awkward, if not ridiculous position before the world, and would, besides, expose him to much jealousy and prejudice." Clay, Crittenden went on, was "the candidate of the Whig party"; the people had already settled the question.

---

*The occasion was to investigate the case of one Alexander McLeod, a Canadian who boasted a role in the destruction of the *Caroline,* and who was about to be tried in New York, causing an international crisis.

Still, Crittenden felt that he had to warn Clay about Scott's reaction to his eventual disappointment:

> I understand that Scott has lost all hope, and I wish he could be saved from all further disappointment or difficulty on the subject; he is a good Whig and a good fellow, and will eventually support you heartily. It is not to be wondered at if, in the first moments of disappointment, he should show some little impatience, and his wounded vanity not permit him to take the most prudent and proper course. In common with the rest of us, he has his portion of vanity, and that may be excused on account of his other great and good qualities. I like him, and am sure he will do right at last.[4]

Developments unfolded exactly as Crittenden had predicted. By April of the following year, well after all of Scott's hopes had vanished, he was again writing to Crittenden with that boastful, joshing style that the modern reader finds so perplexing. "It has been just a month today," he began, "since you, Archer, and others turned your backs upon me, leaving me to my fate. . . . In revenge, I have a great mind to turn *Tyler-man* and seek consolation in the pure circle about him." And a couple of months later, in light-hearted protest of one of Crittenden's public appearances, Scott again playfully raised the threat: "I shall have to cut your acquaintance or take the other tack and become a *Tyler-man*." But then quickly, "I'll cut my throat first!" Both letters are full of gossip and of indirect criticism of President John Tyler. The Whigs had disappointed Scott in his unrealistic ambitions, but he was in no mood to cut his ties with them.

When the Whig convention of 1844 got under way, Crittenden proved once again to be a shrewd prognosticator. On May 1, the Whigs gathered at Baltimore and nominated Henry Clay for president and Theodore Frelinghuysen, of New Jersey, for vice president. The Democrats met soon thereafter at Baltimore and after a complicated series of maneuvers on the part of the Southern "discontents," nominated James K. Polk of Tennessee for president and George M. Dallas of Pennsylvania for vice president. Polk, a true disciple of Andrew Jackson, was an avowed expansionist and advocate of Texas annexation. President Tyler was also nominated by a group of loyal states'-rights Democrats, almost all of whom owed him patronage from his four years in office.

The presidential election of 1844 turned out to be more than the choice between two party nominees; it was a serious referendum on the subject of Texas annexation. It was saddled with another issue as well, the question of the quarrel between the United States and Britain over the U.S.-Canadian boundary in the Pacific Northwest, then known as the Oregon Territory. East of the Mississippi River the boundary between the United States and Canada ran along the 49th parallel to Lake of the Woods, Michigan, but the border west of that lake was in dispute, the United States claiming territory as far north as 54°40' north latitude, and the British claiming territory as far south as the Columbia River. Both sides claimed the whole of Vancouver Island.

For some thirty years both sides had been content with a joint occupation of the territory, but in recent years British troop strength had been building up while American settlers had been pouring in. In 1841 Scott had noted that the British had 20,000 troops in the British North American provinces. Both sides were relatively happy with a simple extension of the boundary along the 49th parallel to Puget Sound, leaving only the island of Vancouver as a point to be resolved. However, in an effort to placate the voters in the northern states, who cared little for the question of Texas, someone in the Democratic ranks managed to inject the Oregon issue into Democratic campaign rhetoric. Hence the unrealistic American demand for all the lands south of 54°40' north latitude. The dramatic slogan "Fifty-four forty or fight" would face whoever was elected as the new president.

The second controversy, between the United States and Mexico, grew out of the future of the Republic of Texas, a one-time state of Mexico that had attained its independence from Mexico City in 1836. It was a matter of long standing. Many Americans, especially Southerners, had always contended that the purchase of Louisiana from Napoleon in 1803 had included the territory that now comprises East Texas. In 1819 the United States and Spain signed a treaty in which the Americans relinquished all claim to the Texas region, and Spain relinquished claims to Florida. After Mexico became independent of Spain in 1821, thousands of Americans, self-proclaimed "Texans," overran the territory, and in 1836 they declared their independence. Citizens of other parts of the United States felt free to send weapons and volunteers into Texas to aid in the cause of Sam Houston and Stephen Austin. With the Texan success at the battle of San Jacinto, most of the world's nations recognized Texan independence. The American government had not promoted the migration that changed the status of Texas, but it had done nothing to discourage it either.

In the years following de facto Texas independence, Mexican president

Santa Anna refused to recognize its legality. He continued to conduct a low-scale border war across the Rio Grande, a war that kept the Texans in a belligerent mood, and, since the reporting of news in the United States was all done from a "Texan" viewpoint, it inflamed American public opinion against Mexico and gave Americans cause to annex the young republic as a state of the Union. President John Tyler was among those anxious for this to come to pass.

Tyler had two secretaries of state after the resignation of Daniel Webster. The first was Abel P. Upshur and the second, after Upshur's unexpected death, was John C. Calhoun. Both Upshur and Calhoun were staunch advocates of Texas annexation, and both conducted negotiations with the Republic of Texas to that end. By April 1844, Calhoun had negotiated an annexation treaty with Texas, which President Tyler sent to the Senate for ratification. The Senate rejected the treaty, however, less on its merits—annexation was a popular issue in the United States—than as an expression of antipathy for an increasingly unpopular president.

In November 1844 James K. Polk was chosen eleventh president of the United States. Though the margin that elected the underdog Polk was provided by the emergence of James Gurney's Liberty Party in New York, which split the Whig vote, the election, in the public perception, mandated aggressive United States positions on Texas and Oregon, and Polk considered himself justified in pursuing both.

John Tyler, however, would not be out of office until March 1845, four months away. Interpreting the election in the same way as Polk, Tyler now theorized that a formal treaty would not be necessary to effect an annexation, and on that basis he went ahead and finally secured a congressional resolution inviting Texas to join the Union.* Tyler signed the resolution and sent it to Washington-on-the-Brazos, Texas, the night of March 3, 1845, the eve of the Polk inauguration.

These developments were being watched closely in Mexico, where Polk's election was seen as a virtual declaration of war between the two countries. When Congress passed the annexation resolution—and Tyler signed it—the Mexican minister in Washington demanded and received his passports.

---

*Congress actually passed two resolutions, as the version of the Senate and that of the House of Representatives varied considerably. But the Congress obliged by permitting the President to choose whichever version he preferred.

Diplomatic relations between the United States and Mexico were officially broken.

Scott was involved only peripherally in the various decisions that brought these events about. As the new general-in-chief he was busy inspecting the various posts on the frontiers, checking on the state of his troops.

He also had domestic matters on his mind. Maria Mayo Scott, with the Scotts' four daughters, returned from Europe on the packet *Argo.* They had been gone for five years, during which time Scott had lived alone at Elizabethtown, New York, and Washington. It was no secret that Maria Scott, a woman who had never gotten over the days when Richmond society had been at her feet, found herself happier in the high society of Europe than in the suburb of Elizabethtown, where much of her husband's social life was confined to male company. But now that Scott was stationed in Washington, it was a different matter. How much that fact influenced her decision to return must, of course, remain conjecture. She arrived at Washington on October 21, 1843.

Scott never complained about his wife's absences, but he was visibly upset over his favorite daughter's decision to take the vows and enter a Catholic convent. Virginia Scott, while living in Paris, had become attached to a young man who shared her deep religious convictions. Together, so the story went, the two lovers decided to express their love for each other by becoming consecrated to the service of God. They were reported to have met later in church, at which time they showed no recognition of each other. Scott's unhappiness on hearing of Virginia's plans was reported in the diary of his friend Philip Hone:

> I cannot imagine a more severe trial for a heart as susceptible as his, than that which he is about to undergo. His daughter, a lovely young woman, 22 years of age, has determined to take the veil in the Convent at Georgetown, and shut herself out of the world forever. No entreaties of her parents have the least effect to divert her from her rash resolution, and their tears are unavailing to save her from self-immolation.[5]

Unfortunately, Virginia Scott was in frail health, unequal to the rigors of convent life. She died on August 26, 1845, a cause of further grief to her father and mother.

Another death in 1845 carried meaning for Winfield Scott. On June 8, General Andrew Jackson died at his home, the Hermitage, near Nashville, Tennessee. Scott received word of the old warrior's passing while he was supervising the conduct of an examination at West Point. Immediately Scott terminated the examination and issued a statement:

> Major Delafield, Superintendent. I suspend the further labors of this examination till-morrow, in honor of an event interesting to all Americans. A great man has fallen among us. Andrew Jackson, after filling the world with his fame, and crowning his country with glory, departed this life on the 8th instant. . . . Orders [for special honors] will soon arrive from Washington.

Andrew Jackson was the only man who ever humbled Scott and still retained Scott's esteem and respect.

22

❧❧❧

"A Hasty Plate of Soup"

*A politically minded President James Polk makes
Scott a laughingstock—for the moment.*

JAMES K. POLK and Winfield Scott were an unlikely pair of men to work
together. Never admirers of each other, they had vastly different personalities which did not complement each other. Instead, they caused friction.
Polk—diminutive, secretive, and calculating—could not abide the bluff,
outgoing, egotistical Scott; nor did he have any intention of trying to. Their
professional experiences and assumptions were antithetical. Polk was a partisan Democrat, a disciple of Andrew Jackson, who had instilled in him a
profound distrust of regular army officers. Scott, the Whig, was contemptu-
ous of the militia in which Polk held the courtesy rank of "colonel." Scott
was not awed by the presidency; he had served many presidents before Polk
and expected to serve more after him, if indeed he did not succeed Polk as
President himself.

When these two were teamed as President and general-in-chief at a time
of crisis, the potential for trouble was considerable. The ultimate responsibility lay with the President, who possessed the power, at least theoretically,
to remove Scott from his high post. Polk may have considered doing that,
but he did not. First, it would be impossible to find another officer who possessed Scott's military knowledge and experience. Second, Scott's unques-
tioned prestige in the military field was recognized by Democrats as well as
Whigs. Finally, what other officer of the U.S. Army on the current scene
would be any more acceptable politically? All of the regular army generals
were Whigs. Besides, if the conduct of the war ran into trouble, Polk could

always lay the blame on Scott, a potential opposition candidate for the presidency in 1848. The best course, Polk concluded, was a balancing act: to keep Scott on as general-in-chief, but to prevent, if possible, his attaining any additional glory on the battlefield.

This distrust between Polk and Scott meant that the general-in-chief did not participate in the presidential decisions that led up to the war with Mexico. Another general, Brevet Brigadier General Zachary Taylor, would move into the spotlight, shoving aside his military superior.

James Polk's first days in office were eventful. In his inaugural address he reiterated his determination to carry through the annexation of Texas to the Union. He scoffed at Mexican protests, declaring such an annexation to be a matter "between Texas and the United States alone." He thus showed no concern when, following his address, Mexico's minister demanded his passports and officially broke diplomatic relations between the two countries, threatening war if the United States followed through on Polk's intentions.

Since President Tyler had sent an annexation proposal to Texas, the issue lay for the moment in the hands of the Texans themselves. Polk knew that the vast bulk of the population were eager to join the United States, if only to attain protection against the ever-present threat of Mexico. Certain interests beclouded the issue, however. The British, attempting to prevent annexation to the United States, were striving to secure Mexican recognition of Texas's independence from Mexico. Some Texan politicians such as Sam Houston and Anson Jones also realized that their personal standings would dimininish if their independent nation should become merely another state of the Union. Their professions of support for annexation, therefore, were not always wholehearted. To give the Texans a shove toward a favorable vote, President Polk appealed to their longing for United States protection. He sent a small army to the eastern bank of the Sabine River, the border between Texas and Louisiana, at the same time putting the Mexicans on notice that the United States would step in if they undertook a major invasion of Texas. To command this army Polk selected Zachary Taylor.

"Zack" Taylor was, like Scott, an old-time regular army officer, a veteran of the War of 1812, the Black Hawk War, and the Seminole War. Unlike Scott, whose interests lay mainly in the East, Taylor had served the bulk of his years in the West, where he owned two plantations in Louisiana. Like Duncan Clinch in Florida, Taylor had managed for years to combine farming with military duties, and longed for the days when he could retire from service and devote full time to his plantations. In person Taylor was informal, courtly in manners, and pleasant to converse with. As shown in his letters, he possessed a keen understanding of politics, but he seemed detached as he viewed the current Washington power struggle. Polk realized that Taylor was a Whig, but he had never been an active one. And Polk's selection of Taylor had been encouraged by Andrew Jackson, who had advised that Taylor should be the general to lead United States forces in case of war. For the moment Polk was content that in Taylor he had the right man on the scene.

Taylor's orders were purposely vague. He was to take about 2,200 men— a quarter of the Army—to Fort Jesup, in western Louisiana, there to remain until he received clearance from the American minister to Texas, Andrew J. ("Jack") Donelson,[1] before moving into Texas territory. This was a strange order, and Scott, when he finally saw it, flew into a rage. The prospect of an Army field commander being placed under the orders of a diplomat, independent of the Army chain of command, was anathema to him. Donelson, however, was a West Point graduate, sensitive to such military nuances, and he was careful to couch his dealings with Taylor in the form of consultations and requests. No harm resulted, except to encourage Scott's growing mistrust of his civilian superiors.

As it turned out, the Texans voted overwhelmingly to join the Union. In late June, therefore, Taylor and Donelson agreed that Taylor's "Army of Occupation" should move forward. Taylor took his force by water to the small settlement of Corpus Christi, at the mouth of the Nueces River on the Gulf of Mexico. He located his camp on the far side of the river, thus purposely occupying territory then claimed by Mexico, emphasizing the Texan contention that the Rio Grande was the proper boundary between the two countries. On arrival, Taylor immediately set up camp and began drilling his troops. The Army of Occupation spent a profitable, though increasingly uncomfortable, winter there during 1845–46.

Bringing Texas into the Union was only the first of Polk's objectives as President. His second objective was to expand the borders of the United States by assimilating what is now the American Southwest all the way to the Pacific Ocean. As Mexico theoretically owned all that territory, expansion meant acquisition of vast tracts of land from her. Polk very much desired to effect the acquisition peaceably. In late 1845, therefore, he sent a prominent Louisianian, John Slidell, to Mexico City with a set of proposals for purchase of much Mexican land. Slidell went armed with a set of alternatives, the most extensive of which visualized a boundary including upper California to include Monterey, for which payment would come to $25 million. Those various offers, while probably reasonable by the monetary standards of the day, ignored one important fact: the Mexicans had no desire to sell any lands for any sum.

Slidell ran into difficulties from the moment he reached Mexico City. Mexican President José Joaquin Herrera refused to receive him.[2] Frustrated, Slidell protested Herrera's snub and threatened United States action. He soon left the capital for Veracruz, where he sulked for some months before returning to the United States. His rebuff, however, may have been expected; it provided the excuse for Polk and Secretary of State James Buchanan to appear deeply offended. On January 13, 1846, therefore, Secretary of War William Marcy sent orders to General Taylor to "advance and occupy, with the troops under your command, positions on or near the east bank of Rio del Norte."[3]

Taylor and his men were relieved; they were more than ready to leave Corpus Christi. Their camp on the sandy beach had provided many benefits, including the opportunity for intensive drill, but they had become tired of their lengthy wait and tempers were beginning to flare.

One incident brought Scott into conflict with Polk. Taylor, though no parade ground soldier, decided, in late autumn 1845, to hold a review of his army, which had now grown to 3,550 men. As "commander of troops" for the review, he designated Colonel David E. Twiggs, commanding officer of the 2d Dragoons, on the basis that Twiggs ranked higher on the Army's regular promotion list than did Colonel William J. Worth. Worth, who held a brevet rank of brigadier general, protested what he interpreted as Taylor's slight, insisting that the criterion for seniority should be brevet, not regular rank.

Such a matter might cause some grumbling under normal circumstances, but in the bored atmosphere of the Nueces River encampment it caused a furor. The officers of Taylor's camp split into factions, those supporting Worth and those supporting Twiggs. So Taylor, exasperated, canceled the review and wrote to the President through the Adjutant General requesting a ruling on the brevet matter. Scott intercepted the message and, claiming his authority as the Army's senior professional, issued his own directive, that brevet rank should take precedence over regular rank. The proponents of

Twiggs, furious, sent a petition protesting Scott's decision to the president of the Senate. When Polk finally learned of the matter, he became enraged over Scott's intercepting a message addressed to him. He reversed Scott's directive, calling it "highly exceptional" and asserting that it "amounted to insubordination."[4]

Taylor began the overland trek from Corpus Christi to the Rio Grande on Sunday, March 8, 1846, arriving on the Rio Grande in late March 1846. There, at Matamoros across the river, he found himself confronted by a belligerent Mexican force slightly larger than his own. For a month the two armies sat glaring at each other while the Mexican commander built up his force to the point where he felt ready for battle. He issued an ultimatum for Taylor to withdraw from Mexican territory by April 15, on which date the two nations would be at war. Taylor not only refused to leave; he ordered the two naval vessels under his command to blockade the mouth of the Rio Grande, cutting off Matamoros from access to its principal source of sustenance, the Gulf. On April 26, 1846, the Mexican commander, General Mariano Arista, sent a force of 1,600 cavalry across the Rio Grande. Unaware of the size of the Mexican force, Taylor had sent a patrol of 63 dragoons to intercept him. In an unequal battle, 16 of the dragoons were killed or wounded, while all the rest were captured.

Taylor immediately sent a message back to Washington, "Hostilities may now be considered as commenced." At the same time he called on the governor of Texas for four regiments of volunteers.

On Saturday evening, May 9, 1846, President Polk was conferring with his cabinet as to the next move, following the return of his emissary, John Slidell, from Veracruz. Polk now planned, on the strength of the insults Slidell had sustained, to ask Congress for a declaration of war against Mexico. "Young Hickory," as Polk was called, was uneasy; it was a shaky basis, he knew, on which to declare war. That evening, however, word came from General Taylor, telling of the action on the Rio Grande. Polk's problem had evaporated. "American blood," he claimed in his war message to Congress the following Monday, "has been shed on American soil!" A state of war existed, he trumpeted, because of the actions of Mexico.

The reaction in the United States was electric. The people cried for revenge against Mexico and determined to send all possible aid to Taylor, whose 3,500 hundred men, many miles from bases in the United States, were facing a nation of seven million people. The members of Congress, many of whom had been resisting Polk's efforts to push the country toward war, received his war message with a mixture of anger and resignation—anger at both Mexico and Polk, resignation to the inevitability of war. Both houses of Congress were forced to accede to Polk's "confirmation" of the state of war[5] and to appropriate funds for its prosecution. So frenzied was the atmosphere that the legislators authorized the President to call up 50,000 volunteers, to serve for one year or to the end of the war—twice the number he had asked for.

Enter Winfield Scott for the first time. By the evening of Wednesday, May 13, Polk realized that he had done all he could without the advice of his foremost professional soldier, so he sent for Scott and Secretary Marcy to come to the White House. When Scott and Marcy arrived, the discussion centered on how to organize the 50,000 volunteers that the Congress had that day authorized. The meeting was inconclusive, and Polk was dissatisfied, considering Scott's plans not complete enough. In the course of the meeting, however, the President offered Scott the command of whatever army would eventually take the field against Mexico. Scott accepted gratefully, unaware that Polk had made the offer solely because he could not justify choosing anyone else.

At eight o'clock the next evening, the three officials met again for four hours. Polk outlined his own concept of the war, which was simply to occupy large spaces of northern Mexico, thus hoping to force Mexico into a negotiated peace. Neither Polk nor anyone else wished to conquer Mexico; the concept was to "conquer a peace," not a nation. To accomplish that limited goal, Scott proposed calling up 20,000 of the men that Congress had authorized, and Polk reluctantly agreed. Such a force was too big for his limited purposes, he later recorded, but he was "not willing to take the responsibility of any failure of the campaign by refusing to grant to General Scott all he asked."[6] At least the plans, in a general way, had been laid.

Scott returned to his office a couple of blocks from the White House and began the fabulous schedule that always amazed his associates. He stayed at his office eighteen hours a day, sometimes interrupting his labors with a full dinner but more often eating at his desk. His tasks were enormous. In a country that was almost completely unprepared for war, he was responsible for calling up, clothing, equipping, and training the 20,000 volunteers. The new recruits had to be transported to their places of mobilization and training, and later transferred to the regions in which they were expected to operate. All this had to be done with a minimum staff, without modern conveniences such as the recently invented telegraph or, for the most part, even railroads.

Trouble soon began. As Scott's conversations with Polk had failed to produce any mutual confidence between the two men, they had not fully communicated. Scott did not concern himself over what Polk expected him to do during the next few months. Though Polk keenly desired to get Scott out of Washington, Scott had no intentions of leaving Washington for several months. He had much work to accomplish, and he wanted to ensure that when he left for the Rio Grande, he would take with him substantial reinforcements. He wanted to ensure that Taylor, whose conduct had been creditable, would be perceived as having been incorporated into a larger force, not replaced. To assemble those reinforcements would take time.

Unfortunately, Secretary Marcy was of no help as a bridge between president and general. Although he was well acquainted with Scott from the days when they had traveled to Buffalo together during the Patriots' War in 1838, and from their associations in New York, he seemed unable to interpret the two men to each other. Had he been able, he might have saved much difficulty.

On May 19, ten days after their second White House meeting, Polk instructed Marcy to warn Scott that he must proceed to his new post "very soon." If he failed to do so, Polk warned, he would be superseded as general-in-chief. Marcy did not act at once; he was busy attending to another of Polk's assignments, conspiring with the powerful Democratic senator from Missouri, Thomas Hart Benton, to increase the number of the Army's general officers. Two new major generals (making a total of three) and four new brigadiers (for a total of six) would give President Polk latitude to appoint Taylor to a rank coequal with Scott's. The third appointment as major general might well go to Benton himself. If Benton could take command in the field, a Democrat rather than a Whig might gather the laurels of military victory.

The bill got nowhere, but the debate alerted Scott. Having "smelt the rat," as he put it in a letter to Crittenden, Scott confronted Marcy. Only then did Marcy inform Scott of the President's ultimatum regarding his continued presence in Washington.

Scott's Achilles heel, his sense of pride, had been pierced. On May 21 he wrote Marcy a lengthy letter which, while it contained a great deal of wisdom, was all too open, too frank, and too quotable. He had learned that "much impatience" had been felt, perhaps in high quarters, that "I have not already put myself in route for the Rio Grande." His explanation was unfortunate. He was "too old a soldier," he went on, not to feel the importance of securing himself against "the most perilous of all positions: A fire upon my rear, from Washington, and a fire, in front, from the Mexicans."[7] Such a direct accusation—for that is what it was—would later prove utterly correct, but it understandably brought hostilities on the Washington front to a new level.

On the evening of May 23, 1846, word came from Zachary Taylor that he had, on the May 8 and 9, fought two successful battles with Mexican forces on the left (north) bank of the Rio Grande, thereby eliminating the Mexican threat to Texas. Mexican losses had been high; many soldiers drowned in the Rio Grande in their hell-bound retreat. The country went wild with that heady news. Zack Taylor—"Old Rough and Ready"—was now the hero of the day. No longer was Polk compelled to justify denying Scott the command of the troops of the frontier; he could now just keep Scott in Washington. Marcy wrote Scott a stern letter to that effect.

But the drama had not yet played out. When Scott received Marcy's letter, he exploded. Giving vent to his lifelong habit of describing the circumstances in which he received a letter, he began his reply, "Your letter of this day, received at about 6 PM, as I sat down to a hasty plate of soup . . ."

That did it! Polk and Marcy published the letter in the *Congressional Globe.* The validity of its complaints was lost. The public laughed at the spectacle of a pompous general simpering at not getting what he wanted. Trivial as the matter was, Scott never lived it down. In the meantime, humiliated, he remained in Washington.

Fortunately, Scott never allowed personal frustrations to interfere with his military duties. He continued to carry out his heavy responsibilities, mobilizing for a war for which the United States was ill prepared. As he described those responsibilities to a friend,

> I was needed [in Washington] to make a thousand arrangements with the Secretary of War and the chiefs of the general staff, which could be made nowhere else and by nobody but the commander in constant contact with those persons, to distribute, to apportion, to settle rendezvous and routes, subsistence, medicines, means of transportation, camp equipage, and to raise troops, have them properly organized, put in motion at the right time, and put upon the right points, etc.

On the personal side, Scott was also required to maintain a cheerful front as he watched the Whigs beginning to court Zachary Taylor for the 1848 presidential nomination. Shortly after receiving news of Taylor's victory at Resaca de la Palma, a number of leading Whigs came to visit Scott, visibly upset—in a "panic," as he described them. Their question did not pertain to Scott but to Taylor. Was Taylor indeed a Whig? If so, could Taylor be substituted for himself, Scott, as the Whig candidate in 1848? Scott later claimed he was "more amused than offended" at their lack of tact and proceeded to tell them a homely story designed to establish Taylor's very high sense of honor and integrity.

There may have been some histrionics in Scott's benign treatment of the visiting politicians, but he was sincere in his insistence that Taylor be amply recognized for his victories on the Rio Grande. Thus, when Congress voted that a special medal be struck for Taylor, Scott gave the matter his thorough attention—the medal's materials, design, bust, inscriptions, and events to be depicted. Writing more than fifteen years after the event, Scott devoted four full pages of his *Memoirs* to describing his specifications for Taylor's medal.

He would have been out of character, however, had he accepted his professional eclipse lying down. He therefore took recourse to his pen, writing Marcy from West Point[8] on September 12, 1846, requesting that "I might be sent to take the immediate command of the principal army against Mexico, either today or at a better time the President may be pleased to designate." The horse regiments, he said, were now within fifteen or twenty marches from the Rio Grande, and the season for consecutive operations was at hand. He added that his presence was "neither unexpected nor undesired" by Taylor and that he could be on the Rio Grande by the end of the month.

Marcy was not convinced. His reply, a model of curtness, turned Scott down without explanation.

Scott now gave vent to private indignation. He wrote his friend John Crittenden, enclosing copies of the correspondence, terming Marcy's letter "vulgar and cold-blooded" and insisting that he had written only in the knowledge that Taylor has "all along expected and desired my presence." His conspiratorial turn of mind now developed a theory that Polk intended to relieve Taylor and replace him with General William O. Butler, a Democrat, with the objective of building Butler up as a presidential possibility. In fairness, Scott added that Butler himself would be "incapable of any machinations of *that* sort." Two weeks later, he was writing Crittenden again in the same vein, adding his favorite self-pitying couplet,

True as the dial to the sun,

Although it be not shone upon.

While all this was going on in Washington, Zachary Taylor, on the Rio Grande, was busy organizing his army for further operations in Mexico, incorporating the new volunteer regiments into his force, volunteers who came from seven states.[9] These new units arrived complete with officers and a sort of organization. They remained separate from the regulars. The two components would live in separate camps; they would be treated in separate hospitals. Taylor would command two armies, one regular and one volunteer.*

Given freedom to select his first objective in Mexico, Taylor decided to march on the city of Monterrey (in those days spelled Monterey), in the state of Nueva Leone. In early August his army concentrated at Camargo.[10] A month later, with pressures for action building up in Washington, he took about half his force, 6,000 men, in the direction of Monterrey, reaching it on September 19, 1846. He began an assault on the city two days later.

Monterrey turned out to be an unexpectedly hard battle. The Mexicans, in strong positions, exacted a severe toll. In the end, it was not the troops so much as the commander, Pedro Ampudia, who was defeated. In the light of severe American losses and low supplies, Taylor accepted a truce as part of his generous terms of surrender.

In Washington, Scott was elated by Taylor's victory at Monterrey, calling the bloody and partially mismanaged battle "three glorious days." Polk, however, received the news with anger, his mind concentrating solely on Taylor's acceptance of a truce, which Polk had forbidden in advance. Polk wasted no time in sending orders to Taylor terminating the truce, orders that reached Monterrey on November 2, 1846, at almost exactly the time the truce was scheduled to expire anyway.

It was now Zachary Taylor's turn to incur Polk's wrath. The process had begun almost a month earlier, actually, when Taylor had received orders to detach a force of 4,000 volunteers, under Major General Robert Patterson,

---

*One regular who missed the first battles was William J. Worth, who had resigned his commission. When he learned that a war had begun, Worth withdrew the resignation and returned to rejoin Taylor's army.

to assist Commodore David Conner in seizing the Mexican port of Tampico. As the War Department sent the order directly to Patterson, Taylor interpreted the action as an attempt to undercut his own authority. He responded by advising Marcy on October 12 that he could not comply with the secretary's instruction; the troops supporting Conner at Tampico would have to come from elsewhere—which they eventually did.

Scott himself added to Taylor's disenchantment with the Polk administration. On September 26, three days after Marcy's message to Patterson had been sent, Scott wrote Taylor a personal letter warning that plots were afoot to replace Taylor with that same volunteer officer, Patterson, who had innocently become the target of Taylor's wrath. Taylor expressed his frustration in a letter he wrote to his son-in-law and confidant, surgeon Robert C. Wood:

> There is, I hear from high authority [Scott], an intrigue going on against me, the object of which is to deprive me of the command; my only sin for this is the want of discretion on the part of certain politicians, in connecting my name as a proper candidate for the next presidential election, which I very much regretted.[11]

Taylor was already feeling persecuted when Marcy's orders to terminate the truce arrived on November 2.[12] He promptly notified the Mexican commander of the end of the truce and followed that message up by sending General Worth ahead to Saltillo. On the day of Worth's move, a letter came from Marcy strongly suggesting that Taylor occupy no territory in advance of Monterrey, but Old Zack merely pocketed the letter. He also wrote "personal" letters of questionable propriety to Senator Crittenden and his close friend Edmund Gaines. Crittenden kept Taylor's letter confidential, but Gaines turned his over to a local New Orleans newspaper, which published it. That letter reached Washington too late to affect the strategy for the future prosecution of the war, but it sufficed to make Taylor, not Scott, the prime target of Polk's pique.

Winfield Scott, meanwhile, was comporting himself with the utmost decorum. Outwardly correct in support of Zachary Taylor—as was Polk also, in public—he made sure not to commit himself on anything, especially to the press. He moved the headquarters of the Army from West Point, where he had been staying out of sight, and returned to Washington. It was important for all concerned that he participate in any future planning for the conduct of the war.

Polk and his cabinet were now reappraising the strategy for the future conduct of the war. With the escape of the Mexican army from Monterrey, and with Santa Anna's return to power in Mexico, the Americans were reconciled to the fact that a substantial Mexican army would be in the field for the foreseeable future. To avoid escalating the war, Polk tentatively settled on a plan euphemistically termed "masterful inactivity," which envisioned occupying an east-west line running from Tampico on the east, through Monterrey in the center, and Chihuahua farther west. Polk, his cabinet, and other Democrats hoped that the Mexicans, faced with indefinite occupation of large parts of their territory, would eventually give way and make peace. That was essentially the strategy originally urged by Taylor.

"Masterful inactivity," however, died aborning. When Polk showed it to Senator Benton, that worthy Democrat objected. The whole idea of a sedentary occupation of northern Mexico, he argued, was contrary to the temper of Americans whereas it was ideally suited to the Spanish temper. He pointed out that the Spanish, who "loved procrastination," had outwaited the Moors for 700 years in the south of Spain and the Visigoths for 300 in the north. Their descendants, the Mexicans, could easily outwait the Americans. The alternative, Benton insisted, was to deliver a strong blow against Mexico from the port of Veracruz, with a subsequent push on to Mexico City. Under Benton's influence, Polk set aside the concept of "masterful inactivity," much to the chagrin of many in his government.

Four days later, Polk asked Benton's advice regarding the future command of the amphibious invasion of Mexico. Benton liked none of the possibilities; none of the generals was satisfactory. The position of expedition commander, he said, "required a man of talents and resources" and it depended more "upon the talents and energy of the officer than upon mere bravery. He then said that if such an office was created by Congress, he would be willing to accept the command himself."[13] The President did not seem the least taken aback by Benton's presumption; he remarked that he would be pleased should that eventuality come about.

Polk and Benton soon realized, however, that Congress would never stand for such an arrangement. Scott, who was keeping an eye on the whole proceedings, therefore saw his chance. To prove how thoroughly he supported the concept of an invasion at Veracruz, he began drawing up plans designed to convince Polk that he, Scott, was the man to carry out this option. In a plan that resembled Benton's, Scott recommended following the route that Hernando Cortés had used over three hundred years earlier, from

Veracruz on the Gulf of Mexico to Mexico City. During the week following November 10, 1846, Scott submitted no fewer than three plans to that effect to Secretary Marcy.

Still Polk was unconvinced, casting about for anyone's name but Scott's as the commander, but as Congress was not prepared to create a special lieutenant generalcy for Senator Benton, the field of possible alternatives to Scott was narrowed down to only three: Taylor, Patterson, and William O. Butler.

The prospects were not pleasant for James Polk. Taylor was out of the running by this time; his petulant refusal to send Patterson to Tampico had convinced Polk that he was no longer "in sympathy with his administration." Butler had been seriously wounded at the battle of Monterrey and was unfit for field duty in the near future. Patterson was foreign-born, an Irishman by birth and therefore ineligible to stand as a Democratic presidential candidate in 1848. Secretary of War Marcy, Secretary of the Treasury Robert J. Walker, and others therefore agreed that Scott was the inescapable choice. Polk, despite his preference for nearly anyone else, agreed. As he put it, he did not see how Scott's appointment could be avoided.

Polk still wished to sound Scott out. He sent for the general to come over to the White House "once or twice daily" during the third week of November 1846, during which visits he exuded "warmth and emphasis of his profession [of friendship]," thereby winning Scott's "confidence."[14] Scott, of course, reciprocated. He wrote a letter addressed to the Whigs in Congress, telling how handsomely he was being treated by the President and the secretary of war—at the same time begging that the nine new regular regiments that Polk had requested be authorized without delay.

On November 19, 1846, Polk formally offered Scott the command of the Veracruz operation. Scott accepted gratefully, "so much affected that he almost shed tears." Scott left the White House "the most delighted man" Polk had seen for some time.[15] He was determined now to leave Washington as soon as possible, before anything could happen to change the President's mind.

Scott's euphoria was dampened, ever so slightly, by his desire to remain on friendly terms with Zachary Taylor, whom he was in many ways replacing. His conscience was reasonably clear that he had never done anything ungentlemanly to secure his present position. Admittedly, he had a few days earlier criticized Taylor's tone in his letters to Marcy, and had even said that Taylor should explain them, but that incident had occurred after Scott's appointment. Taylor, not he, was to blame for Taylor's fall from grace.

When Scott reached New York on November 25, therefore, he penned Taylor a long letter explaining the new situation. He was on his way to New Orleans, he said, expecting to be there by December 12. He planned to visit Taylor's base at the Brazos on the mouth of the Rio Grande, and from there to go up the river to Camargo, arriving on December 23. He regretted that he would not be able to come all the way to Monterrey to congratulate Taylor in person for his "many brilliant achievements" but hoped that they might meet later somewhere in the interior of Mexico. He recognized that Taylor might not be able to come to meet him on the Rio Grande. He was quick to give assurances as to the nature of his own mission:

> I am not coming, my dear general, to supersede you in the immediate command on the line of operations rendered illustrious by you and your gallant army. My proposed theatre is different. . . .
>
> But, my dear general, I shall be obliged to take from you most of the gallant officers and men (regulars and volunteers) whom you have so long and so nobly commanded. . . . This will be infinitely painful to you, and for that reason distressing to me. But I rely upon your patriotism to submit to the temporary sacrifice with cheerfulness.
>
> No man can better afford to do so.[16]

Scott had written such letters before, to Atkinson during the Black Hawk War and to Clinch in the early days of the Seminole War, and he was always sincere in doing so. But Scott was not dealing with Atkinson or Clinch now; he was dealing with a man who had won significant victories and had been bitten by the presidential bug.

Nevertheless, Taylor's first answer to Scott's letter was cheerful. On December 26 he replied from his headquarters between Monterrey and Victoria telling of his dispositions in delivering troops in the direction of Tampico, and ending,

> When my presence shall be no longer required at Victoria, I propose, unless otherwise instructed, to return to Monterey, which may be early in February. At all times and places I shall be happy to receive your orders, and hold myself and troops at your disposition.

At that point, fate stepped in to tear the previous friendship between Scott and Taylor asunder. The vessel on which Scott was traveling was held up by adverse winds, and by the time he arrived at Camargo on January 3, 1847, Taylor was already at Victoria, well out of communication. Scott now had to take what troops he needed without Taylor's participation in the choosing; he could do nothing else. In a letter to Butler, Taylor's second-in-command, he specified the units he would take:

> Regular cavalry (1st and 2d Dragoons): 500 men
> Volunteer cavalry: 500 men
> Two batteries of light field artillery
> Regular infantry (Worth and Twiggs): 4,000 men
> Volunteer infantry (Patterson): 4,000 men

At the same time that Scott ordered those troops to march to Tampico by way of Victoria, he wrote Taylor, allowing himself only a bit of pique:

> I am sorry that mine of the 20th ultimo had not been received by you, as it would, I think, have brought you back to Monterey. As it is, I am much embarrassed by your great distance from me. That circumstance, and the great pressure of time, has thrown me upon the necessity of giving direct instructions, of a very important character, to your next in command. Please see herewith a copy of my letter to Major General Butler, of this date.

Unaware of the consequences of this act, Scott ended with an optimistic note: "I believe my arrangements of every sort to be complete; Providence may defeat me, but I do not believe the Mexicans can."[17]

23

꧁꧂

Triumph at Veracruz

"The flag of the United States was this day . . ."

WINFIELD SCOTT was now at the summit of his career. He had been a general officer for thirty-two years; he had participated in the War of 1812, the Seminole War, and several peaceable Indian removals; he had performed invaluable service as his country's peacemaker on the northern frontier. Now, at the age of sixty but in full vigor, energy, and enthusiasm, he was about to embark on the expedition that, more than any other, has enshrined his name.

He had been general-in-chief for only four years, but those years had been productive. He had not changed the organization of the Army radically, but he had developed the light, or "flying," artillery to a new level of efficiency. In that all-important arm the U.S. Army was the finest in the world.[1]

The invasion of Mexico through the port of Veracruz was a vast undertaking, up to that time the most ambitious amphibious expedition in human history.[2] Scott planned to transport a large force by sea to Veracruz, land on a hostile shore under the guns of the formidable Castle of San Juan d'Ulloa, take a major port, and then advance over two hundred miles through a practically unknown countryside to seize Mexico's capital city of about 80,000 souls. All this would have been difficult enough even had Scott enjoyed the full backing of the President and the secretary of war, but Polk and Marcy were intent on cutting corners, demanding the most from their generals for the least cost. As a result, as time went on, Scott would find himself short of men and supplies that he had counted on—and on which he had made his rosy predictions of success.

Scott had first estimated, back in October, that he would need a force of 20,000 men to subdue Mexico by way of Veracruz. Later, when faced with the need to conduct his campaign on a shoestring, he shaved his troop requirements to make the project acceptable to Polk. His third and final memo did not contain any more reductions, because the prospects were improving for Congress to authorize the nine additional volunteer regiments being requested by the administration, making an augmentation of about 7,000 men.

Scott, as general-in-chief, had begun planning for the invasion even before President Polk had resolved the issue of command. Fortunately, Scott's small staff was competent. Thomas Jesup had been the Army's quartermaster general for thirty years, and during that long tenure had placed the office on a sound military and business basis, with procedures codified into Army regulations as early as 1821. The falling-out between him and Scott a decade earlier had never been fully healed, but Jesup knew his job and was willing to perform it as a professional.

A full month before Scott's appointment, Jesup had left Washington for New Orleans to purchase or lease large numbers of ships,[3] boats, wagons, and animals. It was well that Jesup started early, for he had to contract for ships and equipment without the advantages of the modern telephone or telegraph.

By the time of Scott's appointment, all requirements for the expedition had been calculated. Scott specified that he would need 50 transports with a capacity of 500 tons each and 140 flatboats, sufficient to carry an assault wave of 5,000 men. The transports were being chartered, but the flatboats had not even been designed yet, so Scott performed that task himself. He also, before leaving New York, wrote to Commodore David E. Conner, commander of the Home Squadron blockading the Mexican coast, asking for advice. He needed recommendations as to suitable landing spots, routes of approach, and means of avoiding the guns of San Juan. Conner had given Zachary Taylor invaluable help in establishing his base at Brazos Santiago, Texas, and Scott felt comfortable in counting on the naval officer's continued cooperation.

Scott's troubles with his civilian superiors were not over, however. When his ship docked at New Orleans on the way to the Brazos, a stranger approached him and delivered a letter from an old friend, Alexander Barrow, saying that President Polk had again asked Congress to establish the rank of lieutenant general in the Army. Presumably that lieutenant generalcy was to be conferred on Senator Benton. Scott, trusting Polk's professions of friendship, brushed Barrow's doubts aside, sure that Polk intended to bestow that exalted rank on himself. He continued to write to Secretary Marcy personal as well as official letters, one of which almost pleaded for reassurance:

> Private letters from members of Congress were received at the moment of my departure from New Orleans (not addressed to me) stating that Colonel Benton would be appointed *Lieutenant General* and sent to Mexico. I do not believe a word of it, and have unlimited confidence in the kindness and sincerity of the President and yourself. I say so on all proper occasions ... besides writing to that effect in Washington—to Crittenden, J. M. Clayton, Corwin, Archer, Morehead, Barrow, Washington Hunt, etc., etc.[4]

Rumors persisted, however, and Scott's naiveté finally gave way. He now realized that, as he had forecast, he was indeed being subjected to "fire from his rear as well as fire from his front." In later years he would describe Polk's actions with venom: "A grosser violation of human confidence is nowhere recorded." Fortunately for the interests of the United States, Congress refused even to consider Polk's proposal.

Barrow's warnings were understated. In Washington, the president was not only attempting to establish a lieutenant generalcy for Senator Benton; he now suspected Scott of subversion, his suspicions arising partly from a trivial incident. It involved Colonel William Selby Harney, commander of the 2d Dragoons, a dashing, fiery officer, who tended toward the insubordinate and who carried a personal animus toward Scott. Scott was aware of Harney's feelings, and when he learned that Harney was among those officers coming to his command from Taylor, he ordered the hotheaded subordinate to return to Taylor. Harney refused to obey Scott's order and was placed under court-martial. Scott was not vindictive. He allowed Harney to select the members of the court, and when the court recommended a severe reprimand, Scott reversed the decision, restoring Harney to his position as commanding officer of the 2d Dragoons, part of the invasion force.

Polk knew nothing of Scott's generosity. When he received word of Harney's impending trial, he recorded in his diary that Harney was "known to be one of the most gallant and best officers in the service. . . .

He was, however, a Democrat in politics. . . . I can conceive of no reason but this for the arbitrary and tyrannical conduct of General Scott."[5] He ordered Harney's reinstatement, which had already been done. Even when he learned the facts, Polk never seemed to feel at all apologetic for the injustice of his attitude.

Important events were meanwhile transpiring in northern Mexico. On February 22, 1847, Zachary Taylor's army of about 6,000 men, almost all of them volunteers, were facing the battle of their lives. Mexican President Antonio López de Santa Anna had marched an army of 25,000 men from San Luis Potosí across three hundred miles of desert to hit Taylor's overextended position. Though Santa Anna lost over half his men on the long, grueling march, and the remainder were tired and hungry, the disparity in strength between the two armies was still great.

The armies made contact at Buena Vista, a hacienda a few miles south of Saltillo. Taylor had not been ordered to Saltillo, much less to Buena Vista; Scott had urged him to stay back at Monterrey. Taylor's reasons for ignoring Scott's urgent plea were probably personal, involving rage against being relegated to a secondary theater and possible political eclipse.

The Battle of Buena Vista began late on February 22, 1847, a date Taylor's troops considered auspicious as George Washington's birthday. The first actions were indecisive, but the next morning fighting began in earnest. Despite the advantages of a strong defensive position, determined troops, superior artillery, and extraordinary good luck, Taylor's army barely survived the day's battle. On awakening the morning of the 24th, the Americans were astonished to find that Santa Anna had left the field, his ammunition low and his men exhausted. Of Santa Anna's original force, less than 10,000 men would make it back to San Luis.

On February 15 the other American force, under Scott, was at the Brazos Santiago on the Rio Grande. Scott was feeling discouraged; he had returned from Camargo in late December, expecting the troops he had taken from Taylor to arrive ready to continue on to Tampico. Not all of them had arrived. Quartermaster-General Jesup, despite energetic efforts, had been unable to secure transports in time; in fact the first of the large ships began arriving at the Brazos only on February 11. The problem was cost. Ship owners, aware of the government's dire need for transports, ran the prices up, with the result that every purchase was a confrontation.[6] Scott therefore left Worth behind to bring the regular troops as they arrived and set out aboard the *Massachusetts* with a few accompanying vessels for Tampico, where he was to assemble that portion of his army that was not coming directly from home ports.

The *Massachusetts* arrived at Tampico during the evening of February 18, 1847, and Scott went ashore the next morning. There, he was glad to find that 6,000 men were on hand. The troops were in a festive mood, having been paid the previous day. Soldiers lined the banks to cheer their commander, and a band brought from Governor's Island, New York, played martial tunes. The artillery in the marketplace fired salutes, while large details of troops held back the crowds of curious Mexicans, who wished to get a glimpse of the great American. Scott declined to ride the horse that had been provided for him, preferring to walk to his quarters, his huge frame dwarfing his staff. That evening a full moon provided the inspiration for more festivity.

Scott stayed only one night at Tampico, and on February 20 was again aboard the *Massachusetts*. He and his staff then set sail for his major rendezvous point, Lobos Island, 70 miles down the coast from Tampico and another 200 from Veracruz. The *Massachusetts* arrived there on February 21, but Scott stayed aboard the ship when heavy weather prevented debarking. The next day was Washington's birthday. Scott could not know—and would not know for some time—that Zachary Taylor was beginning the fierce fight at Buena Vista that same afternoon.

At Lobos Island, Scott was again disappointed to find that many of his volunteers, some of whom were to come directly from their home ports in the United States, had not yet arrived. (He knew that the regulars were behind him.) The necessary landing craft were also missing. Scott could only wait, drill his troops, and hope. He also needed time for his troops to recover from an epidemic of smallpox that had broken out among them. Fortunately, that scourge dissipated before he was forced to move on.

By early March, most of Scott's expected transport ships and about sixty-five flatboats had arrived at Lobos. Though that number represented only half of those he had ordered, his patience was nearing its end, and he decided that time considerations overrode the need to put maximum strength ashore in the first wave; he would make do with that reduced number and press on. He organized his available force into three divisions, two of regulars and one of volunteers. The regular divisions were commanded by Brevet Major General William J. Worth and Brigadier General David E. Twiggs, the volunteer division by Major General Robert Patterson.[7]

On March 3, Scott's fleet set sail from Lobos, the personal red flag of a major general flying from the mast of the steamer *Massachusetts.* Scott himself stood dramatically at the prow, soldiers and sailors cheering. By March 5, 1847, about seventy sail had appeared off the island of Anton Lizardo, where Commodore Conner kept his headquarters south of Veracruz.

The sight greeting Scott and his armada from the water was spectacular. Off in the distance, behind the spires of the beautiful "City of the True Cross," stood the magnificent 15,000-foot peak Orizaba. Between the ships and the city stood the menacing fort of San Juan d'Ulloa. The air was clear, the weather brisk. Standing out to meet the convoy were the sloops *Albany* and *John Adams,* sent by Commodore Conner to guide Scott's ships into the anchorage of Anton Lizardo lagoon. Anton Lizardo was twelve miles below Veracruz along the coast.

From the outset, Scott and Conner worked together harmoniously. Conner, who had reconnoitered several landing sites before Scott's arrival, had narrowed the number to two. Scott examined the reports on both and tentatively decided to use the beach called Collada, a site near the city but out of range of the guns of the fortress of San Juan. The beach sat behind Sacrificios Island from the ocean and therefore was expected to provide relatively calm conditions for the debarkation.

Collada had one drawback; its harbor was too small to handle Scott's large transports. Conner had an answer to that; he could, he said, transfer Scott's troops from the transports to his naval vessels, and from them he could transfer them a second time to the flatboats. The arrangement seemed reasonable to Scott, and they decided on that plan.

On March 7, two days after Scott's arrival, he and Conner decided to reconnoiter Collada Beach in person. Taking members of their staffs with them, they set out on a small ship to verify what they had concluded on paper. For some reason—perhaps they were preoccupied—their boat sailed too close to Fort San Juan, and the Mexican gunners opened fire, several shots coming dangerously close. Had the boat been hit, that one round would have greatly affected history, for the passenger list included names that would become famous as the future leaders in the Civil War: Captain Robert E. Lee, Lieutenant George G. Meade, Major Joseph E. Johnston, and Lieutenant P. G. T. Beauregard. George Meade, ever the worrier, later wrote home that "one shot, hitting the vessel, might have been the means of breaking up the whole expedition." A sterner view of the incident was provided by Captain E. Kirby Smith in a letter home to his wife:

> The stupidity of the enemy alone saved them. The enemy should have used their entire water battery and thrown solid shot alone, opening on the boat when nearest and they must have sunk it,—but they waited until she was going off and then with no effect sent only the eleven shots spoken of.[8]

It is doubtful that the Mexican gunners had any idea whom they were firing at.

The actual landing was closely observed by George Ballantine, a literate young Briton in one of David Twiggs's regiments. Ballantine, a good soldier, was no glory hound; he was quite content that it would be Worth's, not Twiggs's, troops who would lead the assault on Collada Beach. He had not the slightest inclination, he frankly recorded, to "earn high fame or distinction." Still he was keenly interested in the landing procedure.

Ballantine had heard through the grapevine that General Scott had demanded the surrender of Veracruz and San Juan d'Ulloa on the night of March 7—and that the Mexican commander had spurned the demand outright. Scott had been ready for the landing the next day, but once more there had been a delay; one of the dreaded "northers" had forced Scott's armada to ride out the storm. Nothing happened on March 8. On the morning of March 9 the sun was out bright and clear, and there was no doubt that the landing would occur that day.

All commanding officers had readied their men for the forthcoming operation. Each carried two days' rations in his haversack, and each man carried a full canteen of water, a blanket, or, as a substitute, his greatcoat; the rest of his clothing and possessions were to remain aboard the vessel he was leaving.

Ballantine was impressed by the surfboats that Scott had designed for this landing, though he may not have known who had designed them. Each boat was strong, light, and roomy, carrying about a hundred men with ease. He was aware that his regiment would be transferred from his transport to the brig *Porpoise,* on which they would await their turn to go ashore in a flatboat on one of the follow-up waves.

The harbor at Sacrificios Island was jammed full with ships of war, both

American and foreign. Ballantine could identify—or have pointed out to him—an English man-of-war brig, a French vessel of the same type, and a Spanish sloop. The officers of these vessels were all at the quarter-decks, and the men were all in the rigging, eyeing the whole proceedings with much curiosity. Turning to the landward, Ballantine could make out the objectives—a series of thirty-foot sand hills that had been formed by drifting and the violent gales of the frequent northers. The transfer to the *Porpoise* was completed by about 11:00 A.M.

By early afternoon the time came for the transfer from the naval vessels to the flatboats. Ballantine timed it: Worth's 5,500 men, who were to lead the assault, took about a half hour. As Twiggs's men watched the preparations, they felt a wave of excitement sweep over them. Ballantine now believed that many would have gladly gone ashore with that assault wave.

It was an exciting and imposing sight. At a given moment in late afternoon, a cannon roar from the *Massachusetts* ripped through the air. It was the signal for the assault to begin. The military bands from the regiments struck up "Yankee Doodle," "Hail Columbia," and "The Star-Spangled Banner." The flatboats started ashore, and Scott savored the cheers of his men as they passed the *Massachusetts,* each flatboat being rowed by sailors from Conner's squadron. Ballantine could see American men-of-war anchored near the shore, ready to open on the enemy should he appear.

The fire never came. Worth's division, as it neared the shore, reached a point where the water was only knee-deep. Worth, in the lead, jumped into the calm water and headed for shore, his men following him. Once ashore they quickly reorganized and dashed to take possession of the line of sand hills a few hundred yards inland, encountering almost no Mexican resistance. Without a single loss 5,500 men landed safely at Collada Beach at 5:30 P.M. Another trip or two sufficed for the Navy to deliver the rest of Scott's force, which came nearly to 12,000 men. Scott and Conner had made history.

Scott could go about taking Veracruz in one of three ways: he could assault the walls of the city by frontal attack; he could reduce it by starving it out by a passive siege; or he could reduce it by an active siege, cutting it off from resupply and reinforcement while his heavy guns took it under fire. Any one of the three methods, he believed, would eventually be successful. A direct attack would of course consume less time than a siege—an important factor—but it would be costly in the lives of his soldiers. Aside from the humanitarian aspect, always important with Scott, he believed he could not afford to so weaken his army. A passive siege, on the other hand, while more humane to all involved, would be too slow to meet Scott's timetable for leaving the unhealthy lowlands. He therefore decided to conduct an active siege. The city was small—only about 15,000 people spread behind a mile of coastline—and the heavy guns expected to arrive from the United States could easily render it untenable.

His decision was not universally popular. William J. Worth publicly ridiculed Scott's caution, comparing it unfavorably with Taylor's aggressive attack on Monterrey the previous September. Scott, however, was firm in his resolve, so upon landing he set out to cut the city off from the Mexican interior by moving his three divisions around to the west. Once that was accomplished, he could begin building up supplies and bombarding the city. He began the movement on the morning of March 10, 1847.

The first stage, surrounding Veracruz on the landward side, would be a tiring and tedious undertaking; the sand was soft, and pulling supply wagons and guns through it was back-breaking. So Scott did what he could to equalize the burden. Worth's division had landed in the vanguard of the army, but Scott did not plan to send him further inland. Instead he passed Patterson's division through Worth's lines and, after Patterson had reached his destination, he sent Twiggs through Patterson, all the way to the northeast end of the line. Thus each division could at least travel over the ground already broken by its predecessor. This scheme also kept Worth's division back at Collada Beach, where Scott maintained his headquarters, near Conner.

Difficult as these movements were, the planned encirclement was completed by the end of the third day, when Twiggs reached the town of Vergara, on the far end of the line. The next day, March 13, another norther hit, forcing Conner's naval vessels to take refuge in open waters. The storm lasted only a day, however, and soon the sailors were delivering the first of the mortars, artillery, and horses to the beaches. It was now time to begin the bombardment.

Again Scott was to suffer frustration. He had only light field guns on hand; the heavy mortars scheduled to arrive from the United States had not yet come. Scott sent futile letters of complaint and finally decided to give up. He turned to his friend Conner for help once more. Could he borrow some heavy guns from Conner's ships to supplement the fire from his other four artillery batteries? Those naval guns, far heavier than anything Scott had at the moment, would be invaluable.

Conner, always helpful, exacted a price this time. His own men were suffering from intense boredom aboard their blockading ships, he said, and it would constitute a severe blow to their pride to give up their treasured guns for the use of the Army. Conner agreed to loan the guns, but he stipulated that they be manned by his own seamen. Scott readily accepted that arrangement. The siege would now have punch.

The transfer of the guns to the siege line did not, however, take place during Conner's tenure of command. Past retirement age and in poor health, he had been scheduled to return home for a long time but had always been kept on his post for just a little longer. Now his successor arrived, and all the army officers could do to express their gratitude was to pay calls on Conner, wishing him well in the future. Fortunately, the officer who replaced Conner, Commodore Matthew Perry,[9] continued with his predecessor's policies.

The naval guns were soon ashore and being tugged into place under the supervision of Captain Robert E. Lee, an assistant engineer. It was hard going, and it took so long that Scott's patience gave out. On March 22, before the guns were even installed, he issued an ultimatum to the Mexican commander, General Juan Morales, to surrender the city. Morales defied the ultimatum; so did the foreigners in the city, who seemed also to take Scott's threats lightly. Though free at that moment to leave, most of the foreigners remained, to their intense sorrow during the next few days.

The naval guns opened fire on Veracruz during the evening of March 23, 1847, under the command of Captain J. H. Aulick of the Navy, Perry's second in command. The 6,300-pound monsters, each of which threw solid shot of 32 pounds each, were heavy enough to soften the walls around the city. The Paixhans, named after the French naval lieutenant who had designed them, were even more powerful. The shots they fired each weighed 62 pounds. The sailors were delighted with this new activity. Commodore Perry rotated the crews so as to give every man possible a chance to participate. Even when a Mexican shell killed four of their number, the tars were only stimulated, not discouraged.

Inside the city, the devastation was severe. The people accused the Americans unjustly of targeting churches and hospitals. Mexican batteries from Forts Santiago, San José, San Fernando, Santa Barbara, and San Juan d'Ulloa returned the fire, though with little effect.

While the exchange of fire was going on, Scott toured his lines. In one instance he was walking the lines and spotted some men peeping over the parapet. "Down—down, men!" he shouted. "Don't expose yourselves!"

MAJOR GEN. WINFIELD SCOTT.
Of the United States Army

Winfield Scott, 1815, pictured as a young major general still short of his thirtieth birthday. *(After Joseph Wood; National Portrait Gallery, Smithsonian Institution)*

A. BURR, ESQ.

Aaron Burr, former Vice President of the United States, whose trial for treason Scott witnessed as a young law student in 1807. *(Enoch Gridley, artist; National Portrait Gallery, Smithsonian Institution)*

Thomas Jefferson, President of the United States 1801–1809. His imagination foresaw the vast continental empire that Scott would do so much to build. *(James Akin, artist; National Portrait Gallery, Smithsonian Institution)*

Major General James Wilkinson, Scott's bête noire— a man who, though on active service, accepted stipends from the government of Spain. *(Charles Wilson Peale, artist; Independence National Historical Park, Philadelphia)*

James Madison, President of the United States 1809–1817. An inept commander-in-chief, he nonetheless recognized Scott's true worth as a combat commander. *(Chester Harding, artist; National Portrait Gallery, Smithsonian Institution)*

Tecumseh, the great Shawnee chief who attempted to unify the Indian tribes against the United States. *(Artist unknown; Benson J. Lossing,* Pictorial Field-Book of the War of 1812*)*

Sir Isaac Brock, the aggressive British commander, killed at Queenston in October 1812; respected by British and Americans alike. *(J. W. L. Forster, artist; Government of Ontario Art Collection)*

Brigader General Stephen Van Rensselaer, prominent citizen of New York State, commander of American troops at Queenston, October 1812. *(Artist unknown; Benson J. Lossing, Pictorial Field-Book of the War of 1812)*

John E. Wool, Scott's contemporary and friend from Queenston to the Civil War. *(U.S. Army Military History Institute)*

Thomas Jesup, Scott's aggressive regimental commander at Chippewa and Lundy's Lane, July 1814; later Army Quartermaster General. *(U.S. Army photo)*

General Andrew Jackson, President of the United States 1829–1837. The only man who ever humiliated Scott and yet retained his admiration and respect. *(Charles Torrey, artist; National Portrait Gallery, Smithsonian Institution)*

Martin Van Buren, President of the United States 1837–1841. Known as "the Little Magician," he did not allow political differences to destroy his long friendship with Scott *(John Langerdoerffer, artist; National Portrait Gallery, Smithsonian Institution)*

Henry Clay of Kentucky, three-time nominee of the Whig party, and therefore sometime rival of Scott. *(Albert Newsam, artist; National Portrait Gallery, Smithsonian Institution)*

Osceola, the fiery Seminole chief who largely perpetrated the Second Seminole War. *(George Catlin, artist; National Museum of American Art, Smithsonian Institution)*

Edmund P. Gaines, Scott's lifelong rival in the Army and probably his bitterest enemy. *(U.S. Army Military History Institute)*

Winfield Scott, at about the time of his campaign in the Second Seminole War, 1836. (*A. H. Ritchie, artist; Scott,* Autobiography*)*

James Monroe, President of the United States 1817–1825. Scott's friend and confidant from the days following the War of 1812 to Monroe's death in 1831. *(John Vanderlyn, artist; National Portrait Gallery, Smithsonian Institution)*

John Quincy Adams, President of the United States 1825–1829. Scott's friend from 1816, but one who must have had second thoughts about the friendship from time to time. *(Philip Haas, artist; Mead Art Museum, Amherst College)*

Winfield Scott at the beginning of the War between the United States and Mexico, 1846–1848, showing his age but with energy and faculties undiminished. *(Library of Congress)*

James Knox Polk, President of the United States 1845–1849. The purposeful protagonist of Manifest Destiny, his obsessions with domestic politics damaged his effectiveness as commander-in-chief in the War with Mexico. *(Library of Congress)*

(Above) William Marcy, Secretary of W₁ under James Polk. He manfully faced t challenge of maintaining some sort of harmony between President and Gene in-Chief. *(Artist unknown; National Portrait Gallery, Smithsonian Institutio*

(Left) Nicholas Trist, President Polk's emissary with Scott's army, a man with whom Scott developed a close relation ship after a bad start. *(Library of Congress)*

Antonio Lopez de Santa Anna, Mexican dictator and general-in-chief during the War with Mexico, 1846–1848. (American History Magazine)

Captain Robert E. Lee, Scott's most trusted subordinate during the War with Mexico, and the man Scott was grooming to succeed himself as general-in-chief of the U.S. Army. *(Library of Congress)*

Major General William J. Worth, Scott's one-time aide and close friend, who turned against Scott when his lust for advancement and recognition overcame him. *(Charles Fenderick, artist; National Portrait Gallery, Smithsonian Institution)*

Franklin Pierce, President of the United States 1853–1857. He was Scott's subordinate during the War with Mexico, but subsequently he humiliated Scott in the presidential election of 1852. *(George Peter Alexander Healy, artist; National Portrait Gallery, Smithsonian Institution)*

Jefferson Davis, Secretary of War under Franklin Pierce, later President of the Confederacy, 1861–1865; his ego clashed violently with Scott's. *(William Sartain, artist; National Portrait Gallery, Smithsonian Institution)*

Winfield Scott about 1852. An idealized painting, probably designed for use in the political campaign of the same year. *(New-York Historical Society)*

Abraham Lincoln, President of the United States 1861–1865. At first dependent on Scott's military prowess, he was later aware of the need to replace the aging General with more youthful men. *(Library of Congress)*

William Seward, Secretary of State under Abraham Lincoln. Scott's apparent political ally, he ruthlessly took advantage of Scott's trusting friendship. *(Library of Congress)*

Major General George B. McClellan, who professed to be Scott's loyal subordinate, was to become the man who most severely undercut him the beginning of the Civil W *(Currier and Ives Lithograph National Portrait Gallery, Smithsonian Institution)*

Winfield Scott in 1861. This image, showing Scott in his old age, is unfortunately the one that has most frequently charac- terized him in the public mind. *(Photo by Matthew Brady; National Portrait Gallery, Smithsonian Institution)*

One of them, almost as if he had been planted for the purpose, shouted back, "But General, *you* are exposed." That was Scott's cue: "Oh," he answered theatrically, "generals nowadays can be made out of anybody, but *men* cannot be had."[10]

The bombardment proved to be highly effective. A witness in the city described it graphically:

> From that time the horrors of a bombarded city commenced. The surgical hospital, which was situated in the Convent of Santo Domingo, suffered from the fire, and several of the inmates were killed by fragments of bombs bursting at that point. While an operation was performing on a wounded man, the explosion of a shell extinguished the lights, and when others were brought, the patient was found torn in pieces, and many others dead and wounded. . . . On the 24th the [naval] battery opened its fire. The battery was composed of four mortars of 68 pounds and four of 36, taken from the steamer *Mississippi.* Six pieces were turned against the battery of Santa Gertrudis. A shower of grenades and balls then fell, which spread death and despair. . . . The firing was prolonged through the whole night, and the same on the 25th. Vera Cruz then presented a sad sight. Fathers of families, who had lost their houses, their fortunes, and their children, unhappy infants, who now had no parents, wounded men, without food, without surgical aid. . . . The people were hungry. . . . Such was the spectacle presented by Vera Cruz.[11]

After two days of this bombardment, the foreign consuls of England, France, and Prussia in Veracruz sent out a message appealing to Scott for a cease-fire to allow them to move the noncombatants out of the city. Scott would have none of this plea: the consuls had defied his earlier ultimatum and they could now suffer the consequences. The consuls, however, were determined to stop the danger to their nationals. On receiving Scott's refusal of their request, they turned on General Morales, demanding that he surrender. Morales was ready to do so, but honor forbade. He therefore feigned illness and turned the command over to his deputy, General J. J. Landero. Landero immediately sent Scott a message proposing that the two sides establish a commission to arrange a "convention." Scott ceased fire and the commission met on the afternoon of March 26, 1847.

For two days the Mexican and American commissioners haggled. The Mexican demands, made while the guns were silent, were generous to themselves: the 3,000-man garrison was to be permitted to leave the city, carrying arms and accoutrements, without being forced to sign paroles. In addition,

Morales had given Landero authority to surrender only the city, not the fortress of San Juan. When Scott prepared to recommence the bombardment, however, the Mexicans relented, and on the evening of March 27, 1847, they signed the surrender agreement. Both the city and the fortress were to be handed over to Scott's force; all the garrison's arms were to be turned over in a formal ceremony, representing the honorable terms of the surrender. The Mexican troops were all to be paroled until regularly exchanged, and the religious and civil rights of the city's inhabitants were to be respected.

Through all these negotiations, which were being conducted by Captain Aulick, Scott had been tense. When he received news of the signing, he exuberantly clasped the messenger with joy, nearly tearing him from his mount. His decision to take Veracruz by siege rather than by assault had been amply justified.

The siege of Veracruz, however, was not an end in itself; the port was merely a way station on Scott's path to Mexico City.

24

❧❦❧

Cerro Gordo:
Almost According to Plan

"The enemy army has ceased to exist."

O N THE FIRST Sunday in April, 1847, Major General Winfield Scott
donned his full dress uniform to participate in an unusual ceremony.
Together with his staff, he left his headquarters near Collada Beach, Mexico,
to join the local Mexican governor for Catholic services at the Veracruz
Cathedral. Attending religious services on a Sunday would not ordinarily be
considered noteworthy, but this event would be fraught with political significance. Scott knew that his attendance at Catholic services would seriously damage his chances to attain the Whig presidential nomination in
1848. One of his principal sources of political support, the anti-Catholic,
xenophobic group known as the "Native Americans" or "Nativists,"[1] would
be irate on reading of it. Yet Scott was not deterred by that prospect. Though
he had never dropped his interest in seeking the presidency, his current military mission took precedence over all other considerations.

The priests conducting the service made the most of Scott's presence.
They thoughtfully placed a bench against the wall for his use—the rest of
the congregation stood—and one of the priests brought a lighted candle
down from the altar and gave it to Scott. Other priests gave smaller candles
to his aides. Soon Scott found himself marching in a procession around the
church, an active participant. His loyal and respectful staff found it difficult
to suppress their smiles.

The general's attendance at Catholic mass was part of a calculated campaign to win the friendship of the Mexicans. Though Scott and Polk agreed

on very little else, they shared a common goal of keeping the war between Mexico and the United States as limited as possible. Scott's army, which never exceeded 12,000 men, would stand little chance of achieving his ends if seven million Mexicans were lined up solidly against him. In order to convince the people of Mexico that the Americans had come as friends, therefore, Scott set out to ensure that the rights of the Catholic Church were respected. American soldiers were required to salute priests when meeting them on the street, and Scott's attendance at church was part of this effort.

Moreover, Scott made sure that his order proclaiming martial law stressed the benign nature of the occupation. To enforce Mexican rights he soon found it necessary to restrict his troops to the city, where foraging soldiers would find it impossible to kill domestic animals belonging to the Mexicans—a source of great anguish among the population. He enforced iron discipline. Colonel Ethan A. Hitchcock witnessed the hanging of an American soldier for rape a couple of weeks after the surrender of the city.

Though Scott had taken Veracruz with remarkable ease, he spared himself no time for savoring success. It was necessary to remove the bulk of his army from coastal Mexico before the *vomito* (yellow fever) season set in. He planned to march to Puebla by the so-called National Road, the same route Hernando Cortés had taken three centuries earlier, up the coast from Veracruz, into the Sierra Madre to Puebla, by way of Jalapa.* Mexico City, beyond Puebla, was the final objective; taking Veracruz would be meaningless without seizing Mexico City. His most urgent requirement, for the moment, was to move his troops into the relatively healthful climate of Jalapa.

Scott's most serious problem was his lack of transportation to carry supplies. His army had been conveyed and supplied by ships up to this point, but the campaign into the interior of Mexico would require him to carry great amounts of food and ammunition. He estimated that he needed about eight thousand mules and about a thousand wagons just for the delivery of supplies.[2] As it was, he lacked wagons, mules, everything.

Scott made no effort to be diplomatic in his complaints to Quartermaster Jesup or to Secretary Marcy. He was particularly angry when he received a hypocritical letter from Marcy communicating "views in regard to preserving health of the troops in the insalubrious season which is approach-

---

*Another route to Puebla, the Orizaba Road, was also available. Scott's information convinced him that the National Road was better maintained and was being improved. The relatively new National Bridge, which crossed the River Antigua, stood as evidence of that contention.

ing." The President, Marcy informed Scott gratuitously, was "very solicitous that the valuable lives of the patriotic men who have entered public service . . . should not be wasted by the ravages of malignant disease." A few mules and wagons would have helped Scott a great deal more than such advice from Washington.

Since no supplies were arriving from the United States, Scott set about to remedy his shortages on his own. He sent John Quitman's brigade, from Patterson's division, to search the Gulf coast at Alvarado for wagons and mules. Another expedition was dispatched to Antigua. Neither effort was really productive. Scott's army still had only about a quarter of the transportation he believed he needed.

Yet he could not afford to delay leaving Veracruz pending the resolution of his supply problems. On April 8, he began the move by sending one-third of his army, Twiggs's division, along the National Road toward Jalapa. Twiggs had occupied the northernmost sector of the army during the siege, and his division was therefore the one nearest the National Road, a logical selection.

Not everyone, however, agreed with Scott's logic. William Worth, who had customarily led the vanguards of both Taylor's and Scott's armies, had come to consider the leading role as his right. He regarded Twiggs's designation as a personal affront.* Taking advantage of his long and close association with Scott, he confronted the commanding general with his complaint. Scott did not bother to remonstrate; he brushed his brash subordinate off with a terse remark that other generals were also entitled to the "position of honor." Worth was already in a touchy mood, still smarting from having been proved wrong in advocating a frontal assault on Veracruz, a position he had advocated almost to the point of insolence. He felt that Scott's sending Twiggs in the vanguard was a form of reprisal—and that the man for whom he had named his own son was punishing him. From that point on, the relations between Scott and Worth cooled rapidly.

Mexican resistance to the American landing at Veracruz had been light, but that situation was about to change. On March 9, 1847—the day the Americans landed at Collada Beach—Mexican President Santa Anna

---

*Worth had been the first man to cross the Arroyo Colorado with Taylor a year earlier. He had later crossed into Matamoros to confer with the Mexicans on Taylor's behalf. And Worth, as noted above, had personally led Scott's first wave at Collada Beach on March 9.

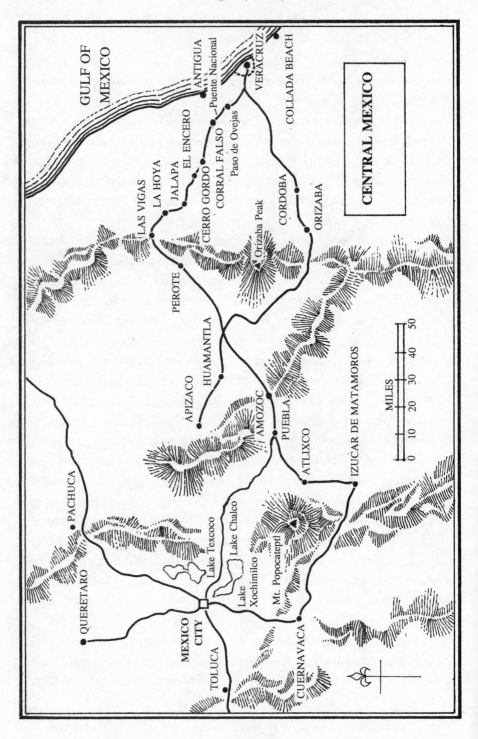

had led what remained of his starved, parched army into his base at San Luis Potosí. Though the Buena Vista campaign had cost him some 10,500 men, over half his army, the one-legged dictator was still a masterful recruiter and organizer. Miraculously, he had managed to reconstitute a respectable Mexican force during the month that Scott had been busy at Veracruz.[3]

Not everyone in Mexico City had been deceived by Santa Anna's claims of victory at Buena Vista. Therefore he had been forced to spend a few days putting down a near insurrection fomented by his vice president, Gomez Farias. Paradoxically, the news of Scott's landing at Veracruz came to Santa Anna not as a cause for alarm but as a pleasant surprise. He would, he promised his people, follow up his recent "victory" with a similar one over Scott. "My duty," he loudly proclaimed,

> is to sacrifice myself, and I will know how to fulfill it! Perhaps the American hosts may proudly tread the imperial capital of Azteca. I will never witness such opprobrium, for I am decided first to die fighting![4]

The people applauded. With his newly organized army, whose growing ranks would soon include many troops Scott had paroled at Veracruz, Santa Anna left Mexico City on the National Road to Veracruz on April 3, 1847.

Brigadier General David E. ("Old Davy") Twiggs got off to a bad start in the first stages of his march to Jalapa. Following the National Road, he set a rapid march rate through the heavy sand, but he soon found that the troops could not cope with the pace. Nearly 30 percent of them fell out along the wayside. The damage, however, was slight. A few stragglers were killed by Mexican irregulars, but most of the exhausted men rejoined their units by the end of the day.

The next morning things went better. Twiggs broke camp early and slowed down the pace. After a few miles the road turned inland toward Jalapa; leaving the heat of the lowlands, the division began to ascend the Sierra Madres. Soon the Americans entered into what George Ballantine, the articulate Englishman, described as a scene of "picturesque beauty." A comrade Ballantine referred to as a "Glasgow gallant" exclaimed, "Scotland or damn me!" Ballantine agreed, calling the panorama "exceedingly like the section of a Scotch river glen." As they continued on, Twiggs's men descended a steep slope that led to the National Bridge over the Antigua River. They crossed the Antigua unopposed by any Mexicans; General Valentin

Canalizo, who had been sent by Santa Anna to hold the bridge, had prudently decided to leave the scene.

By noon of the next day, April 11, Twiggs's division reached the town of Plan del Rio, which was situated on the east bank of the confusingly named Rio del Plan. Twiggs knew that a Mexican force was occupying the hill of Cerro Gordo several miles away, but he decided to brush it aside with his advance guard. The advance force, however, was stopped in its tracks by small arms and even artillery; Santa Anna's entire army was facing them. Twiggs pulled his forward units back and began to plan an all-out attack for an assault on April 14, three days away.

"Old Davy" Twiggs was popular among his men in a rough sort of way. He was a great showman, and the troops enjoyed his profanity and even his violent outbursts of temper. They did not, however, hold his mental capacities in any awe, and they questioned his judgment in bringing on a major engagement under these circumstances. They did not protest openly, of course, but they began writing their "last letters home," as soldiers customarily do when they fear they might be killed the next day. Twiggs went ahead with his plans, ordering his three engineers—Joseph E. Johnston, Pierre G. T. Beauregard, and Zealous B. Tower[5]—to make a thorough reconnaissance of the front in preparation.

On the evening of April 13, as Twiggs's men resigned themselves to attack the next morning, Major General Robert Patterson, leading the Volunteer Division, arrived at Plan del Rio. Patterson, as a major general, was now in command, but he was sick with fever and gladly turned temporary command over to Twiggs while he took to his bed. No sooner had he lain down, however, than he heard of Twiggs's plans for attack the next morning. Unwilling to assume the responsibility himself, and certainly unwilling to let Twiggs act in his behalf, Patterson roused himself, temporarily resumed command, and called off the attack pending the arrival of Scott in person.

At eleven o'clock that evening George Ballantine entered one of the tents occupied by downcast soldiers. What he saw was not cheerful: "various groups of anxious-looking faces in the flickering light of the bivouac fire, gloomily watching their unleavened cakes, and thinking bitterly of the morrow." But then, when word of the cancellation came,

> the announcement produced one of the most sudden illuminations of the human countenance divine among these groups, which I ever recollect to have seen. The cakes were either abandoned, or carried away half-baked, to be fin-

ished at some other opportunity, and all retired to sleep, carrying their news to their dreaming comrades, that the attack was deferred until Scott came up.

The next day, at about noon, Scott himself arrived at Plan del Rio, accompanied by the head of Worth's division. The troops "now expected that something would be done, and all seemed to feel a revival of confidence and anticipation of success." Scott felt that confidence as he rode into camp. "No commander," he later wrote, "was ever received with heartier cheers—the certain presage of the victories that followed."

Scott's total strength at Cerro Gordo, including Worth's division, was about 8,500 men; he estimated he was facing about 12,000. Scott was certain that Santa Anna would never attack, despite his superior numbers, because his hastily organized army was much too unreliable for offensive actions. Scott's assumption turned out to be correct; Santa Anna had decided simply to make a stand at Cerro Gordo.

Cerro Gordo, or El Télégrafo,* was the name of a round hill about 1,000 feet high that lay seven miles west of Plan del Rio. Behind the hill, at its base, lay the town by the same name, Cerro Gordo. Both the town of Cerro Gordo and Plan del Rio are located on the left (north) bank of the Rio del Plan, which runs east-west in a straight line. The National Road joins the two towns but it does not follow along the banks of the river. Instead it meanders off to the northeast immediately after leaving Plan del Rio and only later does it return and run along the river just before reaching the town of Cerro Gordo. In its initial stages, where a considerable space lies between the National Road and the river bluffs, Santa Anna had selected three prominent cliffs, on which he placed three artillery batteries to command the National Road as it approached him (see map, p. 253).

Those three batteries, however, were merely an outpost; Santa Anna established his main defensive position a couple of miles behind them, on El Télégrafo. Since the Americans approaching along the National Road would be exposed to deadly artillery fire from that prepared position, Santa Anna could say, from the porch of his comfortable villa nearby, that he had selected an excellent position indeed.

Santa Anna's position, however, had one weakness. An extensive tract of

---

*For convenience, "El Télégrafo" will be used for the hill, "Cerro Gordo" for the town. The topography of the region is unchanged during these past 150 years.

wilderness ran up to his left (north) flank, the vegetation along it so dense that it denied Santa Anna any reasonable observation in that direction. That flank was therefore vulnerable, provided an enemy could make his way through that tangled woods with guns and ammunition. The complacent Santa Anna was not concerned about that threat, however. Having decided that the woods in that direction were impenetrable, he ignored the pleas of his subordinates, who urged him to fortify a somewhat smaller hill called La Atalaya, which could have protected that flank. He sent only an observation post of two dozen men to occupy it.

As Scott studied Santa Anna's position, he decided to attack it along the National Road only as a last resort. A less professional officer, concluding that the Mexican left flank could not be reached, might have settled for that obvious but costly approach. Given the high quality of Scott's officers and men, such tactics might have succeeded in carrying the position, but it was plain that the casualties would have been heavy, and Scott had only a minimum number of troops in his army. So as soon as he arrived at Plan del Rio on April 12, Scott began seeking alternate plans.

Lieutenants Johnston, Beauregard, and Tower had done a thorough job of scouting the area along the National Road during the time that Twiggs was planning his own attack on Cerro Gordo. Most of their work had concentrated on the Mexican artillery positions between the National Road and the Rio del Plan; the trail that led to Cerro Gordo from the northeast through the wilderness had been accorded only second priority. Scott now began concentrating on turning Santa Anna's left flank, and sent a new scouting party, led by Major John L. Smith, chief engineer, and Captain Robert E. Lee.

It was not an easy task for the engineers. At the outset they were uncertain that they could reach the point where the old trail rejoined the National Road. Lee had hardly begun his mission when he had a narrow escape. Pushing far forward, he came upon a clear spring, a local watering hole. Just as he arrived, a party of Mexican soldiers sauntered into the glade to fill their canteens. Lee dove for the cover of a nearby log, next to the pool, well camouflaged with a large bush. For hours he remained motionless, not daring even to brush the insects from his brow, while the Mexicans came, drank, made casual conversation, and wandered off. It was dark before Lee made it home in the inky blackness over rough country.

Lee and the other engineers brought encouraging news. That sector, they concluded, was undefended and a road could be built through it to support

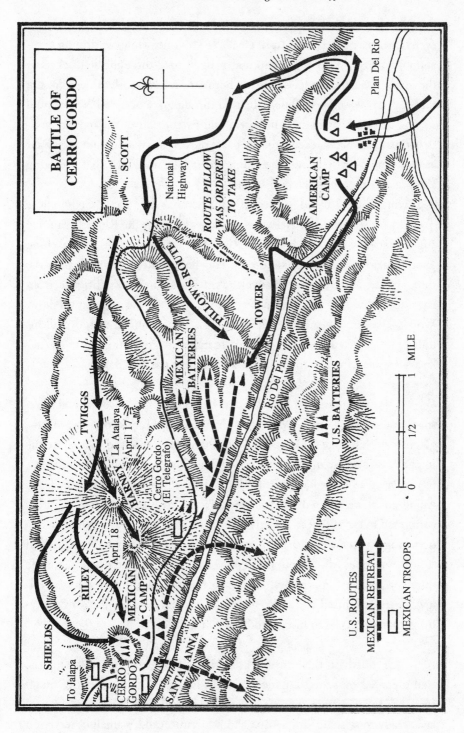

BATTLE OF
CERRO GORDO

SCOTT

Plan Del Rio

National Highway

ROUTE PILLOW
WAS ORDERED
TO TAKE

AMERICAN
CAMP

PILLOW'S ROUTE

MEXICAN
BATTERIES

TOWER

TWIGGS

La Atalaya
April 17

HARNEY

Cerro Gordo
(El Telegrafo)

Rio Del Plan

U.S. BATTERIES

MILE

RILEY
April 18

MEXICAN
CAMP

SHIELDS

To Jalapa

CERRO
GORDO

SANTA ANNA

U.S. ROUTES

MEXICAN RETREAT

MEXICAN TROOPS

1/2

0   1

an attack from that direction. Based on their information, Scott sent out an even larger party on Friday, April 16, 1847. This one, while continuing to reconnoiter, was also to begin building a rough road through the thickets to the town of Cerro Gordo, bypassing both La Atalaya and El Télégrafo. On that day, Lee was able to follow the trail through to a point where he could see the National Road and the town; and by the end of the day the construction party had hacked a road capable of carrying wagons and even light artillery most of the way. By evening Scott had no doubt that attacking along that route would be his best plan.

Having thus decided to attack Santa Anna's left flank, Scott chose Twiggs's division to lead, as Twiggs was already across the Rio del Plan. He augmented Twiggs's two brigades (Riley and Persifor Smith) by attaching James Shields's brigade of volunteers. For the secondary attack against the three artillery batteries near the river, he chose Gideon Pillow's brigade, from Patterson's division. The rest of Patterson's division was to follow Pillow; Worth, just arriving, was to follow Twiggs. Scott planned to move all his units into advanced positions—that is, to move Twiggs all the way to La Atalaya—on the 17th. The main attack would come the next day.

While issuing verbal orders late on the 16th, Scott ran across a snag. Brigadier General Gideon Pillow insisted that his mission was too dangerous—a "desperate undertaking," he told Scott. Scott tried to reassure the impetuous young man, pointing out that he was not to attack until the rest of the Mexican front had been hit by Twiggs. Pillow was not satisfied. He would go where ordered, he declaimed, "if he left his bones there," but he continued to claim that two of his regiments were "too raw" for such an undertaking. Scott rejected that argument, but it was only when he mentioned something about "discipline" that Pillow relented.[6] He said no more for the moment. As James Polk's one-time law partner in Columbia, Tennessee, Pillow regarded himself as the President's "representative" in the army; anything that happened to him would not go unnoticed.

Early in the morning of April 17, Twiggs set out, following the trail prepared by Scott's engineers. It was hot, slow going over the rough road, but by noontime Twiggs's lead troops had reached the base of La Atalaya, ready to seize it. Santa Anna had not reinforced his small observation party, so the Americans cleared the top of the mesa with little difficulty. That was as far as Twiggs had been ordered to go that day; La Atalaya was only a way station. The final objective was the town of Cerro Gordo, in Santa Anna's rear.

But once Twiggs was committed, he could not or would not stop. As the Mexicans scurried over the crest toward the safety of El Télégrafo, someone yelled to Twiggs, "How far do we go, General?" "Charge 'em to Hell!" was the reply.[7] Twiggs's men took him seriously. Onward they went toward El Télégrafo. When they reached a point about halfway between the hills, however, Mexican fire began to make itself felt. Twiggs's men were stuck; they could not retreat and they could not advance. They spent a miserable time until the arrival of nightfall allowed them to slink back in the darkness to La Atalaya.

Twiggs's precipitate action in fighting beyond Atalaya on April 17 had altered Scott's original plans; that position could no longer be bypassed. So the fighting on Atalaya resumed early in the morning of Saturday, April 18, 1847. Persifor Smith's brigade, with C. F. Smith's "red-legged infantry" attached, began driving toward El Télégrafo.[8] Persifor Smith himself was down with a fever, so Scott placed Colonel William S. Harney in command of Smith's brigade. In that action, Harney more than justified Scott's generosity in retaining him as a major commander back at the Brazos. He led his brigade down the swale and up the slopes of El Télégrafo under heavy Mexican fire. Tall and athletic, he cut an inspirational figure for his men as he waved them on with his sword. It was said that his shrill voice could be heard above the din. The Mexicans held their positions for a while, filling vacant ranks as their men "fell in heaps in the midst of the confusion."[9] But American numbers told; in the hand-to-hand combat the Mexican defenders were soon overwhelmed by cheering Yankees, and when Brigadier General Ciriaco Vasquez fell, they were left without strong leadership. After a feeble attempt at a counterattack, they panicked and fell back, the masses of men trying to escape. Their retreat degenerated into a rout. El Télégrafo had fallen to the Americans.

In the meantime, the two brigades of Shields and Riley, straining along the final stretches of the path to the town, burst out to the National Road at Cerro Gordo.

On the left side of Scott's line, however, everything went wrong. Gideon Pillow, despite the protests of Lieutenant Tower, abandoned the route they had reconnoitered together the previous day and led his two regiments along a path visible to the Mexicans at the three gun positions. Shouting at Colonel Wyncoop of the Pennsylvania regiment, he alerted the unsuspecting Mexican gunners, who began pouring grapeshot into the 2d Tennessee infantry. To save his men, Colonel William Haskell, the commander, began attacking what guns he could see. Seven or eight hidden pieces began firing, however, and his men fell back in confusion. Pillow, on suffering a minor wound in the arm, left the field. Leaderless, Wyncoop and Haskell began looking for somebody to give them orders to attack, anxious for their troops to participate in the sweet taste of victory.

Pillow and Patterson remained unavailable, so the Pennsylvanians were preparing to attack without official orders. It became obvious, however, that the entire Mexican army had collapsed, and Wyncoop relented. The regiments of Pillow's brigade later occupied the Mexican positions without resistance. Everything was over by 2:00 P.M. Scott had cleared the way to Jalapa, Perote, Puebla, and Mexico City.

Scott's battle had been fought almost according to his original plan. And it made little difference whether he had succeeded by penetrating the Cerro Gordo defense directly—as was the case—or had succeeded in turning it before attacking it. He had taken too many prisoners of war as it was. He reported that he was

> quite embarrassed with the results of victory—prisoners of war, heavy ordnance, field batteries, small arms and accoutrements. About 3,000 men laid down their arms, with the usual proportion of field and company officers, besides five generals, several of them of great distinction.

Scott was elated. In the aftermath of the Battle of Cerro Gordo, he lavished praise on many, including Harney, for their roles in the victory. And, perhaps with an eye to his political leaders at home, he was more than generous with Pillow, giving his brigade credit for having twice assaulted the enemy's batteries on our left "with great daring." Conceding that Pillow's assaults were "without success," he said they "contributed much to distract and dismay our immediate opponent."

But it was on the field that Scott showed his greatest care for his men—and his appreciation of them. As George Ballantine was emotionally savoring his deliverance from the battle, he saw Scott and a few of his staff riding up to his position. Scott stopped to shake hands with all who approached him, congratulating them loudly on their victory. When a number of men and officers crowded around him, he spoke as familiarly as he was capable:

> Brother soldiers, I am proud to call you brothers, and your country will be proud to hear of your conduct this day. Our victory has cost us the lives of a number of brave men, but they died fighting for the honor of their country. Soldiers, you have a claim on my gratitude for your conduct this day which I will never forget.

As he spoke, Scott held his hat in his hand, though still on horseback. He was, according to Ballantine, "very much affected, and tears rolled over the furrowed cheeks of the majestic old hero, the sight of which caused sympathetic drops to start to the eyes of many a rough and weather-beaten countenance." Scott then rode slowly off, bowing and waving his hat.

Scott and his men did not take long catching their breath after the battle. General Robert Patterson, bracing himself against the symptoms of the fever, took to his horse and led his division of volunteers ahead to occupy the pretty little town of Jalapa. The rest of Scott's army went through the grisly task of burying the dead and cleaning up the battlefield. American soldiers were somewhat shocked to discover how many young Mexican women had died in that battle; they were by the sides of their husbands and lovers, often sharing the same fate.[10]

The disposal of the dead, horrible as it was, was a routine matter. Disposing of the living, however, especially of the 3,000 Mexican prisoners, was something else. Feeding the American force was difficult enough as it was; adding so many captives to his ration requirements would unacceptably hamper Scott's future operations. And he could not afford to detach troops to escort large numbers of prisoners to Veracruz for shipment to the United States. He therefore advised Washington that he was releasing his prisoners on parole. Considering the time it took for a message to go back and forth, Washington was in no position to protest. Many of Scott's troops, however, thought that decision to be an error. Even his admirer George Ballantine joined the rest.

Despite the decisiveness of Scott's victory, the Mexican dictator Santa Anna escaped capture. Once he realized the extent of his defeat, the Napoleon of the West left the field by descending the steep banks of the Rio del Plan and crossing it to the south, later turning westward toward Mexico

City. Santa Anna's life was in danger throughout his flight; his stock with the Mexican populace was low.

In his abandoned luggage back at Cerro Gordo, Santa Anna had left many items of treasure to the Americans, not the least of which was one of his spare wooden legs, formally dressed. The leg was discovered by Illinois volunteers, who confiscated it, much to the envy of the regulars. It was proudly displayed in Chicago for some years afterward.

25

➤➤✦❦✦◄◄

The Long Summer of 1847

*Having cut himself off from Veracruz, Scott loses and
then rebuilds his army in the center of Mexico.*

IN THE COURSE of six weeks, from March 9 through April 18, 1847, the
army under Winfield Scott had landed at Collada Beach, exacted the surrender of Veracruz, moved inland, and shattered the Mexican army at Cerro
Gordo. Since Santa Anna had no strong defensive position to fall back on, it appeared that Scott's way was clear, at least to the Valley of Mexico, in which stood
Mexico City. It was not to be so easy. Scott still had many obstacles to overcome, the most serious of which were created by the Americans themselves.

As soon as the Americans had cleared the field of Cerro Gordo,
Scott moved his army to the nearby town of Jalapa for refitting. He had selected a delightful place to do so. Captain E. Kirby Smith, a forty-year-old
West Pointer in Worth's division, waxed eloquent as he described it. Jalapa,
he recorded, was the "prettiest town I have ever seen, surrounded by the
finest country with the most delicious climate in the world, the thermome-
ter never rising above eighty degrees or falling much below sixty, more than
four thousand feet above the level of the sea." Fruit and vegetables, he noted,
were abundant and cheap. He was impressed by the presence of "some very
ancient buildings . . . a chapel built by Hernando Cortés," with a monastery
and college attached. And yet, Smith saw dangers among the beauty:

> What a stupid people [the Mexicans] are! They have lost six great battles; we have
> captured six hundred and eighty cannon, nearly one hundred thousand stand of

arms, made twenty thousand prisoners, have possession of the greatest portion of their country and are fast advancing upon their capital which must soon be ours— yet they refuse to treat! "Those the gods wish to destroy, they first make mad."[1]

Scott had little time for such philosophical ruminations; his victorious army was about to be critically reduced, not from battle or even from disease, but from the short-sighted provisions of the "war bill," which had been enacted on May 13, 1846. The volunteers it had raised had served faithfully, but their term of service, for one year, was about to expire. Few if any of them had any taste for continuing further in service. Scott had them polled, with overwhelming negative results. On May 3, 1847, therefore, he published his General Order No. 135:

> The general-in-chief regrets to learn . . . that, in all probability, not one man in ten of those regiments [polled] will be inclined to volunteer for the war. This predetermination offers, in his opinion, no ground for reproach, considering the long, arduous, faithful, and gallant services of these corps.

Seven regiments were about to leave, three from Tennessee, two from Illinois, and one each from Georgia and Alabama. But Scott accepted that development philosophically. Concerned to get his volunteers through the port of Veracruz before the height of the *vomito* season arrived, he sent them home a month early. On May 6 he had them on the road, leaving behind only those too sick to march. Scott was now left with only 7,000 effective men.

The town of Jalapa, while beautiful, was small, and the resources it afforded for sustaining troops were limited. Moreover, Scott's men were becoming bored in that small area. So Scott decided to move part of his army forward, under the command of Worth, to his next major objective, the city of Puebla. Worth left Jalapa on May 6, the same day as the volunteers. After dropping a regiment off at the fortress of Perote, just beyond Jalapa, he was scheduled to arrive at his destination, sixty miles away, on May 19. Scott planned to follow with the rest of his army in a little over a week.

Scott was being bold, even rash, in dividing his small army. He felt confident, however, that the risk was justified. Santa Anna could not present any threat for the immediate future, and Scott was counting heavily on cooperation from the hierarchy of the Catholic Church, whose members were violently opposed to Santa Anna because of his habit of raiding their coffers for funds. At first the church had encouraged the Mexicans to resist the Yankees, hoping that Santa Anna might be killed in battle. But with Santa Anna's ability to survive and to retain his hold on power, the prelates had decided to cooperate with Scott, a lesser evil. In this, Scott's judgment would prove correct.

An even more difficult decision now presented itself. Scott's communications line to the Gulf of Mexico could no longer be maintained. Defending his way stations—Veracruz, Jalapa, Perote, and Puebla—would reduce his strength by 5,800 men, an unacceptable loss. So on June 4, 1847, Scott withdrew all the wayside garrisons he had stationed between Veracruz and Puebla, cutting himself off from the Gulf Coast. In London, the aging Duke of Wellington noted the move as he followed Scott's progress. Wellington reportedly declaimed, "Scott is lost! He has been carried away by successes! He can't take the city, and he can't fall back on his bases!"[2]

On that eventful day of May 6, 1847, as Worth and the volunteers were marching out of Jalapa in opposite directions, an official from Washington, Nicholas P. Trist, set foot ashore at Veracruz, prepared to join Winfield Scott's army at Jalapa. His presence with Scott, at first far from welcome, would divert much of the general's attention from more important matters for some weeks to come.

Trist had come as a personal envoy of President Polk himself, sent to negotiate a treaty of peace with Santa Anna should the opportunity arise. Polk had been encouraged in hoping for a quick peace by recent visits from a Mexican colonel, Alexander T. Atchota, who purported to be a friend of Santa Anna's. The Mexican president, Atchota claimed, was amenable to talking of peace terms. To give himself credence, the colonel had brought a letter from the Mexican foreign minister, José Maria Monasterio. The talks with Atchota had come to naught—the Mexican preconditions could never be met—but the visits had raised the possibility of a negotiated rather than a military peace.

Word of Scott's success at Veracruz, which arrived in Washington on April 10, had prompted Polk to take immediate action. The question was, whom should he send to negotiate a peace? In a cabinet meeting that day Secretary of State James Buchanan said he would like to go in person but that he could not afford so much time away from the United States. Senator Benton had offered to go, but his demands for unlimited power could not be met. Finally, Buchanan suggested that Trist be sent. Polk had approved, and Trist had accepted the mission enthusiastically.

Trist's official title sounded modest: chief clerk of the State Department. In reality he was a man of standing. As chief clerk, he was the highest ranking professional in the State Department, second only to the secretary. A one-time West Point cadet who had later been a law student under Thomas Jefferson, he had married the venerable man's granddaughter. He had been Andrew Jackson's private secretary and later United States consul at Havana, attaining his position with the State Department partly through the influence of Andrew Jackson ("Jack") Donelson. Trist possessed personal charm, spoke fluent Spanish, and was well acquainted with the Latin American way of life. He seemed ideal.

Trist, however, had corresponding weaknesses, not readily apparent. His judgment while he was consul in Havana had been brought into question, even by his brother-in-law, Thomas Jefferson Randolph.[3] He was vain, fancying himself as a clever, witty writer. But if Polk knew of these matters, he was not deterred. He intended Trist's mission to be limited to delivering a proposed treaty to the Mexican authorities, with little or no authority to negotiate its terms.

Polk also saw an extra benefit in appointing Trist. He was known to be a dyed-in-the-wool Democrat, and Polk could count on him to prevent Winfield Scott from attaining any more glory in Mexico than absolutely necessary. Polk played on Trist's ambition. If he handled things well, Polk hinted, why he might even find himself the Democratic nominee for president in the 1848 elections!

Thus Trist arrived at Veracruz with a hostile predisposition against Scott. Yet the two men might have avoided confrontation had Trist not become sick on arrival. Unable to come to Jalapa immediately, he commandeered a convoy and sent armloads of abstruse and sometimes contradictory documents to Scott, omitting from the collection the most important of all, from Scott's viewpoint: Scott's unsealed copy of Buchanan's message to the Mexican minister of foreign relations. Had Trist sent Scott the copy—and had Scott read it—the caveats included therein would have put the general's mind at ease. Instead Trist sent Scott a letter of his own.*

---

*Trist's letter to Scott has unfortunately been lost, but as the eminent scholar Justin Smith evaluates the results, "it proceeded from a truly amiable but high-strung, top-lofty man, who felt expressly Called by Destiny to perform a Great National Act and immediately place Winfield Scott where he belonged." Justin Smith, *The War with Mexico*, 2:128.

Scott reacted as one might expect, negatively. One of the documents Trist had sent was a poorly worded one from Marcy defining Trist's status with Scott's army. Trist, it said, came "clothed with such diplomatic powers as will authorize him to enter into arrangements with the government of Mexico for the suspension of hostilities." What alarmed Scott most, however, was the encroachment on his own authority:

> Should [Mr. Trist] make known to you, in writing, that the contingency has occurred, in consequence of which the President is willing that further active military operations should cease, you will regard such notice as a direction from the President.[4]

Scott took once more to his pen. He wrote Trist complaining about that gentleman's commandeering the armed escort to deliver his message to Jalapa and decrying the fact that he had not been permitted to see the letter addressed to the Mexican minister of foreign affairs. He mentioned the new Mexican law, passed after Cerro Gordo, that deprived the executive of any power to conclude a treaty or even an armistice.[5] On that basis he doubted whether he could send Buchanan's letter on to Santa Anna. On a note of self-pity, he continued,

> I see that the Secretary of War proposed to degrade me, by requiring that I, commander of this army, shall defer to you, the chief clerk of the Department of State, the question of continuing or discontinuing hostilities.

Finally, insisting rightly that his army must take measures to provide for its own military security, he stated that "the question of an armistice or no armistice is, most peculiarly, a *military* question, appertaining to the commander of the invading force; consequently I shall demand, if the enemy should entertain your overtures, you refer that question to me." The safety of the army, he concluded, "demands no less, and I am responsible for that safety, until duly superseded or recalled."

Scott sent a copy of this letter, with only a brief cover note, to Secretary Marcy.

Though his reactions were explosive, Scott was acting much as any military commander might be expected to act under the circumstances. His command was under great danger, and it is obviously better to be punished by one's own government than to lose an army.

Trist received Scott's harsh letter at San Juan del Rio, on the way to Jalapa. Immediately he sat down to pen a long, laborious letter of his own, nearly

5,000 words long. Much of his argument made sense, but he gave vent to his well-known cleverness, including much sarcasm. Referring to Scott's observation that the secretary of war was degrading him, he snarled,

> I have to state that the order conveyed to you in the letter of the Secretary of War, did not originate with that officer, but emanated from him, who, if the constitution of the United States be anything but an empty formula, is "the commander-in-chief" of this army, and of the whole armed force of the United States."[6]

Having no time to send the letter en route, Trist kept it, to be dispatched to Scott immediately after his own arrival at Jalapa. On May 20, at Jalapa, he found he had more to add. He did not call on Scott, nor did Scott call on him. Moreover, Scott returned the documents Trist had sent him for transmission to Mexico City. So Trist appended his original letter to another one, giving vent to even more sarcasm.

Scott was now worried as well as furious. On the same night as he received Trist's second letter, he wrote Marcy again. Because of the infrequency of the mails, his letter dealt with much other information, practically all of it more important than the Trist matter. From the letter's tone, however, it was obvious that the Trist issue was foremost on his mind. He conceded that his earlier communications had been written in haste. To strengthen his case, he passed on the rumors that Senator Thomas Benton had publicly declared that if he (Benton) had been appointed general-in-chief in Mexico, the President would have given him the power of negotiating an armistice, even concluding a treaty of peace, a much "higher power."

In contrast, Scott complained, he had been deprived of "all voice or advice in agreeing to a truce with the enemy," placing him "under the military command of Mr. Trist," requiring him to "respect the judgment of Mr. Trist here on [military] events." Finally he entreated "to be spared the personal dishonor of being again required to obey the orders of the chief clerk of the State Department as the orders of the constitutional commander-in-chief of the army and navy of the United States."

Fortunately for all, Secretary Marcy finally came through as a balance wheel between Polk's fury at Scott, Scott's fury at both Polk and Trist, and Trist's fury at Scott. As an old social companion of Scott's but a loyal administration man, Marcy kept the controversy under control until such time as it could rectify itself. He knew his men. When he first learned that Scott and Trist had taken to the pen, he exclaimed, "I hear that Scott and Trist have got to writing. If so, all is over!" But he kept his humor; when Scott wrote "begging to be recalled," Marcy simply set the letter aside.[7]

When Scott reached Puebla in late May 1847, he was disappointed to see how bad the situation was. He could not accuse the Catholic priests of letting him down; they had certainly done everything he could ask to facilitate the American occupation. The local bishop had, in fact, arranged for the removal of the town governor, a man known to be a dedicated patriot,[8] and replaced him with a man "dedicated to the cause of peace." The civic officials of Puebla had found it necessary to receive Worth coldly when he arrived, but the causes of difficulty lay not with the Mexicans but with Worth himself.

Worth had entered Puebla triumphantly on May 15, 1847, as ever with a bit of panache. He left the bulk of his troops outside the city, taking with him only a small guard of seventy mounted men, an act of defiance. He then began acting with great pomp, assuming "the powers and airs of a Spanish generalissimo."[9] On the other hand, his terms for the city's capitulation were exceedingly lenient, even allowing the Mexican courts to try cases of civilians accused of murdering American soldiers. The Mexicans were quick to abuse that privilege, and the measure took a severe toll on the morale of the occupying troops.

At the same time, Worth apparently developed a certain paranoia toward the Mexicans, imagining plots to poison the water the soldiers were drinking. He allegedly overreacted to every vague report that the enemy were approaching the city in force. His drums alerting the troops on such occasions beat so frequently that they gave a name to these alarms—"Worth's scarecrows." Thus it was that Scott's men welcomed the arrival of the commanding general with all the enthusiasm they had exhibited on his appearance at Plan del Rio the previous April.

Worth's misconduct in governing the city of Puebla could not be overlooked. Scott therefore convened a court to evaluate Worth's misdeeds. On June 24, the members found that Worth's terms of capitulation had been "improvident and detrimental to the public service" and that a circular from him warning of the poisoned water was "highly improper and extremely objectionable." Though Worth was given only a reprimand, he was so angered that he appealed to Washington to give him justice. Worth was no longer Scott's trusted friend and ally.

To rectify Worth's mistakes, Scott was required to start almost from the ground up to build a degree of confidence between the Mexican population of Puebla and the American occupying forces. He approached the task in as low a key as possible. He did not, for example, make a point of refuting the rights of Mexican courts to try cases of murder. Instead he simply reissued his old General Order No. 20 from Veracruz, which had established martial law. He reversed the policy of "hot pursuit" in every case of a threat to an outpost. And once again he instituted his policy of friendship and respect for the Mexican Catholic Church. Before long, the atmosphere was much improved.

Scott was fortunate that his long period of enforced inactivity due to lack of troops placed him in such a pleasant city as Puebla. The climate, while of course hot in the summer, was tempered by its 5,000-foot altitude. The large city of 60,000 people was pleasant, with wide, tree-lined streets. The imposing Cathedral of the Immaculate Conception and the Church of Santo Domingo, among many others, lent a feeling of genteel antiquity to the city. Accommodations for high-ranking American officers in sumptuous Spanish *casas* were of course agreeable to Scott. The air was clear, and from Puebla one could see four major peaks—Orizaba, Popocatepetl, Iztaccíhuatl, and La Malinche—that looked close despite being many miles away.[10] It was a favorable atmosphere in which to face his manifold problems.

One of those problems was the continuing feud with Nicholas Trist. For a month after their arrival in Puebla, the two men avoided each other. Scott took pains to look after Trist's comfort and welfare at the mess of Persifor Smith, but the two prima donnas never met. In the meantime, Trist went about his business alone, sending messages to the Mexican government through the British minister, Charles Bankhead, and Bankhead's representative, one Edward Thornton. On June 14, Trist received a message from Bankhead lending encouragement that Santa Anna might be willing to discuss terms of peace—provided that an emolument in the form of gold would accrue to his personal benefit.

Trist needed Scott's cooperation in this matter, as the general held physical possession of the necessary money. He therefore wrote Scott a courteous letter explaining the situation, belatedly appending a copy of his authority to act as commissioner. Scott was so pleased by the tone of the letter, together with Trist's conciliatory attitude, that he responded cordially and made a personal overture. Knowing that Trist was ill, he sent a box of guava marmalade to his host, Persifor Smith:

My dear Sir:

    Looking over my stores, I find a box of Guava marmalade which, perhaps, the physician may not consider improper to make part of the diet of your sick companion.[11]

That exchange of favors caused Scott and Trist to meet for the first time in nearly two months. Both men, having been chastised by their superiors, were ready to make amends.[12] Over and above the observances of the proprieties, however, they found that they liked each other. From that time on they became friends and partners.

Scott now reversed his attitude, showering favors on his new friend. He accorded Trist an ample supply of a commodity he personally cherished: fanfare. He decreed that Trist was now to be treated as the American minister. All the guards in the headquarters were to turn out and render appropriate honors whenever Trist should approach them. He referred to the man he had earlier called "the personification of Danton, Marat, and St. Just," as "able, discreet, courteous, and amiable," asking that "all I have heretofore written about Mr. Trist should be suppressed." Nor was Trist to be outdone. At about the same time, he wrote to Buchanan that Scott's conduct had been "characterized by the purest public spirit, and a fidelity and devotion which could not be surpassed." The way was now open for the two men to work in earnest to bring the war to an end.

It was well that they had arrived at a rapprochement, for the problem at hand was a knotty one, to find a way to deal with Santa Anna's demand for a bribe of a million dollars in exchange for a treaty of peace. Both Scott and Trist, desiring to end the war without further casualties, were favorably disposed to the idea. They were personally aware, of course, that the United States had bribed the Barbary Pirates early in the century and the Winnebagos in the northwest territories much later. Neither appeared to have great difficulties as to the morality of such a bribe,[13] though Scott was uncertain as to its appearances. On July 16, Scott called a meeting of his general officers to discuss the question. They had already taken a preliminary step. Santa Anna's agents had demanded an "advance" of $10,000 and Scott and Trist had already forwarded that sum to them as a down payment.

The meeting included all of Scott's general officers, except for Worth and Persifor Smith. Worth was not invited because the bad feelings over his recent court-martial had not yet subsided. Persifor Smith had been sent eastward to meet Brigadier General Franklin Pierce, whose brigade was running into trouble on the road from Veracruz. Of those who attended, Twiggs might also just as well have stayed home. Not interested in political affairs, he simply voted in favor of accepting Santa Anna's proposition and left. But Scott had the men he wanted: Gideon Pillow, John Quitman, James Shields, and George Cadwalader. Pillow and Quitman, both promoted to the grade of major general by President Polk, represented the Polk administration. The rest were also staunch Democrats, personally loyal to President Polk, men of prominent civilian backgrounds.[14]

With the exception of Pillow, all of these men, despite their politics, were also intensely loyal to Scott. When it came time to vote, therefore, only Pillow supported the bribery scheme wholeheartedly. The rest were defensive of Scott, concerned by the possible consequences this act might have on his future career. The politically sophisticated Quitman said he did not like the payment, as the people at home would not understand it. Shields disliked the scheme but said he would support whatever Trist decided, being anxious to keep Scott isolated from the decision. Scott agreed, explaining that "though he approved of the use of the million, and would under all circumstances defend Mr. Trist in that use of it, still the use proposed was a matter for Mr. Trist to determine altogether by himself." Scott "offered the money from the contingent fund only because Mr. Trist could not do it."[15]

For several days Scott and Trist awaited word from Mexico City. On July 21 some encouragement came; the British minister, whose subjects were being vastly inconvenienced by the war, was working hard to make the scheme come about. On July 25, word came in that Santa Anna was having difficulties inducing the Mexican Congress to agree to peace negotiations. The next day official word arrived that the scheme, in the words of Colonel E. A. Hitchcock, Scott's inspector general, had been "knocked into a cocked hat." Santa Anna was reportedly convinced that the new army he was recruiting could defeat the Yankees and he was afraid to defy the Mexican law, which made it a matter of treason for a Mexican to treat with the Americans.

Santa Anna was now $10,000 richer, having pocketed the advance bribe. Scott, perhaps relieved, prepared to continue the war.

By early August 1847, Scott's army had received all the reinforcements it was going to get. On that day Franklin Pierce's brigade, accompanied by that of Persifor Smith, marched into Puebla. Pierce's 2,400 men, plus the 4,500 that Pillow had brought in on July 8, brought Scott's strength up to 14,000 men, though of these 3,000 were reported sick and 600 more convalescing. Since all peace prospects had collapsed, Scott now concluded that the time had come to move forward, "naked blade in hand."[16]

He organized his army into four divisions, largely to conform to the number of high-ranking commanders on hand. The 1st Division (regular), under Brevet Major General William J. Worth, was a powerful force, consisting of two brigades totaling six maneuver (infantry and artillery) regiments. The 2d Division, under Brigadier General David Twiggs, was also strong, with two brigades totaling six regiments. Major General Gideon Pillow's division, considered "regular" but consisting of newly recruited men with volunteer officers, had two brigades of five maneuver regiments. Major General John Quitman's division included two brigades with only three volunteer regiments, though supplemented by William Harney's cavalry brigade of two cavalry battalions.[17]

Arrayed against this force Santa Anna was reported to have gathered an army of 36,000 men with a hundred cannon. Though the numbers were overwhelming on paper, Scott was not concerned, as he knew such an army would be unreliable. He had few qualms when, on August 7, 1847, the first elements of his army marched out of Puebla on the way to the Valley of Mexico. Harney's dragoons led the way, followed by Twiggs's division. Quitman's volunteers followed the next day, Worth's division on the ninth, and Pillow's brought up the rear.

Scott himself started out with Quitman's division, the usual position of the commander. Soon, however, he became impatient and rode to the head of the column. He had no idea what lay ahead.

26

The Valley of Mexico

Scott shatters the Mexican army at Contreras and Churubusco.

THE MORNING of Tuesday, August 10, 1847, broke clear and cold in the high reaches of the Sierra Madres. Scott's lead division, under Twiggs, was approaching the Rio Frio, a powerful mountain stream that Scott was half expecting to find defended. But Twiggs's scouts detected nobody. Relieved, the division moved on toward the crest of the mountain range, only a few hours away.

When Scott and his men reached the crest later that morning, everyone gasped. There spread before them was the Valley of Mexico, a sight that moved many to express their impressions in writing. One was George Ballantine, who rhapsodized, "Description is tame when one tries to convey the impression which this scene makes on all who see it for the first time. It is certainly the most magnificent view in Mexico; perhaps the first in the world."

They were standing at a point 3,000 feet above the floor of the valley, which was itself more than 7,000 feet above sea level. The valley, once the floor of a great lake, was a large round basin, of 120-mile circumference at the base and 200 miles at the crest of the mountains. One glance showed the spectator everything in a single view. The remarkable transparency and purity of the atmosphere made the most minute details discernible—the towers and spires of the city of Mexico twenty-five miles distant "peering out from the foliage and trees." The valley, Ballantine continued, looked like "a large green plain, dotted with white churches, spires, and haciendas, and containing several large sheets of water, the remains of lakes which are said to have once covered the whole valley."

The aspect of the scene that awed most witnesses, however, was the new perspective it afforded of Popocatepetl and Iztaccíhuatl. The two great volcanoes, perceptible at Puebla, were here only about twenty miles away, rising a full 7,000 feet above the rim of the surrounding hills. Owing to the bright atmosphere and the sun shining on the snow, they seemed only two or three miles distant. This "circle of stupendous, rugged, and dark mountains, the rough but sublime setting of nature," formed what to Ballantine was "a most perfect combination of the sublime and beautiful."[1]

Scott's reaction was less poetic than Ballantine's but by no means less enthusiastic. As he sat astride his horse, he saw not a panorama but a prize, "the object of all our dreams and hopes—toils and dangers." He admitted that the numerous steeples in the distance, overshadowed by Popocatepetl, filled his mind "with religious awe." Recovering himself, he exclaimed exuberantly, "That splendid city soon shall be ours!"

Mexican dictator Antonio López de Santa Anna, meanwhile, was feverishly preparing to defend Mexico City against Scott's advance, exercising to the fullest his genius for inspiring his zealous if disorganized people. "It is," he declaimed, "much more glorious to submit fighting than to leave the gates of Mexico [City] open, without firing a gun at the North Americans." The people responded. In the words of the Mexican historian Ramón Alcaraz,

> The spirit of the inhabitants of the capital, who had been thrown into great consternation by the news from Cerro Gordo, began to recover confidence, hoping that the day was near for the vindication of our honor and the triumph of our arms. Joy was seen in the faces of good citizens; selfish men and the evil-minded carefully concealed their sentiments, pretending to partake of those of the immense majority of Mexicans. The partisans of peace, ashamed, dared not to confess their feelings, and the cry of war was heard from one extremity of the city to the other.[2]

Santa Anna had been busy consolidating the various small "armies" that had been scattered around the Mexican countryside. Foremost among these was the Army of the North, at San Luis Potosí, which boasted 4,000 regulars and twenty-two guns. It was commanded by the temperamental General Gabriel Valencia, a man who was not impressed by the charisma of the current Mexican president. Six years earlier, in 1841, Valencia had, in fact, been Santa Anna's co-conspirator in seizing the reins of power in Mexico City. More recently he had come to view himself as a presidential possibility. Santa Anna had therefore kept him in the north, but he was now forced to bring him down to a position just north of Lake Texcoco, to guard Mexico City from an attack from the north.

To augment Valencia, Santa Anna sent for two other regular formations, the Army of the South and the garrison of Mexico City, which each comprised 10,000 men. With the addition of several smaller formations, Santa Anna's total force now came to at least 25,000 men, and perhaps as many as 30,000. The reports Scott had received were somewhat exaggerated but essentially correct.[3]

As Santa Anna was trying to organize his army and discipline his officers—which was no small order—he was also busy planning. Mexico City, he reasoned, was readily open to invasion, lacking walls or even significant fortifications. Since he wished to spare it destruction, he decided to push his army out to the east and defeat Scott in the open. The problem was narrowed somewhat, as Scott would have to approach Mexico City along the National Road as far as the hamlet of Buena Vista, thirty miles to the east of the city. Once Scott reached that crossroads, he would have options that Santa Anna could not predict with assurance. In the absence of definite information, therefore, Santa Anna decided to gamble that Scott would continue his approach along the National Road. He concentrated his main defense on a single hill known as El Peñón, which dominated the National Road.

Santa Anna's reason for concentrating so much effort on one position was influenced by domestic, political, and psychological factors. By preparing defenses on a single position, he could focus the efforts of his people, who were desperate to take part in some action. Always the politician, he placed his National Guardsmen on this all-important position. Even though they were his least experienced troops, they were "bound to the inhabitants with the strongest ties of friendship and kindred. Almost every family had among them a father, a lover, or a husband, and it was very natural that their demonstrations of interest should fall principally upon those who by so many titles possessed their consideration."

On August 10, 1847, the day that Scott was exulting at the crest of the valley, Mexican troops marched through the streets of Mexico City, through the Zócalo, or Grand Plaza, as citizens crowded the balconies of the townhouses, cheering. "The band music of the 11th Infantry," wrote one observer, "filled the air with its inspiring martial sounds; a thousand *vivas* answered it, and all the National Guard marched, bearing with them the good wishes of all."[4] In the morning Santa Anna and his brilliantly uniformed staff came to El Peñón with great fanfare, past the crowds, the new grocery stores, eating houses, and even liquor stores, that had appeared overnight, supplied by converting the roadside ditches into canals! He climbed the impressive El Peñón amid the cheers of his people. The inhabitants of Mexico City approached the next few days of terrible battle with an emotion bordering on ecstasy.

David Twiggs's division arrived at Buena Vista on Wednesday, August 11. Scott accompanied Twiggs, for he had serious decisions facing him that could not be made from the rear. Specifically, he must decide which of three routes he would take from Buena Vista to Mexico City.

Scott had been thinking seriously about this problem for a long time. Back at Puebla he had designated two officers, Major William Turnbull and Captain Robert E. Lee, to study the routes. Perhaps whimsically—or perhaps to test these officers—Scott had directed them to begin their studies independently, using their own sources, only later pooling their efforts. Their individual performances were never compared for the record, but together Turnbull and Lee amassed much information about Santa Anna's dispositions around Mexico City, concentrating at first on the defenses of the vaunted El Peñón. They had also studied the road net that ran southward from Buena Vista, around Lakes Chalco and Xochimilco. If El Peñón turned out to be strongly held—which they suspected it would be—then Scott might be well advised to take a southern route into Mexico City, bypassing Santa Anna's main defensive position.[5]

Based on these studies, Scott had tentatively decided to turn his army south at Buena Vista. He needed more concrete, confirmed information, however. Once Twiggs had passed Buena Vista, heading for El Peñón, Scott sent Worth, who had been following Twiggs, to reconnoiter the southern route that ran south of Lakes Chalco and Xochimilco. Meanwhile Twiggs was to continue westward to the small adobe town of Ayotla and probe the defenses of El Peñón. So by August 12, Worth was at the town of Chalco, with Pillow's division behind him. Quitman's division was tentatively scheduled to follow Twiggs.

Scott was still not sure, however, that the inferior southern route should be followed. He placed his entire engineer detachment under Lee's supervision and instructed Lee to confirm his previous conclusions. Lee began scouting on the 12th and by the end of the 13th came back convinced that the information he and Turnbull had put together was reasonably accurate. He confirmed that El Peñón was the anchor of Santa Anna's main defense, and he estimated that Santa Anna had placed about 7,000 men and thirty cannon on it, a force comparable in size to Scott's entire army. The confident Americans, though sure that they could take the position, all agreed that it would be too costly. So Scott ordered Lee and others to continue scouting for other routes.

By August 15, Scott had all the information he needed. Rejecting a third route that ran south of El Peñón to the town of Mexicalzingo, Scott confirmed his tentative decision, made at Puebla, to turn southward at Buena Vista and follow the secondary road that Lee and Turnbull had recommended and that Worth's engineers, together with Colonel Duncan, had confirmed.[6] That road ran south of both Lake Xochimilco and Lake Chalco about seven miles south of Ayotla, joining the Acapulco Road, a major artery, directly south of Mexico City. With this change of direction, Worth's division was now leading the army, leaving Twiggs to demonstrate in front of El Peñón for a day to screen his movements.[7]

Santa Anna was of course keenly interested in what Scott was doing. There was no mistaking that something was afoot; Scott's scouting parties were hardly any secret to the Mexicans. On August 14, the day before Scott turned southward, Santa Anna's spies reported suspicious Yankee activity that indicated that Scott was intending to bypass El Peñón. At first Santa Anna refused to believe them, his mind being set on a defense along the National Road. Two days later, however, a Mexican force clashed with elements of Twiggs's division that were marching eastward, not westward, away from El Peñón. Only then did Santa Anna concede what was happening. Once convinced, however, he acted energetically. He abandoned El Peñón and marched his badly demoralized men back into the city. There they found "empty streets, untenanted balconies and bolted windows; and the silent, sombre, fearsome aspect of a besieged city." But the Napoleon of the West did not seem discouraged; he prepared to fight on a new front.

Santa Anna's defensive position on the south was not so formidable as that at El Peñón, but it was still a strong one—provided he conducted his defense sensibly. The Churubusco River, really a canal, flowed from the west into Lake Xochimilco about five miles south of Mexico City. Its steep banks were virtually impossible to cross except by bridge. Only three such bridges crossed the Churubusco, and they were all located within two miles of each other. Santa Anna, therefore, could mount a strong defense by merely concentrating enough force at each of these bridges. He did not, however, wish to make his final stand so close to the capital; he therefore crossed the Churubusco to meet Scott on the south bank.

The terrain south of the river was also favorable for the defense. Just two miles south of the banks of the Churubusco lay a fearsome volcanic lava bed, known as the Pedregal, whose surface rendered it nearly impenetrable. Infantry could cross it with great difficulty, but supporting artillery and supplies could not. The Pedregal was oval in shape, its long axis extending east-west about five miles, across which no known road ran. Only two ran north-south around it; one of these, the Acapulco Road, was a main artery, over which much trade had been conducted between Mexico City and Acapulco over many years. On the west of the Pedregal was the San Angel Road, a far less impressive route that led nowhere beyond the town of Contreras.

Maneuver along each of these roads was extremely limited. The Acapulco Road was restricted on the east by water, which came close to the Pedregal at the Hacienda of San Antonio, about three miles south of Churubusco. The San Angel Road ran through a narrow neck with the Pedregal on the east and precipitous cliffs on the west. Thus Santa Anna could, he felt, block both roads by holding the towns of San Antonio on the east and San Angel on the west. He could fall back and defend behind the Churubusco River as a final, last-ditch defensive position.

Santa Anna knew that Scott would soon have possession of San Agustín, the town on the Acapulco Road where it joined the route south of Lake Xochimilco. Assuming that Scott would approach Mexico City by way of the Acapulco Road, he stacked the bulk of his available forces on that road. He moved his strongest single force, the 5,500 men of Gabriel Valencia, to Coyoacán, about halfway between the Acapulco and San Angel roads, where he would be able to reinforce Mexican forces holding either.

It was not a bad plan, assuming that Santa Anna's subordinates would carry it out. It fell down because Valencia was never disposed to obey any of Santa Anna's orders without question, especially where the attainment of military glory was involved. So as soon as he received orders to move to Coyoacán, Valencia began to protest. The threat along the San Angel Road was also a real one, he argued, and he should take position further down that

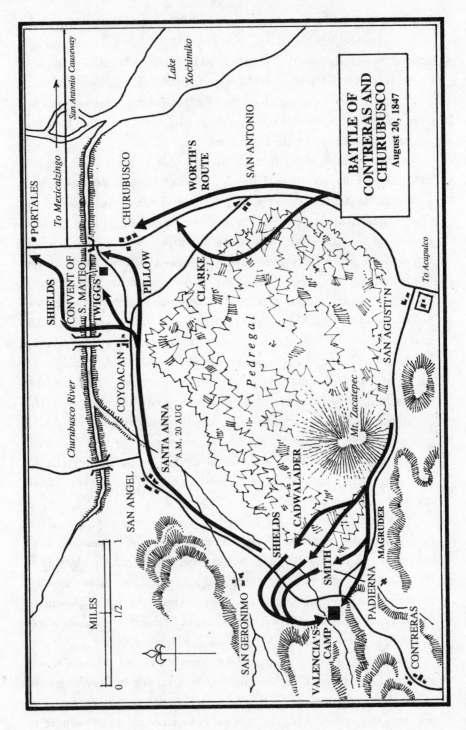

BATTLE OF CONTRERAS AND CHURUBUSCO

August 20, 1847

road, at San Angel. Santa Anna could not enforce his will upon his subordinate. At the point of exasperation, he finally gave permission for Valencia to occupy San Angel. Valencia, however, was still not satisfied. Perhaps in a show of bravado, he moved his division ahead another four miles down the San Angel Road to a hill in the vicinity of the Indian village of Padierna. From there he could fight his own battle.[8]

By Wednesday, August 18, Worth's division, leading Scott's army, reached San Agustín, on the Acapulco Road. At that point Worth turned and headed northward toward San Antonio, and Mexico City eight miles beyond. At San Antonio, however, Worth found the approach to the town confined to a narrow causeway, with water on both sides. Even if he could cross the causeway he would have to move troops along the eastern edge of the Pedregal in order to flank it. The east (right) flank was all water. So again Scott decided to bypass a position even though he believed it could be taken. He ordered Worth to halt in place, and merely "threaten and mask" the place.

Scott's situation was now becoming serious if not desperate. He had left Puebla with a small army and no reliable source of supply, depending on a quick victory to eliminate danger to his army. But now his way to Mexico City was blocked, and his army was running out of sustenance. As Hitchcock put it, "We have no forage for our horses; our hard bread is getting musty; we have four days' rations for the army and some beef on the hoof. . . . Our men were exposed on the wet ground before San Antonio, and the General-in-Chief appeared discouraged as we rode along the road lined with men, horses, and wagons—the men without tents, the evening cold and a menace of rain." And the discouragement reached down through the ranks. Kirby Smith, the barometer of the army's morale, wrote, "Mexico must fall or we must all find a grave between this and the city."[9]

Scott never made a costly frontal attack when given the option of turning a position; this case was no exception. As at Cerro Gordo, he began seeking ways to bypass the San Antonio position as soon as he arrived at San Agustín on the 18th. Even as Worth was probing San Antonio, Scott sent an exploratory mission across the southern rim of the Pedregal to find a road, if such existed, that could carry his army from the Acapulco Road westward to the San Angel Road. For this mission Scott sent not only Lee but Beauregard, Tower, and later Major Larkin Smith, his chief engineer.

By the end of the day Lee and Beauregard had brought in some encouraging information. At Peña Pobre, a village a mile and a half west of San Agustín, they had found a passable road. After following it for some time, they had reached a crest near the peak called Zacatapec. There Lee's escort had encountered a small group of Mexican cavalry and, after a brief skirmish, had dispersed them. But from that point Lee had seen the rest of the road leading to the village of Padierna, on the San Angel Road. Reasoning that the Mexican cavalry they had encountered must have come across a similar road, Lee concluded that a passable road ran all the way to the San Angel turnpike. So the next morning Scott decided to exploit that new information.

The Battle of Contreras (Padierna)

What happened on that August 19 was entirely unforeseen. The results, also, were confused—so confused, in fact, that there appear to have been almost as many versions of what happened as there were witnesses. Early that morning, Scott sent out a construction party of 500 men from Pillow's division who, under the supervision of Lee and other engineers, were to build a road westward across the Pedregal. Scott intended for this party only to make a reconnaissance, not to get involved in a fight.

The confusion stemmed, at least in part, from Scott's awkward arrangement of sending two division commanders out to work on the same project. Theoretically, it may have looked good. Pillow's men were to provide the work detail and Twiggs was "thrown farther in front to cover" the operation, two separate missions. As it was, the arrangement worked fairly well until about 1:00 P.M., when work was halted near the peak of Zacatapec by heavy Mexican artillery fire. A strong enemy position—estimated at twenty-two heavy-caliber guns—was sited across a steep ravine, atop a hill near the Indian village of Padierna. Although the Americans did not know it at the time, that position was occupied by some 7,000 men under General Gabriel Valencia. Nor did they know that another large force, led by Santa Anna himself, had cautiously followed Valencia down the San Angel Road to a position about four miles from him. Scott's work party was running up against the greater portion of Santa Anna's army.

With this turn of events, Lee returned to San Agustín to report to Scott. Scott, sensing that something important was transpiring, rode up the road to an observation point near Zacatapec. He arrived at about 4:00 P.M., only to discover that a battle was already under way. Since Lee had left the work party to report to him, Gideon Pillow had, at the first sign of hostile action, begun committing troops without Scott's authority. He first ordered two artillery batteries (Captain John B. Magruder and Lieutenant F. D. Callender) to haul their guns over rough terrain up to a spot where they could take the Mexican batteries under fire. That they had done, and were attempting to maintain fire in the unequal contest. This exchange went on for about an hour before the heavier Mexican guns knocked them out of action.

Pillow had done more than return artillery fire, however. Assuming command of the two divisions over the groans of a reluctant Twiggs, he sent two companies of Mounted Rifles to brush the Mexican position aside. He did not stop to think that such a formidable volume of Mexican artillery might be part of a major formation. The two companies were repulsed, not surprisingly, and they were unable to return from their exposed position. They therefore remained in position between Valencia at Padierna and Magruder's batteries.

Pillow then rode up to Colonel Bennet Riley, of Twiggs's division, and ordered him to cross the Pedregal. Riley, an old soldier who had no more trust in Pillow than did any other regular, asked the general if his own commander, Twiggs, knew of the order. Pillow answered evasively that he did, so Riley led his stumbling brigade across the Pedregal and down across the ravine, and seized the town of San Geronimo at its base. He then continued to a spot between the two wings of the threatening Mexican army. Lacking any specific mission, Riley set about to reconnoiter the territory in order to send information back to Twiggs and Pillow.

In the meantime Pillow became aware of Riley's danger and tried to pull him back, but when he realized that Riley was out of contact, he attempted to reinforce him. First he sent Cadwalader's brigade and Morgan's 15th Infantry, in generally the same direction as Riley, while he personally stayed at Zacatapec. Then Persifor Smith, witnessing Pillow's indecision as to what to do next, took his brigade, with neither orders nor protest from Pillow, across the Pedregal and the ravine. When he found the other brigades, he assumed command of all the troops in the area.

By the time Scott became aware of this situation, he could do little to affect it for the moment, contenting himself with sending Shields's brigade to join Smith. He also gave orders that Valencia's position must not be attacked during hours of daylight, "because, independently of the ravine, our infantry, unaccompanied by cavalry and artillery, could not advance without being mowed down by the grape and canister of the enemy's batteries." Then, satisfied that he could do nothing to remedy the situation on the field, Scott returned to his headquarters in San Agustín, where he could maintain contact with both wings of his army. But from here on, Gideon Pillow was out of the picture. Scott would communicate with Persifor Smith as best he could by messenger.

Brigadier General Persifor Smith, now personally commanding nearly half of Scott's army, was a natural soldier, aggressive but far from rash. Like Scott, he had begun his career as a lawyer, but also like Scott, he had discovered that the military profession was the place where his genius shone brightest. He had caught Scott's eye in Florida, where he had commanded the Louisiana volunteers, and he had distinguished himself at Monterrey under Zachary Taylor. But the battle of Contreras was one of his finest feats of arms. If anyone could be called the "hero" of Contreras, it would be this unpretending Yankee from Louisiana.

When Smith arrived at San Geronimo and assumed command, he had only Cadwalader's brigade and Morgan's regiment in addition to his own brigade, but he soon located Riley as well. He realized that his command was in extreme peril, facing Valencia on the south and a major buildup of Mexican troops threatening from a point less than a mile up the San Angel Road.[10] Rather than wait passively for these forces to squeeze him, he planned to attack them himself, one at a time. He would assault the northern force, leaving only a small force to guard against Valencia in his rear. But he had arrived too late, only an hour before sunset, and darkness was falling. Smith therefore postponed the attack and consulted Riley.

Riley had done his scouting work well. He had found a way around to the rear of Valencia's position that had escaped the Mexican's notice, perhaps because Valencia's thoughts, as well as his guns, were trained on Magruder's battery to the east. Smith decided to attack Valencia from the rear at daybreak. He asked Lee to return to Zacatapec and inform Scott of his plans, at the same time requesting a diversionary attack on Valencia's front. He added, however, that he planned to make the attack in the morning whether or not Scott was able to provide that diversionary attack.

Lee was bone-weary from his exertions during the past couple of days, but he readily accepted Smith's mission. With a few men he stumbled and groped his way through the black night over the rough Pedregal in a storm. Fortunately, the storm provided occasional sheets of lightning that illuminated Lee's main terrain guide, the peak of Zacatapec. Finding Scott gone, he continued for the remaining three miles to Scott's headquarters at San Agustín, arriving at 11:00 P.M. Despite all the confusion, Lee found Scott remarkably confident.

Scott was delighted to receive his first authentic news. Throughout the evening he had been sending messengers—seven in all—to find Smith, but all had given up in the darkness of the Pedregal. Enthusiastic about Smith's plans for the morning, Scott held a small council with the several officers present, including Pillow, Twiggs, and Lee. Based on Lee's information, Scott decided that the action near Padierna was to be his main effort. He sent word for Worth to withdraw most of his force from San Antonio and follow Pillow's command to the west. On Scott's invitation, Pillow remained overnight in his command post. Twiggs, however, insisted on rejoining his division, so Scott sent Lee with him. The two were to find troops to conduct the morning demonstration that Smith had requested. Eventually Lee found Franklin Pierce's brigade near Zacatapec and after some difficulty got Pierce's men placed into position.

During the night, Shields finally found Persifor Smith and, though he was the senior officer, yielded to Smith's greater experience and familiarity with the ground. Smith thereupon posted Shields at San Geronimo to watch the Mexican force to the north while he and Riley made preparations for the early morning attack on Valencia. The next morning, at 3:00 A.M., Smith's force, led by Riley's brigade, began their surreptitious march around to the rear of Valencia's position. Following Riley was part of Cadwalader's brigade, followed by Morgan's regiment.

Valencia's men, in the meantime, were in no condition to fight a battle, feeling the effects of a night of wild celebration, brought on by Valencia's illusion that he had won a major battle the previous day. Further, they were suffering from the cold rain and frightened by the fact that the Mexican force they had seen coming to their rescue from the north had withdrawn. Some had already begun to desert before dawn broke. In any case, they did not see Riley's men during the three hours the Americans struggled to reach their attack position. By dawn the rain had ceased and the sun was up, with Smith's force still undetected.

At 6:00 A.M. the Americans struck. The merciless slaughter lasted only seventeen minutes. Valencia's men offered no resistance as they broke and ran. Many of them were intercepted by Shields at San Geronimo. The Americans pursued the fugitives all the way to San Angel. At that point, the battle of Contreras over, Gideon Pillow rode into San Angel to reassume command of his division.

The battle of Padierna (Contreras) was a resounding victory for Scott's army. Persifor Smith's 4,500 men had shattered Valencia's 7,000—all this transpiring with another 12,000 Mexicans under Santa Anna within easy supporting distance. The Mexican losses were not enough to destroy Santa Anna's army, but Scott's experience led him to believe, correctly, that the panic engulfing Valencia's men would quickly spread to the rest of Santa Anna's force. All this meant that the battle of Churubusco, fought later that afternoon, would, though costly, be a mopping-up operation. The day had been won at Padierna.

Churubusco, August 20, 1847

One of Santa Anna's skills as a commander, honed through much practice, was his ability to recover from devastating military defeats. Whatever weaknesses he exhibited—and there were many—he possessed a keen understanding of his troops, knowing when they would fight and when they would not. The period immediately following the disaster at Padierna serves as a case in point. Santa Anna realized that, even though only a fraction of his army had been destroyed, defeatism would spread among his other troops and he could expect them to perform only very limited tasks. Even such a modest undertaking as the reestablishment of a strong defense along the line of the Churubusco River would be unrealistic. Because crossings existed at the Churubusco Bridge, at Coyoacán, and at a point north of San Angel, he would be forced to split his army in order to defend all of them. Scott would then be at leisure to concentrate overwhelming force on whichever of the three he chose, and Santa Anna's men would lack the heart to resist effectively.

Santa Anna did the sensible thing under the circumstances: he withdrew the bulk of his army into Mexico City, leaving only such forces at each of the Churubusco River crossings as could achieve maximum delay. From Santa Anna's viewpoint, therefore, the battle of Churubusco had become a mere delaying operation.

Scott, on the other hand, was elated. As he rode through San Angel toward Coyoacán, he was described as "in his glory, enjoying every moment of his triumph and giving his orders rapidly and with a quick understanding of each new development."[11] As the situation was fluid, developing rapidly, he had much to decide. His first order involved Worth and Pillow. In order to make use of the Acapulco Road as well as the San Angel Road, he ordered Worth to recall whatever units he had sent behind Twiggs and to turn once more to the north on the Acapulco Road toward San Antonio. Quitman was to follow him. Scott, however, was ever conscious of Worth's rashness; he specified that his aggressive subordinate was not to attack until Pillow's division, coming around the north end of the Pedregal from the west, should take the Mexican position at San Antonio in the rear.

When Scott reached Coyoacán, he issued verbal orders for attacks on his two main objectives, the San Mateo Convent and the *tête de pont* over the Churubusco, two strongpoints in the town of Churubusco, about 300 yards apart. Giving priority to the San Mateo Convent, he threw four brigades against that position. Two of them, Persifor Smith's and Riley's, came from Twiggs's division. To surround the convent and to cut off the garrison's retreat, Scott sent a "temporary division" under command of Shields, consisting of Shields's own brigade and that of Pierce, to cross the Churubusco River at Portales, then to turn southward to take the convent in the rear. Since Pillow had been sent down the Acapulco Road to take San Antonio in the rear, the *tête de pont* would have to be neglected for the first part of the battle. Scott and his staff followed Twiggs, as that officer's brigades were making the main effort.

The San Mateo Convent was harder to reduce than Scott had anticipated. Not only were the walls solid, but the defenders were determined. Giving steel to their backbone were over two hundred men of the notorious San Patricio Battalion, American soldiers, largely of Irish birth, who had deserted the American army from various places and had joined to fight for Mexico. These men knew that they would be tried for treason if they were captured by the Americans, and they fought accordingly.[12] After two hours of fighting, the convent held firm.

To the south, at San Antonio, William J. Worth was becoming tired of waiting for Pillow to arrive on the scene. He therefore sent one brigade, under Colonel N. S. Clarke, westward into the Pedregal to flank San Antonio. Clarke made good progress and soon returned to the Acapulco Road, only to discover that the Mexican garrison had departed, leaving the way clear. That meant that Worth could head northward immediately and, with Cadwalader's brigade of Pillow's division, begin the attack on the *tête de pont*. This Worth did, and with the zeal of his troops he succeeded in reducing that strong position within a half hour.

Shields and Pierce, enveloping the convent from the north, ran into a strong force at Portales, north of the river. Scott, now with Twiggs, immediately sent the Rifle Regiment and a couple of troops of cavalry to Shields's help. That attack successful, Shields was now able to turn on the convent. With six brigades now amassed on the convent—and with the fires from Worth's division supporting—the San Mateo Convent surrendered, thus bringing the bloody 20th of August to a close.[13]

Scott had crossed the entire Valley of Mexico, winning two stunning victories and temporarily destroying Santa Anna's army. But he had yet to "conquer a peace."

27

❧❦❧

Truce, Tragedy, and Triumph

Mexico City falls to Scott at great expense.

B Y THE EVENING of August 20, 1847, Winfield Scott was satisfied that the battle of Churubusco was indeed finished. But his men were exhausted from two days of continual activity, so he made no attempt to take Mexico City that evening. He moved his headquarters from San Agustín to the sumptuous Bishop's Palace overlooking the town of Tacubaya, though first penning a note to Santa Anna demanding that he surrender Mexico City without the need for a fight.

He did not demand that Santa Anna surrender his army, however. Command of that army constituted the dictator's only source of power in Mexico, and keeping Santa Anna in office was necessary, as Scott saw it, to his own ends. He needed a Mexican government with the authority to sign a truce, if not a final peace. If Santa Anna was ousted from the Mexican presidency, who would be left to negotiate a settlement?

Santa Anna was a jump ahead of Scott. Aware that his disorganized army was incapable of repulsing an American assault, and calculating correctly that the American goverment was becoming desperate to end the fighting in Mexico, he resorted to diplomatic negotiation. Even before Scott sent his demand for surrender, Santa Anna had instructed his minister of foreign relations, Don Francisco Pacheco, to write a formal reply to Secretary of State James Buchanan's message of the previous April.

Pacheco's note was transparently a ruse. Everyone realized that weeks would pass before an answer could arrive from Washington. Santa Anna's real addressee was Trist, to whom he wrote another note asking that Scott's army be restrained from entering Mexico City. At the same time Santa Anna sought support from diplomats from other nations whose legations were in Mexico City. He informed the Spanish minister of his actions and sought the services of Edward Thornton and Edward Mackintosh of the British legation.

To carry his dispatch to Trist, Santa Anna chose General Ignacio Mora y Villamil, who turned out to be a good emissary indeed. Mora rode through the gates of the city during the morning of the 21st in a well-appointed carriage, looking far from defeated. He encountered Scott by chance at Coyoacán, as the general was busy supervising the emplacement of an artillery position to fire on Mexican positions around the city. Scott stopped his labors to examine the message, and on his own authority rejected it out of hand. Pacheco's tone was too arrogant for Scott to suffer; worse, Pacheco had proposed a truce lasting a whole year—out of the question. Scott knew that Trist would agree with him.

General Mora, however, had made personal contact. He gained Scott's confidence by appealing to him as soldier to soldier, and intimated that Santa Anna would welcome any suspension of hostilities. Scott quickly consulted with Trist and together they wrote a counterproposal calling for a short truce. Scott then appointed Quitman, Pierce, and Persifor Smith as commissioners to negotiate it, along with Trist. An enthusiastic Santa Anna seized on the chance for an armistice, and by August 23 an agreement had been reached, to take effect on the 25th.

The provisions of the truce were fairly simple. All hostilities within a radius of seventy-eight miles from Mexico City were to be suspended. Either side could terminate the truce with a notice of forty-eight hours. While it was in effect, neither side was to reinforce or strengthen its positions. Americans were to allow the passage of supplies through the gates of Mexico City, and in response American quartermasters were to be allowed to purchase provisions within the city. Scott happily agreed to release all Mexican prisoners of war he had taken.

Despite Scott's logical reasons for desiring an armistice, many of his officers and men were taken aback by his action. Unaware of Scott's need to preserve Mexico's political structure, and probably as yet unaware of the army's low levels of supply, most of them were anxious to destroy Santa Anna while he was still off balance. The prospective comforts of a grand city were also enticing, of course, but Scott's more thoughtful troops were concerned for the preservation of their lives.

If the American troops resented the truce, the Mexican civilians resented it even more. On August 27, only two days after the truce was signed, a convoy of supply wagons from Scott's army was turned back at the gate to the city. Santa Anna quickly sent out a delegation to apologize and assure Scott that such an infraction would not occur again. On the very next day an even more dramatic encounter took place. An American convoy, escorted by Mexican lancers, successfully entered the city, only to be set upon by a mob of Mexican citizens at the Grand Plaza (Zócalo). Several American teamsters were wounded and two wagons were lost. Significantly, the people's fury was directed as much toward Santa Anna as it was toward the Americans. "Death to Santa Anna" was shouted in the same breath as "Death to the Yankees." Santa Anna, in their view, was the villain who had made the truce.

Santa Anna pretended to be as disturbed by these incidents as was Scott. He arranged for supplies to be delivered at night, with pack mules substituted for wagons, and escorted by Mexican troops. The new arrangement worked. Supplies began to flow from the city, and the ticklish matter of specie (hard currency) was solved.* Santa Anna, however, was using this cooperation to cloak his other activities. On August 31, Inspector General Ethan A. Hitchcock heard reliable rumors that some 18,000 men had been assembled in the city; Santa Anna had even held an impressive review of his troops in the plaza. Still the Americans took no immediate action. Supplies and specie continued to flow, and the truce remained in effect for the moment.

During this time of relative inactivity, Scott had to decide on the disposition of those seventy-two San Patricio deserters his troops had captured at Churubusco. It was a difficult matter, because the offense of desertion was clearly one that called for the death penalty by hanging. Most of the accused men were foreign by birth, but that fact carried no legal weight. They had, after all, joined the so-called San Patricio Battalion to fight for Mexico against their former comrades. Scott was not a cruel man, and the

---

*The question of specie, hard currency in silver and gold, points up that the war between Mexico and the United States was no total war, as has been the twentieth-century experience. As the Americans had decided to pay for all supplies used in Mexico, Scott's army needed the money to do so. But since the two countries still had financial arrangements, he was allowed to draw money on Mexican banks for his necessary purchases. If the system broke down, it is to be presumed that Scott's army would have simply taken what supplies were needed from the populace without payment. Resentment would have become greater, and a situation closer to total war would have developed.

prospect of mass hangings was as repulsive to him as it would be to anyone else. Yet he had an army still facing a dangerous enemy, and he could not afford to show any weakness in the harsh discipline that held it together. He therefore had no choice but to place all the prisoners before courts-martial.

The men were tried in two groups. One court sat at Tacubaya, presided over by Brevet Colonel John Garland; the other, presided over by Colonel Bennet Riley, sat at San Angel. The trials were conducted fairly, but the facts were all too clear; the men had all been captured wearing Mexican uniforms. Seventy of the seventy-two were found guilty and sentenced to hang.

Scott was disturbed at the sweep of guilty verdicts, and he was under some pressure from prominent Mexicans, who had made national heroes of the San Patricios. As one who had never lost interest in the law since his youth, he felt competent to evaluate the details of the case. He therefore sat up nights attempting to find excuses to avoid the universal application of the death penalty.

Finally Scott approved the death penalty for fifty San Patricios but pardoned five men and reduced the sentences of fifteen others, including Sergeant John Riley, whom many considered the ringleader of all the desertions. Riley had deserted from Zachary Taylor's army at Matamoros before war had been officially declared in May 1846.[1] The sentences were scheduled to be carried out in early September.

As time wore on, the truce with Santa Anna became progressively more fragile. On the evening of September 3, 1847, Hitchcock reported that Trist had come back from his regular meeting looking, in his words, "dispirited and fatigued."[2] No meeting was held the next day, and on September 5, Hitchcock noticed an ominous sign. General Scott decided to leave the Bishop's Palace at Tacubaya and move back into his tent. (Tacubaya was only a mile from the hill of Chapultepec, from which Mexican guns could easily hit the palace.) The next day, September 6, Scott reluctantly concluded that all efforts at peace between the commissioners had failed. He issued the required forty-eight hours' notice; the truce was at an end.

That was too much for a nervous Kirby Smith. In anguish he wrote home,

We are now no more advanced than we were previous to the battle of the twentieth last. In the sixteen days during which [Santa Anna] has been flattering us with all the hopes of peace he has been actively collecting his scattered forces, and with all his energies preparing to renew the combat. He has now twenty-two thousand men under arms and the Capital placed in such a state of defence that the enemy loudly boasts that we cannot take it. Fatal credulity! How awful are its consequences to us! By it, the fruits of our glorious and incomparable victory are entirely thrown away . . . and now alas, we have all our fighting to do over again.

During the time the truce was in effect, Scott meticulously refrained from reconnoitering the terrain leading up to Mexico City. By the 6th of September, however, he considered himself free to hold a council of war to discuss the routes the army might take in approaching the city. For the moment he deferred making a decision; his eye had been drawn to a set of flat-roofed buildings located about a thousand yards to the east of Chapultepec. Together the cluster was called the Molino del Rey, or the King's Mill.

The Molino was a mysterious place, and rumors coming out of Mexico City during the previous two weeks had attached considerable importance to it. It had once been a cannon foundry, and the Mexicans, Scott heard, were planning to use it to cast new artillery pieces. Church bells from inside the city, so the rumor went, had been hauled out for that purpose. The mill was also reported to be lightly defended, if at all.

As Scott was pondering during the afternoon of the 7th, he received word that Mexican troops had been spotted moving from Chapultepec to the Molino. With unaccustomed haste, therefore, Scott all but decided to attack it. The action would be nothing much more than a raid, he believed, so he sent for Worth, whose division was located in Tacubaya.

Worth, enthusiastic, agreed that he could take the Molino with no difficulty. He turned down Scott's suggestion of making the attack at night. Scott conceded the point and attached Cadwalader's brigade, Sumner's dragoons, and Duncan's field artillery batteries to him. Worth would attack the next morning.

Not everyone was so sanguine about the reduction of the position as were the two generals. Captain Kirby Smith, whose company of the 5th Infantry would participate, wrote home an impassioned letter:

Tomorrow will be a day of slaughter. I firmly trust and pray that victory may crown our efforts though the odds are immense. I am thankful that you do not know the peril we are in. Goodnight.

Those were the last words that Kirby Smith ever wrote.

Once Scott had assigned Worth the task of capturing the Molino and the nearby Casa Mata, he left Worth to conduct it as he saw fit. Scott remained at a vantage point near Tacubaya and watched the operation from beginning to end, never interfering.

Both Scott and Worth had underestimated the strength of the Mexican resistance. The information that Scott had received was not necessarily false; it was simply outdated. During the last couple of days Santa Anna had decided to shift forces from the southern *garitas* (gateways) of Mexico City to the Molino and its nearby outpost, the Casa Mata. He had brought up five infantry brigades, supported by artillery. He placed a cavalry force of 4,000 men to cover the position to the west. This force was a far cry from the handful of troops that Scott and Worth expected.

While it took Worth only two hours to take both the Molino and the nearby Casa Mata, the American losses were appalling. Worth lost 116 dead, including Major Martin Scott, the commanding officer of the 5th Infantry, and Captain Kirby Smith of the same regiment.[3] Colonel J. S. McIntosh, the 2d Brigade commander, and Major C. A. Waite, the commander of the 8th Infantry, fell wounded. Worth's total losses came to 787 officers and men, double those that Zachary Taylor had sustained at Monterrey a year earlier. Worth's command was only half the size of Taylor's.

Ironically, no cannon foundry was found at the Molino del Rey. The damage to Mexican morale was great, but the damage to American morale may have been greater. Certainly the faith of the American soldiers in their army's leadership was shaken. And Scott and Worth each held the other responsible. The battle of the Molino del Rey was one of the great tragedies of the Mexican War.

Scott had no time to dwell on the losses incurred at the Molino del Rey, for his attention was focused on capturing Mexico City. He had a challenge facing him. His men were to capture a city defended by 15,000 troops, a large amount of artillery, and a hostile population.

In a way, his decision was simplified by the fact that his choices were restricted. The lands south of Mexico City were swampy under the best conditions, and Santa Anna had flooded them further. It would be impossible for artillery to move cross-country, hard going even for infantry. Any approach toward Mexico City would have to be made along one or more of the causeways that led out from the various garitas. These causeways, which consisted of stone aqueducts with double-lane roads on each side, were defended at various points along their lengths.[4]

Only five of these causeways were considered practicable for use. Two of them, the Belén and La Verónica causeways, started at the base of Grasshopper Hill, on the west, under the castle of Chapultepec. Scott realized that if he were to use either of these, he must first capture Chapultepec Castle, a step that he had not yet settled on.

Another possibility existed. Three parallel causeways ran directly into Mexico City from the south. These were, west to east, the Piedad causeway, which ran northward from the town of San Piedad; the Niño Perdido causeway, about a thousand yards to the east; and the San Antonio causeway, which began at Churubusco. Scott's engineers generally favored using one of the three southern approaches in order to avoid having to take Chapultepec Castle.

On September 9, the day after the battle at the Molino, Scott took Captain Lee with him to the Niño Perdido road. From that vantage point they could look eastward across the swampland and study the conditions along the San Antonio causeway. Lieutenants Beauregard, Stevens, and Tower were all sent to a point east of the causeway, hoping to find a way to turn it from that direction. One thing was certain: time was important. The Americans could see the Mexicans actively hauling up artillery to protect the garitas, each of which already contained some eleven pieces but could handle more. Nevertheless, it took two days for Scott to reach a decision.

On the evening of September 11, 1847, Scott called his general officers and staff to confer in the small town of La Piedad. For once Scott departed from his normal procedure by stating his own preference at the outset. He thought it best to take Chapultepec and then follow the Belén and La Verónica causeways into the city from the west. He emphasized the hard ground in that area, which he thought would compensate for the strength of the Chapultepec position. In this he was supported by an artillerist, Captain Benjamin Huger, who thought that Chapultepec could be nearly demolished in the course of one day's bombardment. Scott was concerned about the marshy conditions surrounding the causeways of the southern approaches to the city. Having finished giving his views, he called on his engineers to present the results of their studies.

This time Captain Robert E. Lee disagreed with his chief. In the light of

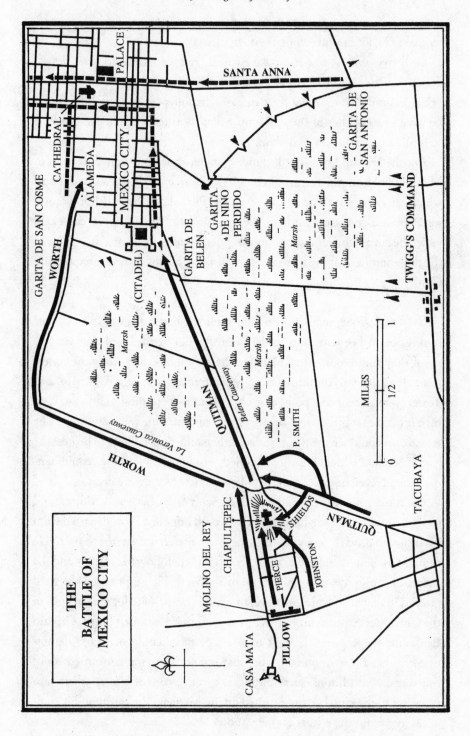

THE
BATTLE OF
MEXICO CITY

the strength of the Chapultepec position—and the feasibility of the southern routes—he argued persuasively in favor of the southern approach. After some discussion, Scott called for an informal vote. Four general officers and the three engineers voted with Lee. Only Twiggs and Lieutenant Beauregard sided with Scott. After the vote, Beauregard, previously silent, rose to present his side. So convincing was he in arguing for the Chapultepec route that one of the generals, Pierce, swung over. Scott, however, was not running an election; having asked for and received the staff's views, he drew himself up to his full height and declaimed, "Gentlemen, we will attack by the western gates. The general officers present here will remain for further orders—the meeting is dissolved."

Scott was not quite so self-assured as he let on before his assembled officers. As the officers left the conference, he turned to Hitchcock and said, "I have my misgivings."

The next day, September 12, Scott devoted his time to supervising the bombardment of Chapultepec, dearly hoping to avoid the need for an assault. He had plenty of artillery to work with: in the course of the previous evening he had established heavy batteries within range, his total pieces of heavy guns having been trebled by recent captures. At the end of the day, however, he was disappointed. The castle, while damaged, was still capable of defense. Scott therefore regretfully ordered his army to assault Chapultepec the next morning, September 13, 1847.

The Chapultepec position included far more than a hill with a castle on top. Though Chapultepec Castle itself was not a strong fortress, its walls too easily damaged by artillery, Santa Anna was defending a large, rectangular piece of ground surrounding it. The area was protected by high walls, three-quarters of a mile long and about one-quarter of a mile wide. Grasshopper (Chapultepec) Hill occupied only the eastern half of the rectangle; the western half, between the hill and the Molino, was covered by a grove of ancient cypress trees, treasures of the Montezumas even before the arrival of Hernando Cortés over three centuries earlier. The cypress grove was critical to the defense of the Chapultepec position because the slope of Grasshopper Hill was gentle from the west and moderate from the south, but precipitate on the north and east. Furthermore, those cypress gardens included the source of water for the castle.

The position was extensive enough that Santa Anna could have committed as many as two thousand men to its defense, with most of them deployed behind the walls surrounding the rectangle. The castle itself could hold only about three hundred defenders, if that many. When Santa Anna visited the castle at noon on the 12th, he questioned the wisdom of holding the position at all. Its commandant, however, was General Nicholas Bravo, a fearless old hero of the Mexican Revolution in 1821, and he was determined to defend Chapultepec to the death.

Only two roads led to the Chapultepec position from the south, both originating in Tacubaya. One ran from Tacubaya to the Molino, from which direction Scott had decided he would make his main effort. Worth's division would ordinarily have received that "honor," and indeed his division was on hand in that town, but Scott decided to commit another division first because of the shock Worth's men had undergone only four days earlier. For the attack from the west, Scott moved Pillow's division from Mixcoac to Tacubaya during the evening of the 11th. The next morning, Pillow moved forward and reoccupied the Molino, which Worth had evacuated after taking it on the 8th. When the attack was launched the next day, Worth was to follow Pillow as reserve and support.

The main road on the west led northward from Tacubaya to the southeast corner of the Chapultepec wall. From there it continued eastward along the Belén causeway to the Belén garita. Scott assigned this route to Quitman's division, much of which had seen no action in the battles of Contreras and Churubusco. Quitman was brought up from San Augustín on September 11 to make an ostentatious demonstration in front of the San Antonio garita. Then, under cover of darkness, he moved to Tacubaya. On that night, September 11, the bulk of three of Scott's divisions were in the vicinity of Tacubaya.

Twiggs's men, still shaken from the fight at the San Mateo Convent on August 20, were assigned a less arduous task. They were to make a demonstration at the San Antonio garita during the morning of the attack so as to mask Scott's true intentions. One of Twiggs's brigades, that of the redoubtable Persifor Smith, was to be attached to Quitman to make an enveloping movement toward Chapultepec from the east of the main Tacubaya road.

Though Scott had assigned the attack on Chapultepec to his two less experienced divisions,[5] he still resorted to the concept of special assault parties—from the ranks of the regulars, with forty marines borrowed from Commodore Perry. He organized two "forlorn hopes," each with over 250 officers and men. Captain Samuel McKenzie, 2d Artillery, was to command the party assigned to Pillow; Captain Silas Casey, 2d Infantry, was to command that attached to Quitman. For some reason—pride, a desire to have a storming party of his own, or because Casey was late in arriving—Quitman organized his own divisional storming party under Major Levi Twiggs, USMC.

At 5:30 A.M. on September 13, 1847, Scott's artillery opened fire on all parts of the Chapultepec defensive position. The bombardment continued until 8:00 A.M., at which time it lifted to permit the attack to begin. Pillow advanced in a column of brigades, Cadwalader leading, with Pierce following behind. At the outset, in order to secure footholds inside the walls to the west of Chapultepec, Cadwalader sent Colonel William Trousdale with two infantry regiments and two field artillery batteries along the San Cosmo causeway, along the northern edge of the Chapultepec position. His mission was to prevent both reinforcement of the position from the north and escape from the castle. At the same time the 9th and 15th Infantries crossed the wall, through the grove.

The critical attacks in the day's fighting would be the voltiguers, or light infantry battalions. While Major T. P. Andrews took one battalion of voltiguers inside the southern wall, Major Joseph E. Johnston took another on the outside (south side) to a point beyond the cypress gardens. There, after reducing a Mexican redoubt, Johnston led his battalion through a gap at the very foot of Chapultepec Hill. He quickly reduced two other redoubts inside the enclosure, leaving the winding road to the summit of the hill open.

While Johnston was making an end run around the southern end of the Mexican position, the progress was slow and difficult through the cypress gardens. Early in the action Gideon Pillow, sensing that the attack would be difficult, sent a message back to Scott, who was observing from Tacubaya, that Worth's division should be brought forward to the Molino, the better to support him on short notice. Scott so ordered Worth, only to learn that his impetuous subordinate had already left Tacubaya on his own volition.

The fighting continued to be difficult. Almost immediately after his regiment was committed at the foot of the hill, Colonel T. B. Ransom, commanding the 9th Infantry, fell dead with a rifle ball through his forehead while leading his troops forward. Pillow, near the front, was hit in the ankle with a painful but not serious wound. Dragged to safety, he called for Worth to make "great haste" or else it would be "too late." Soon Pillow's troops were joined by those of Newman Clarke's brigade, Worth's division.

On the Tacubaya road, Quitman's assault party was held up, due largely to the restricted area he had in which to maneuver. Casey's storming party and Quitman's own party, which included the Marine detachment, were halted about a hundred yards from the Mexican batteries guarding the southeastern gateway to Chapultepec. Quitman sent Persifor Smith's brigade, as planned, to turn the position from the east, but Smith was unable to do anything other than brush aside a few skirmishers; he had been given too little to work with. Quitman finally sent the New York, Pennsylvania, and South Carolina regiments to the west, where they passed through the gap in the wall earlier opened up by Johnston. There they met with elements of Clarke's brigade. Soon a disorganized mass of troops from three divisions—Quitman's, Pillow's, and Worth's—were intermingled at the walls of the castle of Chapultepec.

But the walls had been reached, and the men were fairly safe. Mexican artillery could not hit the bottom of the walls, and American sharpshooters kept the enemy riflemen down behind their walls. When the ladders arrived, they were lined up fifty abreast. The assault troops scaled them. Two officers were killed but eventually Captain Joshua Howard, of the voltiguers, gained the parapet unhurt. Captain McKenzie followed soon after. By 9:30 A.M., less than two hours after the assault began, the flag of Johnston's voltiguers flew above the parapets of Chapultepec.

Mexico City was now doomed. The Americans now possessed the heights that dominate it, and Scott's resumption of the attack so soon after the debacle of Molino del Rey was frightening to the Mexicans and electrifying to the Americans. When Scott rode up the Tacubaya Road toward the Belén causeway that morning, "The men pressed around him. He told them how glad he was, and how proud of them; and how proud their country, their wives, their sisters, and their sweethearts would be; and it seemed as if such cheering had never been heard, anywhere in the world before."[6]

The story, however, has tragic sidelights. The most celebrated of these is the legend of the Mexican cadets, fifty of whom had insisted on remaining to defend Chapultepec Castle against the Americans. Though most survived—even General Bravo lived to surrender his diamond-studded sword—six did not. One, so the story goes, threw himself off the side of the vertical east wall of the castle, clutching a Mexican flag in his arms. The six, known as Los Niños Heroicos, are commemorated by stone pillars that stand at the base of Grasshopper Hill, main attractions of Chapultepec Park below.

Another haunting picture is that of the thirty men of the San Patricio Battalion slated for execution that day. Of the fifty men for whom Scott could find no mitigating circumstances, sixteen had been hanged at San Angel on September 10, 1847, just as Scott was planning his attack on Mexico City. The next day, four others had met their fate at Mixcoac, two miles away. On September 13, the last thirty were scheduled for the same fate.

These unfortunates had been consigned to Colonel Willam S. Harney for execution, and he used his imagination to make the experience as painful as possible for the victims.[7] He placed each one on a mule cart, a rope around his neck, and while the doomed men taunted and jeered him—they had nothing to lose—he fastened the end of each rope to a mass gibbet. When Harney and the men of the San Patricio saw the American flag rise above the walls of Chapultepec, the executioners gave the mules a whack. The mules lurched forward; each left a body dangling.

It was still late morning, and though Chapultepec had fallen, Mexico City had not. So Scott, who was now in a position to supervise the battle from the top of the castle, sent orders to Worth, at the northwest corner of the castle grounds, and Quitman, at the southeast, to continue on the San Cosmo causeway and the Belén causeway respectively, toward the city. He had no need to issue that order, as both officers had gone into action without it. Scott's main function now was to reinforce both commanders with what reserve he had available. To Worth, who was advancing with only John Garland's brigade, he sent N. S. Clarke's, then George Cadwalader's, with the heavy guns to follow. To Quitman he sent Pierce's brigade, from Pillow's division, as well as some additional siege guns.

Scott intended for Worth, whose division was still his best, to make the main effort. Worth's route would take him to the Citadel, near the Belén gate, which Scott believed would be the center of Santa Anna's defense. Accordingly, he accompanied Worth along that wide causeway toward the San Cosmo garita.

Scott had not reckoned with Quitman, whose resentment at being left out of Cerro Gordo, Contreras, and Churubusco was high. Quitman drove on with special zeal, even though his was supposedly only a "feint" attack. During the afternoon, Scott sent Quitman several messages urging caution.

He was too tactful to order him to stop or to withdraw. Eventually Quitman was in a position to assault the Belén garita.

Santa Anna, in the meantime, had retreated to the Belén garita after the fall of Chapultepec. While there he brought some artillery pieces up from the Piedad road and then headed for the San Cosmo garita without leaving anyone in charge of the position he had just left. In Santa Anna's absence, the local commander, General Andrés Terrés, abandoned the garita and took his eighty men back into the Citadel. He and Quitman faced each other, at an impasse.

Santa Anna, at the San Cosmo garita, soon learned of the loss of the Belén garita. He hurried back with three infantry battalions in time to help halt Quitman but not to retake the gate. In his rage, he made Terrés the scapegoat for the loss of the capital, relieved him of command, and placed him before court-martial.[8]

By now it was getting dark, so both Worth and Quitman settled down for the night, each in possession of a garita. Of the two, Worth's prospects for taking the city were better than Quitman's, because no citadel lay in his path; the streets would be open to his troops when they moved out in the morning. Scott was also convinced that nothing more would happen that day, so he returned to his headquarters at Tacubaya and sought a few hours of well-deserved rest.

Before the light broke on September 14, Scott's slumber was interrupted. At 4:00 in the morning a delegation of Mexican officials arrived at his headquarters with a request to see him. An aide roused him.

Shortly after midnight the previous evening, the delegation explained, Santa Anna had called a meeting at the Citadel. There he had reviewed his options, and in the light of the poor condition of his army, his low supplies, and the danger of destroying Mexico City by further resistance, he had decided to evacuate. The evacuation had begun at once, and by one o'clock in the morning of Tuesday, September 14, the army was on its way to Guadalupe.

Scott considered the delegation's request for a surrender on favorable terms and set forth his own:

> that I would sign no capitulation; that the city had been virtually in our possession from the time of the lodgments effected by Worth and Quitman the day before; that I regretted the silent escape of the Mexican army; that I should levy

upon the city a moderate contribution for special purposes; and that the American army should come under no terms, not *self*-imposed.

In other words, "unconditional surrender." The levy that Scott finally exacted was $150,000.

Scott hurriedly sent word to Worth and Quitman to advance "slowly and cautiously" toward the heart of the city. He then joined Worth, whose division he still considered the main effort. He and Worth followed the general route of the present-day Paseo de la Reforma, along the northerly side of the Alameda, then south into the Plaza. At sunrise they halted at the present site of the Opera House.

Scott now prepared for the most dramatic moment of his career. He joined Worth at the Alameda, ready for the triumphal entry into the Plaza of Mexico City. He took his place at the head of Worth's division, with Harney's mounted dragoons as escort, and left the Alameda amid the clatter of cavalry hooves and the cheers of the troops. Scott was resplendent "in full-dress uniform, snowy plumes, and glittering epaulets, riding a superb bay charger." Harney's musicians played "Yankee Doodle." Even the Mexicans could not restrain themselves from a ripple of scattered applause.

There, in the Plaza, they found Quitman's men, who had beaten Worth to their destination by a full hour!

Scott was up to the occasion. He doffed his hat, reined in his horse, and solemnly reviewed all the troops, Worth's and Quitman's. He dismounted and entered the palace by the main doorway. He then turned and said impressively, "Let me present to you the civil and military Governor of the City of Mexico, Major General John A. Quitman. I appoint him this instant. He has earned the distinction and he shall have it."[9] He entered the palace and occupied one of the ornate apartments, seating himself at a desk to write out his order announcing the result of his victories. Two days later he issued his General Order No. 286:

> The General-in-Chief calls upon his brethren in arms to return, both in public and private worship, thanks and gratitude to God, for the signal triumphs which they have recently achieved for their country.

28

Peace with Mexico

The end of the "unnatural war."

S COTT HAD defeated the Mexican army under Santa Anna and had taken possession of the streets of Mexico City. But now, in mid-September 1847, there was still much to do. First he had to establish order in Mexico City and in the surrounding countryside; second, he must lay plans to administer Mexico in a manner satisfactory to the Polk administration at home. Finally, he must support Nicholas Trist in his all-important efforts to negotiate a peace with Mexico. Though these tasks were major undertakings, none seemed overwhelming to a veteran soldier and administrator such as Scott.

The first task, to pacify the streets of Mexico City, was more difficult than Scott had anticipated. Santa Anna, as one of his last acts before leaving Mexico City, had released thousands of prisoners and convicts from the city's prisons; a large number of them were armed. Many of these convicts joined the ever-present léperos (homeless mobs) in roaming the streets and sniping at the Americans. Some shots had already been fired even before Scott reached the Plaza; Colonel John Garland, a veteran of many a battle, was hit in the leg by a sniper's bullet. Even as Scott was reading his triumphal edict to his officers, an uproar broke out in the street just below the National Palace.

Scott was not amused. As soon as he satisfied himself that the disturbances were not caused by American soldiers on a spree, he ordered draconian measures: squads of American troops were sent through the streets with orders to use artillery to blast houses where firing had been spotted. No mercy was shown to any occupants of buildings from which firing had occurred. Scott also placed sharpshooters of his own in church towers and windows, with orders to pick off Mexicans seen bearing arms.

Scott also dealt with the Mexican authorities. He notified the *ayuntamiento* (mayor) that whole blocks of houses would, if necessary, be destroyed. If forced to take extreme measures, he notified them, he would turn the whole city over to unrestrained looting. To make his measures both legal and as palatable as possible, he issued General Order No. 384, warning his troops that the war was not yet over, and exhorting them to be "sober, orderly, and merciful."

Fortunately for Scott and the Americans, the anxious city officials took Scott's warnings to heart and did their utmost in urging the people of the city to cease resistance. The clergy also believed that Scott meant what he said. Since much church wealth was concentrated in the city, its officials cooperated eagerly with the civilian authorities. As a result, the unrest in Mexico City began to subside in a few days, and by October 1, two weeks after Scott had entered the city, a reasonable degree of tranquility was restored.

The long-term occupation of Mexico City, which stretched out over nine months, seems to have been neither more nor less severe than most other military occupations throughout history. Although the streets were generally quiet, it was still inadvisable for American soldiers to wander through them during the hours of darkness. The greatest threat to American troops was ennui. Many of the soldiers, with too little to keep them tired and busy, fell into habits of gambling, drinking, and soliciting prostitutes. Some even fell prey to the temptation to desert, despite Scott's reminders of the fate of the San Patricios the previous September.[1] The tradesmen who accompanied the army showed remarkable enterprise in providing instant and convenient vice. Ethan A. Hitchcock later recalled that, as inspector general of Scott's army, he broke up "a gambling-table established by a follower of the American army in the palace in the city of Mexico on the 14th of September—the very day we entered."[2]

Scott left these matters to the man he had appointed as governor of the city, John A. Quitman. He had broader matters to be concerned about, especially the overall position of his army in Mexico. Though Santa Anna had fled Mexico City to save the remnants of his army from destruction, he did not regard his flight as signaling the end of the war. He realized that Scott's occupying army was very small and his supply line to Veracruz was tenuous at best. Napoleon I had suffered his greatest debacle, losing almost the entire Grand Army after having taken Moscow, only thirty-five years before. Though Mexico City was the heart of the country both politically and financially, nobody, including Scott or Santa Anna, assumed that its occupation, in itself, would automatically end the war. With that in mind, Santa Anna took a force of about 5,700 men to Puebla, intent on destroying the American garrison there. On September 21, having surrounded the city, he issued an ultimatum to Colonel C. F. Childs. Though the garrison consisted of only about 2,200 men, many of them sick, Childs stood firm. Santa Anna, unable to make his dispirited men attack, settled down to a siege, which eventually evaporated.

In the meantime, Scott's reinforcements continued to flow into Mexico City. A large detachment of 2,500 men under Brigadier General Joseph Lane encountered resistance in Huamantla, north of the National Road.* While that battle was in progress, Santa Anna received orders from the new Mexican president, Manuel Peña y Peña, to turn over command and face courtmartial. That would have been contrary to Santa Anna's nature. For a while he considered rebelling against the government, but when he found no support for such an undertaking, he faded into the countryside to Tehuacán, a spa some seventy miles southwest of Puebla. He later escaped to Jamaica, awaiting a more fortuitous day to return to Mexico.

Though Lane's command stopped off at Puebla to protect it from further attack, additional reinforcements to Mexico City raised the strength of Scott's force to about 15,000 men by the end of December.[3] Still, despite the overcrowding that resulted, he did not enlarge the size of his holdings in Mexico. It would take "intolerable work," he explained to Marcy, to bring his new recruits to such "respectable degrees of discipline, instruction, and conduct" as to justify sending them to occupy outlying districts. Scott was not being totally frank. A key factor in his reasoning was the need to accommodate Nicholas Trist. Any expansion of United States–occupied territory would, Scott believed, jeopardize the status of Trist's efforts to negotiate peace.

Nevertheless, Scott complied with Polk's demands that the Mexicans be forced to pay for the American occupation. The public back in the United

---

*The action is notable chiefly for the loss of the intrepid Captain Sam Walker, of the Texas Rangers, who had survived many a battle, beginning with Zachary Taylor's actions around Point Isabel in May 1846, only to fall in this minor fracas.

States was becoming daily more weary of the war, and it would help the President to defend his policies if he could show that expenditures for the occupation were being kept to a minimum. Scott had therefore levied the arbitrary assessment of $150,000 on Mexico City on September 14, the day he established his occupation, and studied the amount that each Mexican state had paid to the Mexican government in 1843. He then demanded that the same amount be paid to his own coffers. By the end of the year 1847, he announced an annual assessment of over $3 million on the nineteen states of Mexico. The federal district of Mexico, in which stood the capital, was assessed $668,000.

During this period, Scott was mindful of the morale of the men under his command, officer and enlisted alike. To that end he encouraged the *American Star*, a newspaper previously published in Jalapa, to move to Mexico City. That paper, along with the *North American*, a lesser publication, provided at least some contact with the outside world. It reproduced articles from such newspapers as the *New Orleans Picayune* and others. Though such a limited access to American thought could and did cause mischief, it was the only contact a soldier had with home, other than the sporadic mails.

On December 8, 1847, Scott hosted an elaborate dinner in honor of General David Twiggs, who was leaving to take command at Veracruz. The night was memorable principally for a toast that Scott gave to the United States Military Academy, an institution for which he felt a proprietary interest. Only three former cadets were present at that dinner: Colonel Ethan A. Hitchcock, Colonel Jones M. Withers, and Nicholas Trist, who had attended but not graduated. Scott admonished those three to pretend they were elsewhere, and then declared at length that but for the science of the Military Academy "this army, multiplied by four, could not have entered the capital of Mexico." The senior officers present seconded Scott's generous opinions.

There was a certain irony to this festive occasion. The vast bulk of the West Pointers to whom Scott felt indebted were relatively junior officers. Those young men, who included Robert E. Lee, Pierre T. Beauregard, Zealous Tower, Ulysses S. Grant, and others, were too low-ranking to be included in the guest list.

The occupation of Mexico City was not being conducted as an end in itself; its only purpose was to promote Trist's efforts to negotiate an acceptable peace with the Mexican government. The efforts were delayed for a time, because Trist could find no Mexican government to deal with. After Santa Anna abdicated the presidency, a state of limbo prevailed until the leaders of the Moderato Party prevailed on Manuel Peña y Peña, the senior member of the Mexican Supreme Court, to assume the office. A temporary government of Mexico was set up at Toluca, west of Mexico City, on September 22. It moved to more comfortable surroundings at Querétaro in early October but was not sufficiently organized to do business until November 11, when a formal election named General P. M. Anaya as acting president and Peña as minister of foreign affairs. Peña and Trist had been working for only five days, however, when startling word arrived from Washington: Trist was recalled and Scott was ordered to "prosecute the war anew"—against whom was left unsaid. Both Scott and Trist were aghast.

The principal reason for this reversal of United States policy was a gross misunderstanding, caused by a combination of slow communications and mutual distrust between Polk and his two subordinates in the field. Scott was partly at fault for failing to give more attention to dispatches home, his last letter having been written on July 25, before he had left Puebla. Lacking direct word from Scott, the only sources of information available to Polk, Marcy, and Buchanan were grossly distorted letters from Gideon Pillow and the often-slanted articles in the nation's newspapers. Polk's decision was made on October 5, based not on news of the victorious valley campaign but on receiving word of Santa Anna's refusal to negotiate even after having received the beginnings of a substantial bribe. Convinced that the Mexicans would not "treat for peace upon the terms which the United States can accept," Polk felt it necessary for Trist to be recalled and for Scott to increase the levies on Mexico to support the occupation—indeed to prosecute the war "with increased forces and increased energy."[4] At that time Polk seemed to hold no rancor toward Trist personally.

After another two weeks, however, Polk's attitude toward Trist had degenerated markedly. On October 21, having received dispatches from Trist admitting his failure to get negotiations going, Polk jumped to the conclusion that the Mexicans were simply being recalcitrant, not fumbling from internal confusion. Polk had also been informed that Trist was considering a treaty that would grant to Mexico the territory of Texas between the Nueces and the Rio Grande. Two days later Polk's pique had reached a crescendo. Trist, he raged, had "managed the negotiation very bunglingly and with no ability." He had exceeded his instructions, and had invited proposals from the Mexican government that the United States could never accept. "I directed Mr. Buchanan," he wrote, "to prepare a despatch expressing in strong terms my disapprobation, and to repeat his order of the 6th instant for his immediate recall." Due to the infrequency of the convoys running from Veracruz to Mexico City, the two messages arrived together, on November 16.

Fortunately, Trist was under no pressure to act on his orders of recall instantly. Scott could not provide him an escort to Veracruz before December 4, so he had at least two weeks to consider. His first reaction was to obey orders and depart; after all, Polk and Buchanan might benefit from a firsthand report of conditions in Mexico. As time passed, however, he began to develop second thoughts. On November 24, a week after receiving his summons back to Washington, he received a note from Peña advising him that President Anaya had appointed commissioners to treat. The astonishing thing about this note is that Peña had sent it from Querétaro in the full knowledge that Trist had been officially relieved of his duties.

Others joined in a chorus of persons wishing Trist to stay on to complete his negotiations. Most influential among these was Bernardo Couto, one of the recently appointed commissioners, and one who had served on the truce commission of the previous September. Couto argued with Trist for several days, urging him to get on with the peace proceedings. Scott agreed with Couto, saying he believed that "any treaty Mr. Trist might sign would be duly ratified in Washington."[5]

By December 3 Trist had decided to stay on. He passed the word quietly to Couto, who then transmitted it to Edward Thornton of the British legation. And by the next day Trist had rolled the dice. He wrote to Thornton, "I am now resolved . . . to carry home with me a treaty of peace, if the Mexican government feel strong enough to venture upon making one on the basis, as regards boundary, of the project originally presented by me."

Two days later he sent a long, elaborate letter to the State Department, in which he went so far as to castigate the character of Gideon Pillow, thus sealing his fate with the Polk administration.

Though Trist had gone all out in defying the authorities at home, partly at the urgings of the Mexicans, Peña was unable to act promptly to take advantage of his decision. Further negotiations, the Mexicans contended, would have to wait for the confirmation of the commissioners by their senate, and Peña was not a bit sure that all of them would succeed. That argument was plausible on the surface, but other considerations were obviously at work in the minds of the Mexicans. Rumors were rife that the Whigs in the United States were intent on forcing President Polk to accept terms far more lenient than those Trist had previously insisted upon. In sharp contrast, another rumor had it that the United States was now intent on occupying all of Mexico. A third rumor was a compromise; it held that the right of conquest could leave the United States in possession of Chihuahua, Veracruz, and other key points in the postwar years without even the formality of a treaty.

Still Trist and Scott remained optimistic on the whole. On December 29, 1847, Trist wrote to Buchanan that he expected to sign a treaty within a week, and Scott told Hitchcock on January 7 that he expected a treaty within three days. After all, Trist and the Mexican commissioners were agreed that the future boundary between the United States and Mexico should run along the Rio Grande until it reached 32° north, at which point it should run westward to the Pacific coast.

Every day Trist made progress, and by the end of January 1848, the Mexicans were ready to sign a treaty; but they demanded $30 million for the territories the United States was assuming, a figure Trist had never been authorized to meet. Even at that late date, Trist declared the negotiations to be at an end. Nobody believed him.

The negotiations were conducted in a surprisingly cordial atmosphere. Couto would later comment on the feelings the Mexicans had toward Trist—of "grateful and honoring recollections."[6] More remarkable was the fact that on January 30, 1848, at about the time that Trist was calling the negotiations "at an end," the city council of Mexico City invited Scott to make a formal, though festive, visit to the ruins of a Carmelite convent about fifteen miles outside Mexico City. Scott, though wary, accepted.

Ethan Allen Hitchcock, one of those invited to accompany Scott, later described how the Mexican city council rode out in their carriages while Scott, William O. Butler, and Persifor Smith rode out on horseback, escorted by two troops of dragoons for protection against guerrillas and robbers. First the parties stopped to view the Carmelite convent, which Hitchcock called "the most interesting ruin I have ever seen." The party then gathered for a meal "embracing every delicacy which the country affords— a multitude of cooks, dishes, and every variety of wines and the greatest abundance of everything." The chief *alcalde* (councilman) sat at one end of the table, with Scott and Butler on either side, others distributed around the table. A band greeted Scott's arrival; a small group of guitar and flute players entertained during dinner.

Most amazing to Hitchcock was the nature of the speeches that followed dinner. Scott made general remarks, to the effect that he desired peace, but two or three of the Mexican speakers "expressed the hope that [the Americans] would not leave the country until we had first destroyed the influence of the clergy and the army!" At the end of the day, Scott returned. He had stationed a regiment of infantry five miles outside the city, just in case.

The atmosphere prevailed. Two days after the outing, Scott learned that Trist was joining the Mexican commissioners at Guadalupe Hidalgo, just north of Mexico City, for the purpose of signing an agreement.[7] By that evening, February 1, 1848, copies of an agreed-upon text arrived at Scott's headquarters. The next morning, Trist and the Mexican commissioners signed the treaty. Upon receiving notification, Scott pledged to suspend hostilities.

The Treaty of Guadalupe Hidalgo was a truly historic document, one that set the boundary between the two countries almost as it stands today.* The treaty called for a border that ran along the Rio Grande to the southern boundary of the then Mexican state of New Mexico, thence west along the Gila River to the Gulf of California. From there it would run westward to the Pacific. The United States would assume the debt owed by Mexico to American citizens and pay Mexico $15 million for the territory thus transferred.

For Scott and Trist the Mexican War was over. The Treaty of Guadalupe Hidalgo caused President James Polk a great deal of anger but, as Scott had predicted, the chief magistrate sent it to the Senate with little delay. It was duly ratified on March 10, 1848; on June 12, 1848, the last American troops sailed from Veracruz, bound for home.

For Scott there was a strange sequel. Shortly after the Treaty of Guadalupe Hidalgo was signed, a deputation of Mexican leaders approached him with the proposal that he declare himself dictator of Mexico for a term of four to six years, his authority to be maintained by the 15,000 or so American troops that even Scott agreed he could raise.[8] Scott, accord-

---

*The Gadsden Purchase, made in 1852, rounded out the southern area of Arizona to accommodate the railroad being built there.

ing to the deputation, would have the power and the ability to establish order in Mexico long enough to allow "politicians and agitators to recover pacific habits, and learn to govern themselves." Since troops currently under Scott's command were already in control of all the principal forts, arsenals, foundries, mines, and seaports, he could, with such troops as he could recruit for the purpose, control the country.[9]

Scott contemplated the offer, but only to savor the flattery. In the end he politely turned it down. He was too old and dedicated a soldier to enter into an arrangement so questionable in terms of his own country's interests.

29

※※

Fire from the Rear

*A petulant president manages to replace Scott but not
to discredit him.*

> Successful as was every prediction, plan, siege, battle, and skir-
> mish of mine in the Mexican war, I have here paused many weeks
> to overcome the repugnance I feel to an entrance on the narrative
> of the campaign it was my fortune—I almost said *misfortune*—
> to conduct, with half means, beginning at Vera Cruz on March
> 9, and terminating in the capital of the country, September 14,
> six months and five days.
>
> —Scott, *Memoirs*

WINFIELD SCOTT'S recollections of the campaign of 1847 from Veracruz to Mexico City are remarkably bitter. Describing his brilliant
military campaign in his *Memoirs* seventeen years later, Scott revealed his
pain from the events following the end of hostilities in Mexico.

The war with Mexico had been a triumph for both President Polk and his
generals, most notably for Scott. It had been costly: 13,000 dead, thousands
wounded, and a monetary cost of $100 million. It had been even more costly
to the Mexicans in both casualties and loss of territory.

From a national point of view, however, especially in territorial gains, the
war had greatly benefited the United States. The shared success might have
healed old wounds of antagonism, but it did not. Hard feelings, between
Polk and his generals in particular, were far too deeply embedded to allow
them to feel charitably toward one another. When a chance to humiliate

Scott presented itself to Polk, therefore, he seized upon it avidly. The main tool at his disposal was, not surprisingly, the disposition of his loyal friend Gideon Johnson Pillow.

Pillow was not a malicious sort of man, but he lived by a set of values that neither Scott nor most of the rest of the officer corps could understand. He was enthusiastic about the tasks that Scott and the army faced, but for his own ends. Law required that his commission as a major general would expire once the Treaty of Guadalupe Hidalgo was ratified. His every act in uniform, therefore, was directed toward reaping glory from his military service, glory that would serve as an asset for a future career in public life, even leading to the presidency itself. Unfortunately, his ambition was not inhibited by any noticeable set of moral principles or compunctions.[1] By his very nature, he was bound to create trouble in the somewhat inhibited atmosphere of Scott's army.

Scott's army had barely entered Mexico City when Pillow ran into trouble. One of the two Mexican howitzers taken at the storming of Chapultepec was found to be missing from Scott's inventory of captured weapons, and one of Pillow's subordinates found it in Pillow's baggage wagon. Pillow attempted to get rid of the weapon, but someone preferred court-martial charges against him. Pillow, realizing that he was trapped, tried unsuccessfully to throw the blame on two young lieutenants, and he was duly reprimanded on October 27, 1847. The court, while admitting that Pillow had returned the souvenir, held to the "impression" that Pillow had taken such action only when caught. The ruling was, however, immediately countermanded in Washington by President Polk himself. That appeared to be the end of the story.

Other matters of even greater concern arose, however. In Pillow's official report of the battle of Contreras, he had portrayed himself as exercising total command over Scott's whole army, with hardly a mention of Scott. He also claimed to have given the order for Quitman and Worth to move on toward Mexico City along the causeways after Chapultepec had fallen. As Scott was still inclined to treat Pillow with kid gloves, he reproved Pillow very mildly. On October 2, he sent a letter expressing his compliments and inviting Pillow's attention to several pages in Pillow's reports of August 24 and September 18, pointing out the glaring misrepresentations but calling them "inadvertent" and presuming that they had been "silently corrected."

Pillow answered the next day, gushing over Scott's "kindnesses" and expressing "no hesitation" in correcting anything in his reports. His implied price, however, was that Scott pay a call on him to discuss the matter, as he was "unable" to call on Scott. Scott bristled at the prospect of subjecting himself to calling on a subordinate, so after another fruitless exchange he dropped the matter with a shrug.

Later in October, however, the *American Star* reprinted an article that had originally appeared in the New Orleans *Delta* on September 10, just before the attack on Chapultepec. Signed by an anonymous person who called himself "Leonidas," the article included some startling sentences:

> [Pillow's] plan of battle [at Contreras] and the disposition of his forces, were most judicious and successful. He evinced in this, as he has done on other occasions, that masterly military genius and profound knowledge of the science of war, which has astonished so much the mere martinets of the profession. . . . During this great battle, which lasted two days, *General Pillow was in command of all the forces engaged,* except General Worth's division, and this was not engaged. . . . (General Scott gave but one order and that was to reinforce General Cadwalader's brigade.)[2]

The fat was now in the fire; Pillow had hit Scott in his most vulnerable spot, his vanity. His pique was hardly assuaged by a humorous sidelight. The *Picayune* edition, sensing what an exaggeration all this was, had added another tidbit:

> [A Mexican] made one terrible charge at our General with his lance, which the latter evaded with great promptitude and avidity, using his sword, tossed the weapon of the Mexican high in the air and then quietly blew his brains out with his revolver.

The officers and men of Scott's army were both amused and angered by Pillow's presumption, for there was little doubt as to who the author of the *Delta* article was.

At about the same time as the "Leonidas" article appeared, another one, also carried in the *American Star,* added to Scott's discomfiture. Pillow as an individual could be brushed off, perhaps, but this piece, which originated in the *Pittsburgh Star* and was later reprinted in Tampico, proved that dissension in the command went even further. It involved Scott's decision of August 15, one in which he took pride, to turn south from the National Road to avoid the risk of attacking Santa Anna's position on El Peñón directly. The wise move, the article stated, was not Scott's at all. It gave full credit to Worth and to James Duncan, who had supposedly saved Scott from his own ineptness. It was followed by another article eulogizing Pillow, this one signed "Veritas."

Scott was now infuriated. On November 12, 1847, he published General Order No. 349, which called the attention of "certain officers" to an 1825 regulation that forbade them from writing for civilian publication on military operations. In vituperative language, it said that only "two echoes from home had reached the army regarding the brilliant operations of our arms," the New Orleans article ("Leonidas") and the Tampico (Pittsburgh). It required "not a little charity" to believe that the principal heroes of the scandalous letters did not either write them or "specifically procure them to be written," and it would be easy to conjecture the "authors—chiefs, partizan, and pet familiars." In writing the order, Scott made the mistake of making it too graphic:

> "False credit may, no doubt, be obtained at home, by such despicable self-puffings and malignant exclusion of others; but at the expense of the just esteem and consideration of all honorable officers, who love their country, their profession, and the truth of history."

While Scott's accusations certainly applied to Pillow, Worth was at least technically innocent. Already in a state of pout with Scott, he wrote an angry letter stating that he had learned

> with much astonishment that the prevailing opinion in this army points the imputation of "scandalous" contained in the third and of "the indignation of the great number," in the fourth paragraph of orders No. 349, printed and issued yesterday, to myself as one of the officers alluded to.

He then demanded to know whether the general-in-chief applied to him, Worth, the epithets contained in the order. Scott brushed him off with a noncommittal answer, and a frustrated Worth sent a letter to President Polk, correctly providing a copy to Scott. In it he appealed for redress "from the arbitrary and illegal conduct, the malicious and gross injustice, practiced by the general officer, commanding-in-chief, this army, Major General Winfield Scott. He accused Scott of acting in a manner "unbecoming an officer and a gentleman" and enumerated his complaints in detail.

Scott now exploded. He placed Worth in arrest and preferred court-martial charges against him for "behaving with contempt and disrespect toward his superior and commanding officer."

Scott's wrath soon extended still further. James Duncan, in support of Worth, promptly wrote a letter to the local *North American* admitting that he himself had written the so-called Tampico letter. Scott therefore preferred charges against Duncan also. Then, when he learned that Pillow had written Secretary Marcy in connection with his alleged theft of a howitzer at Chapultepec, Scott did the same with him. Two of Scott's four division commanders, plus his most noted artilleryman, were now in arrest, awaiting the convening of a court. President James K. Polk, in Washington, now saw his chance.

On New Year's eve, 1847, Polk conferred with two influential Democratic senators, Lewis Cass and Jefferson Davis. Both senators claimed to deplore the conflicts that had arisen among the high-ranking officers of Scott's army. Doubtless to the pleasure of Polk, both were loud in condemning Scott's conduct and in recommending his recall as general-in-chief in Mexico. The next day Secretary of War Marcy was more specific. Scott, he said, should be superseded in command and replaced by General William O. Butler. That evening both Postmaster General Cave Johnson and Attorney General Nathan Clifford came to the same conclusion.

Polk was now assured of the unanimous support of his cabinet in dealing with Scott, so he nullified Scott's court-martial charges against Worth and directed that all three officers Scott had arrested—Worth, Duncan, and Pillow—should be released from arrest. He did not yet feel free to nullify the charges against Pillow and Duncan, but a few days later he appointed a court-martial to investigate the charges, with the same court continuing to sit as a court of inquiry to rule on the mutual charges between Scott and Worth. Finally he reduced the investigation of Pillow and Duncan to a court of inquiry, a watered-down hearing that bore no criminal implications. Scott was now completely repudiated.

On January 13, 1848, Secretary Marcy sent Scott three separate communications. The first simply implemented the president's decision to nullify Scott's charges against Worth for insubordination on the basis that Worth's conduct had been correct. Worth, so the argument went, had been offended by the wording in Scott's General Order No. 349, had attempted to redress his wounded honor by appealing to Scott first, and only then, when that avenue had failed, had he written to the President. Worth's appealing to a "common superior" could not, Marcy argued, be interpreted as an insubordinate act. All other procedures would have to wait, however. "The charges which General Worth has presented against you must be disposed of before any proceedings can be had on that which you have presented against him." He finished by directing Scott to release all three officers from arrest.

The second communication, War Department General Order No. 2, set up the court of inquiry, the members of which were to be Brigadier General N. Towson, paymaster of the Army; Brigadier General Caleb Cushing; and Colonel E. G. W. Butler, 3d Dragoons. The court, which consisted of officers all vastly inferior to Scott in rank, was to meet at the Castle of Perote, Mexico, on February 18, or "as soon thereafter as practicable."

The third communication, stiffly formal, dwarfed the others in importance:

Sir: in view of the present state of things in the army under your immediate command, and in compliance with the assurance contained in my reply to your letter of the 4th of June, wherein you asked to be recalled, the President has determined to relieve you from further duty as commanding general in Mexico. You are, therefore, ordered by him to turn over the command of the army to Major General Butler; or in his absence, to the officer highest in rank with the column under you.[3]

In Mexico City, Scott had received unofficial news of these actions even while the details were being worked out in Washington. As early as February 9, he wrote Marcy saying that newspapers and magazines had told him of Polk's intention "to place me before a court, for daring to enforce necessary discipline in this army against certain of its high officers!" He was, however, pleased that his successor would be General Butler. But then a touch of bitterness: "Perhaps, after trial, I may be permitted to return to the United States. My poor services with this gallant army are at length to be requited as I have long been led to expect they would be."

When official word came on February 18, therefore, Scott was prepared. His farewell message was generous toward General Butler, calling him "a general of established merit and distinction in the service of his country." He did not stage an elaborate departure ceremony. He simply published this order and then retired for a month to prepare his case for the forthcoming court of inquiry, which was to be held, by dictate from Washington, first at the Castle of Perote, near Jalapa, then at Puebla, and finally in Mexico City.

But though Scott went quietly, the army in Mexico was enraged. Hitchcock, a caustic intellectual who revered no one, wrote,

So far as I can discover, there is in the army a feeling of unmitigated condemnation of the late change, universal except among the immediate partisans of Pillow, etc. We all see the enormity of the conduct of the President—deplore and abhor it.

The next evening, at a dinner given for Scott at the British legation, Hitchcock quoted senior British foreign officers as "deploring" the order relieving Scott and observing that it "would be bitterly condemned in Europe, as the result of low and vulgar intrigue by inferior men."

Robert E. Lee took a more temperate view of Scott's relief, but his feelings also were strong. In a letter to his brother, he wrote,

> The great cause of our success [in Mexico] was in our leader [Scott]. It was his stout heart that cast us on the shore at Vera Cruz; his bold self-reliance that forced us through the pass at Cerro Gordo; his indomitable courage that, amid all the doubts and difficulties that surrounded us at Puebla, pressed us forward to this capital, and finally brought us within its gates.
>
> I agree with you as to the dissensions in camp; they have clouded a bright campaign . . . and ought to have been avoided. The whole matter will soon be before the court, and if it had been seen that there is harshness and intemperance of language on one side, it will be evident that there has been insubordination on the other.[4]

By the time the court of inquiry convened in Mexico City in mid-March 1848, Scott was ready to drop the whole thing. As the commanding general administering necessary discipline to keep his army functioning, he had preferred court-martial charges against three insubordinate officers the previous November, but he was no longer in command; the nature of the court had since been downgraded to a court of inquiry; the charges against Worth and Duncan had been nullified; and Pillow's commission as a major general would soon be terminated by the end of the war. Worst of all, the authorities in Washington had so couched the terms of the trial that Scott, while still acting as prosecutor, was also a defendant. Accordingly, he opened by saying that he declined to prosecute the charges and specifications against Pillow without the court's "special orders, or the further instructions from the President of the United States."

Gideon Pillow, however, was now confident that he had an overpowering advantage over Scott. He therefore refused to let the charges be dropped.

Since he had entered the army to promote his political standing at home, it would be far better for him to be exonerated by due process (which Polk would ensure) than to merely have the charges against him dropped. Accordingly, he answered that he saw no need to justify Scott's dropping the case. Since Scott had expressed no doubt as to his guilt, he continued, he demanded the "opportunity to investigate the facts." If Scott persisted, he would hold himself "acquitted of his accusations, and the world must so regard it." He asked the court to "protect" him from such consequences.

Scott now found himself in a quandary. If he simply waited the sixty days for his statement to make the round trip to Washington, the delay would be unbearable. Besides, the return voyage to the United States would then occur during the worst of the *vomito* season in Veracruz. So Scott assented, wearily, to go ahead with the trial.

Testimony began on March 21, 1848. The first charge to be taken up was a clear-cut one, Pillow's allegedly being the author of the notorious "Leonidas" letter. The second, less clear-cut one would come later, charging "conduct unbecoming an officer," with many specifications, most of which centered around his claims to have won the battles of Contreras, Churubusco, and Chapultepec almost single-handed.

The case involving "Leonidas" was hazy. James Freaner, the respected correspondent from the New Orleans *Delta,* testified that he recognized the wording of the "Leonidas" article as identical to one that Pillow had asked him to file under his own, Freaner's, signature. When Freaner had refused, he concluded that someone had inserted the article in his dispatch case. Freaner's testimony, however, was partly nullified by that of Major Archibald Burns, a protégé of Pillow's, who testified that he had been the author of the letter.

Nicholas Trist then appeared as one of Scott's most effective witnesses. Since Trist held Pillow responsible for poisoning the President's mind against him, his venom toward Polk's one-time law partner exceeded even his rage over the intensity of Pillow's cross-examination. His testimony finished, Trist left for home on April 8, 1848.

The specification regarding the alleged falsehoods in Pillow's "puffing letters" was even more difficult to establish, as it involved, at least to some extent, a matter of weighing the testimony of one witness against that of another. Ordinarily, the weight of the evidence, as presented by such highly respected officers as Hitchcock and Lee, would have worked heavily in

Scott's favor, but it was doubtful that even they would convince a court carefully selected by Polk and Marcy for its hostility to Scott.

Colonel Ethan A. Hitchcock was another of Scott's most effective witnesses. His direct testimony, however, was overshadowed by the contents of two letters he had written, which unequivocally supported Scott's superb leadership throughout the Mexican campaign. One of the letters, ten pages long, had found its way into the New York *Sun* the previous January. In it Hitchcock had dealt harshly, even sarcastically, with Worth, Duncan, and Pillow alike, causing Pillow to describe it as "infamously false and scandalous . . . calculated and intended to prejudice the public mind, and causing it to prejudge the very questions on which [Pillow] was to be tried." Pillow's attack on Hitchcock centered not so much on him or the contents of his letters as on the fact that he had written them at all. His doing so, Pillow contended, violated the 1825 law as egregiously as Pillow would have— if, as he denied, he had actually written the "Leonidas" letter.

Pillow attacked Hitchcock violently in his cross-examination, and he seemed to believe he had attained the upper hand. "I have convicted him [Hitchcock] of the very offense with which [Scott] charges me while I have proved myself entirely innocent," he wrote his wife. "Scott has raved with passion & tried to bully the court and browbeat me; but he is now so thoroughly whipt that he is quiet as a lamb."

Hitchcock, however saw the exchange differently. As one experienced in Army politics, he proved to be more than a match for Pillow. And despite Pillow's private boastings, Hitchcock appeared to take the general's abuses in stride.

On balance, there was no question that Hitchcock's conduct and the material contained in his letters were telling evidence. So effective was Hitchcock's testimony that Worth, watching on the sidelines, angrily demanded that General Butler, as commanding general, place Hitchcock in arrest. But Butler, a prudent man, held off pending the end of the court. By then, Worth had developed second thoughts and did nothing more. Hitchcock was a formidable antagonist and he knew things about Worth's conduct at the battle of Monterrey that "would require a strong man to bear." As Hitchcock wrote somewhat smugly in his diary of April 4,

[Pillow] used every effort to irritate me, but in vain. I was perfectly at home and answered all his questions. . . . I claimed that I had violated no regulation; that I felt perfectly free to use my considerable knowledge of the campaign and I expected to continue to use it as occasion might require. I was on oath, and took care to remind the court that I was aware of it.

As the hearings were winding down in Mexico City, a further inquiry came in. President Polk, through Secretary Marcy, was asking for details regarding the conference at Puebla and the offer of a bribe to Santa Anna. On this one, Scott refused to answer. He would divulge the details only to the President, he declared, and *possibly* to Marcy. The court could do nothing; the matter simply had to drop.

By April 21, 1848, the court of inquiry decided that it had taken all the testimony necessary in Mexico; it had sat there only because of the availability of the witnesses. It would reconvene at Frederick, Maryland, the customary place for courts of inquiry to be held. The next day Scott departed Mexico City by mule wagon, accompanied by a disabled soldier as an aide. He requested that his departure be marked with no fanfare, but word was out that he was leaving. A crowd of officers surrounded his wagon, and many brought their horses so that they could follow him a few miles out of the city. By one eyewitness account, all joined in a cry of "God bless you, General!"[5]

When Scott and his aide arrived at Veracruz on May 1, he immediately called on Commodore Matthew Perry. Perry offered him the use of a new steamer to take him to the United States, but Scott characteristically demurred; the steamer could be put to better use carrying wounded and sick soldiers. He took passage on an old sailing craft, the *Petersburg,* which was loaded with guns, mortars, and ordnance stores. On May 20, 1848, the captain of his vessel steered the ship through the Narrows at New York. Scott managed to procure a rowboat to take him home to Elizabethtown, New Jersey, where his wife, Maria, and three daughters awaited him.

Scott could have taken passage to New Orleans, where Mayor A. D. Crossman had previously sent him a pressing invitation to be the city's guest. The state of Louisiana had also voted him a ceremonial sword with lavish endorsement. Scott was doubtless pleased with the invitation, which had reached him just at the end of the court session in Mexico City, but his earlier orders directed him to return to Washington. Further, he was sick from the case of *vomito* he had contracted during his short stay at Veracruz; he therefore tactfully passed up the invitation.

Despite the implied disapprobation of President Polk, Scott was not wanting in outbursts of support and admiration from other quarters. Soon after he reached Elizabethtown, "in great want of repose and good nursing," he was "overpowered" by delegations from New York and invited to a dinner given by the city in his honor, a "magnificent reception, both military and civil."[6] He could also derive satisfaction from the fact that Congress had voted its thanks to him and to the officers and men, both regulars and volunteers, who had fought under him, enumerating his various battles. The Congress had further requested the President to cause an appropriate medal to be struck in Scott's honor, "emblematical of the series of brilliant victories achieved and to cause the foregoing resolutions to be communicated to Major General Scott, in such terms as he may deem best calculated to give effect to the objects thereof." Ironically, those instructions had been sent to Polk on March 9, just as the court of inquiry was about to begin in Mexico City!

The court of inquiry reconvened at Frederick, Maryland, on June 5, a little over two weeks from the day Scott had landed at New York. Starkly contrasting with the outpouring of adulation Scott had received on returning to his homeland, it proved to be even more of an ordeal for him than had been the session at Mexico City. Scott was still worn out from the *vomito* he had contracted at Veracruz; Pillow, who had ridden home in luxury aboard a steamer in the company of the members of the court, was in fine fettle. Pillow was, more than ever, feeling impending triumph.

The attitude of the court, apparently stiffened by its new proximity to the political powers in Washington, now became more hostile to Scott than ever. Scott had few by the way of allies among the high-ranking officers. Of the four division commanders in the Valley of Mexico, Pillow was one and Worth another. Quitman, while a gentleman and friendly to Scott, was primarily beholden to President Polk, with whose views he was familiar. Scott's greatest support, therefore, came from David E. Twiggs, whose testimony, had he been a more convincing witness, would have been important. Questioned on June 9, he produced the following testimony:

Q: Before the arrival of Major General Scott on the field in the afternoon of August 19, in front of the entrenched encampment of Contreras, who was first, and who was second in army rank on that field?

Twiggs: I don't know when General Scott arrived. General Pillow was a major general, commanding the 3d division, and I was a brigadier general, commanding the 2d division.

Q: Was the witness made acquainted, by Major General Pillow, that afternoon or day, with any general plan of attack, or original order of battle, against the enemy's forces in or about the entrenched camp at Contreras, emanating from the said Pillow?

Twiggs: I was not.

Later, when Pillow cross-examined Twiggs, he tried to browbeat him. "Has it escaped the witness's memory," he asked, "that General Pillow held a conversation" with Twiggs pointing out the position of the enemy and giving orders for Twiggs to advance and that Pillow would not interfere with his operations? To that and further elaborations on Pillow's performance, Twiggs simply stated, "No such conversation as that in this question took place between us."

That, however, was almost the only high point for Scott. A parade of witnesses, even including Marcy himself, did his case no good. Finally, on July 1, 1848, the court announced its finding. It called Pillow's conduct on August 19 at Contreras "meritorious" and said it was "emphatically approved by General Scott at the time." Finally, "the court is of the opinion that no further proceedings against General Pillow in the case are called for by the interest of the public service."[7]

Pillow and Polk had both triumphed, not from the strength of their case but through the sheer manipulation of governmental power. Neither man, however, showed any signs of remorse. Pillow returned from Frederick to Washington to celebrate his acquittal at a White House dinner with his friend James K. Polk, President of the United States.

Winfield Scott had one more disappointment to bear, even while he was still at Frederick. As the court of inquiry was winding down, the Whig presidential convention met and nominated Zachary Taylor for President of the United States. The Whig choice of general, engineered largely by Senator John Crittenden, would seem on the surface to be unfair. Scott's military campaigns in the recent war had, after all, far overshadowed those of Taylor. But the Whigs had chosen their second general over their first for reasons other than sheer military prowess. For Taylor, despite his homespun ways, was an astute politician; Scott was not. Taylor was known to his troops as "Old Rough and Ready"; Scott was "Old Fuss and Feathers." Practical politics, far more than Scott's involvement with the court at Frederick, had made the difference.

30

⊱⚜⊰

The Last Whig Candidate, 1852

A superb soldier makes an inept politician.

> In this defeat, I presume General Scott has felt a deeper depression than he has ever before experienced in all his life. I would not undergo his feelings of disappointment at the defeat for all the honors of the world put together and all the wealth of the world added.
> —Ethan Allen Hitchcock, *Fifty Years in Camp and Field*

WHEN THE COURT of inquiry closed in Frederick, Scott reassumed his administrative duties as general-in-chief of the Army. He had no wish to be around Washington, however, so in early July 1848 he moved his headquarters back to New York. He had still not recovered completely from the fever he had contracted in Veracruz, so he welcomed the chance to rejoin Maria and to settle down once again at Elizabethtown. He managed to stay away from President James Polk for the rest of the latter's term, which still had eight months to run. He was sensitive to Zachary Taylor's new status— a presidential nominee while still an officer on active duty. To avoid embarrassment to himself and Taylor, Scott temporarily gave up his command of the whole Army, administering only the Eastern Command, while leaving Taylor to command the West without reporting to him.

In November 1848 Taylor was elected President of the United States by a small majority over the Democratic candidate, Lewis Cass. Scott expressed little opinion on the subject, and he found an excuse to avoid Taylor's presidential inauguration ceremony; being part of the backdrop for an occasion honoring both Polk and Taylor was more than he could stomach.

A few days after the inaugural, however, Scott heeded the advice of his faithful friend Philip Hone and went to Washington. He called at the White House to pay a formal, highly visible call on the man who had been his subordinate for thirty years. In a cordial meeting Scott secured permission to keep the headquarters of the Army in New York. Taylor accepted that arrangement, probably with a sense of relief.

Scott had been undergoing one frustration after another, so he was pleased when, in early 1849, Congressman Robert Toombs of Georgia introduced a bill in the House of Representatives authorizing the rank of lieutenant general to be created for him. That honor, as it turned out, would be years in coming to fruition, but the recognition served as a palliative to Scott's wounded pride.

Scott remained out of sight for the next year, attending to the duties of shepherding the Army from a wartime to a peacetime footing. During that time, events were transpiring on the national scene of great interest to him. The Mexican War had brought on a crisis, as predicted, between free states and slave states. The Wilmot Proviso, introduced by Democratic Pennsylvania Congressman David Wilmot in late 1846, had called for the prohibition of slavery in those territories obtained from Mexico. The proviso had failed to pass, but its principle remained as a watchword for some of the more radical elements of the Whig party.

As President, Zachary Taylor attacked the problem of slavery expansion head-on. A slaveholder himself but opposed to the extension of the institution, he encouraged the two new territories, California and New Mexico, to organize for statehood with a view to entering the Union as free states. Taylor's actions so infuriated the South that support for New Mexican statehood quickly backed off,[1] and it fell to Henry Clay, the "Great Compromiser," to come up with a formula to settle the question. In February 1850 Clay introduced on the floor of the Senate a series of measures designed to address the conflicts.

The "Compromise of 1850" encompassed various provisions, some of which favored the position of the Southern planters and others of which were favorable to the North. It provided for California to be admitted to the Union as a free state, but the rest of the new territories were to be administered without provision for their future status, free or slave. It settled the boundary issue between Texas and New Mexico by placing the western boundary of Texas along today's lines.[2] It required the federal government to assume Texas's debts. The District of Columbia was to cease functioning as a depot for interstate slave trade, but slave ownership was not to be abolished within its borders.

At first glance, those provisos seemed to be balanced enough, but to make the package more acceptable to the South, Clay upgraded an old law of 1793 confirming the right of a slaveholder to pursue a fugitive slave into free territory, there to bring him before a magistrate, whose duty, once the facts were known, was to restore the slave to the rightful owner. This more rigorous Fugitive Slave Act was anathema to the abolitionists of the north.

Even without the Fugitive Slave Act, the members of the Senate realized the impossibility of passing the compromise as a single act; the extremists on both sides could bind together to vote it down. In late 1850, therefore, Clay submitted the provisos as individual bills, so the combined votes of the moderates and the more extreme supporters would be enough to push each individual measure through.

Zachary Taylor saw no use for Clay's Compromise of 1850, as he had already put forth his own answer to the problem. Further, he was reported to be ready to go to war with those who threatened secession over the issue. There were no more battles for this general, however, because in July 1850 he died suddenly of a gastrointestinal disease. Clay's path was now clear. The compromise package was passed piece by piece in September.

On Zachary Taylor's death, Scott's attitude toward the atmosphere in Washington underwent a drastic change. He took charge of Taylor's funeral arrangements and participated flamboyantly in the parade that was held on July 15, 1850. So impressive was he that even the Washington *Union*, a Democratic organ, observed,

> The noble and commanding figure of the General-in-Chief, mounted on a spirited horse and shadowed by the towering plumes of yellow feather which mark his rank, presented an object well calculated to fill the eye and swell the heart with patriotic pride. . . . It is at once an elevating sight to behold such a Hero as Taylor followed to the grave by such a Hero as Scott.[3]

The ceremony completed, Scott reported straight to the White House, where he was happy to see his old friend from Buffalo, Millard Fillmore, now installed as the thirteenth president of the United States. Fillmore had long been aware of Scott's tribulations, and upon meeting him, he broke out, "Now, General, your persecutions are at an end!" Scott forthwith packed up his family, closed the house in Elizabethtown, and moved the headquarters of the Army from New York back to Washington.

For a month Scott held the post of acting secretary of war, pending the acceptance and arrival of Charles Magill Conrad, a representative from Louisiana. But he never aspired to hold that position on a permanent basis; his real interest lay in the passage of Clay's compromise—or compromises. He overstepped his bounds as a military man by lobbying for Clay's measures among Whigs, but his political prominence, or potential political prominence, was such that nobody protested. He worked hard in tandem with Daniel Webster in pushing passage of that important legislation.

As time went on, Scott's name figured once more in political circles. A majority of the American population, Scott among them, was satisfied with the Compromise of 1850, with all its faults, and hoped it would avert secession and civil war. But one group, the antislavery wing of the Whig party, was not. Its leader was William H. Seward, one-time governor of New York State and since 1849 its junior senator. A Whig throughout the life of that party,[4] he was, at age fifty-one, ambitious for the presidency and sincere in his desire to end slavery. Seward was a practical politician first of all, and he realized that if the Whig party were to dissolve over the compromise issue, he could accomplish nothing. He said little about the Fugitive Slave Act, while he looked about for a candidate who could fill the presidency in 1852, before his own planned candidacy at a later period. He needed a popular figure, one whose views regarding the compromise were not well known. Scott had, admittedly, lobbied for the compromise bill among members of Congress, but he was not publicly identified with it. Seward therefore settled on him.

As the year 1850 drew to a close, it became apparent that Scott was a serious contender for the Whig nomination in 1852, second only to incumbent President Millard Fillmore, who cheerfully accepted the prospect of competing politically with his general-in-chief. Henry Clay was out of the running—aged, sick, and failing. John C. Calhoun had died at the end of March 1850. The only other candidate was Daniel Webster, but that statesman's famous Seventh of March Speech, in which he had advocated compromise with the slaveholders, had cost him the support of his native New England. Nevertheless, Scott did not run overtly. At such times as army administration and politics did not occupy his time, he relished the convivial social life of Washington, in which he was ubiquitous, loquacious, and invariably hungry.

In late 1850 Scott attended a dinner in Wilmington, given in honor of John Middleton Clayton, favorite son of Delaware Whigs for the 1852 election. The honoree, strangely, was called on to speak not of himself but of Scott, which he did with a remarkable willingness. Clayton's speech was taken as a nomination of Scott, on the part of the Delaware Whigs at least. The accolade had its drawbacks. Clayton was known to be close to Seward, who had many enemies, and the association was not universally considered favorable to Scott. In writing of Seward, the editor of the *New York Herald* was sharp:

> [Scott] could not place himself in worse hands. They [Seward and Thurlow Weed] are in bad odor throughout the country. . . . Our advice to the old hero is to withdraw, as soon as he possibly can, from the clique, or they will drag him down with them. No plan which they form can succeed, and no candidate whom they may nominate can be elected.

The *Herald* was right, at least insofar as Seward's intentions were concerned. Scott, who had a "past untainted by any positive stand on the slavery question," was his choice, but not Thurlow Weed's. Concluding that not even a hero such as Scott could save the disjointed Whigs from disaster in 1852, Weed left the political scene for a trip to Europe.

Scott paid little attention to attacks on Weed and Seward, and at some point, at least by late 1851, he came to a tacit understanding with them. In recognition of his own tendency to injure himself politically whenever he opened his mouth or picked up his pen, he agreed to put his political future in the hands of his friends and to make no public statements. Word of his understanding leaked out, and Scott was soon attacked by the partisans of President Millard Fillmore and Secretary of State Daniel Webster. A strange scenario now presented itself; the only three Whig candidates for the presidential nomination of 1852 were the President himself, his secretary of state, and the general-in-chief of the Army.

The Democrats were also busily planning for the 1852 presidential nomination, but in a calmer atmosphere, since the compromise, including the Fugitive Slave Act, was almost universally to their liking. The core of Democratic kingmaking centered around the former adherents of James Polk, for even though Polk was disliked personally while in office, his legacy, territorial expansion from which to create more slave states, had a great following in the Democratic party. It was not surprising, then, that a chief player in the Democratic sweepstakes was Gideon J. Pillow.

In the summer of 1851 Pillow joined with a group of prominent Democrats, among them Jefferson Davis, John A. Quitman, Thomas L. Clingman, and Caleb Cushing,[5] in an effort to find a candidate satisfactory to all. Their common criterion for a candidate was one who would "support the Compromise of 1850 and the preservation of the Union."[6] Stephen A. Douglas, James Buchanan, Willam L. Marcy, and even Sam Houston of Texas were among the possibilities. Pillow also worked secretly at securing the Democratic nomination for himself. He expected Scott to be the Whig nominee, and he considered the general's support among Whigs to be weak. The election of 1852 might provide him a chance to do further injury to Scott.

Eventually, however, Edmund Burke, Cushing, and Pillow agreed to work on behalf of Franklin Pierce. What Pillow stood to gain from this arrangement remains unclear. He could not help noting the parallel between this situation and 1844, however, when he had been instrumental in making another relatively unknown politician, Polk, into a man seriously considered for the presidency.

The Democrats met at the hall of the Mechanics Institute in Baltimore in early June 1852, with Lewis Cass, Stephen A. Douglas, James Buchanan, and William L. Marcy the leading candidates. Though all were popular, none of them could muster the necessary two-thirds majority. So again, as in 1844, a long series of ballots finally resulted in turning to a dark horse, this time Franklin Pierce. In his acceptance speech, Pierce supported the Compromise of 1850 without reservation. To Pillow's disappointment, the vice presidential nomination went not to him, but to William Rufus King of North Carolina.

The Whigs met in the same Mechanics Institute, Baltimore, later in June. As the delegates gathered, President Fillmore, the man who had signed the Fugitive Slave Act, was the front-runner, supported by the Southern wing of the party. Webster was supported only half-heartedly by New England because of his Seventh of March Speech, and Scott was the choice of the Seward-Weed group.

Most Whigs would have preferred to find some candidate other than Scott. Congressman Meredith P. Gantry of Tennessee spoke for many as the convention was meeting. While conceding Scott's superiority as a soldier over former presidents William Henry Harrison, Zachary Taylor, and even Andrew Jackson, he worried that Scott lacked

> those attributes and qualities which make the people love him as they loved Jackson, Taylor, and Harrison. Should he be nominated, he will prove to be the weakest man ever run for the Presidency. He will be more overwhelmingly defeated than any man who has ever been placed in that position by any considerable political organization.

If that spirit was pervasive, either Webster or Fillmore should have been nominated. Both were favorable to the 1850 compromise, but the feelings of their followers were so strong that neither could attain a single vote from the other.

Before the Whig convention turned to electing a nominee, however, it addressed the matter of a party platform. Here, without the benefit of the presidential candidate, it came up with a platform somewhat resembling that of the Democrats by supporting, though less enthusiastically, the 1850 Compromise. With that issue at least partly defused, the rest of the nomination and election process hinged largely on the matter of personalities.

The balloting among the three candidates was stubborn; no wing was in any mood to compromise. President Fillmore began far ahead, with Webster claiming only a splinter. As time went on, however, the less stubborn delegates gravitated, not from Fillmore to Webster or vice versa, but to Scott. After a week—and fifty-three ballots—Scott, the compromise candidate, was nominated on Monday, June 21, 1852.

Although the reaction of most Whigs was apathetic, the hard-core party stalwarts, elated that an acceptable candidate had been selected, celebrated by touring the streets of Washington in gangs. First they went to Scott's house on H Street, where he made a short and innocuous talk. They then went to the home of Secretary of the Navy William A. Graham, the vice presidential nominee. From there they surged to the White House, where a congenial Millard Fillmore, who still seemed not to resent Scott's candidacy, told them to honor the "rising, not the setting sun." They then went to the home of Daniel Webster, who masked his bitter disappointment heroically. Four months later, even before the election was held, Webster was dead.

When word came of the nomination, Winfield Scott's elation overcame his promise to avoid making public statements. Flushed with success, he cast aside the statement prepared for him by Horace Greeley, which had been carefully crafted to avoid offending the liberal Whigs, and without even awaiting official word of his nomination, he sent off a message to the convention:

> Having the honor of being the nominee for President by the Whig National Convention, I shall accept the same, with the platform of principles which the Convention has laid down.

Seward and Greeley must have groaned at Scott's blunder. His words were bound to infuriate the northern Whigs, whose attitude toward the convention was expressed in a phrase: "We accept the candidate, but we spit on the platform." Seward did not feel that Scott had any obligation to abide by the platform, but his "good soldier" had openly declared that as President he would put it into execution.

Matters were made worse in August when a group of highly respected antislavery men—Charles Francis Adams, Charles Sumner, and Joshua Giddings among them—broke ranks from the Whigs and held a "Free Soil"[7] convention at Pittsburgh, nominating Senator John Parker Hale of New Hampshire for president. The Free Soilers could not command many votes, but their action did much to cast a pall on the Whig campaign.

By September, President Fillmore realized that Scott's candidacy could use all the help it could get. He obligingly sent Scott as head of a board of officers on a tour of the West to Lewistown (Pennsylvania), Pittsburgh, Cleveland, Columbus, and Cincinnati, ostensibly to find suitable sites for planned "soldiers' asylums."[8] Whig organizations, notified in advance, ensured that Scott received considerable fanfare at every important city. It was an obvious ruse, and one member of the touring board, Brigadier General John E. Wool, shunned all the welcomes. Wool was a loyal Democrat.

Since both parties had endorsed the Compromise of 1850, the 1852 presidential campaign hinged heavily on the qualifications of the individual candidates. In such a setting, Scott was bound to suffer because his long record, spanning over forty years, was known; Pierce was a relative unknown. In their efforts to attack Pierce, the Whigs had little to go on. They accused him of drunkenness, which may have been justified but was difficult to prove. They also tried to ridicule Pierce as "the fainting general," recalling his passing out at the Battle of Contreras. The implication of weakness on Pierce's part was totally unfair. Pierce had fainted from the pain from a wound in the ankle. The wound was much more severe than either of the two that had put Gideon Pillow out of action; Pierce's mistake was in being too conscientious. He had looked weak while trying to stay on duty.[9]

Such accusations, however, paled in contrast to those leveled against Scott. Not only was his nickname of "Old Fuss and Feathers" exploited to the hilt, but every unfortunate thing he ever did or said was brought to the forefront. Even his court-martial in 1809, forty-three years earlier, was exhumed for the public's gaze. His unfortunate clash with Jackson, with Jackson's challenge to a duel and Scott's refusal, was brought out, along with Scott's subsequent challenge to Governor DeWitt Clinton. Attackers mocked his wound at Lundy's Lane as having been incurred "in the rear." Trivial slips in verbiage such as the "fire upon my rear" and the "hasty plate of soup" were derided. More serious matters were raised as well, such as his hanging of the San Patricio men in Mexico, which was cynically used to infuriate those of Irish extraction. Nothing was spared.

Scott's campaign speeches, while sincere, were unconvincing. They dwelt on his past, harking back to battles fought long ago. They did not make up for the Democrats' personal attacks. Nor was he able to describe his true accomplishments as a fighter and as a peacemaker in sufficiently convincing language. His friends tried to treat his lackluster performances humorously. Scott had "never learned to run," they said, referring to running from the battlefield.

Still there were at least two men who, as the election neared, believed that Scott had a chance. One was President Fillmore, who for some reason had regained his confidence.* The other optimist was Scott himself.

The voters went to the polls on November 2, 1852. Thanks to the telegraph service, which had been developed around the country for the previous eight years, Scott had strong indications of his defeat the very night that the votes were cast. The results were appalling. The Democrats carried every state except for four: Kentucky, Tennessee, Vermont, and Massachusetts. Pierce received a total of 254 electoral votes as against Scott's 42, a popular vote of 1,601,474 as against Scott's 1,386,578. Even Scott's home state of Virginia went against him.

Scott's disappointment was great, but he never showed it in public. Al-

---

*On October 15, Fillmore wrote to a political leader, "I see the prospect is very fair for the election of General Scott, and those who give the most attention to the subject here are quite confident of his success." *Ohio State Journal,* 1 Nov 1852. Elliott, *Winfield Scott,* p. 641.

ways the survivor, he later expressed profound thanks that politics had now been eliminated from his concerns.[10] But the Whig Party, in contrast to Scott, never recovered from the 1852 election. The Whigs never produced another candidate for president after 1852.

On February 28, 1853, four days before the inauguration of Franklin Pierce as president of the United States, the outgoing president, Millard Fillmore, hosted a dinner at the White House. It was notable for the good will that prevailed between former and future political rivals. The cabinet members were mixed, along with congressmen of both parties. Two of them, ultra-Whig John Crittenden and ultra-Democrat Caleb Cushing, chatted amiably. Scott, the recently defeated Whig candidate, was "especially fraternizing" with his one-time tormentor, William Marcy, the former secretary of war. At that time, one paper recorded, "the 'hasty plate of soup' was forgotten in the champagne."[11]

31

>>◆◁<

Relegated to the Sidelines

Pierce and Buchanan preside over the dissolution of the
Union while using Scott on only one mission.

During the thirteen years following the peace with Mexico, but
few incidents of historic interest to the autobiographer occurred.
—Scott, *Memoirs*

Hᴵꜱ ᴅᴇꜰᴇᴀᴛ ᴀᴛ the polls did little to diminish Scott's stature. Though
rejected in his quest to become the nation's chief executive, he remained a revered figure on the American scene, treated respectfully whenever he appeared on the streets of Washington or New York. Meeting him
was considered an event; the distinguished novelist Henry James recorded
such an encounter as an unforgettable experience, not so much for what was
said but for the awe in which his father held the Great Man.

It was on Fifth Avenue, New York, on a November day, shortly after the
1852 election. James's father, a staunch Whig, had recently voted for Scott
and was still smarting from the outcome. James was only nine years old at
the time, and he could later recall little but the "proud little impression of
having 'met' that high-piled hero of the Mexican War." He recalled, however, being awed by Scott's size:

. . . for some moments face to face while from under the vast amplitude of a dark
blue military cloak with a big velvet collar and loosened silver clasp, which spread
about him like a symbol of the tented field.[1]

Despite the loyalty of his friends, however, Scott was feeling his defeat heavily, and when writing his autobiography a decade later, he refused to discuss the events of that entire, cataclysmic decade in American history. As the precious federal Union disintegrated before his eyes, he could do little but watch from the sidelines.

Scott's wounded pride encouraged his isolation from the new President. Immediately upon Franklin Pierce's inauguration, Scott secured the President's permission to move the headquarters of the Army once again from Washington to New York City. Though Scott bore no resentment toward Pierce personally, he preferred to avoid the President's company.

Yet Scott might have been able to serve harmoniously under the amiable Pierce had it not been for the personality of the new secretary of war, Jefferson Davis. Twenty-two years younger than Scott, once a son-in-law of Zachary Taylor's, and a rabid Democrat, Davis was not cowed by Scott's prestige. Rather than following the precedents set by George W. Crawford and Charles M. Conrad, the secretaries of war in the two previous administrations, Davis elected to meet Scott's foibles head-on. Scott's move to New York, rather than easing the tensions, only increased them, for it required them to communicate in writing, and the written word was Scott's Achilles' heel.

On May 20, 1853, less than two months after Pierce's inauguration, the secretary of war inserted himself in a dispute between Scott and a War Department auditor, who contested Scott's right to claim mileage compensation in connection with recent travel. Mileage allowances were to be paid only to officers, he insisted, "who travel under written and special orders from their proper superiors." Scott had submitted no such written orders. More than the money was at stake for Scott; his right as the head of the Army to travel on his own recognizance was being challenged. Scott claimed that he had no "superior" in the Army; his only "proper superior" was the President himself.

Davis ruled with the auditor and did so in a cool, disdainful manner. In approving the denial of reimbursement, he advised Scott that he did "not perceive a just ground for the complaint you utter, because a literal interpretation of the law and regulation made under it has recently been insisted on."

Scott would not give in. He refused to appeal to the President, however, and for two years his outstanding claim of $577.60 stood. In the meantime, he charged his travel expenses to the Army Asylum Commission, over which Davis had no control.

Expenses having to do with Scott's expenditures from the Mexican War were a far more serious matter. In November 1854 Scott submitted an itemized statement of his receipts and expenditures during the occupation of Mexico City, admitting accountability for about $261,700. The money had come to him from various sources. Some had come from the War Department, of which $30,000 had been earmarked to finance secret service (espionage) activities. From tribute that Scott had levied on Mexico City "in lieu of pillage" came $150,000. Another $50,000 had come from the sale of captured Mexican tobacco. Of this amount he had actually disbursed about $250,000, about $11,000 less than the amount claimed. Scott insisted that the balance was rightfully his on the basis that the "usages of war and prize money in the naval service" authorized him to a commission of 5 percent, or about $11,000—the same amount as the shortfall in his expenditures. Davis referred Scott's claim to the $11,000 to the President. After much haggling, Scott finally ended up losing money for his efforts in Mexico.[2]

In early 1855, however, Scott won a significant triumph over Davis. The bill submitted in Congress in 1849, granting Scott a brevet of lieutenant general, was finally passed. On February 15, Congress passed a joint resolution putting it into effect, and on March 7, 1855, Scott was appointed to the grade of lieutenant general, with the full pay and allowance, retroactive to March 29, 1847, the day that Scott had received the surrender of Veracruz. Davis did all in his power to prevent the honor from coming to fruition, but he was helpless. And when the President and Attorney General Caleb Cushing approved Scott's sizable claim for the eight-year pay differential, Davis was so furious that he refused to endorse the President's order. He seriously threatened to resign his office of secretary of war, and it took much effort on the part of Pierce to dissuade him.

Franklin Pierce was an unlucky president. He was neither malicious nor particularly indolent, but he was a mediocre man thrust into office at a time when the problems were well-nigh insurmountable. His early years in office were marked with certain accomplishments. One involved laying the groundwork for the expansion of the railroad systems westward. In the early 1850s four transcontinental railroad lines were being planned to join cities in the East with those on the Pacific. One of these, the southern route, ran from New Orleans, through Texas, thence along the Gila River to San Diego.*

The southern route presented difficulties in that its proposed tracks ran for some distance through Mexican territory, south of the boundary between the two countries as set by the Treaty of Guadalupe Hidalgo in 1848.[3] Davis and Pierce therefore called on James Gadsden, minister to Mexico and Andrew Jackson's one-time agent with the Seminoles, to purchase a large strip of land south of the Gila River from the ever-greedy President Santa Anna. The price was $10 million. Many Mexicans deeply resented that transaction, but the Americans considered it necessary to the development of the southwestern part of the country.

Another accomplishment under Pierce was the opening of Japan to foreign commerce by Commodore Matthew C. Perry, the naval officer who had cooperated so effectively with Scott at Veracruz in 1847. Pierce sent Perry to the Far East with seven powerful warships on a mission to "pry open the bamboo gates of Japan." This Perry accomplished with a combination of force and tact. Though the event went practically unnoticed at the time, it foreshadowed the beginning of modern Japan.[4]

It was in domestic issues, particularly the growing North-South rift over the slavery issue, that Pierce ran into a solid phalanx of disasters. Antislavery sentiment was inflamed by the publication of *Uncle Tom's Cabin,* by Harriet Beecher Stowe, in 1852. Granted, the book was in circulation before Pierce's election and serialized before that, but its full effects began to be felt a little later. It eventually sold a million and a half copies and became one of the most popular plays ever produced on the American stage. It transformed the slavery question, which to many Northerners had been an abstract moral issue, into a concrete, personal one.

Pierce's downfall was brought about largely by his supporting the Kansas-Nebraska Act of 1854, which involved both the railroads and the slavery question, now increasingly an emotional issue. The bill's chief proponent was Senator Stephen A. Douglas of Illinois, a short, barrel-chested man nicknamed the "Little Giant." Douglas was intensely interested in pro-

---

*The others were, first, the northern, from Chicago, up the Oregon Trail, to Portland; a second ran through present-day Kansas; a third ran through present-day Oklahoma. Morison, *Oxford History,* p. 587.

moting Chicago as the central hub of the northern transcontinental railroad line, which was to run north of Texas and Oklahoma, and for the safety of the railroad it was deemed necessary to "organize" the territories through which it was to run. His answer was the Kansas-Nebraska Act, which he introduced on the floor of the Senate early in 1854. The bill would divide all the lands between the Mississippi River and the Rocky Mountains, then known as "Nebraska," into two unequal areas, the southern portion being Kansas and the much larger, northern portion being Nebraska. Kansas, it was presumed, would later become a slave state; Nebraska would presumably become a free state. To make his bill palatable to the slaveholders, whose votes he needed, he included an additional proviso that allowed future settlers in Nebraska the option of deciding the slavery issue for themselves— "squatter sovereignty." The concept of "squatter sovereignty" flew in the face of the Missouri Compromise of 1820, which forbade slavery north of the 36°30' latitude.

The majority of the American people were apathetic, at best, about the Kansas-Nebraska Act. Yet Scott was worried about its potential repercussions. Combining self-interest and national interest in the same breath, he wrote his friend Crittenden in mid-March 1854,

> My bill [for promotion to lieutenant general] is held back, that it may not be swamped in the whirlpool of passion created by the Nebraska question. God grant that the revival of the slavery question may not dissolve the Union. The excitement caused by the *compromise* [of 1850] *measures* had nearly died out, and I was in favor of *letting well enough alone.*

What that apathy meant was that Douglas needed the President's support to get his bill passed.

Aggressive, even duplicitous, Douglas trapped the President. He caught Pierce off guard on a Sunday morning in early 1854, securing his tentative endorsement, contingent on the important proviso that Secretary of State William Marcy approved also. Though entrusted by Pierce to consult Marcy before introducing the bill in Congress, Douglas neglected to do so, and submitted it while claiming it enjoyed presidential approval. When Pierce signed the Kansas-Nebraska Act into law on May 30, 1854, he unwittingly destroyed any hope he had of a second term as president.

For a while it appeared that Scott might be called into action to quiet the unrest that erupted in Kansas following the passage of the Kansas-

Nebraska Act. Northern "Free-Soilers" entered the state, armed with the new Sharps rifles, to contest the presumption that the territory should enter the Union as a slave state. They were outvoted in the election of 1855, however, by hordes of settlers from Missouri, who crossed the Missouri River in droves just to vote. By early 1856, violence had broken out between the two groups, violence that was echoed as far away as Washington where, on May 22, 1856, Congressman Preston Brooks of South Carolina entered the Senate chamber and attacked Senator Charles Sumner of Massachusetts, beating him unmercifully with his cane. Sumner had earlier made a harsh speech criticizing slavery in general and Brooks's uncle in particular.

The day after the attack on Senator Sumner, the worst massacre in the Kansas unrest occurred at Pottawatomie, Kansas. There a fanatical abolitionist named John Brown took six men (four of them his sons) to Pottawatomie County, where on the next day they killed five people and hacked their bodies to pieces. From then on, Brown became known as "Old Osawatomie," a name bestowed because of Brown's temporary residence, a byword for terror.

In these circumstances, an alarmed citizenry sought someone to restore stability to "bleeding Kansas." On June 10, 1856, Senator Crittenden offered a resolution to the Senate calling for Scott to be sent. The popular disturbances, the resolution began, caused "insurrection and obstructions to the due execution of the laws." It called for the application of military force in the territory, which "should be conducted with the greatest discretion and judgment, and be under the command of an officer of [adequate] rank and reputation"; be it therefore

> *Resolved,* by the Senate of the United States, that the President be, and is hereby, requested to employ the military services of Lieutenant-General Scott in the pacification of Kansas, and the immediate direction and command of all the forces to be employed for that purpose.

General Scott's high station and character, Crittenden continued, would enable him to do more than any other man to rectify what could now be called a civil war. The peace of the country was seriously threatened. "General Scott, in going to Kansas, would carry the sword in his *left* hand" and in his right hand "*peace,* gentle peace. . . . It would be better to employ the name of a great warrior to make peace than with the sword."[5]

Despite Crittenden's urgings, the Pierce administration was unwilling to take such action. Despite the urgings of the *New York Times* and other papers, Scott was never sent.

The presidential election of 1856 left the country as leaderless as it had been under Franklin Pierce. The weakened Democratic Party nominated James Buchanan, who was able to win only because the opposition was even more divided. Opponents of the Kansas-Nebraska Act, both Whigs and Northern Democrats, had banded together in Ripon, Wisconsin, to form the new Republican Party. It was not, however, fully organized. Its nominee that year, Senator John C. Frémont of California, was almost a joke, a glamorous explorer whose main qualification was his lack of involvement in the Kansas dispute. Another party was also formed, the American Party, which nominated former president Millard Fillmore. As in 1844, the split among the Northerners placed a Democrat, James Buchanan, in office. Buchanan was aged and indecisive. Nothing was solved by that election.

Buchanan evokes a certain amount of sympathy. Most presidents are afforded at least a short honeymoon period after entering office, but he received none. On March 6, 1857, only two days after his inauguration, the United States Supreme Court handed down a ruling that was destined to inflame the country even further, the Dred Scott decision.

Dred Scott, the aging slave of an army doctor from Missouri, was suing for his freedom on the basis that his owner, now deceased, had kept him for some six years in the free territories of Illinois and Michigan. On the basis of the Missouri Compromise, Scott sued in the state courts of Missouri for his freedom. He had won in the lower courts but on appeal he had lost.

The public interest in the case was not focused on the fate of Dred Scott, however, but on the political issue behind it. Had the justices of the Supreme Court considered the Missouri Compromise to be the law of the land, Scott would have gone free. Six judges declared that it was not, but a significant three thought that it was. The resulting furor reached a new crescendo.

The Buchanan administration was not known for doing evil; it was known for doing nothing. It let the two parts of the country continue to drift apart.

Such political and judicial questions, of course, lay outside the purview of the general-in-chief, who had kept his headquarters in New York despite the improved atmosphere that came with the Buchanan presidency. He was engaged in supervising the continuing missions against the western Indians and striving to train his army, routine duties that did not tax him. He continued to live the good life in New York.

One evening in 1859 a young man named Charles Haswell, at the stylish theater called the Conservatory of the Arts, got a glimpse of the old hero, and he was favorably impressed. Edwin Booth was starring that evening in a production of *Hamlet,* and Haswell noted that General Scott "won almost more attention than did the play." Haswell observed the general closely, noting that because of his age, he had waited after the play for the rest of the audience to leave. When he discovered that most of the people were waiting for him in the lobby, with a space left for his convenient exit, he passed down this space slowly,

> bowing to the right and left, amid silence and the respectful regard of the company. The general at this time was past eighty [actually seventy-three], but his noble proportions were scarce harmed by age, his courtesy was becoming, and the behavior of the casual company was a notable instance of good breeding.[6]

The old warhorse was enjoying his fame and respect.

In the early fall of 1859, as threats of Southern secession grew stronger, General Scott received a message in New York ordering him to report to Washington for an important assignment. His new mission would take some time, a fact that probably did not bother him much; Maria and their daughters were off again in Europe.

The new mission would be arduous. A potentially dangerous situation had arisen between Britain and the United States at Puget Sound, in the Pacific Northwest. The confrontation had grown out of a long-standing boundary dispute over the ownership of the San Juan Islands, located between the southern tip of Vancouver Island (British) and present-day Bellingham, Washington. The islands were small, but their location enabled anyone possessing them to dominate all maritime traffic coming into Puget Sound from the Pacific Ocean. The Americans claimed the San Juans on the basis that they lay south of the 49th parallel; cession of the tip of Vancouver Island to the British, they contended, had been granted only as an exception to the proper boundary. Unable to settle the question easily, President James Polk and the British prime minister, Sir Robert Peel, had swept the argument under the rug in the hasty compromise they signed in May 1846. During the intervening thirteen years the islands had lain nearly empty, inhabited by only a few squatters of both nationalities.

The issue had suddenly become acute, however, because of a trivial incident; an American settler had shot a hog owned by the British Hudson's Bay Company, and the two sides could not agree on a proper price to be paid as damages. Trivial or not, the incident pointed up the unsatisfactory nature of ambiguous sovereignty and it quickly became a crisis. Relations between the United States and Britain were becoming strained to the point of possible war.

When word of the crisis reached Washington in September 1859, President James Buchanan instantly became alarmed. True, a foreign crisis might possibly exert a unifying effect on a nation being torn apart by the slavery question, but it was far more likely to encourage rabid Southerners to secede from the Union. In an effort to defuse the situation, Buchanan called on the "Great Pacificator," General Scott.

Buchanan, Scott learned in Washington, had already taken steps to conciliate the British government. But the President was too experienced a diplomat to trust the information he had received in Washington, and he ordered Scott to travel to Oregon, supersede General William S. Harney in the Oregon command, and attempt to negotiate an agreement with the British. From his days as secretary of state under James K. Polk during the Mexican War, Buchanan knew that Scott could be difficult but also that Scott thrived on exercising personal responsibility. Scott's orders reflected that confidence:

> It is impossible, at this distance from the scene, and in ignorance of what may have already transpired on the spot, to give you positive instructions as to your course of action. Much, very much, must be left to your discretion, and the President is happy to believe that discretion could not be entrusted to more competent hands.

Scott had just passed his seventy-third birthday. He was also partially disabled from a recent fall. Nevertheless, he rose to the occasion, accepting this mission with his old-time enthusiasm.

He left New York on September 19, 1859, aboard the side-wheeler *Star of the West.* He crossed the Isthmus of Panama to the Pacific Ocean on the newly built railroad and in early October boarded the Pacific Mail steamer *Northerner,* bound for the Oregon territory. Among the four hundred passengers aboard the ship were twelve Holy Name nuns, who were said to be awed by the salutes and fanfare that greeted the general every time the vessel hove into port. The ceremonies were particularly elaborate in San Francisco, where in late October a multitude followed as Scott, accompanied by a band from the 3d Artillery and the California Guard, proceeded from the Oriental Hotel to the wharf. As the *Northerner* pulled out, the U.S. steamer *Shubrick,* with dignitaries on board, fired a fifteen-gun salute while flags were lowered and bells were rung in the city.

On October 21, 1859, the *Northerner* reached the Columbia River. At Fort Vancouver, near Portland, Scott disembarked to confer with General Harney. Captain George E. Pickett, who had been commanding a force sent by Harney to San Juan Island, was on hand to assist in the conference.

Harney supplied the details of the situation. The San Juans, before the crisis, had been occupied only by an outpost of the Hudson's Bay Company and by sixteen American squatters, who had staked out claims earlier that year. The two nationalities had ignored each other until, in June, one Lyman Cutlar, an American, shot a hog that had been rooting in his potato patch. The hog belonged to the Bellevue Farm, the Hudson's Bay outpost. Cutlar offered to pay $10 for the hog, but the operator of the farm haughtily demanded $100, an unreasonable price. Cutlar appealed to General Harney, claiming that British authorities were planning to arrest him and remove him to Victoria for trial.

The impetuous Harney took immediate action. After a futile discussion of the matter with Sir James Douglas, the British governor at Vancouver, he proceeded to San Juan Island and secured a petition for protection from the American settlers. Then, with the support of the governor of Oregon, he sent a company of infantry from the garrison at Bellingham to San Juan Island to "protect the inhabitants of the island from the incursions of the northern Indians" and from "attempts at interference by the British authorities." Cutlar, having had enough of this foolishness, left the island.

On August 22, 1859, a company of 68 soldiers and 50 civilian workers, under Captain Pickett, landed on San Juan Island.[7] Its strength soon grew to 500. It was not a happy camp for those troops. Conditions were miserable; drunkenness, desertion, and even suicide were commonplace; and the work on the fort was exhausting. But nothing much had happened recently when Scott arrived.

Sir James Douglas, of course, was little concerned with the hardships of the Americans on San Juan Island. He responded to the American "occupation" by sending three British warships to San Juan, their guns threatening "Camp Pickett." Pickett scoffed at the British commodore's demand for surrender, and the situation became a dangerous impasse.

As a result of the meeting with Harney, Scott concluded that Harney himself constituted the main cause of the problem. His experience with Harney in Mexico was enough to bear that out. With a renewed determination to settle matters amicably with the British, therefore, Scott left Fort Vancouver, still aboard the *Northerner,* to visit U.S. Army garrisons at Steilacoom, Olympia, and Port Townsend, where he transferred to the U.S. ship *Massachusetts* for the trip to Bellingham Bay. There Scott sent his aide, Lieutenant Colonel George W. Fay, with a message to the British governor. In it he proposed a joint military occupation of San Juan Island to protect against Indian depredations.

Sir James, though pleased by the conciliatory tone of Scott's message, refused his proposal, arguing that he possessed no authority from his government to agree to a joint occupation. But Douglas, a sagacious administrator, realized that the Americans represented a potent force with their heavy guns and nearly completed earthen fortress. He sent a counterproposal for a military evacuation by both sides, with a joint civil administration. He discounted the threat from the Indians.

Finally, Scott substituted action for words. Ignoring Douglas's claim of "insufficient authority," he sent word that, being confident of British intentions to settle matters peaceably, he would

> not hesitate at once to order the number of United States troops, on [San Juan] Island, to be reduced to the small detachment originally sent there for the protection of the American settler against neighboring and Northern Indians.

Once Scott had made good on his promise, an abashed Sir James decided that he had to follow suit, so he removed the warships from Griffin Bay. Relations between British and Americans had been personally cordial throughout the episode, and both sides heaved a sigh of relief.[8]

Scott's mission was now complete, and the San Juan Islands question was back in diplomatic channels.* On the way back to Panama he stopped at Camp Pickett, on San Juan Island, where he delighted in personally informing the happy soldiers that most of them would soon leave, their backbreaking work on the fort finished. By the first of December 1859, most of the American troops were gone, and no further trouble ensued. The only casualty of the Pig War had been the late lamented pig itself.

On the way back from Puget Sound, Scott visited San Francisco once more, and one of his callers was his old aide, E. D. Keyes. Scott received his visitor with his "usual cordiality," and Keyes was happy to note that "the exhilaration of the voyage, the success of his mission, and the enthusiastic reception he had everywhere met, revived his spirits, and except that his bulk

---

*In 1874, the German emperor mediated the San Juan Islands to the United States.

had greatly increased at the expense of his bodily activity, the signs of old age were not very apparent, although he was then 74 years old."

Scott had been pleased with what he had seen at Puget Sound, and like the old gastronomer he was, he raved about the quality of the silver salmon and the various trout that were found in its waters. The general ate and drank with a good appetite, Keyes reported, and held forth with many anecdotes and observations of his voyage. All his guests "retired full of admiration for the old hero."

Scott was back in New York by December 17. In his annual message to Congress, President Buchanan admitted that he had perforce placed great discretion in the general's hands. Repeating the words he had used in his order, he said that this discretion "could not have been intrusted to more competent hands."[9]

The settlement of the Pig War, fortunately so quickly forgotten, was another of Scott's triumphs, but it seemed to make little impression on him. Instead the old man, writing five years later, remembered only the verses that his wife Maria wrote in Paris:

> Sail on, gallant Scott! true disciple of virtue!
> Whose justice and faith every danger will breast
> Nor swerve in the conflict. Heaven will not desert you,
> There are angels on guard round the "Star of the West."

Scott had saved the Union from one danger, admittedly a side issue. He was now headed to participate in graver national crises.

32

The Lincoln Inaugural

"If any of the gentlemen who have become so troublesome
show their heads, I shall blow them to hell!"

WHILE SCOTT was away in Vancouver, an event back in Virginia made an impending civil war nearly inevitable. On the night of October 16, 1859, just a month after Scott's departure, the fanatical abolitionist John Brown, "Old Osawatomie," led a group of followers from a farm outside Harpers Ferry, Virginia (now West Virginia), to the center of town to seize the United States armory. Ironically, when a firefight broke out on Brown's approach the first man killed was a free Negro, a baggage master at the railroad station.

Brown and his men took some prisoners but then found themselves trapped in town by some local militia from nearby Charles Town. That night Colonel Robert E. Lee arrived on the scene, accompanied by Lieutenant James E. B. Stuart and a company of marines. They found sporadic firing going on, with Brown, his followers, and prisoners holed up in the railroad engine house. Hoping to avoid killing any of Brown's prisoners, Lee held off attacking that evening.

On the morning of October 18, Lee decided that this episode could be brought to a close only by force. He sent "Jeb" Stuart with a message for Brown, on the understanding that Stuart was to pass it through the door of the engine house and then signal if the demand for surrender had been accepted or not.

It had not. Stuart stepped back, waved his hat, and the attack was on. The Marine company of twenty-five men, under Lieutenant Israel Green, assaulted the door of the small fortress with a battering ram. The first effort failed, but on the second try, the door broke in. It required only three minutes after Stuart had given the signal for Green's men to make a prisoner of Brown and release his dirty, hungry hostages. Two marines were killed by Brown's gunmen. Lee ordered Brown to be jailed in the Charles Town courthouse.

After a quick trial by the Virginia authorities, Brown was sentenced to be hanged. The execution was carried out on December 2, 1859, after much dramatic oratory, a great deal of it on Brown's part. Thomas J. (later "Stonewall") Jackson witnessed the execution.

John Brown's death did not mark the end of his cause, however; it launched it. Instantly his name became a symbol that would motivate the Union armies throughout the oncoming Civil War. His impeccable, if calculated, demeanor throughout his trial and execution stirred emotions on both sides of the slavery issue. His previous history as a horse thief and murderer of innocents was overlooked by extremists in the North, some of them going so far as to refer to him as "Saint John" Brown. More important, his martyrdom pushed some moderate Northerners closer to the radical abolitionist camp. In the South, of course, he was vilified. His raid widened the sectional rift.

Nevertheless, despite the rumblings across the country, business in the North went on as usual; only in the South were real preparations made for secession and war.

On his return from Vancouver in December 1859, General-in-Chief of the Army Winfield Scott did not return to Washington; Buchanan himself was not hostile to Scott, but the bulk of his cabinet, being Southerners, were suspicious of him, and the secretary of war, John B. Floyd, almost insisted that Scott stay away from Washington. Floyd, a Virginian, was bent on obstructing rather than assisting President Buchanan's efforts to hold the Union together by compromise. Scott returned to the home in New York City that friends had purchased for him after the 1852 election.

For a while, incredible as it may seem, Scott seemed to harbor an ambition to run for the presidency once again despite his age and the magnitude of his defeat in 1852. Distressed over the weak leadership in Washington and apparently convinced that his talents were necessary for the rescue of his country, he wrote to Crittenden in January 1860, seeking encouragement:

If I had aspirations, it might be profitable to *show myself* at once; for, instead of being superannuated, I am in the most vigorous of health. In bright weather I read and write without spectacles. I dine, sup, drink, and sleep *like a young man,* and if I don't walk as well, it is only because I am a little lame in my left knee. If once elected I fear I shall find it difficult to avoid a second term. I give you leave to retort, "Sufficient for the day is the evil thereof."[1]

Crittenden did not rise to the bait. If he responded to the idea of Scott's reentering politics, his answer has been lost. Another run for president was never mentioned again.

Everyone realized that the election of 1860 would be a crucial one, far from ordinary. It would also be complicated by the various shades of opinion regarding slavery. In April, when the Democrats gathered in Charleston, South Carolina, they came as two distinct wings, the Northern and Southern. After a lengthy effort to agree on a platform and nominee they gave up and decided to meet again in Baltimore.

In early May another political group gathered at Baltimore calling themselves the Constitutional Union Party. That group consisted of the men from the border states—Virginia, Maryland, and Kentucky—who had once been Southern Whigs. In an effort to get around the devastating slavery issue, the group nominated one-time secretary of war John Bell of Tennessee, with a platform calling only for "the Constitution of the country, the union of the states, and the enforcement of the law." They were significant principally for splitting off the border states from the Deep South.

The Republicans, meeting in Chicago later in May, nominated Abraham Lincoln of Illinois over William Seward of New York. Seward was the admitted head of the party, but his strong advocacy of an immediate abolition of slavery worked to his disadvantage; Lincoln, who stood for the more moderate position of "containment," was considered a more reasonable choice. The party's platform was broadened to include positions on the tariff, the Homestead Bill, and the Pacific Railroad, thus rescuing it from the one-issue position of Frémont four years earlier. The result was a far stronger Republican Party than had entered the polls in 1856.

Only after the Republicans had met did the Democrats convene again, this time in Baltimore. There the Northern, Stephen A. Douglas wing of the party prevailed. Upon Douglas's nomination, the Southern wing, disgusted, met and nominated the current vice president, John C. Breckenridge of Kentucky, for president. The election shaped up to be a choice between four

candidates: Lincoln (Republican), Douglas (Northern Democrat), Breckenridge (Southern Democrat), and Bell (Constitutional Union). The old Democratic Party was split three ways, for some of the Constitutional Unionists
had been Democrats.

In the election held on November 6, 1860, Abraham Lincoln was elected
president with a popular vote of 1,866,000, only 44 percent. The Northern
Democrats (Douglas) polled 1,375,000; the Southern Democrats (Breckenridge) polled 845,000; and the Constitutional Unionists (Bell) polled
590,000. Despite those popular numbers, Douglas received only 12 electoral
votes to Lincoln's 180; Breckenridge received 72 and Bell received 39. In
some of the states the voting was close, but in the tally of electoral votes,
Douglas carried only Missouri.

The Deep South was not ready to accept that outcome; the idea of secession was already too far advanced, and Lincoln, despite the fact that his
views toward slavery were moderate compared to those of Seward, had been
much demonized. Southerners immediately began to consider breaking up
the Union.

Scott, in New York, could not resist the impulse to advise President
Buchanan despite the fact that his views had not been solicited. On October
29, 1860, even before the election ballots were cast, he wrote a memorandum
to the President which he pompously called "Views suggested by the imminent danger of a disruption of the Union by a secession of one or more of the
Southern States." He started out with almost inane political advice, not only
recognizing the possibility of secession but going so far as to visualize a
breakup of the present Union into four separate confederacies, each having
contiguous territory. He advocated that the United States government refrain from the use of force against any of these confederacies unless an "interior state" should secede, thereby destroying the continuity of the federal
territory. He advocated that warships continue to collect revenue at sea,
while leaving exports "perfectly free."

Despite such outlandish political advice, he was on firmer ground when
he turned to military matters. He noted that eight forts in the Southern har-
bors, including Pickens and Sumter, were virtually unmanned.[2] Without
specifying where he would get the troops, he urged that "all of these works
should be immediately so garrisoned as to make any attempt to take any one
of them, by surprise or *coup de main,* ridiculous."[3]

Scott posted that letter and sent a second one along the same lines to
Secretary of War Floyd the next day. They had no effect on Buchanan's ac-

tions, however, as neither the President nor the secretary was interested. Buchanan was currently preoccupied by his efforts to keep at least the border states of the South in the Union, and he feared any move that would imply preparations for war. The gist of Scott's letters did leak to the press, however, and gave at least a touch of encouragement to some of the more radical elements in the Deep South, who were declaring reconciliation to be by then impossible.

In November 1860 Major Robert Anderson was sent to take command of the federal garrison at Fort Moultrie, just outside Charleston, South Carolina. He was an outstanding officer, and his Southern background, it was hoped, might soften the feelings of the South Carolinians with regard to his task. Writing years afterward, Erasmus Keyes described him:

> Of all my acquaintances among men, Anderson had the fewest vices of any one of them. In fact, I doubt if he had any quality which the world *ordinarily* denominates *a vice*. Certainly he had none which are embraced under the sweeping phrase, "Wine, women, and play." . . . In all things he was rigorously temperate and moderate, and he was as honest and conscientious as it is possible for a man to be. . . . A pattern of order . . . [who] always had a reason for what he did. . . . Generally, while we served together in the staff, I was the only Northern man attached to it. Our chief, Pegram, and Shaw were all Southerners.[4]

Despite his southern Kentucky upbringing and general sympathy for the Southern viewpoint, however, Anderson would adhere to his oath as long as he wore the Union uniform.

On November 13, before leaving for his new post, Anderson visited Scott in New York, and they discussed the lack of interest on the part of the secretary of war in Scott's military advice. With that in view, Scott refrained from issuing Anderson any immediate orders, agreeing that he should make a study of the situation at Charleston. However, he advised that it might later be necessary to move the garrison from Moultrie over to the more defensible position at Fort Sumter. When Anderson went to Washington, he found the Buchanan cabinet divided as usual. He surmised that the Northern cabinet members[5] had finally persuaded Buchanan to reinforce the forts but that the President was reluctant to do so without Scott's personal advice. Developing a touch of resolution—and a mistrust of Floyd—Buchanan ordered Scott on December 2 to move his headquarters from New York to Washington.

Scott was sick in bed when he received the order, his physical condition having degenerated considerably since his trip to Vancouver, and was therefore unable to leave at once.[6] But on the 12th, despite his gout and dropsy, he boarded a dirty, rumbling train for Washington, accompanied only by a single aide. On arrival, he found space for the headquarters of the Army in the old Winder's Building on Seventeenth Street, just west of the White House and next to the War Department.[7] Taking residence nearby, he left every morning, struggled into his carriage, epaulets and all, and made his way to work. Scott's presence on the scene, despite his infirmities, gave confidence to the population, as Margaret Leech was to note:

> The presence of the old General was reassuring to the worried residents of Washington. . . . As Scott limped to Winder's Building from his low coupé, drawn by a powerful horse, the passers-by lined up, removed their hats, and cried, "God bless you, General."[8]

During the delay before Scott reported to Washington, however, President Buchanan again changed his mind about reinforcing the Southern forts; doing so, he fretted, would be "coercion." Secretary of State Lewis Cass submitted his resignation in protest on December 8, and at about that time Secretary of the Treasury Howell Cobb did likewise. He left for Georgia, boasting that he had emptied the treasury before leaving. Most important, however, was the departure of Secretary Floyd, who left Washington under a cloud for fraud at the end of the month, clearing the way for a pro-Union Democratic cabinet. With that change in orientation came the restoration of Winfield Scott into the inner circle of the President's advisers.

In the meantime, however, the tragedy that all unionists feared came to pass. On December 20, 1860, the South Carolina Convention unanimously adopted the Ordinance of Secession. The Charleston papers exulted, "The Union is Dissolved!" The Palmetto flag immediately replaced the Stars and Stripes over all the flagpoles in South Carolina. It was only a matter of time before South Carolina would be joined in secession by the rest of the "cotton states" of the Deep South, the states that had voted for John C. Breckenridge in the recent election. Confident that the weak Buchanan administration would give in to their demands, three commissioners were immediately sent from South Carolina to Washington to speak with the President and to the Congress.

The next surprise, however, was caused by Northern rather than Southern initiative. On Christmas, Major Robert Anderson, at Fort Moultrie, South Carolina, decided that his garrison was too much exposed to surprise attack from the land. The next day, without consulting Washington, he moved his troops from Moultrie across Charleston Harbor to the newly constructed Fort Sumter, a far stronger position. Immediately, howls of protest arose in Charleston. Fort Sumter presented no real threat to anyone, but the very fact that the Northerners were contemplating military action at all was seen as an act of war. At the same time, South Carolina's commissioners in Washington discovered that Buchanan's cabinet had switched its leanings away from the South. They quickly departed, increasing the threat of war even more.

By New Year's Day, Winfield Scott had decided that Anderson, at Sumter, should be reinforced and resupplied. He had demurred before, acceding to Buchanan's conviction that the move would be provocative, but he now decided that there was no turning back. He consulted with the new secretary of state, Jeremiah Black, and the new secretary of war, Joseph Holt, and with their concurrence obtained the President's permission to charter a merchant vessel to sail from New York with a contingent of men. When Scott's assistant adjutant general arrived in New York he secured the same vessel that had taken Scott to Panama eighteen months earlier, the *Star of the West*. By the 5th of January the ship with its cargo was headed for the open seas with 200 recruits aboard bound for Charleston. At the same time Scott took action to reinforce Fort Pickens in Pensacola Bay. When the *Star of the West* was driven off by shore-based batteries at Charleston four days later, tempers rose.

Scott's next concern was to provide for the safety of the delegates to the electoral college, who were to meet in the Capitol on February 13. From his contacts he learned that plans were afoot to interfere with the college by force. Scott secured approval from Secretary of War Holt and brought several regiments into the city from Fort Monroe and elsewhere. Many congressmen and senators from the South were still in Washington, including Vice President Breckenridge, and the more rabid among them were incensed that Scott was providing extra security. Typical was the reaction of Daniel C. De Janette, from Virginia, who attacked the general-in-chief on the floor of the House:

There was a time in her history when Virginia, like the mother of the Gracci, when asked for her jewels, could point to her sons. There they stood, Jefferson, Henry, Madison, Monroe, and the immortal Washington. . . . She too, in this age, has been proud of another son, whom she gave to this nation as the commander-in-chief of its armies. That son I, together with her representatives in the

Legislature, in her name, have honored with a sword for his brilliant achievements in arms. Little did I think, little did Virginia think, that that sword was so soon to be drawn against her who gave him birth.[9]

Eloquent and high-sounding as such declamations may have been, they did nothing to weaken Scott's resolve.

The electoral ceremony went off without difficulty, or at least violence. Vice President John C. Breckenridge performed his duties to the letter, presiding over the ceremony that included declaring the victory of Abraham Lincoln over his opponents, Breckenridge included. But once the ceremony was over, the visitors in the galleries gave vent to their rage, surprisingly directing their wrath against Scott rather than Lincoln. "Superannuated old dotard," "traitor to the state of his birth," and "free-state pimp" were among the epithets.[10] The noise was soon quieted down and the dignitaries left the chamber. By evening the city was calm.

On February 18, 1861, Jefferson Davis was sworn in at Montgomery, Alabama, as president of the Confederate States of America. Davis had remained in Washington as a senator until the secession of Mississippi on January 9, then had taken his leave and sadly returned to his native state. There he had hoped, if war came, to command troops in the field. His fellow Southerners, however, had rightly judged that his political skills were more noticeable than his military—Winfield Scott would have conceded the existence of neither—and had elected him a little over a week earlier to the presidency. It has sometimes been said—falsely, of course—that Scott's loyalty to the Union stemmed largely from his animosity toward Jefferson Davis.

When the time began to draw near for President-elect Abraham Lincoln to travel eastward from Illinois for inauguration, both Lincoln and members of his entourage became concerned over matters of security. Until the election, Lincoln had ignored the various threats to his life that he had been receiving in the mail, but after the votes were counted, their tempo and virulence stepped up to the point where any sane man would pay attention to them. In addition, Lincoln had every reason to seek reassurance of Winfield Scott's loyalty to the Union. Lincoln had known of Scott at least since the Black Hawk War, and he held a great respect for the old gentleman. Scott, however, was a native of Virginia, and if he remained loyal to the Union he would be in the minority of men who came from his home state.

Further, Scott had sent the President-elect a copy of his memo to Buchanan of October 29. That document in itself would have sufficed to plant doubts. It was not unthinkable that Scott could even be among those who wished to prevent Lincoln's inauguration.

Lincoln made prudent inquiries. In late January 1861 he asked General Thomas S. Mather, the young adjutant general of Illinois, if he would be willing to go to Washington on Lincoln's behalf. Mather readily assented, and Lincoln gave him instructions: Mather was to go visit Scott to learn beyond doubt whether or not Scott was taking steps to protect the President-elect when he arrived in Washington. Lincoln realized that Scott had received the highest endorsements from such reliable sources as William Seward, but he wanted Mather to secure a personal interview, look the old man in the face, and note carefully not only what Scott said but also how he said it. Mather left Springfield right away.

On arrival in Washington, Mather ran into difficulties. Scott was ill—as he was much of the time in those days—and when Mather went to Scott's home, he was denied entrance. The next morning he met a similar rebuff, but he decided that his errand was far too vital to brook any more delay. He therefore produced the letter that Lincoln had written, and insisted on its importance. After hearing a commotion from the direction of Scott's bedroom, he was escorted upstairs into Scott's presence.

The hero of Lundy's Lane and Mexico City was indeed sick, lying propped up in bed, his face "grizzled, wrinkled, and pale." His breathing was labored and his hands trembled. Nevertheless, when Scott read Lincoln's letter, he responded with energy.

You may present my compliments to Mr. Lincoln when you reach Springfield. Tell him that I shall expect him to come on to Washington as soon as he is ready. Say to him also that, when once here, I shall consider myself responsible for his safety. If necessary, I shall plant cannon at both ends of Pennsylvania Avenue, and if any of the Maryland or Virginia gentlemen who have become so threatening and troublesome show their heads or even venture to raise a finger, I shall blow them to hell.

Mather was impressed. On his way back to Springfield, Illinois, he reflected on the scene and "how profoundly the old soldier seemed to be wrought up." To Mather, Scott's "trembling frame and flashing eyes betokened his unequivocal and righteous indignation at the perfidy of those who were so willing to destroy the Union for which he had fought so long and ardently to maintain."[11]

Once he had reported his finding, Mather noticed that Lincoln gave the local situation in Washington no further concern.

Scott, along with Lincoln, had been receiving threats to his life, but he gave little thought to them. He was concerned only about the threats to the President-elect. He kept track of Lincoln's whereabouts, and he was alerted when Lincoln left Springfield on February 11, bound for Washington by way of Indiana, Ohio, and Pennsylvania, where he was expected to make speeches and attend receptions. Scott was alarmed to read reports, though admittedly vague, of plots and conspiracies against Lincoln. Neither Baltimore nor the state of Maryland had sent the President-elect any invitations to make speeches or attend ceremonies; neither had they taken any precautions to ensure his safety. S. M. Felton, president of the Philadelphia, Wilmington, and Baltimore Railroad, on which Lincoln was to travel, also reported his concern. Felton had hired the Pinkerton Detective Agency to ensure Lincoln's security, and that agency reported the existence of a dangerous plot, led by an Italian barber named Cypriano Ferrandini, who claimed he was drilling a company of fifteen "Constitutional Guards" in Baltimore, for the purpose of preventing Northern volunteers from passing through the state of Maryland to Washington. Scott had his own sources confirming the reports of the railroad men and the concerns of the local troop commander, Colonel Charles P. Stone. The leg of the journey from Philadelphia to Washington, specifically the transfer between train stations in Baltimore, was believed to be where the greatest danger would lie.

Scott sent Colonel Stone to see William Seward and tell him about the worrisome reports they had received. Seward, Lincoln's secretary of state–designate and recognized representative for the presidential transition, was impressed by Stone's presentations, and he wrote Lincoln, sending his message to Philadelphia by way of his son:

> My son goes express to you. He will show you a report made by our detective to General Scott, and by him communicated to me this morning. I deem it so important as to dispatch my son to meet you wherever he may find you.
>
> I concur with General Scott in thinking it best for you to reconsider your arrangement. No one here but General Scott, myself, and the bearer is aware of this communication.

I should have gone with it myself, but for the peculiar sensitiveness about my attendance at the Senate at this crisis.[12]

The message reached Lincoln at Philadelphia. He had received similar reports from Allan Pinkerton and had, reluctantly, all but decided that he could not resist the weight of the evidence arrayed against him. He was, however, scheduled to raise the flag at Independence Hall the next morning and to address the Pennsylvania state legislature at Harrisburg. He insisted on going through with those events. His original schedule could be altered, however. After the ceremony in Harrisburg his plans called for him and his party to take the North Central Railroad directly to Baltimore, there to pass through the streets from the Calvert Street station to the Camden Street station, through crowds known to contain many violently anti-Lincoln men. But he could keep his Harrisburg appointment, leave the presidential party, and return to Philadelphia to catch a sleeper and pass through Baltimore in the middle of the night. That he elected to do, accompanied only by Pinkerton himself and Ward H. Lamon, his bodyguard. The details of the trip were to be closely held among a very select few.[13]

Lincoln's alternate trip went as planned. He arrived on the morning of February 23, 1861, at the Willard Hotel in Washington, where the posh Parlor Number 6 had been reserved for him. That same morning he went, with Seward, to pay a call on President Buchanan. He then proceeded to Scott's office, only to find the general-in-chief was away. That afternoon Scott went to call at the Willard and, despite his great size, managed a low bow, "sweeping his instep with the yellow plumes of his hat."[14] Scott was immensely relieved that the President-elect had come through safely.

Scott supervised every detail of Lincoln's security arrangements for the period of nearly two weeks that would elapse between the westerner's arrival in town and his inauguration. He recruited help from every possible source. He had brought several regiments of regular troops into the city and he checked on the qualifications and loyalty of the District of Columbia militia who were scheduled to take part. He made use of volunteers from the ranks of young Republicans from the North and West, appointing some of them as guards and some as police. The inaugural route to be followed by the carriage of the incoming and outgoing presidents was to be lined with double files of volunteer cavalry. Infantry from the District followed in its path. Scott also stationed sharpshooters on the rooftops and in windows to provide protection. He even placed a battery of regular flying artillery at the east end of the Capitol. Not only would these forces provide security; they would provide show as well.

Still Scott could not relax. Notified that someone planned to blow up the platform on which Lincoln would stand during the ceremony, he directed Stone to place troops beneath the stands and across the foot of the stairway. To protect the presidential carriage along Pennsylvania Avenue, he stationed riflemen on the roofs of certain commanding houses with orders to watch the windows on the opposite side. A small force of regular cavalry was to guard the side-street crossings and to move from one to another during the passage of the procession. A company of sappers and miners from West Point was to march in front of the presidential carriage, and the infantrymen of the District of Columbia were to follow it. Finally, a battalion of District of Columbia troops were to be placed near the steps of the Capitol.

Then Scott watched the proceedings from the brow of a hill, not far from the north entrance to the Capitol, "commanding both the approach and the broad plateau of the east front," with a battery of light artillery at the ready. From a nearby vantage point Scott observed the scene during the entire ceremonies, ready to take personal command and direction if necessary.

President Buchanan was held up by official business until the last moment, when he barely made it in time to pick up the President-elect at the Willard Hotel for their ride together to the Capitol. On the east front of that building, the central group made a historic foursome: Senator Stephen A. Douglas, the author of the repeal of the Missouri Compromise; Chief Justice Roger B. Taney, the author of the Dred Scott decision; President James Buchanan, whose vacillation had allowed the state of the Union to degenerate so badly; and the incoming President himself, Abraham Lincoln. When it came time for Lincoln's address, the tone was firm but conciliatory. It finished strong:

> In *your* hands, my dissatisfied fellow-countrymen, and not in *mine,* is the momentous issue of civil war. The Government will not assail *you.* You can have no conflict without being yourselves the aggressors. *You* have no oath registered in Heaven to destroy the Government, while *I* have the most solemn one to "preserve, protect, and defend it." I am loth to close. We are not enemies, but friends. We must not be enemies. Though passion may have strained, it must not break our bonds of affection. The mystic chords of memory, stretching from every bat-

tlefield, every patriot grave, to every living heart and hearthstone all over this broad land, will yet swell the chorus of the Union, when again touched, as surely they will be, by the better angels of our nature.[15]

Winfield Scott, from his distant location, missed the drama of the occasion. His absence in the crowd was noted and regretted by many who were there. Among those looking for his commanding figure was young Charles Francis Adams Jr., the son of the diplomat of the same name. Adams attended the proceedings with Senator Charles Sumner, and when the new President was duly inaugurated, the two walked away. There, situated on a street corner commanding a panoramic view of the whole spectacle, was a small carriage, "drawn by a single horse and surrounded by mounted staff officers and orderlies, the whole the centre of a crowd of idlers." Adams quickly perceived that the occupant was "the old General himself, in full uniform, anxiously observing the procession as it passed in the street beyond, and holding himself ready for any emergency."

As the fear of a coup de main had passed, Adams and Sumner felt free to pause and greet Scott through the open window of his carriage. "The old General," he later wrote, "shook hands with us, and seemed in high spirits and greatly relieved, as he watched intently the perfect quiet progress of events below, on Pennsylvania Avenue."[16]

With the inauguration completed, and with the firing of a salute by Scott's guns afterward, Scott was satisfied that all had gone well. The United States had a new president, Abraham Lincoln. He spotted his old friend and political guide, Thurlow Weed, who was leaving. Everything, Weed said, had gone well. Scott, much as he did fourteen years earlier at the fall of Veracruz, exulted outwardly. "God be praised!" he exclaimed.

33

❧

Fort Sumter, April 1861

*Scott's sound military advice proves impracticable
in a real world.*

ABRAHAM LINCOLN did not enter the presidential office with the fury of "Christ cleansing the Temple." Even though the seven cotton states[1] had seceded from the Union by the time of his inauguration, the so-called border states had not yet done so. Until Virginia, Maryland, North Carolina, Kentucky, and Tennessee also seceded, prudent men in the North still hoped to save the Union without resorting to bloodshed.[2] The idea still prevailed that the cotton states would find it impossible to survive alone and would soon return to the fold.

Secretary of State William H. Seward was the leader of the group that held such a hope. Though he had previously been one of the most influential abolitionists, his tactics, if not his views, had changed. As the majority leader in the Senate, he had been given credit—in which he heartily concurred—for inspiring moderation in the leaders of the border states, preventing their joining the others in secession. Further, he had stayed in touch with the members of the Senate who had left to join the new Confederate government and had promised them that federal troops would soon be withdrawn from Fort Sumter. Never mind that he had no authority whatsoever to do so.

Seward needed support from other prominent leaders, however, and the man he needed most in his camp was Winfield Scott.[3] Seward seems to have retained some of his earlier influence over the general-in-chief, and he managed to enlist Scott's support. At Seward's instigation, Scott prepared a letter summarizing his views, which closely paralleled Seward's own.

On March 3, 1861, the day before Lincoln's inauguration, Scott sent Seward a letter outlining the four approaches he thought the new President might take in dealing with the seceded states. The first, unfortunately, was political, "to change the name of the 'Republican' Party to the 'Union'" Party and adopt the so-called Crittenden proposals, which called for a return to the Missouri Compromise of 1820, restricting the growth but not the existence of slavery. The second, to collect the duties on foreign goods outside Southern ports, was innocuous. In the third and fourth, however, he presented a dire set of alternatives: to conquer the South by military force or to say, "Wayward sisters, depart in peace."

His evaluation of the consequences of war between the states was prescient, far more realistic than anyone else in public life would dare to admit. It would take three years to subdue the South, Scott thought, and it would require 300,000 disciplined troops to do so. The consequences would be shattering:

> The destruction of life and property on the other side would be frightful. . . . The conquest completed, at that enormous waste of human life to the North and Northwest, with at least $250,000,000 added thereto, and *Cui bono?* Fifteen devastated Provinces? not to be brought into harmony with their conquerors; but to be held for generations by heavy garrisons, at an expense quadruple the net duties or taxes which it would be possible to extort from them, followed by a Protector or an Emperor.[4]

Scott's estimates of costs would later be dwarfed by what actually occurred, but they were considered far too pessimistic at the time. Scott's main troubles, however, lay in dealing with political matters outside his purview as a soldier and by expressing himself in quotable terms. "Wayward sisters" caught readers' attention much as had the earlier "hasty plate of soup."

Seward passed the letter to an uninterested Lincoln and made sure that his colleagues, both in and out of government, were made aware of the general's written support of his own views. The result was a temporary alliance of Seward and Scott against the inclinations of most Lincoln supporters— and, it later turned out, of Lincoln himself. Strong Union men such as Montgomery Blair, the fire-eating postmaster general,[5] were dismayed to see Scott softening toward the secessionists. Had he not promised to blow traitorous men to hell?[6] The general was not advocating conciliation, but the fact that he could even consider it an option seemed completely out of character.

Abraham Lincoln was not allowed the luxury of contemplating these issues at leisure. On the morning of March 5, Acting Secretary of War Joseph Holt brought a distressing message from Major Robert Anderson at Fort Sumter. The Confederates, Anderson advised, were drastically reinforcing their military defenses around Charleston; the guns from the surrounding heights could force the fort into surrender within a few days. He estimated that it would require an army of 20,000 troops to relieve the Sumter garrison from the threat it faced. On the next day, the sixth of March, Confederate President Jefferson Davis put out a call for 100,000 volunteers to serve for a period of twelve months in the new Confederate army.

Lincoln was alarmed at these developments, especially the situation at Fort Sumter. In his inaugural address he had declared that his powers would be "used to hold, occupy, and possess the property and places belonging to the Government, and to collect the duties and imposts." Protecting what remained of United States property in the South, while striving to resolve the crisis without the use or threat of force, had seemed to be a moderate, even conciliatory course. Now even that prudent policy was being threatened.

While trying to decide how to respond to Anderson's message, the President sent for the general-in-chief. He showed Scott Anderson's message and asked for an evaluation. Scott was not inclined to give a quick answer and asked for a few hours to consider. When he returned that same evening, he was in a glum mood. "Evacuation seems almost inevitable," he declared, "if indeed the worn-out garrison be not assaulted and carried in the present week."

That was not the kind of answer Lincoln was hoping to receive, and it shook his faith in Scott's zeal and energy. Refusing to follow such a course of action for the moment, he directed Scott to "exercise all possible vigilance for the maintenance of all the places within the military department of the United States." He followed up that meeting by writing Scott a blunt series of questions:

> 1st. To what point of time can Anderson maintain his position in Sumter?
> 2d. Can you, with present means, relieve him within that time?
> 3d. What additional means would enable you to do so?[7]

Lincoln did not allow Scott time to answer, however. On that Saturday evening, March 9, he held his first cabinet meeting. Its sole purpose was to discuss the problem of Sumter.

Scott had spent the three days between White House meetings conferring with various people, especially with Secretary of the Navy Gideon Welles, who had primary responsibility, he felt, for reinforcing Sumter. The two did not reach a meeting of the minds, however, and their divergences became apparent that evening. The issue, in short, was the ability of naval vessels to run the shore batteries at Charleston, especially those at Cummings Point and Fort Moultrie, in order to reach Sumter. The Army believed that naval vessels could not survive the fire from those land batteries, and they would have to be reduced by the Army before a relief expedition could successfully be conducted—hence Anderson's estimate of 20,000 men. The Navy believed that it could accomplish the mission without the need for the forts' reduction. That position was pushed, not by Welles himself, but by Postmaster General Montgomery Blair, who had been convinced by his wife's brother-in-law, a "capable seaman" named Gustavus V. Fox. Fox was so certain that he volunteered to lead such an expedition in person.

Two days later, Scott answered the President's questions, apparently unaffected by either the Navy's optimism on reinforcing Fort Sumter or Lincoln's obvious repugnance toward evacuating it. Instead, he simply elaborated on his previous positions. To supply and reinforce Sumter, he insisted, would require a force of 5,000 regular troops and 20,000 volunteers, along with a fleet of warships and transports that would require four months to assemble. He then reiterated his previous recommendation, that "Major Anderson be instructed to evacuate the fort . . . immediately on procuring suitable water transportation, and that he embark with his command for New York." A dissatisfied Lincoln decided to poll his cabinet members, asking each the question: "Assuming it to be possible to provision Fort Sumter, under all the circumstances is it wise to attempt it?" He asked for their responses in writing by March 16.

The results were again disappointing to Lincoln. Even though the question assumed the possibility of relief—which Scott contested—only two of Lincoln's seven cabinet members, Postmaster General Blair and Secretary of the Interior Caleb B. Smith, recommended going through with the operation. All the other five[8] voted against it, concerned that such overt military action would swing the border states into line with their Southern sisters. An unhappy Lincoln set the matter aside for the moment.

During his first month as President, Abraham Lincoln refrained from exerting his authority directly, preferring to listen without imposing his views on his subordinates. This reserve encouraged Secretary of State Seward to promote his ill-concealed desire to play the role of prime minister to the President. Scott also felt secure in his position. While far less brash than Seward, the general was still unchallenged in his position of the President's chief military adviser. That situation, so comfortable to both Seward and Scott, came to an end in the course of only a few days at the end of March 1861.

On March 28, 1861, Lincoln summoned Scott to the White House. Scott went down Pennsylvania Avenue unconcerned. The President had apparently given in, albeit reluctantly, on the matter of evacuating Fort Sumter, and he had so far voiced no objection to evacuating Fort Pickens, in Pensacola Harbor. With the Sumter question quieting down for the moment, Pickens was becoming the main focus of discussion. Scott entered the White House confidently, armed with a set of convincing arguments for evacuating both forts, and plans for doing so drawn up by his military assistant, Lieutenant Colonel E. D. Keyes. Scott expected authority to put the evacuation orders into effect.

Lincoln, however, showed himself to be in no mood to listen to the same old routine. He set Scott's memo aside and told the general-in-chief that he was suspicious that Major Anderson, at Sumter, had played the administration false. Furthermore, he was not satisfied with what he deemed Scott's "want of consistency" regarding the feasibility of reinforcing Fort Pickens, his advocating evacuation when he had recommended reinforcement to President Buchanan.[9] His new administration would be broken up, Lincoln went on, unless some more "decided" policy were carried out.

Lincoln reserved his most crushing warning to the last. The President, Scott told Keyes that evening, had warned that "if General Scott could not carry out his views, someone else might."[10]

That evening the President held his first state dinner at the White House. Scott was one of the invitees, but his dropsy, possibly combined with his upset over the day's conference, forced him to return to his home as soon as he arrived on the steps of the White House. As a result, he missed the important conference the President held with his cabinet after the dinner.

At that informal gathering, Lincoln read Scott's latest memorandum aloud. Unfortunately, though Scott had presented the military difficulties, he had once more based his final conclusions on political considerations. While conceding that a voluntary evacuation of the forts alone might not be decisive in itself, his Southern friends had made it clear "that the evacuation of both the forts would instantly soothe and give confidence to the eight remaining slave-holding States, and render their cordial adherence to this Union perpetual."

At first the members of the President's cabinet listened to his memorandum in silence as the President read. However, Montgomery Blair and a couple of others soon raised voices in violent protest against the political nature of Scott's reasoning. As the discussion went on, Secretary of State Seward became keenly aware that he and Scott were now alone in opposing Lincoln's views on holding the forts. The rest of the cabinet members were following the President's inclinations. At a cabinet meeting the next morning, Seward began to sense that his very position as leader of the Republicans around the President depended on his changing his former position quickly. He resolved to do so but said nothing to Winfield Scott.

Two days later, on Easter Sunday, 1861, Scott breakfasted with Keyes, his mind still disturbed by his rebuke at the hands of Lincoln three days earlier. Seeking support of his conviction that the two forts could not be reinforced in sufficient strength and in sufficient time, he asked Keyes to speak freely on the subject. Keyes took a half hour to present his arguments, at the end of which Scott gave him a roll of papers that included maps of the Pensacola Harbor. "Take this map to Mr. Seward and repeat to him exactly what you have just said to me about the difficulty of reinforcing Fort Pickens."

Keyes felt no sense of urgency in those instructions. He strolled unhurriedly from Scott's home at Sixth and "D" Streets toward the Treasury Building, confident that he had ample time to confer with Secretary Seward and still make it to Saint Matthew's Church for Easter services. When he arrived at Seward's house on "F" Street, however, he found the secretary standing alone in the middle of the parlor. Keyes gave a "respectful salutation" and announced, "Mr. Seward, I am here by direction of General Scott, to explain to you the difficulties of reinforcing Fort Pickens."

Seward had no time for such niceties. Brushing aside the "difficulties," he ordered Keyes to find Captain Montgomery C. Meigs and bring him back to Seward's home without delay. Keyes's plans for church could be put off, he said impatiently.

Keyes resented receiving such arbitrary orders from someone outside his own chain of command, but on reflecting that Seward spoke with the authority of the President, he held his tongue and complied. Within ten minutes, he and Meigs were standing together before the secretary.

Seward made himself clear from the start: "I wish you two gentlemen to make a plan to reinforce Fort Pickens, see General Scott, and bring your plan to the Executive Mansion at 3 o'clock this afternoon."

Keyes and Meigs decided to do what they were told. Hastily they went to Meigs's office and with the maps on hand began to make detailed plans.[11] It took them the full four hours, leaving no time to report back to Scott, much to Keyes's discomfort. They arrived at the White House five minutes before the specified time of 3:00 P.M., to find Lincoln and Seward waiting for them.

Keyes was a keen observer, and he was fascinated to watch the new President, who was seated behind the end of a table, his right leg and gigantic foot on the table, his left leg on a chair, and his hands clasped behind his head. As they talked, Lincoln changed position frequently. Keyes had never, he wrote later, seen a man who could so "scatter his limbs." When Seward rather formally asked if the two men were ready, Keyes balked. "I am ready, but I have not had time to see General Scott, who is entirely ignorant of what I have been doing. As I am his military secretary, he will be angry if I don't let him know." Meigs, however, suffered from no such inhibitions. "I'm not General Scott's military secretary, and I am ready to report," he declared.

On Lincoln's orders, then, Keyes and Meigs made their reports. Neither Seward nor Lincoln had any comments. At the end, Lincoln said, "Gentlemen, see General Scott, and carry your plans into execution without delay."

As Keyes had feared, the old general was fretting when he, Meigs, and Seward arrived at his door. Seward, however, ignored Scott's pout and turned directly on him. "You have formally reported to the President your advice to evacuate Fort Pickens," he said. "Notwithstanding this I now come to bring you his order, as Commander-in-Chief of the Army and Navy, to reinforce and hold it to the last extremity."

Scott hid his astonishment at the President's surprising decision, and if he felt anger toward Seward for reversing his position on retaining the forts without disclosing his switch, he concealed it. Drawing himself up, he declared with a flourish, "Sir, the great Frederick used to say, 'When the King commands, all things are possible!' It shall be done." He then went over the plan prepared by the two younger officers, made some additions, and approved their plan. The next day he drew up formal orders for the operation.

After Seward and Meigs departed that evening, Scott turned to Keyes for an explanation of what had happened. Keyes described his experience in detail, hardly noticing Scott's silence. Excited by the major role he had played in "unleashing the dogs of war" and famished from missing lunch while working at the Engineer office, Keyes enjoyed the evening's food and drink. Three weeks later, however, while he was at New York harbor putting his plan into reality, he received a message from Scott. Referring to the Easter incident and to recent "acts of rudeness" on Keyes's part, it concluded,

> I think it necessary to terminate our official connection without further correspondence or irritation. . . . Wishing you and yours all happiness. . . . Yours, Winfield Scott.[12]

His dismissal was not totally unexpected to Keyes. He knew he was falling from the general's good graces because he was still too outspokenly New England in his views for Scott's taste.

It was now becoming evident, even to Scott, that his days as general-in-chief were numbered. Nevertheless, he continued, despite his chronic, debilitating sickness, to be at his desk for long hours every day. For though he was able to move around only with pain and hardship, he was still the only officer with the expertise to address the myriad details of organizing an army. No other officer, not even the veteran John E. Wool, possessed the professional stature of Winfield Scott.

Seward also was to be put in his place. His position as secretary of state was never seriously threatened, but his ambition to be the powerful figure of the Lincoln administration evaporated. Impatient with Lincoln's apparent vacillation and inaction, and having successfully invaded the province of both the War and Navy Departments in the Pickens affair, he wrote a memorandum that he dubbed "Some Thoughts for the President's Consideration, April 1, 1861." Many of his recommendations fell within his purview as secretary, but then, seizing on recent reports of French and Spanish intrusions into Mexico and Haiti, he recommended that the President "demand explanations from Spain and France, . . . and if satisfactory explanations are not received, . . . convene Congress and declare war on them."

Urging an "energetic prosecution" of this policy, he concluded,

> it must be somebody's business to pursue it and direct it incessantly.
> Either the President must do it himself, and be all the while active in it, or

Devolve it on some member of his cabinet. Once adopted, debates on it must end, and all agree and abide.

It is not my especial province. But I neither seek to evade nor assume responsibility.[13]

Lincoln reacted instantly to this blatant power play. On the day he received it he answered. Referring to the portion of the message that pertained to "somebody's business to pursue and direct," Lincoln wrote,

I remark that if this must be done, I must do it. When a general line of policy is adopted, I apprehend there is no danger of its being changed without good reason or continuing to be a subject of unnecessary debate.[14]

Seward knew when he had been chastised. Neither he nor Lincoln mentioned the subject again. Indeed, Seward's fellow cabinet members never learned about it.

Areas of responsibility in Lincoln's cabinet were still so fluid as to cause another serious problem. An incident occurred that concerned the employment of the *Powhatan*, the Navy's most powerful vessel, which the Navy was counting on as the backbone of any expedition to Fort Sumter.

In planning the reinforcement of Fort Pickens and Fort Sumter, Lincoln, Seward, and Scott, in the interests of secrecy, organized two separate task forces, neither of which was aware of the other. Unfortunately, none of the three bothered to notify Secretary of the Navy Gideon Welles, who was planning the Sumter relief, that they intended to employ the powerful *Powhatan* to relieve Fort Pickens. Welles, unbeknownst to Scott, had earmarked the *Powhatan* for the relief of Sumter.

On the sixth of April Lieutenant David D. Porter boarded the *Powhatan* and presented orders signed by the President, placing the ship under his command, relieving the former captain, Samuel Mercer. These orders conflicted with others signed by Secretary Welles, but Mercer and Meigs decided that the President's orders took precedence. Soon Porter, at the helm of the *Powhatan*, was putting to sea as part of the expedition to reinforce Fort Pickens. When Welles learned what had happened, he was justifiably enraged. He sped to the White House to protest. Lincoln quickly recognized the seriousness of his error, personally assumed responsibility for "carelessness," and attempted to recall the *Powhatan*. It was too late. The ship was already out of communication.

Lincoln never reprimanded Seward for this brash action. Nor did he reprimand Scott, who might have prevailed on the inexperienced Seward to inform Welles of the President's plans. Instead, Lincoln sent Scott a gentle request: "Would it impose too much labor on General Scott to make short, comprehensive, daily reports to me of what occurs in his department, including movements by himself, and under his orders, and the receipt of intelligence? If not, I will thank him to do so."

By the end of the first week in April 1861, the expedition to Fort Pickens was under way. Time was running out, however, for a decision regarding Fort Sumter. Major Anderson's supply of food was running dangerously low, and President Lincoln was now forced to choose between reinforcing him and ordering him to depart for New York. Evacuating Fort Sumter remained unpalatable to Lincoln, so he decided to resupply the garrison even without the *Powhatan*. He knew exactly the risks he was taking; if Confederate President Jefferson Davis decided to fire on Sumter or the convoy relieving it, war would commence. In an attempt to reduce the tensions, therefore, Lincoln sent a message to Governor Francis Pickens, advising him that "an attempt will be made to supply Fort Sumter with provisions only; if such attempt be not resisted, no effort to throw in men, arms, and ammunition will be made." Though the message was sent to the governor, Lincoln knew who would make the decision: Jefferson Davis.

On April 9, 1861, Davis met with his cabinet in Montgomery, Alabama, to consider Lincoln's message and to make a fateful choice between peace and war. Their choice was war.

Major Robert Anderson, at Fort Sumter, had been working night and day to strengthen his defenses ever since he had moved his garrison from Fort Moultrie the previous December. Despite his labors, however, he realized that prospects for him to hold the fort indefinitely were hopeless. His provisions were nearly exhausted; on April 1 he had issued his last barrel of flour to his cooks. He had been cut off from the outside world ever since March 29, when Confederate Brigadier General Pierre G. T. Beauregard had received orders from Montgomery to stop any further resupply and halt Anderson's mails to and from Washington. Anderson was perplexed as to what was expected of him. His confusion was further deepened by a contradictory order he had received from Secretary of War Simon Cameron early in April:

You will hold out, if possible, till the arrival of the expedition. But whenever, if at all, in your judgment to save yourself and command, a capitulation becomes necessary, you are authorized to make it.

Anderson's suspense was about to end. During the afternoon of April 11, 1861, one of his men spotted a small boat carrying three men, headed for the island. They turned out to be aides of the commander of Confederate troops at Charleston, General Beauregard. The senior officer, Colonel James Chesnut, brought a message demanding the evacuation of the fort. Beauregard's terms were generous, offering to deliver Anderson and his command to any post in the United States that they might select. And his last sentence was complimentary: "The flag which you have upheld so long and with so much fortitude, under the most trying circumstances, may be saluted by you on taking it down." The offer was tempting to Anderson's tired and hungry garrison, but not a man showed any inclination to accept it. Anderson therefore penned a friendly and respectful reply, almost apologizing for rejecting the demand. Only his sense of honor and obligations to his government prevented his compliance with it. He added a personal note, as Beauregard, thirteen years younger than he, had been his warm friend in happier days: "Thanking you for the fair, manly and courteous terms proposed, and for the high compliment paid me, I am, General, very respectfully, your obedient servant."[15]

The business at hand completed, Anderson walked with the three Confederate officers to their boat. As he shook hands, Colonel Chesnut gave assurances that Beauregard would not begin a bombardment without further notice. Anderson then let a piece of information slip: "I shall await the first shot, and if you do not batter us to pieces, we shall be starved out in a few days." Chesnut asked if he could pass that information to Beauregard, and Anderson assented. When Beauregard received that word, he was surprised to learn that Anderson's provisions were so low.

At 4:30 A.M., April 12, 1861, a ten-inch mortar from Fort Johnson, on James Island, South Carolina, fired the first shot of the Civil War. Upon that signal, Confederate batteries from Sullivan's Island, across Charleston Harbor, joined in. These were soon followed by a battery located at Cummings Point, Morris Island, which dominated Fort Sumter from a distance of only a mile. The Civil War had begun.

Throughout the next thirty-four hours, the garrison of Fort Sumter withstood bombardment from over three thousand shells from forty-nine Confederate guns. All this time the naval flotilla, carrying provisions and reinforcements from New York, sat quietly outside the range of the Confederate guns, unable to affect the battle. Yet, even though the batteries at Cummings Point prevented Anderson from returning fire from the top level of the fort, his men managed to fire off about a thousand rounds from the lower level, where the walls were sixty feet thick in places.

By the morning of Saturday, April 13, however, Confederate artillery had found a vulnerable spot in the fort's defenses. A fire broke out in the powder magazine, and Anderson saw the end was near. In early afternoon he lowered his large garrison flag and raised the white flag of surrender. The Confederates on the surrounding heights cheered. Primarily they cheered their victory, of course, but their cheers were also directed toward Anderson and his men, for whom their Southern cousins had become concerned ever since the fire had broken out that morning. By terms of the surrender, Anderson's garrison was loaded on the vessels of the frustrated relief flotilla, bound for New York. None of his men had been wounded.

As the Yankee convoy sailed out of the harbor, the Confederate gunners who had been firing on Anderson's men rendered salutes to the soldiers of the garrison, along with some hisses for the fleet that had stood by and done nothing to help. To the good people of Charleston, the forthcoming Civil War was still something of a lark.

The authorities in Washington, including Winfield Scott, were kept in the dark as to the minute-by-minute developments at Charleston. Scott went on with his heavy schedule for mobilization of militia units, periodically allowing himself the luxury of entertaining guests at one of the congenial dinners prepared by his landlord, known as a "famous French cook."[16] On the evening of April 11, the prominent British journalist William Howard Russell, of the London *Times,* witnessed a dramatic moment.

The guests at Scott's table that evening included Secretary William Seward, Attorney General Edward Bates, and Colonel George Washington Cullum, one of Scott's aides. It was early in the evening, and just as Scott's guests sat down, a group of mounted volunteers from the District arrived outside the door to serenade the general-in-chief. Scott painfully stood up, excused himself for a few moments, and stepped outside to speak a few words of patriotic thoughts to them. When he had finished, a band struck up "Yankee Doodle." At Seward's request they then played "Hail, Columbia" and "The

Star-Spangled Banner." Russell was pleased when he heard the tune of "My Country, 'Tis of Thee," mistaking it for his own national anthem, "God Save the Queen."

Russell was fascinated by the badinage that went on between Scott and Seward, referring back to the touchy subject of Scott's celebrated "hasty plate of soup" letter to Marcy in May 1846. Scott was just about to tell a story. "Bear with me, sir, for a while," he said, "that I may diverge from the main current of my story and proceed to mention . . ."

At that moment an aide stepped in the door carrying a telegraphic dispatch. Scott paused a moment to read it. Then, apologizing to his British guest, he handed the message over to Seward, who was visibly disturbed. Russell watched as Seward looked inquiringly at the general, who responded only by shaking his head. After showing the message to Bates, Scott read it over a second time and put it in his pocket. "You had better not put it there, General," said Seward. "It will be getting lost, or into some other hands." Scott walked across the room and threw the message in the fire, thus destroying for history the original notification of Beauregard's ultimatum to Robert Anderson.

By Sunday, April 14, the news of Anderson's capitulation at Fort Sumter was blazoned across every headline in the country, and the people of the North were aroused to a fever pitch. Gone was any thought of wooing the "wayward sisters" back into the Union with tolerance and concessions. It was not that Fort Sumter itself was so valuable; strategically, Fort Pickens was far more significant. But the city of Charleston had become equated in the public mind with rebellion, and the very act of firing on the American flag roused the nation much as it would be aroused again, eighty years later, by the Japanese attack on Pearl Harbor.[17]

That Sunday morning President Abraham Lincoln convened his cabinet at the White House, with Scott in attendance. In the course of the day, Lincoln drafted a proclamation to be issued the next morning, April 15, convening the absent Congress in emergency session as of July 4 and, for the interim, calling 75,000 volunteers to "repossess the forts and places seized from the Union."

34

⋙⟪⋘

Guardian of Washington

*Scott remains loyal to the Union and protects
the nation's capital.*

The Lion of the North was fully roused. Betrayed, insulted, outraged, the free States arose as with a cry of pain and vengeance.
War sermons from pulpits; war messages in every assemblage;
tenders of troops; offers of money; military proclamations and
orders in every newspaper; every city radiant with bunting;
every village-green a mustering ground. . . . The very children
abandoned their old-time school-games, and played only at sol-
diering.
　　　　　　—Nicolay and Hay, *Abraham Lincoln*

WAR FEVER had indeed engulfed the sixteen Union states. In New
York, Horace Greeley said that the President's quota of 75,000 men
could have been raised in that city alone. The governors charged with raising quotas to meet President Lincoln's call found that their problems were
not a lack of volunteers but an excess. "Ten days ago we had two parties in
this State," wrote the governor of Iowa. "Today we have but one, and that
one is for the Constitution and the Union unconditionally." The governor
of Ohio was no less effusive: "I have already accepted and have in camp
a larger force than the thirteen regiments named as the contingent of
Ohio. . . . Indeed, without repressing the ardor of the people, I can hardly
stop short of twenty regiments."[1]

In the seven cotton states of the South, the response was just as overwhelming—on the other side. The Confederate cabinet in Montgomery,

Alabama, were said to have received Lincoln's proclamation "amid bursts of laughter." In Atlanta, Confederate Vice President Alexander H. Stephens claimed that it would "require seventy-five times the 75,000 volunteers [Lincoln had called for] to intimidate the South." More Confederate volunteers were called up, the individual states turned over federal military posts to the Confederate government, and guns from Fort Sumter were sent to the Mississippi River to assist in blockading the ports.

In the border states, ambivalence still predominated on the question of secession, but there was none on the matter of Lincoln's request for volunteers. Not a state responded. "Kentucky will furnish no troops for the wicked purpose of subduing her sister Southern States," wrote the governor of Kentucky. "I can be no party to this wicked violation of the laws of the country, "wrote the governor of North Carolina. "In such unholy crusade no gallant son of Tennessee will ever draw his sword," wrote Governor Isham Green Harris. And so on.

The two border states that caused greatest concern in Washington were Maryland and Virginia, because the city was located between them. Virginia was the first to act.

On April 17, 1861, Governor John Letcher of Virginia, previously opposed to secession, reversed his position. On receipt of Lincoln's levy for troops, he wrote Cameron, "You have chosen to inaugurate civil war." He thereupon called a convention to meet secretly in Richmond on April 17 to consider its next action. The convention, by a vote of 88 to 55, passed an ordinance of secession, subject to later ratification by the Virginia legislature, by that point a mere formality.[2] Letcher also pledged, among other things, to seize the powerful Union bastion of Fort Monroe, located at Old Point Comfort, across Hampton Roads from Norfolk. All efforts to that end, however, were to prove ineffectual; the fort would remain in federal hands.

While the Virginia convention was in progress, Lincoln called Scott to the White House to discuss the degree to which, if Virginia seceded and Maryland followed suit, Washington would be exposed to capture. Two visitors from Pennsylvania were present in the President's office, and they were astonished to witness Scott's seeming inconsistency. Asked if the city was defensible, Scott answered, No, the city was not defensible. Beauregard, he said, commanded an army at Charleston larger than all the forces available to the Union east of the Mississippi. Furthermore, Charleston was only a couple of days away from Washington by water. Nevertheless, Scott insisted, the capital was not in danger.

The seeming contradictions in Scott's answer caused the Pennsylvanians considerable discomfort. One of them later wrote of his fears, that the "great Chieftain of two wars and the worshipped Captain of the Age was in his dotage and utterly unequal to the great duty of meeting the impending conflict." But they failed to understand what the experienced old general really was saying. Washington as a city was indeed vulnerable to attack, but Beauregard was also facing real difficulties. In that Scott was right. Beauregard, at Charleston, was expecting a massive Northern invasion any day.

Despite Scott's confidence, Lincoln's concerns had a realistic basis. Only half of the regular troops that Scott had brought into Washington to guard his inaugural remained in the city, and of the militiamen who had since been mustered, nearly half of them had refused to take the oath of fealty to the Union.

On April 20, 1861, three days after the Virginia convention voted to withdraw from the Union, a messenger from Arlington, across the Potomac River from Washington, brought a letter that Scott had been expecting with sadness. That morning Lieutenant Colonel Robert E. Lee, the officer Scott had hoped might some day succeed him as general-in-chief of the United States Army, had turned in his resignation to Secretary of War Simon Cameron.

Lee had visited Scott two days earlier, at which time Scott had urged him, if his decision to resign was final, to do so at once. At the moment Lee was still an officer on active duty, and he might be assigned a mission he could not in conscience perform. One purpose of Lee's letter that morning was to explain why he had not acted earlier: "I would have presented [my resignation] at once," he wrote, "but for the struggle it has cost me to separate myself from a service to which I have devoted all the best years of my life and all the ability I possessed." Mentioning the kindnesses he had received from his superiors over a quarter of a century, he came to his main reason for writing:

To no one, General, have I been so much indebted as to yourself for uniform kindness and consideration, and it has always been my ardent desire to meet your approbation. I shall carry to the grave the most grateful recollections of your kind consideration, and your name and fame will always be dear to me. . . . Be pleased to accept my most earnest wishes for the continuance of your happiness and prosperity, and believe me, most truly yours . . .

R. E. Lee

Scott had no time to dwell on his grief; he was soon to have additional cause for unhappiness as the result of his own decision to stay with the Union.

On the same day that Lee resigned his commission, a deputation of citizens of northern Virginia headed by Judge John Robertson, an old friend from Petersburg, came to Scott's headquarters with the obvious intention of enlisting his services in the cause of his home state. The meeting was short. After the usual exchange of compliments, Scott sensed Robertson's purpose and cut the discussion off abruptly. "Friend Robertson," a witness later reported, "go no farther! It is best that we part here before you compel me to resent a mortal insult!"[3] As Robertson left, he chanced upon Senator Stephen A. Douglas on the street. Robertson's account gave Douglas a lift. The old soldier was quoted as saying, "I have served my country under the flag of the Union for more than fifty years, and as long as God permits me to live I will defend that flag with my sword, even if my own native State assails it."[4]

In a way the dilemma confronting Scott was similar to Lee's—two devoted Virginians who had spent their adult careers serving the Union. But Scott's ties with Virginia were far less compelling than those that bound Lee, whose family had been Virginia aristocrats for generations. All of Lee's people still lived in Virginia, while Scott and Maria, with their family, had lived for many years in New Jersey and New York. Scott had never doubted his own obligation to remain with the Union.

When word of the interview with Robertson spread around Virginia, the reaction was virulent. Scott's image was burned in effigy by students of the University of Virginia. At Dinwiddie Courthouse, Virginia, Scott's nephew, Colonel Joseph W. Harper, a six-foot, seven-inch farmer from nearby McKenney, tore his uncle's portrait from the wall of his home and ordered his slaves to chop it to little bits, tie the pieces to a rock, and throw it in the mill pond.[5] Similar sentiments spread over the state. The *Abington Democrat* graphically described Scott's "skinny hands and bony fingers undo[ing], at one dash, the labors of a long and active life." And an anonymous relative, probably a Mayo, wrote him directly that

when the future historian shall record the two great struggles on the American continent, of liberty against oppression and wrong, two names will be held up to the execration of mankind—that of Benedict Arnold and your own. . . . With a sophistry worthy the understanding of a schoolboy, you declare your determination to fight under the flag of your country, when that flag has prostituted to the foulest and most unholy of purposes.

Scott never indicated that any of these attacks and diatribes caused him to regret his course of action. He did not, in fact, have any time for thinking about them; he was too busy setting up the defenses of Washington.

By the third week of April 1861, Scott could see that the most serious long-term threat to Washington would come from Virginia, where the newly seceded state was arming for war at a rapid pace. To counter that threat, he needed a dramatic buildup of Northern militia in the city. To bring those troops in, his most immediate problem was the railroad bottleneck of Baltimore, through which reinforcement by rail would have to pass. Washington could be reached from the North by only two routes, one by water via the Potomac River and the other by the single railway line that linked the capital with Baltimore. As the Potomac could be interdicted by shore-based Confederate artillery at its narrow points, Baltimore became the all-important funnel. Three principal railroad lines converged in the city, one from the Ohio River and the West by way of Frederick and Harpers Ferry, a second from Harrisburg and the lake region beyond, and a third from Philadelphia.

Although most of the 200,000 people of Baltimore supported the Union, many rabid secessionists roamed its streets, and they would be able to make their presence very much felt. Additionally, Baltimore had, through the years, become somewhat notorious for disorderly tendencies. Scott and Lincoln were well aware of the difficulties, if not dangers, that awaited any Northern reinforcements who should detrain and march through it.

Following Lincoln's proclamation of April 15, the first troops that became available to secure Washington were the New Englanders. John A. Andrew, governor of Massachusetts, had begun mobilizing, equipping, and training his four organized active militia units as far back as January, so his were the best-prepared troops on hand when Lincoln's call for volunteers reached his desk. On the very day following the proclamation, the 6th Massachusetts Infantry Regiment gathered on the Boston Commons and, amid much fanfare, shipped out by train. The regiment reached Philadelphia during the evening of Thursday, April 18, 1861.

At Philadelphia, the commanding officer of the 6th Massachusetts, Colonel Edward F. Jones, learned that large numbers of secessionists were planning to oppose his regiment as it marched through Baltimore to change rail lines. Nevertheless, Jones, who considered the orders of Governor Andrew to be non-negotiable, roused his men before dawn the next day and boarded a train from Philadelphia to Baltimore. En route he ordered his men to load and cap their rifles and issued them strict instructions for the march:

> You will undoubtedly be abused, and perhaps assaulted, to which you must pay no attention whatever, but march with your faces square to the front . . . even if they throw stones, bricks, or other missiles; but if you are fired upon, and any one of you is hit, your officers will order you to fire.

Jones and his men arrived at the Philadelphia Street Station, Baltimore, at about 10:00 A.M. on April 19. Arrangements had been made for them to be conducted cross-town to the Washington Station, a distance of about a mile, in railroad cars drawn by horses. Only part of Jones's regiment, however, could go at any one time.

At the outset, the crowds in the streets became unruly. At first the demonstrations were limited to threats; men gathered around the railroad cars brandishing knives and sometimes revolvers. No injuries were inflicted at this stage. When the cars tried to return for the rest of the regiment, however, the railway authorities discovered that the tracks had been blocked and torn up. The remaining companies of the 6th would have to march on foot.

Serious trouble occurred in the latter stage of the cross-city transit, with the second echelon. As the men marched off from the Philadelphia Station they soon met a crowd of 8,000 to 10,000 people, carrying the flag of secession. When the column reached the site of a demolished bridge, the men were forced to pause while their commander sent them across the obstacle single file. During that delay firing broke out, coming from windows in the nearby buildings; the troops, under orders, returned it. Fortunately the police marshal, though a suspected secessionist himself, did his job professionally, and he formed his men in two lines, between which the beleaguered militiamen could pass.

The resourcefulness of the police marshal, plus the discipline of the Massachusetts troops, kept bloodshed at a minimum compared to what it might have been. By the time the troops were loaded on the train to take them to

Washington, Jones counted his losses: four militiamen dead and thirty-six wounded. Casualties among the Baltimore citizens came to some two to three times that number. A prominent Baltimore citizen was among the dead, raising the ire of the people.

When the exhausted men of the 6th Massachusetts reached Washington late that day, their appearance gave ample evidence of the conditions they had faced in Baltimore. As no other accommodations were available, they were billeted in the Capitol itself. The 7th Pennsylvania, which had been following behind the 6th Massachusetts from the Susquehanna River crossing, had been turned back by the Baltimore authorities and forced to return to Philadelphia.

The police marshal and the mayor of Baltimore, George W. Brown, had done all they could to prevent violence during the morning's difficulties, but later in the day their underlying political feelings began to surface. They joined Governor T. H. Hicks in sending a message asking President Lincoln to leave matters in their hands. "Send no more troops here," they pled. "We will endeavor to prevent all bloodshed. . . . The troops of the State and the city have been called out to preserve the peace. They will be enough." That same evening the three men met again and decided, for the sake of peace in the city, to burn the railroad bridges leading from the North into Baltimore along the two lines from Harrisburg and Philadelphia. Several bridges were destroyed, cutting all railroad traffic between Washington and the North. Governor Hicks, though generally a Union sympathizer, was either weak or overwhelmed. In any case, the end result was untold damage.

On receiving the telegraph message from Baltimore that evening, Lincoln immediately called his cabinet, along with Scott, to the White House. All present found the message unacceptable. Scott thereupon sent a message to Union General Robert Patterson, commanding the Pennsylvania militia in Philadelphia: "Governor Hicks has neither right nor authority to stop troops coming to Washington. Send them [the troops waiting in Philadelphia] on."

The next morning, Saturday, Scott again arrived in his carriage at the White House. As the old general was suffering from gout, President Lincoln considerately came downstairs to Scott's carriage, to save him from having to climb to the second floor. As it was now obvious that troops could not go through Baltimore without trouble, Scott simply declared, "Send them around." A committee from Baltimore soon arrived, expecting a reply to the message from the governor and the mayor. Lincoln accordingly penned a letter to Hicks:

> For the future troops must be brought here, but I make no point of sending them through Baltimore. Without any military knowledge myself, of course I must leave details to General Scott. He hastily said this morning, "March them around Baltimore, not through it." I sincerely hope the general, on fuller reflection, will consider this practical and proper, and that you will not object to it.[6]

It was now up to Scott to determine how Baltimore might be bypassed. The railroad authorities helped solve the problem by offering a route that used the previous rail route as far as Perryville, opposite Havre de Grace on the Susquehanna River, and from there by water to Annapolis, where a railroad spur would take them to Washington.[7] Scott readily accepted the plan, and at a White House meeting on Sunday morning, April 21, Mayor George Brown of Baltimore reluctantly agreed.

While all this was going on, troops from the North continued to pour into Philadelphia. On the evening of April 19, only hours after the ordeal of the 6th Massachusetts in Baltimore, Brigadier General Benjamin F. Butler, overall commander of the Massachusetts brigade, arrived in Philadelphia at the head of the 8th Massachusetts. Butler, a devoted Democrat who had striven to make Jefferson Davis the Democratic candidate for President of the United States in 1860, was an energetic man; above all he was a Union man. He held that conviction sometimes with more zeal than judgment.

Butler was challenged rather than intimidated when he received word of the incident in Baltimore that day. His first impulse was to march the 8th Massachusetts defiantly through the streets regardless of the threats of the mobs. That plan fell through, however, when the Baltimore railroad officials refused to conduct his troops into the city. Butler soon learned of the planned alternate route via Annapolis, however, and he sought permission to follow it. In the meantime, Philadelphia became host to another regiment, this one the vaunted 7th New York, whose commanding officer, Colonel Marshall Lefferts, dearly hoped to arrive in Washington before Butler.

Butler waited for Scott's orders before leaving Philadelphia, but Colonel Lefferts, insisting that he was still under his own governor's orders, felt free to hatch his own plans. Without awaiting word from Scott, he boarded his troops on the transport *Boston* and headed down the Delaware River into the Atlantic Ocean to Hampton Roads, planning to continue up the Chesapeake Bay and the Potomac River to Washington. Butler and Lefferts were now engaged in a race.

Lefferts really had no chance. Butler arrived off Annapolis aboard the ferry *Maryland* on the evening of Saturday, April 20, with Lefferts, aboard the *Boston,* twenty-four hours behind him. Lefferts, receiving new word of Confederate batteries on the Potomac, had prudently decided not to try to reach Washington by that avenue, joining Butler instead.

At this point, Governor Hicks, still under pressure, reentered the picture. Protesting that a landing of federal troops at Annapolis constituted a violation of Maryland's rights, he demanded that both Union commanders refrain from disembarking their troops. Butler complied for the moment, spending Sunday, April 21, helping members of the Naval Academy pull the historic USS *Constitution,* then being used as a training ship, safely out to sea. The old vessel could still be used as a privateer by the Confederates, who were well represented in Annapolis. When Lefferts arrived that evening, both officers remained afloat with their troops for the moment.

Washington, meanwhile, was suffering a state of acute anxiety. Whose troops, it was being asked, would arrive at Washington first, the Northern reinforcements or the Confederate forces known to have seized the Gosport Naval Base at Norfolk, Harpers Ferry, and even nearby Alexandria? The feeling of isolation was heightened when, on the evening of April 21, secessionists seized the telegraph office in Baltimore, cutting even wire communication between Washington and the North. Scott, attempting to reach Butler and Lefferts at Annapolis, was forced to send messengers to do so. Over the weekend of April 20 and 21 many refugees, largely women and children, left the capital by whatever means could be obtained, often at extravagant prices. Union sympathizers went north; Confederate sympathizers, including a few remaining military officers, went south.[8]

On Tuesday evening, April 21, 1861, Scott invited Colonel Charles P. Stone for dinner in order to review Stone's latest plans for a last-ditch defense of the capital. Stone's plan called for defending three strong points within the city: the Capitol, the City Hall (including the post office), and the Executive Square, which included the White House.

Scott disapproved. The defense plan was too ambitious, he said. The Capitol and City Hall must be abandoned and all the resources available concentrated at the Executive Square, which included the White House, the Treasury, and the State, War, and Navy Departments. Sandbags must be stacked around that small perimeter, and the members of the government could subsist for some time. The Treasury Building, he pointed out, had a good water supply as well as two thousand barrels of flour. Scott also declared that the President's cabinet would have to remain and weather the crisis in the Treasury Building. "They shall not be permitted to desert the capital!" he pontificated.

Scott sent the President a report that summarized all that was happening and what he was planning to do:

I have but little that is certain to report, viz.: *First,* that there are three or four steamers off Annapolis, with volunteers for Washington; *Second,* That their landing will be opposed by the citizens, reënforced from Baltimore; *Third,* That the landing may be effected nevertheless by good management; and *Fourth,* That the rails on the Annapolis road (twenty miles) have been taken up. Several efforts to communicate with those troops to-day have failed; but three other detached persons are repeating the attempt, and one or more of them will, I think, succeed. Once ashore, the regiments (if but two, and there are probably more) would have no difficulty in reaching Washington on foot, other than the want of wagons to transport camp equipage; and the quartermaster that I have sent there has orders to hire wagons if he can and if not, to impress, etc.

Of rumors, the following are probable, viz.: *First,* That from 1500 to 2000 [Confederate] troops are at the White House (four miles below Mount Vernon, a narrow point in the Potomac) engaged in erecting a battery; *Second,* That an equal force is collected or in progress of assemblage on the two sides of the river to attack Fort Washington; and *Third,* That extra cars went up yesterday to bring down from Harper's Ferry about 2000 other troops to join in a general attack on this capital—that is, on many of its fronts at once.

I feel confident that with our present forces we can defend the Capitol, the Arsenal, and all the executive buildings (seven) against 10,000 troops not better than our district volunteers.[9]

Fortunately for the peace of mind of Lincoln and everyone else in the nation's capital, the threat disappeared the next day after Scott's meeting with Stone. A train came into Washington's Union Station on Wednesday, April 23, carrying hundreds of volunteers. Butler and Lefferts had landed at Annapolis and had worked together to repair the train tracks between that city and Washington. The city was now secure from any immediate danger.

The city of Washington now became host to numerous train-loads of volunteers. The 7th New York and the 8th Massachusetts, the two regiments that had become teammates mending the destroyed railroad tracks from Annapolis, were housed in the Capitol. The 1st Rhode Island, commanded by Colonel Ambrose E. Burnside, arrived shortly after. The 5th Massachusetts, coming in next, was placed in the Treasury Building. The Irishmen of the New York 69th Regiment found themselves billeted at Georgetown University, the New Jersey Brigade on Meridian Hill.

Scott now set about to mold an army out of this conglomeration of three-month militiamen. His problems were varied. Some of the units had come with their arms; others had to be provided weapons from the stocks currently held in the Army's arsenals. Small arms, in short supply, had to be ordered from overseas. Food, however, was ample, and ammunition supply would be no problem in this early stage of mobilization.

Many of the volunteers who had just arrived were gentlemen, who had signed up out of exuberant patriotism, as had their fathers or older brothers in the Mexican War. Despite the menial tasks assigned them, they approached their new lives in good spirits—indeed, too high-spirited in many cases. The most troublesome were the New York Zouaves, dressed in their gray, scarlet, and blue costumes—it would be stretching to call them uniforms. These men carried rifles, bowie knives, and numerous flags. They came with a ready-made organization, as in New York they had been firemen. They knew their business, and on one occasion, when their stock was low in the city because of their boyish antics, they flew into action and saved the Willard Hotel from burning. The people of Washington demonstrated their gratitude by feting and praising them; but the city was still relieved when the Zouaves were moved out of the city limits to the National Insane Asylum, Saint Elizabeth's.

Despite the weight of his responsibilities, Scott was still able to present a picture of vigor to the man in the street. John Motley, a friend of Scott as well as of Lincoln, encountered the general on the street outside headquarters one day. Afterward he remarked on the general's fine soldierly appearance: "He looks vigorous, healthy, and young; there seems nothing senile about him." But one evening shortly afterward Motley dropped into

Scott's headquarters and found a different scene. The old soldier was asleep in his shirtsleeves, two aides waiting for him to awaken, and a big sergeant brushing flies off his brow. When Scott became conscious of Motley's presence, he beat a hasty retreat into the next room, appearing shortly in a frock coat, a "magnificent old fellow."[10]

No matter what his infirmities, the Guardian of Washington knew well the value of a good appearance to the public.

35

➤➤❧❦❦

The Anaconda Plan and Bull Run

*The Union mobilizes but sustains its first
resounding defeat.*

A T THE END of April 1861, Winfield Scott was the man on whom all
others in the Lincoln administration depended, the "old soldier," the
repository of knowledge and understanding of military matters. Edwin
Stanton, never a great supporter of Scott's, wrote to former president James
Buchanan in mid-May, "General Scott seems to have *carte blanche.* He is, in
fact, the Government."[1] So busy was Scott that he failed to keep the President sufficiently informed. Lincoln accepted the unintended slight philosophically, even with a touch of humor. When the historian John Lothrop
Motley visited the White House at about this time, the President observed
almost whimsically, "Scott will not let us outsiders know anything of his
plans."[2]

Scott's main task, to build an army, was an overwhelming undertaking,
especially since most of his beloved regulars would be unavailable to him.
The total authorized strength of the regular army was about 17,000 men,
consisting of ten infantry regiments, four artillery regiments, and three regiments of dragoons. These units were so scattered out that the organization
was counted in terms of companies instead of regiments. On that basis, 15 of
its 200 companies were assigned to man the heavy artillery positions on the
Atlantic Coast and 23 more were working in arsenals. The rest, 160 companies, were strewn over nearly eighty posts on the frontier in detachments of
company size or smaller. Fewer than 13,000 men were thus trying to secure
3,000,000 square miles of American territory. In the emergency attending

the Lincoln inaugural, Scott had been able to scrape together only about 600 regulars.

Without a substantial regular establishment, Scott was forced to rely on a call-up of volunteers to build an army. That process was complicated by the confusion caused by the sudden uprising of the Southern states, the glut in recruits stemming from the enthusiasm among the populace, the large numbers of military resignations, and the conflicting questions and requisitions coming from the sixteen governors of the loyal states. All this was occurring within a "quasi-field campaign" about Washington. "It was a bedlam," wrote Nicolay and Hay, Lincoln's biographers, "compared to the dignified and deliberate red tape and pigeon-hole methods of quiet times."

The forces on hand, however, fell far short of the country's needs, even had Lincoln, Scott, and others been able to bring order out of all that confusion. The 75,000 three-month volunteers in service could never suffice, even to defend against the 100,000 one-year men that Jefferson Davis had called up. On May 3, 1861, therefore, the President decreed by proclamation that the regular Army should be increased by 23,000 officers and men, the Navy by 18,000 seamen, and volunteers on active duty by 43,000 men—a total increase of 84,000 officers and men. Added to the 75,000 already called, the increases would bring the strength of the Army to about 159,000 men. Since Congress was out of session, Lincoln's proclamation of May 3 was obviously unconstitutional. It was, however, necessary, and Lincoln was content to allow Congress, when it convened on July 4, to make it retroactively legal.

The mobilization did not stop there. Part of the great buildup came because the governors of the various states mobilized more volunteers than the federal government had asked for. By July 1, 1861, Secretary Cameron reported an astonishing 310,000 men under arms. On July 4, Lincoln requested another 400,000 men from Congress; it voted him 500,000.

With all these volunteers being mustered, the government had to decide how they should be organized. Scott's distaste for volunteers, left over from his experiences in 1812 and in Mexico, caused him to advocate an immense buildup in the regular forces, which he hoped to train and equip to a high professional level, employing volunteers only as auxiliaries.

President Lincoln, supported by his cabinet, disapproved Scott's concept. The excuse they gave for so doing was time constraint: training a regular-type force such as Scott envisioned would entail a preparatory period of many months, far too long given the impatience of the public for action.

Another consideration, at least as important, probably had to do with the historic American habit of favoring volunteers over regulars. With the generous bonuses being offered by the governors of the states as inducements for men to sign up, it would be difficult to obtain recruits for the more Spartan regular units. The bulk of the fighting of the Civil War would be done by volunteers.

Since Scott could not expand the regulars substantially, he took steps to preserve at least an elite nucleus of professionals. That policy had merit, but Scott carried it to an extreme, denying permission for regular officers to transfer from regular units to the expanding volunteer units, which offered quicker advancement in rank. At one stroke this ruling deprived the volunteers of invaluable cadres, while it penalized regular officers, who found themselves stuck in place, forced to watch their compatriots who had previously left the service rise to fame.[3]

To attain uniformity among the various volunteer regiments as they came into federal service, a table of organization had to be drawn up. For that task, President Lincoln called on Secretary of the Treasury Salmon P. Chase rather than Scott or Secretary of War Simon Cameron. The reason is not clear. Perhaps Scott's known antipathy toward volunteers lessened his usefulness for this project in Lincoln's eyes. Perhaps he was known to be too busy with other things. Normally, Secretary Cameron would have been the logical choice, but he had other problems. Already in trouble for shady financial dealings, he was in danger of losing his position. In early May, therefore, Secretary Chase, with his two military assistants, Majors Irvin McDowell and William B. Franklin, drew up a plan for bringing 300,000 volunteers into service.

The final organization, which was followed throughout the Civil War, did not represent a dramatic departure from the volunteer units of the past. The new regiments would not, as McDowell and Franklin recommended, be organized along the lines of the regular units, which called for a structure of three battalions in each regiment. Nor would they be numbered as regular units. Instead, they would be identified by their states. As a proud Ohio politician, Chase firmly declared, "I would rather have no regiments raised in Ohio than that they should not be known as Ohio regiments." Chase and his assistants made one decision of critical importance, however, when they set the term of service for new volunteers at a full three years. That proviso, by ensuring continuity in the Army's organization for the foreseeable future, was vital. Even the noted military writer Emory Upton, who scorned civilians in general and politicians in particular, later gave Chase credit, through that one decision, for saving the Union.

One of Scott's main functions, aside from supervising day-to-day operations, was to administer policies pertaining to personnel, a sometimes difficult task among a group of prima donnas. One of his more delicate challenges was to bring an influential but difficult militia brigadier general, Benjamin F. Butler, under some sort of control. Butler, the "stout, crafty-looking, forceful little man,"[4] had played a vital role in securing Washington when he brought the Massachusetts brigade through Baltimore in late April. By May, however, that role was completed with the disappearance of secessionist pressures in Maryland. Scott therefore stationed Butler's brigade at a point called Relay House, on the Baltimore and Ohio Railway, eight miles south of Baltimore.

Relay House was a critical point, since it protected the junction where the B&O Railroad line between Baltimore and Washington joined with the branch running west to Harpers Ferry, occupied by a respectable Confederate force. Nevertheless, guarding a railroad junction, regardless of its importance, promised insufficient excitement for the aggressive Butler, and he moved his brigade into Baltimore itself, planting his artillery unopposed on Federal Hill. His excuse for doing so was to suppress a rumored riot; Butler was quite pleased with himself.

The people of Baltimore were justly incensed at this insult, so Scott quickly sent Butler a message of rebuke and acted to remove him from direct command of his brigade. But realizing that Butler was a popular figure—and important to Lincoln as a strong pro-Union Democrat—he proposed placing the general in command of Fort Monroe. At the same time, he promised Butler a promotion to the grade of major general. At first Butler refused the assignment, considering the command of a mere fortress to be in fact a demotion. He stomped into Scott's headquarters, had a severe confrontation with the general-in-chief, went back to his quarters, and burst into tears.

Butler soon changed his mind. He may have known that he could not win a personal vendetta with Scott, and the political leaders, conscious of Butler's substantial popular following, wooed him with profuse flattery. He finally decided that the grade of major general was so prestigious that he called on Scott at his headquarters to accept the offer. The two men visited pleasantly; Scott congratulated Butler on his new promotion and reminded him that Fort Monroe was the home of delicious soft-shell crabs and hogfish.

On May 23, 1861, Virginia's legislature ratified the ordinance of secession. Since the Old Dominion was no longer a state of the Union, President Lincoln felt free to occupy Virginia territory to defend Washington. On the day following the ratification, a column of Union troops crossed the Long Bridge* to set up a defensive perimeter far enough out to protect Washington from artillery fire. During the night, regiments from the District of Columbia, New York, New Jersey, and Michigan marched through the silent streets of the capital to take position on the Virginia side. The city of Alexandria and Lee's mansion at Arlington were both included within Union lines, the latter serving as army headquarters. Irvin McDowell, now promoted to the grade of brigadier general, began directing the buildup of the force that later grew into the Army of the Potomac.

During this time Scott was planning for the future employment of the great armies now coming into being. With Washington safe from immediate danger and Baltimore open to military traffic, his concern now was to secure the Ohio River, which runs between Ohio, Indiana, and Illinois on the west and Virginia and Kentucky[5] on the east, forming the dividing line between the Union and the Confederacy from Pittsburgh to Cairo, Illinois. Holding both the Potomac and the Ohio Rivers would keep the borders of the Union intact.

Fortunately he had a young officer in Ohio in whom he had considerable confidence. George B. McClellan, who had served as one of Scott's engineer lieutenants at Cerro Gordo and other battles of the Mexican War, had been "borrowed" by the governor of Ohio from the Ohio and Mississippi Railroad, of which McClellan was president, and appointed a major general of Ohio volunteers. Applauding the governor's action, Scott had absorbed him into the regular army and placed him in command of the Ohio frontier. With McClellan in command, and with no aggressions on the part of the Confederates in that region, Scott could go on to other things.

Scott hoped to avoid a bloody conflict, and to do so he planned to mobilize a Union army of such size and efficiency that the Confederacy would negotiate a return to the Union without a fight. While that mobilization was under way, he visualized seizing the entire line of the Mississippi and Ohio Rivers, splitting the Confederate states east of the Mississippi from Texas and Arkansas in the west. This he planned to combine with a naval blockade

---

*Long Bridge was located about where the 14th Street Bridge runs today.

of the Atlantic and Gulf of Mexico ports. Tightening that ring around the eastern Confederate states might so weaken the Confederacy that large-scale warfare could be avoided.[6]

Scott's plan came to be known as the "Anaconda" because it visualized squeezing the Confederacy like a giant snake. The plan came to light by an exchange of messages between him and General McClellan, out in Ohio.

McClellan had taken steps to organize United States forces in the West, but his mind was also occupied in formulating ambitious plans for the future. Even before he was inducted into the regular army as a major general he sent Scott an outline of his scheme for a quick blow against the Confederacy. As soon as his troops could be mobilized, he wrote, he proposed to lead them across the Ohio River and up the Kanawha River through western Virginia toward Richmond. Alternatively he could cross the Ohio at Cincinnati or Louisville and enter Kentucky if that state should prove hostile to the Union. He could even continue on from Louisville to Nashville. Either of these alternate plans, he estimated, would require some 80,000 men.

McClellan's proposals were utterly unrealistic. Further, exercising them any time soon would run counter to Scott's strategy, which rejected conducting operations in one region while still unprepared for action in the others. Nevertheless, he passed them to the President who, though a personal friend of McClellan's from earlier days in Illinois, did nothing to pursue them.

Scott then sent the young general the essence of his Anaconda plan. The government, he wrote, was planning to raise an army of 85,000 men (25,000 of them regulars), but until they could replace the unreliable three-month militia and be equipped and trained, the government's strategy would be forced to rely heavily on a complete blockade of the Atlantic and Gulf ports. To supplement the blockade, he envisioned a

> powerful movement down the Mississippi to the ocean, with a cordon of posts at proper points . . . the object being to clear out and keep open this great line of communication in connection with the strict blockade of the seaboard, so as to envelop the insurgent States and bring them to terms with less bloodshed than by any other plan.

Conscious of "Little Mac's" ego, Scott was careful to add that he expected McClellan to play an important part in that operation.

This Anaconda plan was strategically sound; before the end of the Civil War in 1865, the Union would have implemented it in full. It was, however, premature at the time Scott drew it up, because it discounted the impatience of the

American public for immediate, not future, action. Scott foresaw as much. He was, he wrote, concerned about "the impatience of our patriotic and loyal Union friends" who would "urge instant and vigorous action, regardless, I fear, of the consequences."[7] Nevertheless, he stuck to his plan despite its lack of political viability, for he was convinced that it was the correct way to win.

Scott's misgivings about public opinion proved to be all too accurate. Northern newspapers picked up word of his plan and almost universally derided it. As it did not call for an immediate, all-out assault on the Confederate army, some people accused the general-in-chief of allowing his Southern sympathies to becloud his professional judgment. The cry "On to Richmond," was at that moment universal. Horace Greeley's *New York Tribune,* reminding its readers that the Confederate Congress was scheduled to open in Richmond on July 20, 1861, declaimed

FORWARD TO RICHMOND!

The Rebel Congress Must Not be
Allowed to Meet There on the
20th of July.

BY THAT DATE THE PLACE MUST BE HELD
BY THE NATIONAL ARMY

Other newspapers followed the same line.

Whatever the ultimate strategy, the Union force building up on the south bank of the Potomac was in dire need of a commander. Scott, had he been a younger man, would doubtless have taken it himself as he did in Mexico thirteen years earlier. His weakened physical condition forbade such a thing, however, and even his faint hopes to oversee the operations of the army from a carriage, he realized, were impractical. A hands-on commander must be appointed, at least as deputy to himself.

Almost by default the command fell on the shoulders of Brigadier General Irvin McDowell, who had done such useful work as military assistant to Secretary of the Treasury Chase. At the age of forty-two McDowell was a direct, steady, likeable man, a veteran who had served under John E. Wool in the Mexican War, and one who had been intimately involved with the defense of Washington from the beginning.

Scott was unenthusiastic, at best, about the appointment. McDowell he saw as an unimaginative man who had never commanded any sizable troop unit, his entire service from the end of the Mexican War to 1861 having been in Washington. Scott would have preferred giving the command to Colonel Joseph Mansfield, but that officer, like Scott, was too old for field duty. Scott therefore left Mansfield in the District and reluctantly put McDowell in charge of the troops in Virginia. He was not overly concerned; he intended to oversee the planning for any future operations himself. Expecting that his Anaconda plan would be overridden in favor of more immediate action, he and McDowell began planning a campaign into northern Virginia.

On June 29, 1861, President Lincoln called a meeting of his cabinet and top military officials in the White House. A decision had to be reached soon, he concluded; the federal troops across the river in northern Virginia would soon number close to 35,000,[8] and the militia were soon due for discharge. Although thousands more volunteers were being organized in the various states, public opinion demanded that the men already in uniform should see some action.

At the outset, both Scott and McDowell pleaded for delay. Scott's objection to an immediate forward movement was based on strategy. Scott viewed such a move, executed by only one small force, much as he had viewed Mc-Clellan's scheme—as a piecemeal employment of the federal armies. He preferred his Anaconda plan, of course, but in any case he recommended waiting until the entire weight of the reinforcing volunteers could be brought to bear at one time. McDowell also wanted delay, but for another reason. He, like Scott, recognized that his army was as yet in no shape to fight. He had never maneuvered his troops, and he was all too aware that they needed training. As commander, he pleaded for more time.[9]

Lincoln, however, was forced to contend with the hard fact that General Beauregard, the hero of Fort Sumter, had concentrated 30,000 Confederate troops at the critical crossroads of Manassas Junction, only forty miles from Washington. That force had to be dispersed. Lincoln therefore decreed that McDowell should move forward toward Manassas Junction soon.

Once Lincoln had spoken, Scott's attitude immediately changed. He signaled McDowell, who came forward and spread a large map on the table and began outlining the plan that he and Scott had worked on during the previous weeks. The plan called for McDowell's force to move against Manassas Junction along the Warrenton Pike (present-day U.S. 29), past Centerville, and attack Beauregard's army, which waited behind Bull Run. McDowell planned to make his main crossing of the stream a few miles north of the

Warrenton Pike, making the attack straight down the pike a secondary effort, though making it appear to be the main thrust.

Scott and McDowell's plan was a sensible one, but it depended on two questionable assumptions. The first was that McDowell's army would be able to carry it out. The second was that Major General Robert Patterson, who commanded 15,000 Pensylvania militia at Charles Town, [West] Virginia, would be able to hold down Confederate General Joseph E. Johnston, who commanded a like number at Winchester.

The main weakness of the plan, for which Scott alone was responsible, was the second questionable assumption, that Patterson could hold Johnston in place. Had Patterson been an active, energetic commander, that assumption would have been valid. But Patterson, a veteran of both the War of 1812 and the Mexican War, lacked the force to control his three-month militiamen. He had sent dire warnings to Scott, one after the other, but Scott had paid them no heed.*

A week after that fateful White House meeting, Washington celebrated the Fourth of July with even more zest than usual. Independence Day had always been observed lavishly around the nation's capital, but in 1861 many of the favorite groves and springs just outside the city were occupied by federal troops. The celebrants therefore thronged good-naturedly into the city itself. On Lafayette Square, just north of the White House, crowds lined Pennsylvania Avenue, where the President stood on the stage of a bandstand and the general-in-chief, too bulky to stand for any length of time, sat grandly in front of him. As the Garibaldi Guard passed by, the men saluted the platform by tossing sprays of flowers and evergreens in its direction, missiles that had been uprooted from the gardens of furious property owners whose flowerbeds were located near the Garibaldi encampment.

It was an exhilarating experience. The men looked strong, well drilled, and well quipped. Why, some people wondered, should such an invincible body not sweep to Richmond and stamp out the rebellion? Trivial as the day's outing seems, it spurred the public's demand for action. "They think,"

---

*On June 16, 1861, Patterson had written: "I have to report that the term of service of a very large portion of this force will expire in a few days. From an under-current expression of feeling I am confident that many will be inclined to lay down their arms the day their time expires. With such a feeling existing, any active operations toward Winchester cannot be thought of until they are replaced by three years' men." Patterson to the Adjutant General, 16 June 1861, in Upton, *Military Policy,* p. 244.

wrote William Howard Russell, "that an army is like a round of cannister which can be fired off whenever the match is applied."

Four days later, on July 8, 1861, McDowell's army, organized in brigades, its volunteers bolstered by fewer than a thousand regulars,[10] left the Potomac marching in three columns. Scott was not with them; his health had degenerated too far. He stayed in his office to receive periodic messages, confident that his plan would work.

On Sunday, July 21, 1861, McDowell's force arrived at Bull Run, only to find that Beauregard's and Johnston's Confederate armies had joined. Had Beauregard been alone, without those reinforcements, the sizes of the Union and Confederate forces would have been about equal, with McDowell enjoying a slight edge. As it was, the Confederates possessed a marked advantage, with three brigades from the Shenandoah Valley taking positions facing the points where McDowell was crossing Bull Run.

The battle raged indecisively throughout most of the day. It was not decided until late, when Johnston's last brigade, that of Edmund Kirby Smith, arrived on the scene. The psychological effect was critical. The Union line gave way, and before the evening was over, throngs of Washington sightseers, along with the dispirited and panic-stricken volunteers, were streaming back to Washington. Major George Sykes's small group of regulars retained their formation, distinguishing themselves by covering the Union retreat. The one thing that had gone wrong was the inept Patterson's failure to hold Johnston's force in the valley, away from Manassas.

Scott remained optimistic up to the end. That evening, however, with President Lincoln and his cabinet congregated in his headquarters, the reports became progressively more distressing. One message came to Scott in McDowell's own hand, urging that steps be taken to defend the capital. Scott, as always, contemptuously rejected any fears that Washington might be taken. Shouting that taking Washington would be impossible, he added,

> We are now tasting the first fruits of a war, and learning what a panic is! We must be prepared for all sorts of rumors. Why, sir, we shall soon hear that Jefferson Davis has crossed the Long Bridge at the head of a brigade of elephants, and is trampling our citizens under foot. He has no brigade of elephants, he cannot by any possibility get a brigade of elephants.[11]

Scott's Anaconda plan had been rejected. Its substitute, "On to Richmond!" had gone down to defeat. Scott's prediction of a long war was coming to pass. It was a prediction he would rather have seen proved false.

36

"Hard Is the Fate": October 1861

Age, disease, and a conspiring George McClellan render
Scott incapable of commanding the Army.

The newspapers of yesterday contained the correspondence between Lt. Gen. Scott and the Secy. of War, in which the "Old
Hero" asks to be retired, and the order of the President granting
his request. It does honor to all three individuals. Ever since I can
remember, the name of Winfield Scott has been in my mind the
synonym of valor, honor, and military glory. For more than
twenty years, I have been personally acquainted with him, and I
felt, on read[ing] his withdrawal from active duty, as if a calamity
has befallen the nation—yet it seems to be a necessity, and it was
so admirably done that I could but feel glad that, after so long a
life of heroism, the good old man was to have a season of rest before he should leave a grateful people forever.

—Benjamin Brown French, *Witness to the Young Republic*

THE DEBACLE that befell the Union forces at Bull Run came as a profound shock to the people of the North. The battle itself was relatively
small; it was only a skirmish compared to later battles, dwarfed even by the
first day's battle at Gettysburg two years later. But in July 1861 the people
were not yet inured to carnage and disappointment. Any hope that the
South would give up without a long, hard fight was gone.

Winfield Scott was disappointed, but it never occurred to him, as a military
realist, that all was lost. He now set about to reorganize his army. There was no
time to lose. He quickly located Major George Sykes, whose 4th Infantry had

covered the withdrawal from Centerville. Sykes was assigned the task of guarding the Long Bridge, just in case the Confederate troops under Beauregard and Johnston should appear on the Virginia side. Then, since very few other units remained intact, he designated for each a spot in the city where its members should reassemble. Staff officers galloped about the city, concentrating on such rendezvous spots as hotels and barrooms. The Willard Hotel, for example, held hundreds of dazed and dejected officers, who needed to be told what to do next. Within a short time order had been restored.

The temper of the times called for scapegoats; it could never be admitted that McDowell's army had been sent forward prematurely. As a result, McDowell became the main target for recrimination. Cries for his removal went up immediately. McDowell accepted his bad luck stoically—at least on the outside—and from his headquarters at Arlington began the difficult job of rebuilding his command.

Scott also came in for criticism, and he reacted to it badly, as usual. Within hours of the defeat, he found himself in a meeting with the President, Secretary Cameron, and four Illinois congressmen. Addressing Lincoln, he exclaimed, "Sir, I am the greatest coward in America! I will prove it. I have fought this battle, sir, against my judgment; I think the President of the United States should remove me for doing it."

Everyone present was aghast. Lincoln, also disturbed, responded, "Your conversation seems to imply that I forced you to fight this battle."

Thus challenged, Scott skirted the issue. "I have never served a President who has been kinder to me than you have been."

That exchange, which would have been serious enough had the two men been alone together, was unfortunately played out in front of congressmen not all of whom were Lincoln supporters. William Alexander Richardson, for one, was a strong Union Democrat, and soon the halls of Congress were abuzz with the story that Lincoln had forced McDowell to move forward against the better judgment of his senior military adviser, Scott. On the floor of the Senate Richardson declaimed that Scott had fought the "disastrous" battle "against his judgment." Accusing the Congress of forcing a premature battle, he admitted to having been Scott's political opponent but said that as a soldier, he was "the greatest of them all!"

He fought the battle of Sunday last against his plan. The strategy of General Scott was the finest ever seen. If he had not been forced to precipitate our Army, he would have won a victory without fighting a battle.

If such statements were comforting to Scott, they did not improve his standing with Lincoln. Nevertheless, Lincoln took no action to remove Scott; he simply sent for a man he had known previously in Illinois, Major General George B. McClellan, to replace McDowell. Since McClellan was his own choice, it was not surprising that the President would put more of his trust in his field commander than in his general-in-chief.

McClellan had not been Scott's first choice to replace McDowell; he had advocated sending for Major General Henry W. Halleck, known in the Army as "Old Brains" because of his extensive writings and studies of the military art. But knowing Lincoln's strong predilections toward McClellan, Scott made no protest. He had exchanged complimentary messages with McClellan only a few days earlier, occasioned by McClellan's successful move into western Virginia, clearing it of Confederates. He had added that "the cabinet, including the President, are charmed by your activity, valor, and consequent successes." McClellan had responded warmly:

> All that I know of war I have learned from you, and in all that I have done I have endeavored to conform to your manner of conducting a campaign, as I understand the history of your achievements.
>
> It is my ambition to merit your praise and never to merit your censure.

McClellan arrived in Washington on Saturday, July 27, and he immediately headed for Scott's headquarters to report in. The conference was relatively brief, however. After about an hour, McClellan announced that he must leave; he was due to meet with the President and the cabinet at the White House. Scott, who had not been invited, was taken aback. The handwriting was on the wall: he had been supplanted in the councils of the President.

A period of adulation now began for the young commander of the Division of the Potomac that has rarely had a parallel in the history of the United States. The President, the cabinet, and the Congress, not to mention the people on the streets and his incoming troops, fawned on him. It seems to have come as some surprise, for on the evening of July 28, only the day after his first meeting with the President's cabinet, McClellan wrote home to his wife,

> I find myself in a new and strange position here; President, Cabinet, General Scott, and all deferring to me. By some strange operation of magic I seem to have become the power of the land.[1]

McClellan was, it must be admitted, a supremely successful organizer of the Division of the Potomac, soon redesignated the Army of the Potomac. And his éclat, as described by Margaret Leech, was prodigious:

> McClellan was the man in the saddle—even the saddle bore his name.[2] No one looked at the President, walking through the streets or driving in his carriage in his gray suit and slouched hat. All eyes were on the young commander. He was as different from modest McDowell, walking alone on Pennsylvania Avenue, as from obese, magnificent Scott. Every street lounger knew his stocky, high-booted figure. His passing, in clouds of dust or fountains of mud, was an event, a clatter, a cavalcade. Round the corner, hell for leather, he posted on his favorite horse, Dan Webster, with his staff and escort of dragoons hard put to follow him. He delighted in wearing them out, and thought nothing of a dash from the Chain Bridge all the way to Alexandria, through Virginia encampments which made a continuous military city, more populous than the capital. McClellan wanted his troops to know and trust him. The latest raw recruits were familiar with their general's face, called him "Our George" and "Little Mac," and joined lustily in the shouts which greeted him.[3]

Whatever one may think of McClellan's histrionics, his reorganization of the Army of the Potomac was masterfully done. He realized that, despite the defeat at Bull Run, the brigade commanders had performed about as well as could be expected of men directing large units for the first time. Accordingly—and certainly with Scott's concurrence—a new list of brigadier generals included Samuel P. Heinzelman, William T. Sherman, William B. Franklin, Ambrose Burnside, and E. D. Keyes, among others. Lesser grades included George G. Meade, Joseph Hooker, Don Carlos Buell, John Sedgwick, Winfield Scott Hancock, and Fitz-John Porter. With that group of young professionals he was able to organize the incoming three-year volunteers in minimum time.

In contrast to McDowell, McClellan had a keen eye for Washington politics. To that end, he took up residence at Lafayette Square, in Washington itself, rather than across the river with his troops. And partly to give his troops a sense of belonging—but probably more for the benefit of the Washington populace—he staged grandiose reviews of the Army of the Potomac across the river at a field near Bailey's Crossroads. There "ladies in wide crinolines and tiny bonnets sat marveling in their carriages, and little boys and girls stared pop-eyed at the white gloves and glistening bayonets, the flags, the polished brass, the cannon smoke."[4] One such review, staged late in the fall, comprised a total of 50,000 men.

In his role as the hope of the country, the youthful McClellan lost all trace of deference to anybody—to Lincoln, and even more so to Scott. As early as August 8, less than two weeks after his arrival, he was already complaining to Seward that Scott's negativism, his lethargy, were hindering his own efforts. Seward apparently gave him little support, for McClellan was soon wondering how Seward thought that he could "save this country when clogged by General Scott?" In the same letter he complained to his wife,

> I do not know whether he [Scott] is a *dotard* or a *traitor!* I can't tell which. He cannot or will not comprehend the condition in which we are placed and is entirely unequal to the emergency. . . . I am leaving nothing undone to increase our force—but that confounded old Gen'l always comes in the way—he is a perfect imbecil. He understands nothing, appreciates nothing, and is ever in my way.[5]

On the same day as his visit with Seward, McClellan addressed a letter to Scott advising that the defenses of the capital were totally inadequate to face the 100,000 Confederates he imagined were closing in on the city. The next day an infuriated Scott wrote to Secretary Cameron complaining of McClellan's presumption, criticisms, and insubordination. And then, as he was periodically wont to do throughout his career, Scott asked that he be allowed to retire. He had long been unable to mount a horse, he stated, and since he could not walk more than a few paces, could no longer review troops. Having become an "incumbrance" to the Army as well as to himself, he felt he should give way to a younger commander and "seek the palliatives of physical pain and exhaustion."

Lincoln, however, was not yet ready to dispense with Scott's services, so he attempted to patch up the differences between him and McClellan, thus prolonging the agony of Scott's departure for nearly another two months. During that period McClellan continued his policy of consulting freely not only with the secretary of war but with the President and other members of the cabinet. Nobody was exactly bypassed; McClellan simply observed no chain of command whatsoever.

At the middle of September, a month after the first stage of the quarrel, Scott published General Order No. 17, which forbade such activities as those of McClellan:

There are irregularities in the correspondence of the army which need prompt correction. It is highly important that junior officers on duty be not permitted to correspond with the General-in-Chief, or other commander, on current official business, except through intermediate commanders; and the same rule applies to correspondence with the President direct, or with him through the Secretary of War, unless it be by special invitation or request of the President.[6]

McClellan was immune to such weak applications of power as publication of general orders; he made no change in his way of doing things whatsoever. Three weeks later, therefore, Scott sent his final appeal to Cameron:

Eighteen days have now elapsed, and not the slightest response has been shown by Major-General McClellan. Perhaps he will say, in respect to [the order directing him to make returns of the troops] that it has been difficult for him to procure the exact returns of divisions and brigades. But why not have given me proximate returns, such as he so eagerly furnished the President and certain Secretaries? Has, then, a senior no corrective power over a junior officer in case of such persistent neglect and disobedience?

Scott's letter then suggested arresting McClellan and trying him by court-martial. He immediately dismissed that idea, however, because trying a popular general would create such a conflict of authority at the head of the Army as to be "highly encouraging to the enemies and depressing to the friends of the Union." Hence Scott's long forbearance. But then, admitting that he was only "nominally on duty," he would

try to hold out till the arrival of Major-General Halleck, when, as his presence will give me increased confidence in the safety of the Union . . . I shall definitely retire from the command of the Army.[7]

Three weeks passed, and nothing that Scott had ordered came to pass. Halleck was not called to assume command of the army; Scott was not permitted to retire; and McClellan did not mend his ways. One reason for McClellan's holding out was doubtless a realization that time was on his side, not Scott's.

Every day the old soldier lost zest and vitality. A British journalist, seeing Scott on the street one day, tired and ignored by the passing public, recorded in his diary, "Hard is the fate of those who serve republics."

In the meantime, McClellan was receiving encouragement from his supporters inside the government. On October 19, for example, he wrote his wife, "General Scott proposed to retire in favor of Halleck. The President and Cabinet have determined to accept his resignation, but *not* in favor of Halleck."[8]

Scott finally gave up. On October 31, 1861, he wrote a letter of resignation to Secretary Cameron, citing his usual complaints of "other and new infirmities"—dropsy and vertigo—and then, in circumstances "made painful by the unnatural and unjust rebellion now raging in the Southern States of our so lately prosperous and happy Union, I am compelled to request that my name be placed on the list of army officers retired from active service."[9]

The next morning Lincoln and his cabinet discussed whether to accept Scott's resignation. Unanimously they agreed to do so. All had been aware for some time that the Army could not function with two heads, and that Scott was failing. But Lincoln would not, given the huge reservoir of respect he held for the old general, simply accept the resignation and notify the old man. He sent word he was coming, and then, that afternoon, took his cabinet with him to pay their respects in person.

Lincoln's cabinet arrived at the White House at 4:00 P.M., and soon the entourage—Lincoln, Seward, Chase, Cameron, Wells, and Smith*—were in the hallway of Scott's quarters.

The ceremony was brief. The old general, in full dress uniform, lay on a couch as President Lincoln, sitting in a nearby chair, read the order placing him, "upon his own application," on the list of retired officers of the Army of the United States. "The American people," Lincoln went on, "will hear with sadness and deep emotion that Gen. Scott has withdrawn from active control of the Army." Finally Lincoln expressed a "profound sense of the important public services rendered by him to his country during his long and brilliant career, among which will ever be gratefully distinguished his faithful devotion to the Constitution, the Union, and the flag when assailed by parricidal rebellion."

The old man could not bring himself to stay on the couch to deliver his written reply. Struggling with difficulty to his feet, he stood up, his towering, six-foot, five-inch frame, grossly overweight, filling the room.

---

*William H. Seward, secretary of state; Salmon P. Chase, secretary of the treasury; Simon Cameron, secretary of war; Gideon Wells, secretary of the navy, and Caleb B. Smith, secretary of the interior.

This honor overwhelms me. It overpays all services I have attempted to render to my country. If I had any claims before, they are all obliterated by this expression of approval by the President with the unanimous support of his cabinet. . . . In my retirement, I shall offer up my prayers to God for this Administration and for my country . . . with confidence in its success over all enemies, and that speedily.

Scott lay back down on the couch. The President took his leave. He and each cabinet member came by to shake the general's hand.

In the early morning hours of the next day, November 2, 1861, Winfield Scott arrived at Washington's Union Station. The skies were black—it was only 4:00 A.M. But Lincoln had resolved that Scott would not leave the city unnoticed. Besides his military aides, Scott was to be accompanied on the train by a personage of stature, Secretary of War Simon Cameron, and an entourage including some ladies. A crowd of well-wishers were on hand to see him off.

Out of the dark came the sound of a mounted party. Major General George B. McClellan, Scott's successor as general-in-chief of the Army, had come with his staff to see the old soldier off.

The two generals spoke only briefly. Scott, overlooking the fact that McClellan's plotting had contributed to his own departure, spoke cordially, sending warm messages to the younger man's wife and baby. Then McClellan wheeled off into the dark, and Scott's train pulled out of the station.

37

❧❦❧

Taps

Five years of retirement and a much-lamented death.

Another star has faded, we miss its brilliant glow
For the veteran Scott has ceased to be a soldier here below.
And the country which he honored, now feels a heart-felt woe,
As we toast his name in reverence, at Benny Haven's, Oh!
—"Benny Haven's Oh!" (traditional West Point song)

S COTT DID NOT leave Washington feeling downcast. Perhaps he was even relieved to be freed of the responsibilities he had been carrying without the authority or energy he needed. In any case he was too old a soldier for remorse, having experienced his ups and downs over fifty-three years, under fourteen presidents, a general officer under thirteen of them. He was also pleased by the lavish praise contained in McClellan's General Order No. 19, in which his crafty successor called him "the great soldier of our nation," who had "sanctified with his blood" the fields of Canada, whose exploits in Mexico had eclipsed even those of Cortés, and who, in his declining year, had "given to the world the most shining instance of loyalty, in disregarding all ties of birth and clinging still to the cause of truth and honor." McClellan admitted to his wife that his flowery prose had been a "bit rhetorical," written for a purpose, but Scott took the words at face value.

Scott's comfortable railroad car, provided by the president of the Philadelphia, Wilmington, and Baltimore Railroad, went to New York by way of Harrisburg, since the bridges over the lower Susquehanna had not been fully repaired. Pennsylvania was the home state of Secretary of War Simon Cameron, so the members of his party, except for Scott, left the train for visits and festivities in the state capital. Scott declined, pleading that his infirmities required him to remain aboard. Nevertheless, when the crowds gathered around his train, he made his way to the rear platform, smiled, and shook a few hands. The distinguished party reached New York late in the afternoon of Saturday, November 2, 1861.

Scott had not cut his ties with New York when he had moved to Washington in November 1860. His aide and son-in-law, Colonel H. L. Scott, had kept his house on West Twelfth Street, and for the time being the general accompanied him and Cornelia to their home. The three then prepared for a trip to Europe. Maria Scott had been in France and Italy for some months, seeking relief from her progressive bronchial ailment, and the newly retired general-in-chief wanted to join her. He also hoped to obtain medical treatment for his many physical ailments.[1] Hailed by laudatory newspaper comments that would have warmed the heart of any man, the three Scotts bade New York adieu and boarded the *Arago* on November 9, 1861. On board Scott found his old friend from the political wars, Thurlow Weed. Weed was going to London and Paris as one of a party sent by Secretary Seward to present the Union case to the British and French governments.[2]

The *Arago* arrived at the English port of Southampton on November 24, 1861, amid a flurry of excitement caused by the appearance of a Confederate blockade runner in that port. For a while it seemed as if Scott and the other Americans might be captured. The captain of the *Arago* managed to evade the Confederate vessel, however, and the ship continued its voyage to LeHavre. The Scotts and Thurlow Weed rested a day before continuing on to Paris.

Scott's repose in Paris was interrupted, however, by a serious crisis that came to be known as the Mason-Slidell affair. On November 8, 1861, U.S. Navy Captain Charles Wilkes, commanding the cruiser *San Jacinto,* had stopped the British mail steamer *Trent* in the Bahama Channel and had removed James Murray Mason of Virginia and John Slidell of Louisiana,[3] two diplomatic representatives sent by President Jefferson Davis to the Court of St. James and the Tuileries.

These were important men, but it was not their status that aroused the British public; it was the high-handedness of the American's action in stopping a British vessel on the high seas. The Americans, on the other hand, were largely unimpressed by the British anger. Some of them, remembering the War of 1812, were defiant. When Wilkes brought his two captives to Fort Monroe on November 15, 1861, the people of the North were elated; Wilkes was feted, even presented with the thanks of Congress. Only Wall Street showed nervousness over the implications of the captain's act; the news caused a near panic on the floor of the Exchange.

For a while, emotions aroused by the Mason-Slidell affair threatened to bring on a war between Britain and the United States. On November 30, the British cabinet sent a message to Washington demanding both the surrender of Mason and Slidell and an apology.[4] Lincoln quickly recognized the danger and decided that he would have to accede to British demands—"one war at a time," he was quoted as saying. The decision was made easier, as the British had a good argument on their side. Captain Wilkes had acted in the general spirit of the times, but he had exceeded his instructions. Therefore, Weed and the other Union representatives in Europe deemed it vital to convince the Europeans that Wilkes had acted on his own. The alternative was to presume that Lincoln desired war with Britain.

The American consul in Paris, John Bigelow, agreed with Weed and realized that he must act quickly. He decided to draw on the reservoir of Scott's prestige as the most prominent American then in Paris, to assist in assuring the British of Abraham Lincoln's good intentions. As Scott had recently been at the seat of power in Washington, his voice would be considered authoritative.

Scott was more than willing to help when Bigelow came to see him. Bigelow drafted a letter for Scott's signature, which was distributed to papers in both Paris and London. Perhaps to Bigelow's surprise, Scott signed the draft without change.[5] Its main thrust was contained in this paragraph:

> I am sure the President and people of the United States would be but too happy to let these men go free, unnatural and unpardonable as their offenses have been, if by it they could emancipate the commerce of the world. . . . You may rest assured that an event so mutually disastrous as a war between England and America cannot occur without other and graver provocation than has yet been given by either nation.[6]

The letter, carried in both French and British newspapers, did much to ease the tensions in Europe until Lincoln could turn over the two emissaries to the British minister in Washington and later save what face he could for America.

But Scott did not foresee that the issue would blow over. Fearing that the

British might close the sea lanes to American shipping, he sailed for home on the return voyage of the *Arago,* leaving Cornelia and her husband in Paris to be near Maria. The general arrived back in New York on December 26, 1861, only about six weeks or so after having departed. His health, however, was already much improved.

Scott still seemed unwilling to admit that his days of national service were over. Soon after his return from Europe, he called on his friends in Washington to inquire discreetly whether his services might be needed there in any capacity. They were not. He therefore settled down in New York City.

Of the seven Scott children, only three daughters now survived. His two sons had died as small children; his eldest daughter, Maria, had died in 1833; and Virginia had died in a convent just before the Mexican War. The youngest daughter, Marcella Scott McTavish, lived with her family in Baltimore. With Cornelia remaining in Europe, therefore, only Camilla Scott Hoyt, with her husband, Goold, lived in New York. The Hoyts were socially prominent in the city, but Scott chose to live apart from them. He spent his time in New York alternating between the Brevoort Hotel and Delmonico's, spending the summers in his favorite spot, Frederick Cozzen's hotel near West Point.

Early in June 1862, six months after Scott's return from Europe, his wife, Maria, died in Rome. Scott made arrangements for her to be buried next to their first daughter, Maria, in the West Point cemetery. The general and his wife had been parted much of the time during their later years, and much conjecture had centered around that separation. However, Maria Scott's infirmity was real, and Scott's one-time aide, E. D. Keyes, discounted that any real animosity existed between them.

Later in the same month of June Scott was visited by the President himself. In April 1862, General George McClellan had transported a large army by water to the Yorktown Peninsula of Virginia, where Fort Monroe, still in Union hands, provided a base for a Union advance up the Peninsula toward Richmond. Lincoln was impatient with McClellan's caution, which bordered on timidity, but he was still concerned that McClellan should receive all the assistance by way of troops and supplies that Lincoln could provide. On this visit the President came to seek Scott's advice as to whether to risk exposing Washington to Confederate attack by sending the last large force, McDowell's corps, to reinforce "Little Mac," as he had requested. Scott, never so concerned over Washington's safety as was Lincoln, agreed with Lincoln's professed intention. Lincoln seemed satisfied for the moment, though his plans were later changed by General Robert E. Lee's severe attacks on McClellan, known as the "Seven Days" in the latter part of June 1862.[7]

During this visit by the President, Scott seized the opportunity to recommend that Major General Henry W. Halleck be appointed general-in-chief of the Army to replace McClellan, the field commander. Lincoln assented, and shortly afterward brought Halleck to Washington with that title. Lincoln may not have been satisfied with Halleck's later performance. In addition, his own self-confidence in his role as commander-in-chief was growing. In any case, Lincoln did not seek Scott's advice again; indeed, this was the last time Scott would ever see Lincoln alive.

During the rest of 1862 and through 1863 and 1864, Scott spent much of his time writing. Some of the topics he was forced to deal with were unpleasant. In January 1862 the *National Intelligencer,* in Washington, began a controversy over the question of Scott's advice to President Buchanan in October 1860 recommending the reinforcement of the United States forts in the South. As the stories reflected on Buchanan's judgment, if not his zeal to preserve the Union, Buchanan felt it necessary to write open letters to Scott, to be published in the press. Scott understandably felt compelled to answer. He also felt it necessary to clarify the position he had taken in his "wayward sisters" letter to Seward, which had been published without his permission. As usual, Scott came out second best in his exchange with Buchanan, but neither tempest amounted to anything significant.[8]

His health seemed to hold up well. Ralph Waldo Emerson, visiting West Point in 1863, met the redoubtable general, whom he described as a "huge old lion, aged seventy-seven," possessed of "the stateliest form in America." He added that Scott's behavior was as impressive as his appearance.[9]

Scott's most important literary activity during this time, however, centered around writing his *Memoirs.* Unfortunately, his advanced years prevented his doing justice to his magnificent life's story. His recollection of occurrences fifty years earlier was clearer than that of recent years, so he dwelled on unimportant events of the far past at the expense of more significant accounts of his relationship to the Lincoln administration. The tone he employed in his two-volume work was pompous; most of the time he referred to himself in the third person. Whatever the weaknesses of his efforts, however, Scott was proud of the final product.

Scott wasted no time, after the first copies of his *Memoirs* came off the press in late 1864, in sending a complimentary set to Lieutenant General Ulysses S. Grant, whose armies were besieging Petersburg, Virginia, and marching through the heart of the South to Savannah and northward through the Carolinas.* Scott was particularly proud of the modesty of his inscription, "From the Oldest to the Greatest General," which he later often referred to.

When the Civil War came to an end in April 1865, Scott was still in New York City, preparing for his annual spring move to West Point. When he received news of Lincoln's assassination, he made another public appearance. In full dress uniform, he paid his respects to the body of the fallen President when it lay in state in New York. It was said that the old general, with his gigantic size and trappings, was the most impressive figure at the ceremony.

Shortly thereafter, on June 8, 1865, General Ulysses S. Grant came to West Point to review the Corps of Cadets. Before the ceremony, however, he paid a courtesy call at Cozzens Hotel to visit his old chief. Scott received his visitor dressed in semi-military attire—a "handsome dress coat of blue, with yellow silk lapels and gold buttons." His white Marseilles vest was "buttoned with a regulation eagle." The two generals greeted each other warmly and sat down to a sumptuous luncheon.

Scott spent his last winter in the South. In December 1865, accompanied only by an army surgeon, he sailed for Key West, Florida, and after a month proceeded on to New Orleans, where he enjoyed the warm Louisiana sun, walking along St. Charles and Canal Streets. He returned to West Point in the spring, not realizing that the salutes he was receiving as his ship passed up the Hudson were to be his last.

His health was failing. Although the old soldier began his stay at West Point by indulging in some of his old habits, such as an evening game of whist, he declined rapidly. From time to time he rallied. On the evening of May 28, 1866, his resilience was such that Dr. Marsh felt it safe to allow Scott's daughter Camilla, who had been at his side, to return to New York

---

*Grant was physically at City Point, Virginia, with Meade's Army of the Potomac, besieging Petersburg. Grant was, however, a real, not an imagined general-in-chief, so the army under General William T. Sherman was also under Grant's command.

City. That evening the general suffered a relapse and within twenty-four hours the authorities sent her a telegram advising her to come back. She did so, but she did not arrive in time.

On the morning of Wednesday, May 30, Scott was chilled and trembling, though not in pain. He suffered from troubles in his urinary organs and a slight diarrhea; overall, his strength was simply fading. His skin was discolored, as if by jaundice. And that morning, for the first time, he consented to remain in bed, taking only brandy and water as nourishment. Word went out that the end was near, so the Episcopal chaplain, Dr. J. A. French, came to Scott's room with a prayer book. The academy superintendent, General George Cullum, was also there, along with two servants.

Scott's last words were directed toward one of the servants, James Allen. "James, how is the horse?"

"He is well, General."

"Take good care of him, James."

Dr. French then took Scott's hand and began reading the Order for the Visitation of the Sick, asking the general to press his hand whenever he wished to indicate his understanding. During the reading, Dr. Marsh's journal recorded, "the general breathed his last, so quietly and calmly that it was impossible to note the exact moment."

Two days later, on Friday, June 1, 1866, Lieutenant General Winfield Scott was laid to rest in a corner of the West Point Cemetery alongside his wife, Maria Mayo Scott, and his daughter Maria Scott. In attendance at the rites were the mayor and the bishop of New York. More important for an old soldier, however, was the presence of Generals Ulysses S. Grant, George G. Meade, George Thomas, John M. Schofield, and Oliver O. Howard, as well as Admiral David G. Farragut. The pallbearers were a collection of generals and admirals, besides six strong sergeants.

President Andrew Johnson ordered the national colors flown at half-staff for the day of the funeral; salutes were fired at every Army post in the nation; all offices of the executive branch of the government were closed, as well as the New York Stock Exchange. A giant had passed from the American scene.

Appendix A

Winfield Scott and the Presidents
Under Whom He Served

President	Years of Service	Scott's Position
Thomas Jefferson	1808–9	Captain, 2d Artillery
James Madison	1809–17	Captain, 2d Artillery, to Brigadier General (Queenston, Fort George, Chippewa, Lundy's Lane)
James Monroe	1817–25	Brevet Major General, Commanding General, Eastern Command
John Quincy Adams	1825–29	Brevet Major General, Commanding General, Eastern Command
Andrew Jackson	1829–37	Brevet Major General, Commanding General, Eastern Command (Black Hawk, Nullification, Seminole War, Creek War)
Martin Van Buren	1837–41	Brevet Major General, Commanding General, Eastern Command (Peace missions, Canadian border, Cherokee Removal)
W. H. Harrison	1841	Brevet Major General, Commanding General, Eastern Command
John Tyler	1841–45	General-in-Chief
James K. Polk	1845–49	General-in-Chief (Invasion of Mexico, 1847)
Zachary Taylor	1849–50	General-in-Chief
Millard Fillmore	1850–53	General-in-Chief
Franklin Pierce	1853–57	Brevet Lieutenant General
James Buchanan	1857–61	Brevet Lieutenant General
Abraham Lincoln	1861–65	Lieutenant General
Andrew Johnson	1865–66	Retired. Death, 1866

Appendix B

Cherokee Removal, 1838–39

Leader	Strength	Departure (1838)	Arrival (1839)	Survival[1]
Elijah Hicks	858	Oct. 1	Jan. 4	744
Hair Conrad (Lt. Edward Deas)	858	Oct. 11	Jan. 7	654
John Benge	1,200	Oct. 1	Jan. 10	1,103
Evan Jones	1,250		Feb. 2	1,033
J. Bushyhead	950	Nov. 21	Feb. 23	898
Stephen Foreman	983		Feb. 27	921
Choowalooka	1,150		March 1	970
Mose Daniel	1,035		March 2	924
James Brown	859		March 5	717
George Hicks	1,118	Nov. 4	March 14	1,039
John Drew	231		March 18	219
Richard Taylor	1,029		March 24	944
P. Hildebrand	1,776		March 25	1,312
Total	13,297			11,478

[1]These figures reflect net losses in numbers through deaths and some desertions. A few babies were born along the way, offsetting some deaths. And some Indians transferred between parties along the route.

Appendix C

Sequence of Events,
May 1860–April 1861

May 8, 1860	Republicans nominate Abraham Lincoln for president at Chicago.
May 1860	Democrats, meeting in Baltimore, nominate Stephen A. Douglas for president. Southern Democrats, meeting soon after, nominate John C. Breckenridge of Kentucky.
October 29, 1860	Winfield Scott unsuccessfully urges Secretary of War John B. Floyd and President James Buchanan to reinforce United States forces in Southern harbors, especially Charleston and Pensacola.
November 7, 1860	Abraham Lincoln elected President.
December 12, 1860	Winfield Scott moves Army headquarters from New York City to Washington. Again urges reinforcement of Southern forts.
December 20, 1860	South Carolina secedes from the Union.
December 25, 1860	Major Robert Anderson moves federal garrison from Fort Moultrie to Fort Sumter, S.C.
December 29, 1860	John B. Floyd resigns as Buchanan's secretary of war.
January 9, 1861	*Star of the West,* ship sent to reinforce federal garrison at Fort Sumter, turned back by gunfire in Charleston harbor.
	Mississippi secedes from the Union. Other cotton states follow.[1]
February 10, 1861	Jefferson Davis elected president of the newly organized Confederacy.
February 13, 1861	Ballots for 1860 presidential election formally counted at the Capitol, Washington. Vice President John Breckenridge presiding.
February 18, 1861	Jefferson Davis inaugurated as president of the Confederate States of America in Montgomery, Alabama.
February 23, 1861	Abraham Lincoln arrives in Washington.

---

[1]Florida on January 10, Alabama on January 11, Georgia on January 19, Louisiana on January 27, Texas on February 1.

March 4, 1861	Abraham Lincoln inaugurated 16th President of the United States.
March 6, 1861	Davis calls out 100,000 volunteers for a period of twelve months.
April 13, 1861	Major Robert Anderson surrenders federal garrison at Fort Sumter to General P. G. T. Beauregard.
	Lincoln calls for 75,000 militia to serve for a period of three months.
April 17, 1861	Virginia secedes from the Union. North Carolina, Tennessee, and Arkansas soon follow.
April 19, 1861	The 6th Massachusetts Infantry, marching through Baltimore, is fired on by mob. Soldiers and civilians killed. The 7th New York then proceeds to Washington by water, landing at Annapolis, April 25.

Notes

Chapter 1. The Bugle and the Drum

1. Samuel William Simmons, *The Pegrams of Virginia and Descendants, 1688-1984*, p. 19. Scott may have inherited his great height from the Pegrams, all of whom were exceptionally tall. All this account comes from Scott's *Memoirs*, 1:1.

2. Notably, Ogilvie returned to Scotland to claim a peerage. When the peerage was denied, he committed suicide in 1820. Scott's *Memoirs*, p. 8, mentions the peerage but not the suicide. Other quotes pertaining to Scott's schooling also come from the first chapter of his *Memoirs*.

3. Scott's companions were Thomas Ruffin, future chief justice of North Carolina, and John F. May, head of the bar of southern Virginia.

4. Barron was not the actual captain of the *Chesapeake*, but as the senior officer aboard, he was considered responsible.

5. Henry Adams, *History of the United States*, 4:27.

6. Even though Scott made much of this incident in his *Memoirs*, pp. 19-21, it is not stressed in the history books. It may not have been the only such occurrence along the Virginia coast.

7. "Orders in council" corresponded roughly to the modern American "executive order."

8. The bill was not exactly what Jefferson had requested, but it was significant. It raised the Army's strength to nearly ten thousand men, with $200,000 appropriated for the purchase of arms and equipment. Those funds were to be distributed among the states, who still held the final authority on their expenditure. Weigley, *History of the United States Army*, p. 109.

Chapter 2. A Shaky Beginning

1. Coffman, *The Old Army*, p. 14.

2. The name of the commanding officer was always used rather than a numerical designation.

3. Ganoe, *History of the United States Army*, p. 112.

4. Upton, *Military Policy*, p. 91, breaks the eight regiments down as follows: five regiments of infantry, one of riflemen, one of light artillery, and one of dragoons. He places the Army's strength at 2,765 as of 1810. Each regiment was commanded by a colonel, with one lieutenant colonel, a major, an adjutant, a quartermaster, a paymaster, and two surgeons.

5. Scott, *Memoirs*, 1:31-35. The officers he considered competent included Alexander Macomb, Joseph Gardner Swift, Joseph G. Totten, Sylvanus Thayer, Moses Porter, George

Armistead, Zebulon Pike, and even Edmund P. Gaines, his bitter rival for many years. In mentioning nine new regiments, Scott's memory failed. Only eight new ones had been authorized.

6. Wilkinson later claimed that the messages from the secretary had not reached him before he gave the order for the move, but by the time he made that claim, few people were willing to take his word, given his past history. Wilkinson also exacerbated the situation by adding that even if he had received the secretary's messages, he would not have moved his troops all the way to Fort Adams because "the labor of ascending the river would have diseased nine tenths of the men, the expense would have exceeded twelve thousand dollars, and the position at Fort Adams was ill-suited for the protection of New Orleans." State Papers, Military Affairs, i. 269.

7. Major Henry Atkinson, a close friend of Scott's, lost thirty-two out of a company of sixty-nine men in three months. Coffman, *The Old Army,* p. 28.

8. "Some of these partisans had heard me, in an excited conversation, the preceding summer . . . say that I knew, soon after the trial, from my friends, Mr. Randolph and Mr. Tazewell, as well as others, members of the grand jury, who found the bill of indictment against Burr, that nothing but the influence of Mr. Jefferson had saved Wilkinson from being included in the same indictment, and that I believed Wilkinson to have been equally a traitor with Burr." Scott, *Memoirs,* 1:37.

9. "Specification 1: In threatening the life of his commanding officer at Petersburg, Virginia, sometime in the months of August or September, 1808, by saying that if he went into action under the command of General Wilkinson, he would carry two pistols, one for his enemy and one for his general.

"ADDITIONAL CHARGE: Specification 1: In saying, between the last of December and 1st of January, 1809-10, at a public table in Washington, that he never saw but two traitors, General Wilkinson and Burr, and that General Wilkinson was a liar and a scoundrel.

"Specification 2: In saying, some time about the last of December . . . that he considered a man as much disgraced by serving under General Wilkinson as by marrying a prostitute."

Chapter 3. *"On to Canada!"*

1. Scott managed to study and digest a tome known as *Practical Considerations on the Errors Committed by Generals and Field-Officers, Commanding Armies and Detachments, from the Year 1748 to the Present Time,* by William Armstrong, Esq., late Adjutant-General to His Majesty's Forces. Elliott, *Winfield Scott,* pp. 36-37.

2. Jefferson's last act as he left the presidency in March 1808 had been to sign the repeal of his Total Non-Intercourse Act, or embargo.

3. "The new Congress differed greatly from any previous Congress. It contained some seventy new members [among whom] active leaders were young men. Henry Clay of Kentucky, William Lowndes, John Caldwell Calhoun, David R. Williams, Langdon Cheves of South Carolina, Felix Grundy of Tennessee, Peter Buell Porter of New York, Richard Mentor Johnson of Kentucky, had none of them reached his fortieth year." Henry Adams, *History of the United States,* book 5:122.

4. The United States 4th Infantry, plus militia and volunteers from Indiana and Kentucky.

5. Henry Adams, *History of the United States,* book 6:111.

6. Complaints against Napoleon came to the forefront on March 2, 1812, when the French minister told an infuriated Secretary of State James Monroe that Napoleon's Berlin and Milan decrees, though they had been repealed "in principle," might still be enforced in fact. This despite Madison's conviction, often expressed, that Napoleon's decrees had been withdrawn. As one American official wrote to another, "the Devil himself could tell which government, England or France, is most wicked." Henry Adams, *History of the United States,* book 6:189, 191, 196.

7. Ibid., p. 127.

8. Scott, *Memoirs,* 1:49.

Chapter 4. *Captured at Queenston, 1812*

1. Jefferson wrote as late as August 8 that "the acquisition of Canada this year, as far as the neighborhood of Quebec, will be a mere matter of marching, and will give us experience for the attack of Halifax next, and the final expulsion of England from the American continent." Jefferson to William J. Duane, August 8, 1812. Cited in Henry Adams, *History of the United States,* book 6:337.

2. In spite of the success of this venture, Elliott was one of the more controversial members of the navy of that day. His performance at the famous battle of Lake Erie (October 1813) was far from stellar, though he demanded credit not usually considered his due. See Beach, *The United States Navy,* p. 123n.

3. Among his accomplishments throughout a useful life, Van Rensselaer was a promoter of the Erie Canal, a scientist, and (in 1824) the founder of the Rensselaer Polytechnic Institute.

4. Far back in geological time, Niagara Falls had flowed directly over the escarpment at Queenston. However, the waters of the Niagara River erode the river bed at an estimated rate of one foot every ten years.

5. This process, known as "spiking" a gun, prevented the powder from igniting, thus temporarily putting it out of action. The process was not absolute. The piece could be put back into action if the spike could be removed from the powder hole.

6. Elting, *Amateurs to Arms!* p. 47. The escaped slaves were Runchey's Company of Colored Men, commanded by Captain Robert Runchey, Sr.

Chapter 5. *Captive*

1. Niagara-on-the-Lake is located on the banks of Lake Ontario, and the view today includes the tall buildings of present-day Toronto, then known as York.

2. Jacobs spoke little English, so Brant acted as interpreter. John Brant was no stranger to Americans. His father, Joseph Brant, had been a British ally in the French and Indian War and the American Revolution; and he had been entertained in Philadelphia by President George Washington.

3. Sheaffe's request was soon honored. According to Elliott, *Winfield Scott,* he was soon sent to Montreal in an administrative capacity.

4. Jefferson to Madison, 6 Nov. 1812. *The Writings of Thomas Jefferson,* ed. Ford, 11:271; cited in Elliott, *Winfield Scott,* p. 71.

Chapter 6. *The Capture of Fort George*

1. Berton, *The Invasion of Canada,* pp. 43-44.

2. "I think it my duty to lay before the [War] Department that, on the arrival at Quebec of the American prisoners surrendered at Queenstown, they were mustered and examined by British officers appointed to that duty, and every native born of the United Kingdoms of Great Britain and Ireland sequestered, and placed on board a ship of war then in the harbour. The vessel in a few days then sailed for England, with these prisoners on board. Between fifteen and twenty were thus taken from us, natives of Ireland, several of whom were known by their platoon officers to be naturalized citizens of the United States and others to have been long residents within the same. One in particular, whose name has escaped me, besides having complied with all the conditions of our naturalization laws, was represented by his officers to have left a wife and five children, all of them born within the State of New York.

"I distinctly understood, as well from the officers who came on board the prison ship for the above purposes, as from others with whom I have remonstrated on this subject, that it was the determination of the British Government, as expressed through Sir George Prevost, to punish every man whom it might subject to its power, found in arms against the British king contrary to his native allegiance." Scott, *Memoirs,* 1:73-74. In his *Memoirs* he corrected himself; the number of prisoners was twenty-three, not fifteen to twenty.

3. Henry Adams, *History of the United States,* book 6:426-28.

4. The problem was complicated by the fact that both armies and navies were involved. At the time when Scott and his compatriots were returned home on parole, the United States had only a very few British prisoners, a hundred members of the 1st Battalion, Royal Scots, who had been taken at sea by Captain David Porter, USN. Porter had paroled the Scots and sent them on to Quebec in the same status as that of Scott. When Dearborn proposed that the paroled Americans taken at Queenston be considered as exchanged for the Scots, Prevost refused, claiming that the Scots had already been exchanged for the crew of an American brig taken some time earlier. Secretary of State Monroe eventually stepped in, declaring the Queenston group exchanged and subject to duty. In that impasse, Scott and others went back to duty knowing that capture would mean death.

5. Steele, *American Campaigns,* p. 67.

6. Henry Adams, *History of the United States,* book 7:144-45.

7. Elliott, *Winfield Scott,* p. 92.

8. The Glengarrys were Canadian light infantry, professionally trained militia.

9. Elliott, *Winfield Scott,* p. 101.

Chapter 7. Muddle at Montreal

1. Navy Point, at Sacketts Harbor, was a major base. By early 1815 it employed 1,200 civilian shipwrights. Its naval component came to 5,000 men, one-third of the entire U.S. Navy. The *General Pike* was a 28-gun ship, 145 feet long. It was Chauncey's main hope for continued control of Lake Ontario.

2. Henry Adams, *History of the United States,* book 7:162-63. Canadians honor a woman, Laura Secord, for walking a long distance to warn FitzGibbon of the Americans' approach.

3. Harvey to Lewis, 13 June 1813. Canadian Archives, c. 689, p. 94. Cited in Elliott, *Winfield Scott,* pp. 101-8.

4. Smyth had gone home in disgrace in December 1812, after an unsuccessful attempt to cross the Niagara River and seize Fort Erie.

5. Elliott, *Winfield Scott,* pp. 117-18. Scott, *Memoirs,* 1:98, has a different view: "A landing and search were made, but nothing of value was there. It being certain that the enemy's grand depot of supplies was at York . . . Chauncey and Scott resolved to make a second descent upon that place."

6. Armstrong to Wilkinson, 13 March 1813, cited in Henry Adams, *History of the United States,* book 7:173.

7. That pessimism was shared equally by Wilkinson, who wrote, "But should we surmount every obstacle in descending the river we shall advance upon Montreal ignorant of the force arrayed against us, and in case of misfortune, having no retreat, the army must surrender at discretion." Henry Adams, *History of the United States,* book 7:183.

8. Known also as "Uphold's Creek" and "Hoop-hole's."

9. At the Battle of Chateauguay, Hampton had been stymied by a creditable action on the part of Lieutenant Colonel de la Salaberry, with only 350 men, behind a swamp and in thick woods. Salaberry's feat is rightly a source of pride to the Canadians, but Hampton's lack of energy and his quick decision to withdraw to Chateauguay was based on his lack of conviction that Armstrong, Wilkinson, or anyone else had any intention of pursuing the effort to take Montreal.

Chapter 8. Victory at Chippewa

1. Hickey, *The War of 1812,* p. 142.

2. Lynch, *An Epoch and a Man,* pp. 131-32.

3. Scott's brigade: Infantry regiments: 9th Massachusetts (Henry Leavenworth), 11th Vermont (John McNeill), 22d Pennsylvania (Hugh Brady), and 25th Connecticut (Thomas S. Jesup). Ripley's brigade: 21st Massachusetts (James Miller), 23d New York (McFarlane). Scott, *Memoirs,* 1:118, and Henry Adams, *History of the United States,* book 8:35-37. The regiments were regular army, not state volunteers. Nevertheless, each was recruited and trained in the state it was identified with. Scott, 1:118, notes that not one of those regiments was at more than half-strength.

4. Chauncey had come to be regarded in the Army as the Navy's James Wilkinson. Scott, *Memoirs,* 1:113, describes both Chauncey and Yeo harshly: "These two naval *heroes of defeat* held each other a little more than at arms-length—neither being willing to risk a battle without a decided superiority in guns and men." Beach, in *The United States Navy,* p. 118, takes a more charitable view: "The plain fact was that the commodore with the biggest ship in operation simply took command of the lake, sailed his accumulated fleet upon it—and retired when his opponent commissioned a bigger one."

5. The *Reglement* was only one of the manuals then in use. There were also Steuben's *Blue Book* and Smyth's *Regulations.* See Fredriksen, "Niagara, 1814," pp. 33-41.

6. Scott to Winder, 6 May 1814, *Ohio State Journal,* 26 Oct. 1852. Cited in Elliott, *Winfield Scott,* p. 148.

7. Scott's men present for duty consisted of far fewer: four infantry regiments, the 9th (300 men), 11th (433 men), 22d (229 men), and 25th (370 men), plus artillery—a little over 1,300 men present for duty out of a little over 2,000 on the books. Henry Adams, *History of the United States,* book 8:35; Fredriksen, "Niagara, 1814," p. 51.

8. Riall was in command of the British right wing, responsible for the area between Burlington and Fort Erie, with headquarters in Fort George.

9. At Fort George, 927; at Fort Niagara, 578; at Queenston, 258; at Chippewa, 428; at Fort Erie, 146. Total: 2,337 enlisted. In addition, officer and musician (!) strength came to 332. Henry Adams, *History of the United States,* book 8:38.

10. Scott, *Memoirs,* 1:128, claims that Riall had nine field pieces. Henry Adams, *History of the United States,* book 8:41, mentions only three: two 24-pound field pieces and one five-and-a-half-inch howitzer. Adams may have taken these figures from Riall's report (book 8:43).

Chapter 9. Wounded at Lundy's Lane

1. William James, *A Full and Correct Account of the Military Occurrences of the Late War between Great Britain and the United States of America,* 2 vols. (London, 1818), 2:132. Quoted in Henry Adams, *History of the United States,* book 8:46.

2. Lundy's Lane is now the main east-west street of the Canadian town of Niagara Falls. (Not to be confused with Niagara-on-the-Lake, which was then Newark.)

3. The sun sets at about 8:00 P.M. at Niagara Falls in late July.

4. Jesup, undated letter, Thomas S. Jesup Papers, New York Public Library, cited in Fredriksen, "Niagara, 1814," p. 136.

5. British Colonel Hercules Scott, writing to his brother on August 12, said, "In the last they gained possession of 5 out of 7 of our guns but the fire kept on them was so severe that it afterwards appeared that they had not been able to carry them off, for we found them the next morning on the spot they had been taken. We boast of a 'Great Victory,' but in my opinion it was nearly equal on both sides."

6. They were the second highest of the entire War of 1812, second only to New Orleans in January 1815.

Chapter 10. Hero

1. Scott, in his *Memoirs*, 1:149, has this little piece of self-congratulation: "[Scott] procured a litter, and hired eight men (two reliefs) to bear him on it; but some of the principal citizens drove off the hirelings, and shouldered the litter themselves. It was thus, more than half dead, he was taken in triumph, by the gentlemen of the country, who relieved each other at the edge of every town, some seventy miles, to the house at Geneva, of another dear friend, the Honorable John Nicholas."

2. Brevet promotions were granted in the U.S. Army until well after the Civil War. A brevet rank allowed the recipient to carry the title and wear the uniform of the brevet rank but did not ordinarily provide the pay and actual seniority. The conflict in status between brevet rank and the rank of officers of the same regular grade went on for many years.

3. Scott to Van Buren, 22 Oct. 1814, Van Buren Papers, Library of Congress. Cited in Elliott, *Winfield Scott*, pp. 188-89.

4. For discussion of drill manuals, see Fredriksen, "Niagara, 1814," pp. 31-41.

5. Scott to Monroe, 31 Jan. 1815, Monroe Papers, New York Public Library. Cited in Elliott, *Winfield Scott*, pp. 192f.

6. Scott was incensed that the British were celebrating the burning of Washington, which he considered "an improper act, especially that the Duke of Wellington, whether or not he participated, did not discourage the gathering."

7. Scott, *Memoirs*, 1:166-67.

8. Scott, *Memoirs*, 1:158-60. Scott claimed that Blücher tried to induce the Prussian king to destroy the "Bridge of Jena," a beautiful edifice celebrating the French victory over Prussia in 1806. Baron von Humboldt, according to Scott, succeeded in dissuading the Prussian king from the act.

9. Another revolution, that of Morelos in 1813, had also been put down.

10. The army was still split under two commanders, Andrew Jackson in the south and Jacob Brown in the north.

11. New York City, Plattsburgh, Sacketts Harbor, Fort Niagara, Rome, Watervliet, and West Point.

Chapter 11. Domestic Bliss and a Feud with Jackson

1. Dabney, *Richmond*, p. 98.

2. Scott's *Memoirs* quotes his motto: "When idle, be not alone; when alone, be not idle."

3. The *Columbian* article had actually confused the issue of Jackson's order with another situation pending within Scott's command. Brigadier General Joseph Gardner Swift, who was doubling in brass as the chief of engineers and at the same time acting superintendent of West Point, had allegedly refused to comply with a War Department order to fire Captain Alden Partridge, a perennial troublemaker, from his position at the academy.

4. "The law of the *duello*," Scott later wrote, "requires that the party, first conceiving himself to be insulted, should make such a call—otherwise there would be a mere competition in vulgar abuse, as in the quarrels of fisherwomen." *Memoirs*, 1:199.

Chapter 12. Ridiculous Resignation

1. Ganoe, *History of the United States Army*, p. 156.

2. *American State Papers*, Military, 2:189.

3. Jackson had mellowed, at least for the moment. More important, his objectives had

changed. No longer was he protecting the integrity of a military command; he was now in politics. Jackson had therefore shrewdly used this reconciliation with Scott to show the public a new face. "This [reconciliation] has destroyed the stronghold of those whose minds were prepared to see me with a Tomahawk in one hand and a scalping knife in the other." Jackson to G. W. Martin, 2 Jan. 1824. Jackson, *Correspondence*, 3:222.

4. Margaret Bayard Smith, *The First Forty Years of Washington Society*, ed. Gaillard Hunt (New York, 1906), pp. 182-86. Quoted in Bemis, *John Quincy Adams and the Union*, p. 49. Scott was commanding in the West at this time, so he must have made a special trip east for the occasion.

5. Secretary of State Henry Clay, Secretary of the Treasury Richard Rush, Barbour, Secretary of the Navy Samuel L. Southard, and Attorney General William Wirt.

6. Secretary of War James Barbour, Secretary of State Henry Clay, Secretary of the Navy Samuel L. Southard, and Attorney General William Wirt.

Chapter 13. Black Hawk War, 1831

1. Keyes, *Fifty Years' Observation*, pp. 7, 2.

2. Among them was Captain Abraham Lincoln of the Illinois Mounted Volunteers.

3. Colonel Zachary Taylor, with three hundred regulars and four hundred Illinois militia, followed by water, meeting Whiteside at Dixon's Creek. Unfortunately, Atkinson accompanied Taylor, thus placing himself in a position where he was unable to control the actions of Whiteside's force. Josephy, *The Patriot Chiefs*, pp. 238-47. Bauer, *Taylor*, p. 60.

4. Utley and Washburn, *Indian Wars*, p. 137. Word of the rout, which Zachary Taylor called "the most shameful . . . that troops ever were known to do," spread like wildfire. All but eleven men finally reported back to Whiteside.

5. Scott, *Memoirs*, 1:218. An officer on board later wrote of Scott and the cholera: "He thought . . . that his personal safety must be disregarded to visit the sick, to cheer the well, to encourage the attendants, to set an example to all, and to prevent a panic—in a word to save the lives of others at the risk of his own. All this he did faithfully, and when he could have had no other motive than that of doing good. . . . His conduct exhibited a trait in his character . . . which should not be overlooked." Mansfield, *Life and Services of General Winfield Scott*, p. 211.

6. Taylor sent Black Hawk and a few followers to Jefferson Barracks, Missouri, under the charge of his future son-in-law, Jefferson Davis. Black Hawk went to the East, where he was lionized, and home to Rock Island, where he fought no more.

7. Scott, *Memoirs*, 1:221-23.

8. Mansfield, *Life and Services of General Winfield Scott*, p. 212.

9. Scott had done less well by Alexander Macomb. He had subtly snubbed the general-in-chief by failing to include him in his direct communications with Cass.

Chapter 14. Watching the Nullifiers

1. Henry Clay's "American System," which he had begun promoting as early as 1810, emphasized nationalism, development of industry, and emphasis on interstate commerce, and was in reality a form of new Federalism. It ran counter to the "states' rights" philosophy, and resistance to it grew steadily as the Southern economy came under more pressure from outside sources.

2. The rift between Jackson and Calhoun had been dramatized at a Jefferson Day dinner during which Jackson raised his glass and, looking directly at Calhoun, declared, "Our Union; it must be preserved." Calhoun lacked Southern support outside of South Carolina at that juncture, so he temporarily retreated.

3. Charleston *Mercury*, Saturday, December 1, 1832. The letter, published in the "From

Columbia" column, was dated November 23, 1832. The incident referred to is probably his almost open defiance of President Adams when Macomb was appointed general-in-chief.

4. The leaders on both sides of the issue in Charleston and Columbia were all gentlemen, cut from the same cloth. Governor James Hamilton, one of the more radical nullifiers, never lost his affectionate relationship with Petigru, the leading Unionist with Poinsett.

5. At the turn of the year, Calhoun resigned the vice presidency and assumed Hayne's seat in the Senate.

6. Scott, *Memoirs*, 1:251-52.

7. Scott, *Memoirs*, 1:257.

Chapter 16. Frustration in Florida, 1836

1. The troops, 110 officers and men, consisted of Company "C" of the 2d Artillery, Company "B" of the 3d Artillery, and a few men from the 4th Infantry. All, including the artillerymen, were trained as infantry. With them they brought a single six-pounder gun, dragged along by two teams of horses. Upton, *Military Policy*, p. 163. Also Mahon, *History of the Second Seminole War*, p. 104.

2. Upton, *Military Policy*, pp. 190-92. These figures include the total number of men serving in the Army and Navy from 1836 through 1842. Most of the Army, which numbered only about four thousand effectives, served in Florida at one time or another.

3. Mott, *Journey into Wilderness*, p. 199.

4. There were other incidents. On the night of November 26, 1835, Osceola led a band of Seminoles in murdering a prominent chief, Charley Emathla, for complying with the demands of the government. Then, on December 18, Osceola ambushed a white wagon train, killing six whites and wounding eight.

5. Mahon, *History of the Second Seminole War*, places Seminole losses as only three killed and five wounded. Upton (*Military Policy*, p. 164) cites estimates that place them much higher, 40-60 killed out of an estimated strength of 1,200-2,000 warriors.

6. Fort King had been largely evacuated, its garrison moving to Fort Drane.

7. Gaines's inspector general, Captain E. A. Hitchcock, was especially moved: "The march was continued to Fort King, passing, on the 20th of February, the battleground of the gallant band cut off under Major Dade, on the 28th of December, where we interred the bodies of 106 heroes. No language can do justice to the scene. The remains of our mutilated brothers in arms were found where they had fallen, at their posts—the very position of the advance guard being clearly indicated. Our troops moved to solemn music around the little breastwork which had been hastily thrown up, and where the last of the party were destroyed; each individual lying at the breastworks, where, beyond a doubt, he had fallen in his duty." Hitchcock to Hon. Francis S. Lyon, 11 March 1836. See U.S. Congress, Senate, Exec. Doc. No. 224, pp. 645-47, for Hitchcock's full report on the scene to Gaines, just after its discovery.

8. Gaines was reported to have spit out his teeth, exclaiming, "It's mean of the redskins to knock out my teeth when I have so few." Potter, *The War in Florida*, p. 156.

9. John Bemrose, *Reminiscences*, pp. 78-79.

10. The *right wing* (Clinch), consisting of three battalions of Georgia volunteers, a regiment of Louisiana volunteers, a detachment of regulars, and a company of dragoons (2,000 men), to move from Fort Drane in time to arrive at Fort Izard between March 26 and March 28. The *center wing* (Lindsay), consisting of a regiment of Alabama volunteers, three companies of Louisiana volunteers, and two companies of regular artillery (1,250 men), to move from Fort Brooke and be at the line of departure (Chocochatti, near Inverness) by March 25. The *left wing* (Eustis), consisting of two regiments of South Carolina volunteers and four companies of regular artillery (1,400 men), to leave from St. Augustine and proceed down the coast to Mosquito Bay (Daytona Beach), clearing out all Indian resistance. Eustis was then to

turn westward, cross the St. Johns at Volusia, and be at Piklakaha, near the Dade massacre site, by March 27.

11. Middle Florida, part of the panhandle, was officially delineated by the Suwannee River on the east and the Apalachicola on the west.

Chapter 17. Scott Faces a Court of Inquiry

1. Not all of them, however. Many of the Alabamians apparently feared that they were being recruited for action in Florida, which they wanted no more of.

2. The actions of both Clay and Jesup were strange from the beginning, suggesting an early collaboration to thwart Scott's ambitious plans. Clay never answered the two letters that Scott wrote him on May 31, and Jesup, after his enigmatic letter of June 8, never wrote again until June 17, when he had already arrived at Fort Mitchell, near Columbus. There is no evidence that Clay ever withheld turning over command of Alabama troops to Jesup.

3. General Order No. 65, TAG, 3 Oct. 1836. U.S. Congress, Senate, Exec. Doc. No. 224, p. 8.

4. Scott had long since been reconciled with Macomb; Atkinson was a lifelong friend; and Hugh Brady had commanded the 22d Infantry in Scott's brigade at the battles of Chippewa and Lundy's Lane in 1814.

5. U.S. Congress, Senate, Exec. Doc. No. 224, p. 33.

6. Scott, *Memoirs,* 1:271-72.

Chapter 18. The Great Pacificator, 1838

1. "On this frontier, the citizens enrolled themselves as Canada *patriots* or *sympathizers,* until, perhaps one fourth of all the inhabitants capable of bearing arms were professed friends and abettors of the Canada movement. Itinerant refugees were seen everywhere organizing their friends, with a view to descent upon the Canadas. Thousands and thousands met in lodges all along the border, oaths of secrecy were administered, principal leaders appointed, generals and staff-officers chosen, and at least for Upper Canada, a provisional government formed. The President of the United States issued his proclamations enjoining all good citizens to observe the strictest neutrality towards the British provinces. It had but little effect." Mansfield, *Life and Services of General Winfield Scott,* pp. 287-88.

2. Scott to Poinsett, 3 Feb. 1838, Poinsett Papers, Pennsylvania Historical Society.

3. Mansfield, *Life and Services of General Winfield Scott,* p. 293.

Chapter 19. Along the Trail of Tears

1. John Ross (1790-1866) was the son of a Scottish immigrant and a Cherokee woman who was three-quarters white. He had served under Andrew Jackson at Horseshoe Bend in 1813, had become a member of the national committee of the Cherokees in 1817, and was the principal chief of the Cherokee Nation from 1828 on.

2. Scott, *Memoirs,* 1:323-25.

3. At New Echota, the heart of the Cherokee Nation, near present-day Cartersville, Georgia. Cartersville is northwest of Atlanta, not far from the site of the later Battle of Kennesaw Mountain in the Civil War. Oddly, the Cherokee Agency at Athens and the Cherokee capital at New Echota were far apart.

4. Chief John Ross is known by that name alone. Sequoia was widely known as George Gist, after his Scottish father. In contrast, the Seminole chief, Osceola, was known by that name more widely than by his father's name, Powell.

5. Georgia, for example, had a population of about 517,000 people in 1830 (as contrasted

to the mere 35,000 whites in Florida). U.S. Census, 1830. Cited in *World Almanac, 1992*, p. 74.

6. Governor Gilmer was not alone in calling for immediate Cherokee removal. Governor William Carroll of Tennessee quickly seconded Gilmer's urgings, and Carroll even suggested a bit of bribery to grease the skids with the Cherokee chiefs.

7. The evacuation route became standard. Beginning at Guntersville, it ran northwest along the Tennessee to the Ohio, which it joined at Paducah, Kentucky. It then followed the Ohio to the Mississippi and went down that river to Montgomery's Point, Arkansas. It followed the Arkansas River all the way across the state to Oklahoma.

8. For a complete treatment of the Ridge-Boudinot faction, see Valliere, "Benjamin Currey."

9. Keyes, *Fifty Years' Observation*, p. 134.

10. On June 8, 1838, Scott wrote to General Nathaniel Smith in those same terms. "The general distress caused the emigrants by the want of their bedding, cooking utensils, clothes, and ponies, I much regret as also the loss of their property consequent upon the hurry of capture and removal." He added, however, that the Indians themselves were to blame for having faith in the ability of John Ross to save them.

11. The thirteen thousand people were broken down into thirteen "companies" of about a thousand people each. According to Mansfield, *Life and Services of General Winfield Scott*, p. 312, each company was provided a Cherokee "conductor," assisted by a "sub-conductor and a physician."

Chapter 20. Diplomacy and Politics

1. On November 7, 1838, Scott wrote Poinsett: "My wife and family probably sailed for Europe (on the 8th instant) instead of waiting for me and sailing for New Orleans—the physician objecting to the latter. (Her case is bronchitis.)"

2. Scott, *Memoirs*, 2:331.

3. *Boston Atlas*, 2 March 1839, cited in Mansfield, *Life and Services of General Winfield Scott*, p. 327. Feelings over the Aroostook War had crossed state boundaries to affect others as well. One offer came from J. C. Bennett, commander of the Invincible Dragoons of the Illinois Militia: "Permit me, sir, though a stranger, to ask if you will require any additional troops for the just rights of your state against foreign usurpation. If so, will you be so good as to use your influence with the President to make a call on my brigade? If so, you will much oblige J. C. Bennett, Brig General." Fairfield, *Letters*, p. 253.

4. Martin Van Buren, in this regard, differed greatly from Jackson. However, his peaceable inclinations were not widely known at the time.

5. Scott, *Memoirs*, 2:347-50.

6. Scott, *Memoirs*, 2:353-54.

7. Scott to Worth, quoted in Elliott, *Winfield Scott*, p. 379.

Chapter 21. General-in-Chief at Last

1. Mahon, *History of the Second Seminole War*, p. 116.

2. After Jesup had succeeded Scott in the Florida command, he had, by a ruse that history has deplored, captured the famed Seminole chief Osceola, who died under questionable circumstances at Fort Moultrie, South Carolina, within weeks of his imprisonment there. But Jesup had also become worn out; his last campaign, which ended in May 1838, had resulted in killing only 35 Seminole warriors, though over 4,300 Indians and Negroes were captured or agreed to removal to the West. Jesup had been replaced by Colonel Zachary Taylor, who made a reputation for achieving a spectacular victory in the swamps in December 1837, but

who, at his own request, was relieved in turn by General Lewis Armistead. Colonel William J. Worth, Scott's former aide and confidant, was the final commander in that war. Worth had brought hostilities to a close by refusing to attack bodies of Indian braves; he simply destroyed all the crops they needed to sustain life. The Seminoles were soon reduced to penury.

3. Scott, *Memoirs*, 2:367.

4. Crittenden, *Life*, 1:185-86.

5. Hone, *Diary*, 2:674.

Chapter 22. *"A Hasty Plate of Soup"*

1. Andrew J. Donelson was Andrew Jackson's nephew, a graduate of West Point, and a successful politician in his own right, though for years he subordinated his own career in Jackson's interest, serving as Jackson's aide in retirement. He was one of Polk's staunchest supporters in the critical Democratic convention at Baltimore in May 1844.

2. Polk had given Slidell the title "minister plenipotentiary," which Herrera insisted violated the Mexican severance of relations. Even though the distinction may seem trivial, it entailed respect for the action of Mexico in breaking off relations. The "minister" implied the existence of diplomatic relations, which Mexico had cut off.

3. The Mexicans insisted that the territories between the Nueces River (Corpus Christi) and the Rio Grande (Matamoros-Brownsville) were in the state of Tamaulipas, Mexico. "Rio del Norte" is another name for the Rio Grande.

4. Polk, *Diary*, p. 67.

5. The House of Representatives, after a thirty-minute debate, supported Polk by a vote of 173-14. John Quincy Adams personally led the fourteen, all New England congressmen, all Whigs, to reject Polk's declaration, but they were swamped in the voting against the measure. They later dubbed themselves the "immortal Fourteen." The Senate took a day to support Polk by a vote of 40-2.

6. Polk, *Diary*, p. 94.

7. Scott to Marcy, 21 May 1846, *Congressional Globe Appendix*, 1846, p. 650.

8. In those days, the headquarters of the Army was deemed to be wherever the general-in-chief happened to be. Thus Scott was free to move the headquarters to West Point or anywhere else he wanted to go. Throughout his invasion of the Mexican interior, he always termed his whereabouts the "headquarters of the army."

9. Alabama, Georgia, Maryland, Mississippi, Ohio, Tennessee, and Texas.

10. The month that Taylor's men spent at Camargo was tragic in light of the high number of deaths from disease. One problem was the lack of sanitary discipline among the volunteers, among whom most of the deaths occurred. Another was the lack of real understanding of the causes of infectious diseases.

11. As Wood was stationed back at the Brazos, not directly affected by Taylor's everyday fortunes, Taylor often expressed his views frankly in writing to him. This letter, from Taylor, *Letters*, pp. 66-67, was written on November 10, 1846.

12. Taylor's truce has been the subject of considerable controversy, much of it politically inspired, depending on an individual's feelings toward Taylor himself. Politics affected those judgments, though Taylor's staunchest supporter in this matter was Jefferson Davis, himself an avowed Democrat. (Davis was also once Taylor's son-in-law.)

13. Polk, *Diary*, p. 163.

14. Scott, *Memoirs*, 2:399.

15. Polk, *Diary*, p. 171.

16. U.S. Congress, House, Exec. Doc. No. 60, p. 373.

17. Ibid., pp. 849-50.

Chapter 23. Triumph at Veracruz

1. Much of the credit for the development of the flying artillery has been accorded to Major Sam Ringgold, who was one of the few killed at the battle of Palo Alto, under Taylor, in 1846.

2. At the Battle of Hastings, in 1066, William the Conqueror led only some seven thousand Normans, in contrast to Scott's twelve thousand. Napoleon's 1798 expedition to Egypt was larger, but it did not penetrate into the interior of a major country.

3. Until the Defense Reorganization Act of 1947, the Army always transported troops in its own ships, independent of the Navy.

4. Elliott, *Winfield Scott*, p. 446.

5. Polk, *Diary*, p. 198. The entry for February 20, 1847, contains one of the most amusing political statements ever made: "I have myself been wholly uninfluenced by any reference to the political opinions of the officers of the army in the conduct of the war."

6. Jesup bought the steamer *Alabama* for $75,000 after beating down the owners' original asking price of $90,000. The *Southerner*, a better ship, was offered to him for $180,000, a sum that he thought about $80,000 too much. He paid $45,000 for the *Fashion*, a smaller steamer. Elliott, *Winfield Scott*, p. 449n.

7. The relative strengths are difficult to ascertain, as the units varied in size, each regiment having less than its total authorized number of companies. Most of the units called "artillery" fought as infantry. Upton, *Military Policy*, p. 211, gives the following breakdown:

Worth's Division

Artillery: 9 companies from the 2d Art. and 4 companies from the 3d Art.
Infantry: 4th, 5th, 6th, and 8th regiments (total 25 companies).

Twiggs's Division

Artillery: 12 companies from the 1st Art.; 6 companies from the 4th Art.
Infantry: Regiment of mounted rifles; 2d, 3d, and 7th regiments (total 21 companies).

Patterson's Division

Infantry: 3d Illinois, 4th Illinois, New York Regt., 1st Tennessee, 2d Tennessee, Kentucky Regt., 1st Pennsylvania, 2d Pennsylvania, South Carolina Regt., Mounted Tennessee Volunteers.

Army troops

1st and 2d Dragoons, Engr. Co., Ordnance Co.

8. E. Kirby Smith, *To Mexico with Scott*, p. 112.

9. Matthew C. Perry was the younger brother of Scott's former comrade Oliver Hazard Perry.

10. Mansfield, *Life and Services of General Winfield Scott*, p. 379. Scott's showmanship came naturally to him, but it was also calculated. Lieutenant Ulysses S. Grant, though an admirer of Scott's, realized the amount of staging that the general put on in order to appear impressive to his troops: "General Scott always wore all the uniform prescribed or allowed by law when he inspected his lines; word would be sent to all division and brigade commanders in advance, notifying them of the hour when the commanding general might be expected. This was done so that all the army might be under arms to salute their chief as he passed. On these occasions he wore his dress uniform, cocked hat, aiguillets, sabre and spurs. His staff proper, besides all the officers constructive on his staff—engineers, inspectors, quartermasters, etc., that could be spared—followed, also in prescribed uniform and in prescribed order." Grant, *Memoirs*, 1:138-39.

11. Alcaraz, *The Other Side*, pp. 184-88.

Chapter 24. Cerro Gordo: Almost According to Plan

1. Not to be confused with "Native American," the modern term for American Indians.

2. Specifically, he estimated 1,000 wagons, with five-mule teams, 2,000-3,000 pack mules, and 300-500 draught animals.

3. Santa Anna had managed to portray the battle at Buena Vista as a victory, claiming that he had nearly annihilated Zachary Taylor's army. He lavishly displayed captured battle flags, and his controlled press painted his exploits so favorably that his reputation at home was enhanced by the Buena Vista fiasco.

4. Santa Anna proclamation, 31 March 1847, in U.S. Congress, House, Exec. Doc. No. 60, p. 373.

5. The names of Johnston and Beauregard are well known as generals of the Confederacy during the Civil War. Zealous B. Tower is less famous, though he later became a major general of U.S. volunteers and briefly superintendent of West Point.

6. Hitchcock, *Fifty Years in Camp and Field*, pp. 250-51.

7. Ballantine, *An English Soldier*, pp. 180-82.

8. Persifor Smith was the prominent Louisianian who had distinguished himself while serving under Scott during the Seminole War. The term "red-legged infantry" comes from the fact that the artillery, who wore red stripes on their trouser legs, were often employed in an infantry role.

9. Justin Smith, *War with Mexico*, 2:54.

10. "Among [the corpses] we observed the body of a young and handsome though coarsely attired female, apparently not more than eighteen years of age. She had been the wife of one of the soldiers, and had stayed with him during the action. Perhaps they were newly-married, and had been spending their honeymoon amid the horrid din of war. One could scarcely help wondering which among that group of ghastly corpses had been her husband. For among them he must be; it were impossible to picture him flying on the road to Jalapa, and leaving behind the bleeding corpse of his young and beautiful bride." Ballantine, *An English Soldier*, pp. 199-200.

Chapter 25. The Long Summer of 1847

1. The battles Smith was referring to are Palo Alto and Resaca de la Palma, in Texas, and Monterrey, Buena Vista, Veracruz, and Cerro Gordo. Smith was the elder brother of Edmund Kirby Smith, who was destined to be a renowned Confederate general in the Civil War. E. Kirby Smith, *To Mexico with Scott*, pp. 137, 138.

2. Scott, *Memoirs*, 2:466n. There is no reason to doubt this claim of Scott's, but search for confirmation from other sources has brought no results.

3. "Whatever his errors may have been," Randolph wrote in December 1839, "they have been doubtless of his judgment, but indiscretions may be carried too far." McCormac, *James K. Polk*, p. 490.

4. U.S. Congress, House, Exec. Doc. No. 60, pp. 940-41.

5. "Article 5. Every individual is declared a traitor, who, either as a private individual, or as a public officer . . . shall treat with the government of the United States."

6. U.S. Congress, House, Exec. Doc. No. 60, p. 820.

7. Scott was actually in no hurry for relief. He mentioned that the first moment he could be spared would be November, five months away.

8. Much credit was given to Moses Y. Beach, editor of the New York *Sun*, who had been sent by Polk as a secret agent, for convincing the priests that their best interests lay in supporting Scott.

9. Hitchcock, *Fifty Years in Camp and Field*, p. 258.

10. La Malinche was named after the Indian mistress, interpreter, guide, and adviser of Hernando Cortés.

11. Elliott, *Winfield Scott*, p. 491.

12. Buchanan had written to Trist on June 14 agreeing that Scott's letter to him had been "extraordinary" and "well calculated to wound your feeling," also implying that Trist's secretiveness may have contributed to the misunderstanding. Trist had been taken aback, expecting full backing on any measures he took to cut Scott down to size.

13. On 17 July Scott wrote Trist, "In regard to the morality of the transaction in question, I have, like yourself, not the slightest doubt. We have tempted the integrity of no one. The overtures we propose to meet, if corrupt, come from parties previously corrupted, and we only profit by that corruption to obtain an end (peace) highly advantageous to both the U. States and Mexico. Such transactions have always been considered allowable in war."

14. Pillow's relationship with Polk was well known. Quitman, a New Yorker turned avid Mississippian (and nullifier), had been an interim governor of that state. Cadwalader was also a prominent Democrat. Shields was a Democratic politician from Illinois and one-time rival but now close friend of Abraham Lincoln. In 1836 he had challenged Lincoln to a duel, but the quarrel was settled amicably.

15. Hitchcock, *Fifty Years in Camp and Field*, pp. 267, 268.

16. Scott, *Memoirs*, 2:460.

17. Upton, *Military Policy*, p. 214. The exact breakdown came to:

1st Division (Worth)

Garland's Brigade: 2d Art., 3d Art., 4th Inf.
Clarke's Brigade: 3d, 6th, 8th infs.; Co. A, 2d Art., Light Art. Bn.

2d Division (Twiggs)

P. F. Smith's brigade: 1st Art., 3d Inf., Rifle Regt.
Riley's brigade: 4th Art., 2d and 7th infs., Engr. Co., Ord. Co., Light Co. K, 1st Art.

Pillow's Division

Pierce's brigade: 9th, 12th, 15th infs.
Cadwalader's brigade: Voltiguers, 11th and 14th infs., Light Co. I, 1st Art.

Quitman's Division

Shields's brigade: New York Regt., South Carolina Regt., Marine detachment
Watson's brigade: 2d Pennsylvania Regt.; H Co., 3d Art.; C Co., 3d Dragoons.
Harney's brigade: 1st Bn., Cavalry; 2d Bn., Cavalry.

Chapter 26. The Valley of Mexico

1. Ballantine, *An English Soldier*, pp. 236-37.

2. Alcaraz, *The Other Side*, pp. 238, 240.

3. Justin Smith (*War with Mexico*, 2:87-88), places Valencia's strength at 4,000 men with 22 guns. He estimates the garrison of Mexico City at 2,000 regulars and 8,000 National Guardsmen. Queretaro supplied 500. The Army of the South, under Juan Alvarez, had 2,748, and Canalizo, who had been at Cerro Gordo, a "few thousand" regulars and National Guard. Total 25,000, maybe 30,000.

4. Alcaraz, *The Other Side*, pp. 244, 248, 250, 251.

5. "We were at Puebla, as you know, many weeks, during which time Lee, of the engineers, and Turnbull, of the topographical corps, each prepared a map of the valley of Mexico. . . . These details were first entered in pencil, before being inked, and Lee and Turnbull finally compared their work together and perfected each other's knowledge. I saw those maps grow daily, and almost daily heard General Scott's remarks upon them. In the general's interviews

with the engineers, he was constantly turning their attention upon the Chalco route, ordering them to procure all the information possible with regard to that route, expressing confidently his purpose in taking it, to avoid the Peñón, the strength of which was perfectly well known at Puebla." E. A. Hitchcock letter to Pillow Court-Martial, in U.S. Congress, Senate, Exec. Doc. No. 65, p. 523.

6. See Lee's letter to Mrs. Totten, 22 Aug. 1847, cited in ibid., pp. 461, 462. Worth and Duncan later claimed that they had "discovered" this route themselves. To be charitable, they may have been unaware of the study that had gone on at Puebla.

7. When Twiggs reversed his steps on August 16 to return to Ayotla and thence south, he met a major force twice the size of his own. The force was part of Valencia's army. Twiggs claimed to have "dispersed the enemy," killing and wounding many. The Mexicans had a drastically different view of the action. See Alcaraz, *The Other Side*, p. 266.

8. It is important to note that the Americans always confused the villages of Contreras and Padierna, hence the subsequent naming of the battle, "Contreras."

9. Hitchcock, *Fifty Years in Camp and Field*, p. 275; E. Kirby Smith, *To Mexico with Scott*, p. 197.

10. That force of seven thousand men was under the immediate command of Santa Anna, who was tentatively coming to Valencia's rescue.

11. Freeman, *Robert E. Lee*, 1:267.

12. Not all the deserters had joined the Mexican army. However, these men had found themselves outcasts with the patriotic Mexicans, and the Mexican government offered them generous rewards for enlisting. They were tough men, and particularly adept as artillerymen. In contrast to the American view, they are to this day regarded as national heroes by the Mexicans.

13. Miller, *Shamrock and Sword*, p. 89, estimates that of the 204 San Patricios in the convent, 60 percent had been killed or captured by the time the fighting finished. Eighty-five were taken prisoner, but only seventy-two were later accused of desertion from the U.S. Army.

Chapter 27. Truce, Tragedy, and Triumph

1. Miller, *Shamrock and Sword*, p. 103, claims that the men of Scott's army were almost universally in favor of the death penalty. They particularly resented sparing Sergeant John Riley, who was an expert artilleryman, and whose skills had cost the lives of some of his fellow American soldiers.

2. Hitchcock, *Fifty Years in Camp and Field*, p. 291.

3. The 5th lost 38 percent of its effective strength.

4. Scott described a causeway as "a double roadway on the sides of an aqueduct of stone masonry, and great height, resting on open arches and massive pillars, which, together afford fine points both for attack and defence. The sideways of [the] aqueducts are, moreover, defended by many strong breastworks at the gates, and before reaching them. As we had expected, we found the four tracks unusually dry and solid for the season."

5. Pillow's division, while designated "regular," was comprised of men who had recently volunteered for the "duration." They were led by volunteer officers.

6. Justin Smith, *War with Mexico*, 2:158.

7. The selection of Harney for this task is a subject for conjecture. Though fearless in battle, he was exceedingly unpopular with his colleagues in peacetime. Miller, *Shamrock and Sword*, p. 106, claims, "In the Florida campaign he was accused of indiscriminately hanging Indians without the semblance of a trial, and a soldier said he had 'ravished young Indian girls at night, and then strung them up to the limb of a live oak in the morning.' In St. Louis in 1834, he was indicted for beating a female slave named Hannah, who died the next day from the effects of the blows. One of his officers said, 'For this diabolical murder he would then and there have been strung up by the outraged citizens, but for his precipitate flight from the

city.'" Testimony in War Department correspondence called his character "notorious for profanity, brutality, incompetency, peculation, recklessness, insubordination, tyranny, and mendacity." These remarks may not be substantiated, but they illustrate the low regard in which Harney was held.

8. Bauer, *The Mexican War,* p. 318.

9. Elliott, *Winfield Scott,* p. 552.

Chapter 28. Peace with Mexico

1. "Let all our soldiers, Protestant and Catholic, remember the fate of the deserters taken at Churubusco. These deluded wretches were also promised money and land; but the Mexican government, by every sort of ill-usage, drove them to take up arms against the country and flag they had voluntarily sworn to support. . . . Fifty of them have paid for their treachery by an ignominious death on the gallows." Scott order, 22 September 1847.

2. Hitchcock, *Fifty Years in Camp and Field,* p. 306.

3. The additions were 2,600 men under Major General Robert Patterson, 4,000 men under Major General William O. Butler, and 1,300 under Colonel Joseph E. Johnston.

4. Polk, *Diary,* p. 267.

5. Scott, *Memoirs,* 2:576.

6. Justin Smith, *War with Mexico,* 2:323.

7. The Mexicans, for purposes of honor or prestige, were unwilling to sign the treaty in Mexico City itself. Guadalupe Hidalgo is a sacred shrine. That fact may have had something arcane to do with its selection as the place to sign.

8. With the ratification of the peace treaty, all American soldiers in Mexico, including officers, could become civilians on the spot. The scheme was that they could be paid by the consortium at a rate of 10 percent above regular army pay.

9. Scott, *Memoirs,* 2:582.

Chapter 29. Fire from the Rear

1. In his *Memoirs,* 2:416, Scott described Pillow as "an anomaly—without the least malignity in his nature—amiable, and possessed of some acuteness, but the only person I have ever known who was wholly indifferent in the choice between truth and falsehood, honesty and dishonesty—ever as ready to attain an end by the one as the other, and habitually boastful of acts of cleverness at the total sacrifice of moral character."

2. New Orleans *Delta,* 10 Sept. 1847, reprinted in U.S. Congress, Senate, Exec. Doc. No. 65, pp. 387-88.

3. Marcy to Scott, 13 Jan. 1848, in U.S. Congress, House, Exec. Doc. No. 60, pp. 1044-45.

4. Freeman, *Robert E. Lee,* 1:289.

5. Elliott, *Winfield Scott,* p. 585.

6. Mansfield, *Life and Services of General Winfield Scott,* p. 523.

7. U.S. Congress, Senate, Exec. Doc. No. 65, pp. 281-82.

Chapter 30. The Last Whig Candidate, 1852

1. New Mexico did not become a state until January 1912, sixty-two years later.

2. Texas had been claiming a western boundary along the entire line of the Rio Grande, as far north and west as Santa Fe.

3. Washington *Union,* 16 July 1850, cited in Elliott, *Winfield Scott,* p. 602.

4. Seward had been a member of the Antimasonic Party in 1828. He then was one of the charter members of the Whigs in 1832.

5. Clingman was a forty-year-old fire-eater representing Buncombe County, N.C., in the

House of Representatives. He was a Whig at this time but a staunch supporter of the Fugitive Slave Act and on the verge of switching his party allegiance. Cushing was a politician from Massachusetts, like Pillow appointed a brigadier general by Polk late in the Mexican War. He had reached the Valley of Mexico too late to participate in the fighting but had been a member of the three-man court of inquiry trying the Pillow-Scott case in 1848.

6. Hughes and Stonesifer, *Pillow,* p. 130.

7. A rejuvenation of the Free Soil Party of 1848, ardently antislavery men. "Free soil, free speech, free labor, and free men."

8. Now called "soldiers' homes."

9. Ulysses S. Grant, in his *Memoirs,* wrote of him: "This circumstance [Pierce's fainting with pain from a severe injury] gave rise to exceedingly unfair and unjust criticisms of him when he became a candidate for the Presidency. Whatever General Pierce's qualifications may have been for the Presidency, he was a gentleman and a man of courage."

10. "For his political defeats," Scott wrote in 1863, "the autobiographer cannot often enough return thanks to God. As he has said before, they proved benefits to him." But he was still stubborn or egotistical enough to question, in the light of the much-criticized Pierce administration, "Have they been such to his country? That is a point that may, perhaps, hereafter be doubted by calm inquirers." *Memoirs,* 2:598.

11. New York *Herald,* cited in Elliott, *Winfield Scott,* p. 648.

Chapter 31. Relegated to the Sidelines

1. Henry James, *A Small Boy and Others.*

2. Elliott, *Winfield Scott,* p. 653.

3. The Indians had much to do with that selection. Texas and New Mexico were "organized" territories, protected by U.S. troops. Nebraska, to the north, was still "unorganized."

4. Less successful was Pierce's effort to find justification to take the island of Cuba from its Spanish master. Both the United States and Britain were developing interests in a future Central American canal, and the presence of Spain so close to Nicaragua and Panama, the two possible sites, was considered dangerous. The American pretext for an invasion, however, was soon dispensed with, and Cuba remained in Spanish hands.

5. Crittenden, *Life,* 2:125, 126.

6. Charles H. Haswell, *Reminiscences of an Octogenarian.*

7. Besides Pickett, the engineer in charge of building the fort was also to become famous. Twenty-two-year-old Lieutenant Henry Martyn Robert, a future major general during the Civil War, compiled *Robert's Rules of Order* for parliamentary procedure after retirement from the Army.

8. For a complete discussion of the positions of the two sides, see McCabe, *The San Juan Boundary Question.*

9. Elliott, *Winfield Scott,* p. 671.

Chapter 32. The Lincoln Inaugural

1. Crittenden, *Life,* 2:184.

2. Forts Jackson and St. Philip at New Orleans; Fort Morgan at Mobile; Forts Pickens and McKee at Pensacola; Fort Pulaski at Savannah; and Forts Moultrie and Sumter at Charleston.

3. Scott's "Views," set forth in his letter to Buchanan written on 29 October 1860, were so damaging to Buchanan's reputation that George T. Curtis, in his *Life of James Buchanan,* devotes six pages, in his second volume, to arguments against them.

4. Keyes, *Fifty Years' Observation,* pp. 367-68.

5. Secretary of State Lewis Cass, Attorney General Jeremiah Black, and Postmaster General Joseph Holt.

6. Scott's one-time aide, E. D. Keyes, visited him at about this time. Keyes later recorded, "We were ushered into a large parlor, where the general was seated alone in a spacious arm-chair. Notwithstanding the room seemed to me oppressively warm, he had on over his thick winter clothing a large, knit, woolen afghan. He did not rise from his chair, but he gave to each of us in succession both his hands, and greeted us in terms of warmest regard." And when Keyes reported to Scott for duty the next month, he wrote, "Another contrast to his former self, and a dreadful token of old age, was his bodily inactivity. He moved slowly and with pain, and it distressed him to ascend three or four steps. His bulk was immense, but the expression of his eye and countenance had lost its fire."

7. The War Department and the Navy Department were on the block now occupied by the Executive Office Building of the White House. The headquarters of the Army was across Seventeenth Street, on the west side of the War Department.

8. Leech, *Reveille,* p. 13.

9. *Congressional Globe,* 29 (Jan. 12, 1861): 326, cited in Elliott, *Winfield Scott,* p. 690.

10. Elliott, *Winfield Scott,* p. 692.

11. Weik, "How Lincoln Was Convinced," pp. 593-94 passim.

12. Nicolay and Hay, *Lincoln,* 3:311.

13. Mrs. Lincoln was said to have become hysterical over the separation from her husband.

14. Leech, *Reveille,* pp. 37-38.

15. Nicolay and Hay, *Lincoln,* 3:343-44.

16. Charles Francis Adams, *Autobiography,* p. 98.

Chapter 33. Fort Sumter, April 1861

1. South Carolina, Florida, Mississippi, Alabama, Georgia, Louisiana, and Texas.

2. On February 23, 1861, the day of Lincoln's arrival in Washington, a "Peace Conference," led by former President John Tyler and Salmon P. Chase, paid a call on Lincoln at Willard's Hotel.

3. Seward and Thurlow Reed, it will be recalled, had been the promoters of Scott's abortive run for the presidency in 1839. In 1852 Seward had engineered Scott's nomination by the Whigs, only to desert him over the Fugitive Slave Act.

4. Scott, *Memoirs,* 2:627.

5. Montgomery Blair was the son of old Francis Blair, the editor of Andrew Jackson's organ, the Washington *Globe.* The elder Blair, a staunch unionist, was still on the scene, still wielding influence in a Republican regime.

6. There was a distinct difference; concerning the Lincoln inauguration, Scott was referring to those who would create disorder, not just those who advocated secession. Such subtlety, however, was beyond the reasoning of people whose passions were aroused.

7. Nicolay and Hay, *Lincoln,* 3:379.

8. William H. Seward (State), Salmon P. Chase (Treasury), Simon Cameron (War), Gideon Welles (Navy), and Edward Bates (Attorney General).

9. Scott always insisted on the retention of Forts Jefferson and Taylor, on the Florida Keys.

10. Keyes, *Fifty Years' Observation,* p. 378.

11. "We made out lists of everything a bare fort would require; calculated the weight and bulk of the various pieces and packages, the tonnage needed, and the number of troops of the different arms to place the fort in a state of siege. Meigs made out sailing directions partly, and a requisition for machines to sweeten sea water. We finished our plans almost simultaneously."

12. Keyes, *Fifty Years' Observation,* p. 404.

13. Nicolay and Hay, *Lincoln,* 3:446-47.

14. Ibid., pp. 448-49.

15. *OR*, series 1, 1:13. Anderson and Beauregard were classes of 1825 and 1838 respectively at West Point. Fellow Southerners, they had been friends, serving together, among other places, in the Mexican War.

16. Scott then lived in lodgings at Mrs. Duvall's, on the south side of Pennsylvania Avenue, between Seventeenth and Eighteenth Streets. For some time previously he had boarded at the house of one Cruchet, a French caterer on Sixth Street. Whether Mrs. Duvall was herself the "famous French cook" referred to by journalist William Howard Russell is not clear. Townsend, *Anecdotes,* p. 25.

17. "The response from free states was overwhelming. War meetings in every city and village cheered the flag and vowed vengeance on traitors. 'The heather is in the fire,' wrote a Harvard professor who had been born during George Washington's presidency. 'I never knew what a popular excitement can be. . . . The whole population, men, women, and children, seem to be on the streets with Union favors and flags.' From Ohio and the West came one great eagle-scream for the flag. In New York City, previously a nursery of pro-southern sentiment, a quarter of a million people turned out for a Union rally. 'The change in public opinion here is wonderful—almost miraculous,' wrote a New York merchant on April 18. 'I look with awe on the national movement here in New York and all the Free States,' added a lawyer. 'After our late discords, it seems supernatural.'" McPherson, *Battle Cry of Freedom.*

Chapter 34. Guardian of Washington

1. *OR*, series 3, 1:109, 113, 111, 125-28. Cited in Nicolay and Hay, *Lincoln,* 4:86.

2. Letcher, basically an antislavery man, was called the "Free-soil" Democrat. He supported Stephen A. Douglas in 1860 and opposed secession until Lincoln called for volunteers after the bombardment and capture of Fort Sumter.

3. Townsend, *Anecdotes,* pp. 4-5.

4. Nicolay and Hay, *Lincoln,* 4:103.

5. *Southside Virginia News,* March 1, 1862. Courtesy of L. L. Meredith, Dinwiddie Courthouse.

6. Nicolay and Hay, *Lincoln,* 4: 126.

7. An alternative route was also offered: troops could be taken by rail to Harrisburg, thence south to a point north of Baltimore, then marched around to a point called Relay Station, where they could board a train for the rest of the trip. That way, however, proved to be too tedious, and Scott rejected it.

8. Commodore Franklin Buchanan and Captain John Magruder were among those who went South at this late date.

9. Nicolay and Hay, *Lincoln,* 4:143-44.

10. Motley's favorable impression may have been influenced by the fact that Scott referred to Motley's historical writings as "an honor to the age."

Chapter 35. The Anaconda Plan and Bull Run

1. Stanton to Buchanan, 16 May 1861. Curtis, *Buchanan,* 2:548.

2. Besides all the officers who resigned to join the Cofederacy, the list of West Pointers who reached rank through the volunteer system includes Ulysses S. Grant, William T. Sherman, and George B. McClellan. According to Upton, *Military Policy,* p. 237, 102 officers reentered the Union army from civilian life. Of these, 53 reached general officer rank. Only one-quarter of those who had remained on active duty reached that grade. The comparison would have been worse had not Scott's policies been abandoned later in the war, after his departure.

3. The embittered Emory Upton, an advocate of using the regulars as cadre, later wrote,

"Unfortunately for the country, the General in Chief and the Adjutant General of the Army placed themselves in opposition [to using the regulars as cadre]. So little did they appreciate the value of instructing the volunteers, that officers already in command of regiments and brigades were ordered back to their companies to serve in obscurity, while officers of little or no education at once leaped to the command of divisions and armies." *Military Policy,* p. 235.

4. Leech, *Reveille,* p. 24.

5. It was not known at that time that Kentucky would elect to stay with the Union.

6. The strategy bears some resemblance to the British strategy for the campaigns against Germany during World War II. Prime Minister Winston Churchill referred to it, with satisfaction, as "closing the ring."

7. Scott to McClellan, 3 May and 21 May, 1861. *OR*, series 1, 51 (part 1): 369-70 and 386-87.

8. Some fifteen thousand were located at Harpers Ferry and the rest in Arlington.

9. As McDowell later testified to the Joint Committee on the Conduct of the War, "I had no opportunity to test my machinery, to move it around and see whether it would work smoothly or not. There was not a man there who had ever maneuvered troops in large bodies. There was not one in the Army. I wanted very much a little time, all of us wanted it. We did not have a bit of it."

10. A battalion of eight companies from the 2d, 3d, and 8th Infantry regiments, a battalion of marines, a small detachment of dragoons, and six batteries of artillery—aggregate of eight hundred men. Upton, *Military Policy,* p. 245.

11. Townsend, *Anecdotes,* pp. 58-59.

Chapter 36. "Hard Is the Fate": October 1861

1. McClellan, *Civil War Papers,* p. 70.

2. McClellan had invented the McClellan saddle some years before. It was used in the Army until the end of the horse cavalry.

3. Leech, *Reveille,* p. 110.

4. Ibid., p. 114.

5. McClellan, *Civil War Papers,* p. 81.

6. *OR*, series 3, 1:519.

7. *OR*, series 1, 51:491-93.

8. McClellan, *Civil War Papers,* p. 109.

9. *OR*, series 3, 1:611-12.

Chapter 37. Taps

1. Dropsy, vertigo, and amebic dysentery picked up in Mexico years earlier.

2. Weed was going with Episcopal Bishop Charles P. McIlvaine of Ohio and Archbishop Hughes of New York. Scott had offered to assist this group but Seward had tactfully ignored the offer.

3. Slidell was long familiar from his prominent role in bringing on the war with Mexico back in 1846, when he had been sent to Mexico City and rebuffed. A New Yorker transplanted to Louisiana, he was a particularly unpopular personality in the North.

4. Prince Albert was successful in toning down the message, questioning for the first time whether Wilkes had acted without authority from Lincoln.

5. Scott's reputation for indiscretion in his use of the English language, in which he mistakenly prided himself, was well known to Bigelow, as to all Americans.

6. Elliott, *Winfield Scott,* pp. 751-52.

7. Nicolay and Hay, *Lincoln,* note, "The only record of this visit is a memorandum from

Scott approving the President's own plan of sending McDowell's command to reenforce Mc-Clellan before Richmond, a plan the execution of which was prevented by Lee's attack."

8. As to "Wayward Sisters," Scott wrote to Chase, "I shall extremely regret, if the recent publication (unauthorized) of my letter to Mr. Seward, date March 3, 1861, shall, in any degree, prejudice the Union—having held, from the commencement of this rebellion, that the South had taken up arms, not only without *sufficient cause,* but without the color of right or justice. . . . I have not written a line on the subject till now. I hope not to write another."

9. Baker, *Emerson Among the Eccentrics,* pp. 443-44.

Bibliography

Adams, Charles Francis (1835–1915). *Autobiography.* Boston: Houghton Mifflin, 1916.

Adams, Henry. *History of the United States during the Administrations of Jefferson and Madison.* 4 vols. (9 books). New York: Charles Scribner's Sons, 1890. Reprint. New York: Albert and Charles Boni, 1930.

Adams, John Quincy. *The Diary of John Quincy Adams, 1794–1845.* Ed. Allan Nevins. New York: Longmans, Green, 1929.

Aimone, Alan C., and Barbara Aimone. "Much to Sadden—and Little to Cheer: The Civil War Years at West Point." *Blue and Gray Magazine,* December 1991.

Alcaraz, Ramón, et al. *The Other Side: Notes for the History of the War between Mexico and the United States.* Trans. and ed. Albert C. Ramsey. New York: John Wiley, 1850.

Ambrose, Stephen E. *Undaunted Courage: Meriwether Lewis, Thomas Jefferson, and the Opening of the American West.* New York: Simon & Schuster, 1996.

American State Papers. Washington, D.C.: U.S. Government.

Bailey, Thomas A. *The American Pageant: A History of the Republic.* 3d ed. Boston: D. C. Heath, 1966.

Baker, Carlos. *Emerson Among the Eccentrics: A Group Portrait.* New York: Viking Press, 1996.

Ballantine, George. *An English Soldier in the U.S. Army.* New York: Stringer and Townsend, 1853. Reprint. New York: W. A. Townsend, 1860.

Bancroft, Frederic. *The Life of William H. Seward.* 2 vols. New York: Harper and Bros., 1900.

Banks, Ronald F., ed. *A History of Maine: A Collection of Readings on the History of Maine, 1600–1976.* 4th ed. Dubuque, Iowa: Kendall/Hunt, 1976.

Basler, Roy. *Abraham Lincoln: His Speeches and Writings.* Cleveland: World, 1946. Reprint. New York: Da Capo Press, 1990.

Bauer, K. Jack. *The Mexican War, 1846–1848.* New York: Macmillan, 1974.

———. *Zachary Taylor.* Baton Rouge: Louisiana State University Press, 1985.

Beach, Edward L. *The United States Navy: 200 Years.* New York: Henry Holt, 1986.

Beauregard, Pierre G. T. *With Beauregard in Mexico: The Mexican War Reminiscences of P. G. T. Beauregard.* Ed. T. Harry Williams. Baton Rouge: Louisiana State University Press, 1956.

Bemis, Samuel Flagg. *John Quincy Adams and the Union.* New York: Alfred A. Knopf, 1965.

Bemrose, John. *Reminiscences of the Second Seminole War.* Ed. John K. Mahon. Gainesville: University of Florida Press, 1966.

Benton, Senator Thomas Hart. *Thirty Years' View; or A History of the Working of the American Government for Thirty Years, from 1820 to 1850.* 2 vols. New York: D. Appleton, 1854.

Berg, Dennis E. "Mexican Response to United States' Expansionism, 1841–1848." Ph.D. diss., University of California, Berkeley, 1965.

Berton, Pierre. *The Invasion of Canada, 1812–1813.* Boston: Little, Brown, 1980.

Bill, Alfred Hoyt. *Rehearsal for Conflict.* New York: Alfred A. Knopf, 1947.

Billington, Ray Allen. *Westward Expansion: A History of the American Frontier.* 3d ed. New York: Macmillan, 1968.

Boyd, Mark F. "Florida Aflame." *Florida Historical Quarterly* 30 (July 1951): 1–115.

Brack, Gene Martin. "Imperious Neighbor: The Mexican View of the United States, 1821–1846." Ph.D. diss., University of Texas, 1967.

Buchanan, James. *Mr. Buchanan's Administration on the Eve of the Rebellion.* New York: D. Appleton, 1866.

Burton, E. Milby. *The Siege of Charleston, 1861–1865.* Columbia: University of South Carolina Press, 1970.

Calcott, Wilfrid Hardy. *Santa Anna: The Story of an Enigma Who Was Once Mexico.* Norman: University of Oklahoma Press, 1936. DeGolyer Collection.

Castel, Albert. "Winfield Scott." 2 parts. *American History Illustrated,* June, July, 1981.

Chapman, Helen. *The News from Brownsville.* Ed. Caleb Cocker. Austin: Barker Texas History Center, 1992.

Coffman, Edward M. *The Old Army: A Portrait of the American Army in Peacetime, 1784–1898.* New York: Oxford University Press, 1986.

Coleman, Mrs. Chapman. *The Life of John J. Crittenden, with Selections from His Correspondence and Speeches.* 2 vols. Philadelphia: J. B. Lippincott, 1871.

"Columbia Column," *Charleston Mercury,* Dec. 1, 1832. (Extract of a letter written Nov. 23, 1832.)

Conner, David. *The Correspondence of Commodore David Conner, USN, during the War of 1812 and Mexican War.* Philadelphia: Henkel.

Conner, Philip Syng Physick. "Commodore Conner: Notes on Maclay's History of the United States Navy." *United Review,* 1895.

———. *The Home Squadron under Commodore Conner in the War with Mexico, Being a Synopsis of Its Services, 1846–1847.* Philadelphia, 1896.

Corn, James F. "Conscience or Duty: General John E. Wool's Dilemma with Cherokee Removal." *Journal of Cherokee Studies* 2, no. 1 (Winter 1978): 35–39.

Cruikshank, LTC Ernest. *The Battle of Fort George.* Niagara-on-the-Lake, Ontario: Niagara Historical Society, 1990.

———. *The Battle of Lundy's Lane.* Welland, Ontario: Tribune Office, 1983.

Currie, Emma A. *The Story of Laura Secord.* Niagara, Ontario. Published by the author, 1913.

Curtis, George Ticknor. *Life of James Buchanan.* 2 vols. New York: Harper and Brothers, 1883.

Dabney, Virginius. *Richmond: The Story of a City.* Garden City, New York: Doubleday, 1976.

Donald, David Herbert. *Lincoln.* New York: Simon & Schuster, 1995.

Dufour, Charles L. *The Mexican War: A Compact History, 1846–1848.* New York: Hawthorn Books, 1968.

Ehle, John. *Trail of Tears: The Rise and Fall of the Cherokee Nation.* New York: Anchor Books (Doubleday), 1988.

Elliott, Charles Winslow. *Winfield Scott: The Soldier and the Man.* New York: Macmillan, 1937.

Elting, John R. *Amateurs to Arms! A Military History of the War of 1812.* Chapel Hill, N.C.: Algonquin Books of Chapel Hill, 1991.

Fairfield, John. *The Letters of John Fairfield.* Ed. Arthur G. Staples. Lewiston, Maine: Lewiston Journal Company, 1922.

Fehrenbacher, Don E. *The Era of Expansion: 1800–1848.* New York: John Wiley and Sons, 1936.

Finger, John R. *The Eastern Band of Cherokees, 1819–1900.* Knoxville: University of Tennessee Press, 1984.

Foreman, Grant. *Indian Removal.* Norman: University of Oklahoma Press, 1972.

Fredriksen, John Conrad. "Niagara, 1814: The United States Army Quest for Tactical Parity in the War of 1812 and Its Legacy." Ph.D. diss., Providence College, 1993.

Freeman, Douglas Southall. *Robert E. Lee.* Vol. 1. New York: Charles Scribner's Sons, 1949.

French, Benjamin Brown. *Witness to the Young Republic: A Yankee's Journal, 1828–1870.* Ed. Donald B. Cole and John J. McDonough. Hanover: University Press of New England, 1989.

Ganoe, Colonel William Addleman. *History of the United States Army.* Ashton, Maryland: Eric Lundberg, 1964.

Grant, Rena V. *Three Men from Aroostook: The Story of the Hardison Family.* Berkeley: Brazelton–Hanscom, 1963.

Grant, Ulysses Simpson. *The Papers of U. S. Grant.* Vol. 1. Ed. John Y. Simon. Carbondale: Southern Illinois University Press, 1967.

———. *Personal Memoirs of U. S. Grant.* Vol. 1. New York: Charles A. Webster, 1885.

Graves, Donald E. *The Battle of Lundy's Lane on the Niagara, in 1814.* Baltimore: Nautical and Aviation Publishing, 1993.

Hale, Edward Everett, Jr. *William H. Seward.* Philadelphia: George W. Jacobs, 1910.

Hallahan, John M. "No Doubt Blamable: The Transformation of Captain Winfield Scott." *Virginia Cavalcade,* Spring 1991, pp. 160–71.

Haswell, Charles H. *Reminiscences of an Octogenarian (1816–1860).* New York: Harper & Brothers, 1897.

Hickey, Donald R. *The War of 1812: A Forgotten Conflict.* Urbana: University of Illinois Press, 1990.

Hitchcock, Ethan Allen. *Fifty Years in Camp and Field.* Ed. W. A. Croffut. New York: G. P. Putnam's Sons, 1909.

Hone, Philip. *The Diary of Philip Hone, 1828–1851.* Ed. Allan Nevins. New York: Dodd, Mead, 1927.

Hughes, Nathaniel C., Jr., and Roy P. Stonesifer Jr. *The Life and Wars of Gideon J. Pillow.* Chapel Hill: University of North Carolina Press, 1993.

Humiston, Fred. *The Aroostook War.* Portland, Me.: Guy Gannet, 1965.

Ingersoll, L. D. *A History of the War Department of the United States. With Biographical Sketches of the Secretaries.* Washington: Francis B. Mohun, 1879.

Jackson, Andrew. *The Correspondence of Andrew Jackson.* Ed. John Spenser Basset II. 7 vols. Washington, D.C.: 1926–35.

———. *The Papers of Andrew Jackson, Vol. 4, 1816–1820.* Ed. Harold D. Moser, David R. Hoth, and George H. Hoemann. Knoxville: University of Tennessee Press, 1994.

Jacobs, James Ripley. *Tarnished Warrior.* New York: Macmillan, 1938.

James, Henry. From *A Small Boy and Others* (1913). In James, *Autobiography.* Ed. Frederick Dupee. New York: Criterion Books, 1956.

James, Marquis. *The Life of Andrew Jackson.* Indianapolis: Bobbs–Merrill, 1938.

Johannsen, Robert W. *To the Halls of the Montezumas: The Mexican War in the American Imagination.* New York: Oxford University Press, 1985.

Jones, Oakah L., Jr. *Santa Anna.* New York: Twayne, 1968.

Josephy, Alvin M., Jr. *The Patriot Chief: A Chronicle of American Indian Leadership.* New York: Viking, 1961.

Keyes, Erasmus Darwin. *Fifty Years' Observation of Men and Events.* New York: Charles Scribner's Sons, 1884.

King, Duane H. *The Cherokee Indian Nation: A Troubled History.* Knoxville: University of Tennessee Press, 1979.

Laumer, Frank. *Massacre! An Account of the Massacre of Major Francis L. Dade by the Seminole Indians, December 28, 1835.* Gainesville: University of Florida Press, 1968.

Leech, Margaret. *Reveille in Washington, 1860–1865.* New York: Harper & Brothers, 1941.

Lossing, Benson J. *The Pictorial Field-Book of the War of 1812.* 1869. Reprint. Glendale, N.Y.: Benchmark, 1970.

Lothrop, Thornton Kirkland. *William Henry Seward.* New York: Houghton Mifflin, 1896.

Lynch, Denis Tilden. *An Epoch and a Man: Martin Van Buren and His Times.* Vol. 1. New York: Horace Liveright, 1929. Reprint. Port Washington, N.Y.: Kennikat Press, 1971.

Macartney, Clarence Edward. *Lincoln and His Generals.* Philadelphia: Dorrance, 1925.

Mahan, Alfred T. *Sea Power in Its Relations to the War of 1812.* 2 vols. New York: Charles Scribner's Sons, 1903. Reprint. New York: Greenwood Press, 1968.

Mahon, John K. *History of the Second Seminole War, 1835–1842.* Rev. ed. Gainesville: University of Florida Press, 1985.

Mansfield, Edward D. *Life and Services of General Winfield Scott.* New York: A. S. Barnes & Co., 1852.

McCabe, James O. *The San Juan Water Boundary Question.* Toronto: University of Toronto Press.

McCaleb, Walter Flavius. *The Aaron Burr Conspiracy.* New York: Wilson–Erickson, 1936.

McClellan, George Brinton. *Civil War Papers: Selected Correspondence, 1860–1865.* Ed. Stephen W. Sears. New York: Da Capo Press, 1992.

———. *The Mexican War Diary of General George B. McClellan.* Ed. William Starr Myers. Princeton: Princeton University Press, 1917.

McCormac, Eugene I. *James K. Polk: A Political Biography.* New York: Russell and Russell, 1965.

McDonald, Lucille. "General Scott and the Pig War." *The Sea Chest* 14 (March 1981): 98–100.

McMaster, John Bach. *A History of the People of the United States, from the Revolution to the Civil War.* 8 vols. 1891. Reprint. New York: D. Appleton, 1919. Clifton Miller Library, Washington College.

McPherson, James M. *Battle Cry of Freedom: The Civil War Era.* New York: Oxford University Press, 1988.

Meade, George. *The Life and Letters of George Gordon Meade, Major General, United States Army.* Vol. 1. New York: Charles Scribner's Sons, 1913.

Merk, Frederick. *History of the Westward Movement.* New York: Knopf, 1978.

Miller, Robert Ryal. *Shamrock and Sword: The Saint Patrick's Battalion in the U.S.–Mexican War.* Norman: University of Oklahoma Press, 1989.

———, ed. *The Mexican War Journals and Letters of Ralph W. Kirkham.* College Station, Texas: Texas A&M University Press, 1991.

Morison, Samuel Eliot. *The Oxford History of the American People.* New York: Oxford University Press, 1965.

Mott, Jacob Rhett. *Journey into Wilderness.* Ed. James F. Sunderman. Gainesville: University of Florida Press, 1963.

Myers, William Starr. *A Study in Personality: General George B. McClellan.* New York: Appleton–Century, 1934.

Nevin, David. *The Mexican War.* Alexandria, Va.: Time–Life Books, 1978.

Nichols, Roy Franklin. *Franklin Pierce.* Philadelphia: University of Pennsylvania Press, 1931.

Nicolay, John G., and John Hay. *Abraham Lincoln: A History.* 10 vols. New York: Century, 1890.

Niven, John. *Martin Van Buren: The Romantic Age of American Politics.* New York: Oxford University Press, 1983.

Official Records of the Rebellion. Washington, D.C.: U.S. Government.

Paludan, Phillip S. *The Presidency of Abraham Lincoln.* Lawrence: University of Kansas Press, 1994.

Peck, William A., Jr. *The Pig War and Other Experiences of William Peck, Soldier, 1858–1862.* Ed. C. Brewster Coulter. Medford, Oreg.: Webb Research Group, 1993.

Polk, James K. *Polk: The Diary of a President, 1845–1849.* Ed. Allan Nevins. New York: Longmans, Green, 1929.

Potter, Woodburne. *The War in Florida.* Baltimore: Lewis and Coleman, 1836. Reprint. Ann Arbor, Mich.: University Microfilms.

Remini, Robert V. *Andrew Jackson.* New York: Twayne, 1966.

———. *Andrew Jackson and the Course of American Empire, 1767–1821.* New York: Harper & Row, 1977.

"The Removal of the Cherokees." Unpublished pamphlet. Museum of the Cherokees, Cherokee, N.C.

Rhodes, James F. *History of the United States from the Compromise of 1850 to the McKinley–Bryan Campaign of 1896.* 8 vols. New York: Macmillan, 1920.

Ripley, R. S. *The War with Mexico.* 2 vols. 1849. Reprint. New York: Burt Franklin, 1970.

Rives, George L. *The United States and Mexico.* 2 vols. New York: Charles Scribner's Sons, 1913. Reprint. New York: Kraus Reprint Co., 1969.

Roberts, Albert H. "The Dade Massacre." *Florida Historical Quarterly* 5 (January 1927).

Russell, William Howard. *My Diary North and South.* New York: Harper and Bros., 1863.

Sandburg, Carl. *Abraham Lincoln: The Prairie Years and the War Years.* New York: Harcourt Brace, 1954.

Santa Anna, Antonio López de. *The Eagle: The Autobiography of Santa Anna.* Ed. Ann Fears Crawford. Austin, Tex.: Pemberton Press, 1967.

Schaff, Morris. *The Spirit of Old West Point, 1858–1862.* Boston: Houghton Mifflin, 1892.

Schroeder, John H. *Mr. Polk's War: American Opposition and Dissent, 1846–1848.* Madison: University of Wisconsin Press, 1973.

Scott, Lieutenant General Winfield, LLD. *Memoirs.* 2 vols. New York: Sheldon, 1864.

Sears, Louis Martin. *A History of American Foreign Relations.* New York: Thomas Y. Crowell, 1927.

Semmes, Lieutenant Raphael, USN. *Service Afloat and Ashore during the Mexican War.* Cincinnati: Wm. H. Moore, 1851.

Seward, Frederick W. *William H. Seward: An Autobiography from 1801 to 1846.* New York: Derby and Miller, 1891.

Singletary, Otis A. *The Mexican War.* Chicago: University of Chicago Press, 1960.

Smith, Arthur D. Howden. *Old Fuss and Feathers: The Life and Exploits of Lt.–General Winfield Scott.* New York: Greystone Press, 1937.

Smith, E. Kirby. *To Mexico with Scott: Letters of Ephraim Kirby Smith to His Wife.* Cambridge: Harvard University Press, 1917.

Smith, George Winston, and Charles Judah. *Chronicles of the Gringos: The U.S. Army in the Mexican War, 1846–1848.* Albuquerque: University of New Mexico Press, 1968.

Smith, Justin H. *The War with Mexico.* 2 vols. New York: Macmillan, 1919. Reprint. Gloucester, Mass: Peter Smith, 1963.

Southside Virginia News. Dinwiddie Courthouse. March 1, 1962.

Steele, Matthew Forney. *American Campaigns.* Vol. 1. Washington, D.C.: United States Infantry Association, 1943.

Strode, Hudson. *Jefferson Davis, American Patriot.* New York: Harcourt Brace, 1955.

——. *Jefferson Davis, Confederate President.* New York: Harcourt Brace, 1959.

Swanberg, W. A. *First Blood: The Story of Fort Sumter.* New York: Charles Scribner's Sons, 1957.

Taylor, Zachary. *Letters of Zachary Taylor from the Battlefields of the Mexican War.* Rochester, N.Y.: William K. Bixby. Reprint. New York: Krause, 1970.

Temple, William G. "Memoir of the Landing of the United States Troops at Vera Cruz in 1847." Appendix to P. S. P. Conner, *The Home Squadron* (q.v.).

Tennery, Thomas D. *The Mexican War Diary of Thomas D. Tennery.* Norman: University of Oklahoma Press, 1970.

Townsend, Major General E. D. *Anecdotes of the Civil War.* New York: D. Appleton, 1883.

Turner, Wesley. *The War of 1812: The War That Both Sides Won.* Toronto: Dundurn Press, 1990.

U.S. Congress. Executive Document No. 1. 30th Cong., 2d sess. *Message from the President of the United States to the Two Houses of Congress.* With accompanying documents. Washington, D.C.: Wendell & Van Benthuysen, 1848.

——. House. Executive Document No. 59. 30th Cong., 1st sess. *Correspondence between the Secretary of War and General Scott.* Washington, D.C.: Wendell & Van Benthuysen, 1848.

——. Executive Document No. 60. 30th Cong. 1st sess. *Messages of the President of the United States with the Correspondence, Therewith Communicated, between the Secretary of War and Other Officers of the Government: The Mexican War.* Washington, D.C.: Wendell & Van Benthuysen, 1848.

——. Senate. Executive Document No. 52. 30th Cong., 1st sess. *The Treaty between the United States and Mexico,* 1848.

——. Executive Document No. 65. *Message from the President of the United States Communicating, in Compliance with a Resolution of the Senate, the Proceedings of the Two Courts of Inquiry in the Case of Major General Pillow.* Washington, D.C., 1848.

——. Executive Document No. 224. 24th Cong., 2d sess. *Proceedings of the Military Court of Inquiry in the Case of Major General Scott and Major General Gaines.* Gales and Seaton, 1837.

Upton, Bvt. Major General Emory. *The Military Policy of the United States.* First manuscript 1881. 4th impression. Washington, D.C.: Government Printing Office, 1917.

Utley, Robert M., and Wilcomb E. Washburn. *Indian Wars.* New York: American Heritage, 1977.

Valliere, Kenneth L. "Benjamin Currey, Tennessean among the Cherokees: A Study of the Removal Policy of Andrew Jackson, Part II." *Tennessee Historical Quarterly* 41 (Fall 1982): 239–56.

Van Dusen, Glyndon Garlock. *William Henry Seward.* New York: Oxford University Press, 1967.

Wallace, Edward S. *General William Jenkins Worth, Monterey's Forgotten Hero.* Dallas: Southern Methodist University Press, 1953.

Weed, Harriet A. *The Life of Thurlow Weed.* Vol. 1. 1884.

Weigley, Russell F. *History of the United States Army.* New York: Macmillan Co., 1967.

Weik, Jesse W. "How Lincoln Was Convinced of General Scott's Loyalty." *Century Magazine* 81 (February 1911): 593–94.

Welles, Gideon. *Diary of Gideon Welles, Secretary of the Navy under Lincoln and Johnson.* 3 vols. Boston: Houghton Mifflin, 1911.

Whitehorn, Joseph. *While Washington Burned: The Battle for Fort Erie, 1814.* Baltimore: Nautical and Aviation Publishing, 1992.

Wynn, Dennis Joseph. "The San Patricios and the United States–Mexican War of 1846–1848." Ph.D. diss., Loyola University of Chicago, 1982.

Acknowledgments

THREE PERSONS were of greatest help to me in this project. One was my wife, Joanne Thompson Eisenhower. The second was my friend Professor Louis D. Rubin, Jr., of Chapel Hill, North Carolina, and the third was my secretary, Mrs. Dorothy W. Yentz, of Phoenixville, Pennsylvania.

Of Joanne, I cannot improve on what I wrote in my previous book, *Intervention!:* "To an unusual degree, I am indebted to my wife, Joanne Thompson Eisenhower, for her efforts on behalf of this book. It would be trite to try to describe her role, which far transcended the usual family support. Joanne was practically a coauthor. She reviewed every chapter of the book before its submission and researched many topics. Most important, she arranged trips to [the Niagara frontier, Sacketts Harbor, Montreal, and Quebec, all in connection with the War of 1812; to Florida and Cherokee, North Carolina, in connection with Indian removal; to Mexico City and Veracruz in connection with the Mexican War; and to San Juan Island, in Puget Sound, in connection with the Pig War]. She made sure that I saw the terrain I was writing about."

Louis Rubin performed an invaluable service by reading the entire manuscript in its earlier stages, giving me sound advice on preparing the text for public attraction, and by researching various subjects and sending me the results. In this he was aided by Mary Flinn, one of his former students, who went through libraries at Richmond in search of materials on Maria Scott. Most important, however, was Louis's encouragement at a time when I wondered whether a biography of a nearly forgotten figure was really worthwhile.

Dodie Yentz performed the same functions as she did on previous books, giving untiring efforts. Dodie's patience, willingness, and mastery of modern electronic equipment saved me untold time and aggravation. In addition, she was a fine copy editor, able to catch many errors.

I am also grateful to others who helped:

My daughter, Susan Eisenhower (Sagdeev), took a heartwarming interest, lending encouragement and providing me with real assistance.

Captain David D. Ansel (USN) sent me material pertaining to Scott's misconduct at Terre aux Boeufs in 1809.

Vice Admiral William L. Read sent me a letter of William Price Crighill, USMA 1853, setting forth his reasons for staying with the Union in 1861 despite his North Carolina upbringing. The letter was provided by Carol A. ("Polly") Turner.

Robert Pitt put me in contact with Guy Fridell of the *Virginian–Pilot* and the *Ledger–Star,* of Norfolk, who in turn introduced me to William E. Bolte and L. L. Meredith Jr., both of Dinwiddie Courthouse, Virginia.

The late Colonel Roger Nye, formerly of the History Department, USMA, provided much insight and put me in contact with Alan C. Aimone, mentioned below.

I was also aided by historians with impressive backgrounds.

Professor John K. Mahon, a noted author and historian from the University of Florida, Gainesville, identified the original locations of such important places as Fort King, Fort Drane, and the Cove, in connection with the Seminole War, 1836. He was assisted by Glen Purdy, Garry Ellis, and Brent Weisman.

Patrick Wilder, curator of the museum at Oswego, New York, and an expert on Sacketts Harbor, spent two days showing us around those two important points, accompanied by his wife, Frederika.

John C. Fredriksen assisted me in evaluating Scott's perfomance on the Niagara frontier in 1814. His Ph.D. dissertation on the subject was invaluable.

Of the various librarians who have helped, I would like to mention Louise Arnold–Friend, of the U.S. Army Military History Institute, Carlisle Barracks, Pennsylvania, and her husband, Dave Friend, who so kindly went through *Official Records of the Civil War,* verifying critical information. It was a favor beyond the normal duties of librarians. Louise was of great assistance in locating certain U.S. Army photos of prominent officers, aided by Mike Winey of MHI and Jim Enos of Carlisle.

Alan C. Aimone, assisted by Charlyn Richardson and Judith A. Sibley, of the Special Collections, U.S. Military Academy Library, West Point, made much rare material available. Alan and Barbara Aimone's article on West Point during the Civil War afforded great perspective.

William J. Tubbs, Director of the Miller Library, Washington College, Chestertown, Maryland, was of great help, assisted by Lavinia Slagle and Cynthia Grimaldi.

Other librarians and curators I would like to mention are Dennis Vetock of MHI, Carlisle; Ronald J. Dale, Superintendent of the Niagara National Historic Sites, Niagara-on-the-Lake, Ontario, Canada; Margo Weiss of the Canadian War Museum, Ottawa; Dinah Perry of the Pennsylvania Historical Society, Philadelphia; and Calvin Pitcher, curator of the Martin Van Buren birthplace, Kinderhook, New York.

J. S. D. E.

Index